2

LANGUAGE DEVELOPMENT

COGNITIVE DEVELOPMENT

EARLY COGNITIVE DEVELOPMENT
edited by John Oates

LANGUAGE DEVELOPMENT
edited by Victor Lee

COGNITIVE DEVELOPMENT IN THE SCHOOL YEARS
edited by Ann Floyd

LANGUAGE
DEVELOPMENT

A Reader edited by Victor Lee
for the Cognitive Development Course
at the Open University

CROOM HELM LONDON
in association with
THE OPEN UNIVERSITY PRESS

Selection and editorial material
copyright © The Open University 1979

Croom Helm Ltd, 2-10 St John's Road, London SW11

British Library Cataloguing in Publication Data

Cognitive development.
   Language development.
   1.   Cognition in children
   I. Lee, Victor   II. Open University.   Cognitive
   Development Course Team
   155.4'13   BF723.C5

   ISBN 0−85664−815−9
   ISBN 0−85664−828−0 Pbk

Printed in Great Britain by offset lithography by
Billing & Sons Ltd, Guildford, London and Worcester

CONTENTS

Cognitive Development course team

John Oates (Chairman)
Eve Braley-Smith
Ronnie Carr
Lydia Chant
Chris Cuthbertson
Pam Czerniewska
Phillipe Duchastel

Ann Floyd
Peter Griffith
Victor Lee
Gill Mason
Ken Richardson
Will Swann
Martin Woodhead

Consultants

Peter Barnes
Margaret Berry
Robert Borger
Alan Blyth
Margaret Brown
Ray Derricott
Wynne Harlen
Godfrey Harrison
Michael Howe

Kenneth Lovell
John Newson
Martin Richards
Marjorie Smith
Valerie Walkerdine
Neil Warren
Gordon Wells
Michael Wood

GENERAL INTRODUCTION

This book of readings is the second of three volumes compiled to accompany Open University course E362, *Cognitive Development: Language and Thinking from Birth to Adolescence*. Each volume is independent, being concerned with a different area, and this Reader deals with language development. Although it is designed for students of the above course, it is also intended to stand in its own right as a source book of ideas for anyone interested in language development.

This Reader is divided into two parts: Section One: Language Acquisition, Section Two: Language Variation. The distinction is important. There is a danger that language development might be identified with language acquisition. The inclusion of a substantial section on language variation emphasises the importance of *context* to the acquisition of language. Each of us is born into a particular speech community, family, social group, ethnic group. It is interesting to examine how such environments affect language acquisition, even though we are only at the beginning of understanding such processes.

A profitable way to look at the two areas of acquisition and variation is to consider the former as a vertical dimension and the latter as a horizontal one. So, acquisition is a dimension common to all normal children, although differing rates of development will be noticed. Variation, on the other hand, affects the process of language acquisition in its various stages, so that there may well be features of children's language which are not common to all.

Throughout both parts a central concern is with the relationship between language development and intellectual development. So, there are articles which deal with different 'stages' of language acquisition, but there are also articles which deal with the importance of language to educational performance. Are differences in language just differences or are they deficits? What is the relationship between language and thinking?

Issues such as these cover a wide area and so an inter-disciplinary approach was considered appropriate. So, although a strong base to this selection lies in psychology, there are powerful contributions from sociology and linguistics as well. It is probably fair to say that the psychological contribution is strongest in the language acquisition section, and the sociological element strongest in the variation section. As a general concomitant perhaps, Section One articles are relatively unsophisticated in terms of importance attached to context, while Section Two articles, strong in the importance of context, are sometimes relatively unsophisticated in their assumptions about the psychological process of communication itself. The parts nicely complement each other.

SECTION ONE: LANGUAGE ACQUISITION

Introduction

The opening extract is very different from any other reading in this collection. It presents a very general picture of how language is acquired. What it provides is an excellent introduction to the subject, as it is an overview of language acquisition very simply expressed in language which anyone new to the subject will find readily comprehensible.

Hymes's paper could not be more different as it deals in detail with two ideas. These two ideas — Chomsky's concepts of competence and performance — have been of enormous influence in studies of language acquisition, and Hymes adds a new dimension to them, the social. Hymes argues that Chomsky's theory need not but does neglect socio-cultural factors, and that, because of this, it fails to cope with the difference between the idealised child and the real child. His attempt to broaden the idea of linguistic competence to communicative competence (and do likewise for performance) makes his paper relevant to Section Two Language Variation as well as to the Language Acquisition section.

Any attempt to shed light on language acquisition must try to deal with the relationship between the pre-speech period in the developing infant and the initial stage of language acquisition itself. And this is what the Bruner article attempts to do. Bruner stresses the importance of the interaction between child and parent or caretaker during the first years for the acquisition of language, arguing that the grammar writing procedures of the linguist are not sufficient explanation in themselves. Bruner's paper, a very detailed one, offers a pragmatic approach which attempts to take into account what the child is attempting to accomplish by communicating, and encompasses in some depth such areas as the use of language in joint action between child and mother, and the nature of early reference.

The fourth paper deals with a very important issue, the relationship of language acquisition to thought. Cromer opens this paper by putting the cognition hypothesis into its historical perspective, an interesting and illuminating process for the understanding of current viewpoints on the subject. He reviews some of the experimental evidence for various forms of the cognition hypothesis, and stresses the constant interaction between language and thought. He offers reasons for his choice of a weak form of the cognition hypothesis, but emphasises that this is only a partial hypothesis of language acquisition. This, Cromer argues, reflects the present

13

state of the art.

The influence of Piagetian thinking is widespread in psychology. In the area of language acquisition its influence is less keenly felt perhaps. However, Sinclair-de-Zwart looks at the relationship between language acquisition and cognitive development from a Genevan standpoint. She argues, for instance, that Piagetian cognitive theory can help achieve an explanation of a child's first set of linguistic universals, and could be used to explore the unexpected difficulties of later development. Many of her comments are made in relation to an experiment concerning the subject-object-verb relationship.

In the sixth article McNeill is concerned with four concepts which are central to the Chomsky tradition of transformational generative grammar: the idea of linguistic universals, transformations, and the concepts of deep and surface structure. McNeill distinguishes a weak and a strong type of linguistic universal and discusses them in terms of a child's 'Language Acquisition Device'. The second part of the McNeill extract shows how transformations tie deep and surface structures together, and McNeill gives examples of the ideas discussed.

The main thrust of the Brown extract is that the early sentences a child makes use language in a way similar to the language of telegrams. Brown evaluates some of the evidence both for and against such a description of children's speech, and sees the distinction against the ideas of functors and contentives, the child's 'telegrams' being made up largely of contentives such as nouns and verbs.

The fourth to seventh articles are largely concerned with the acquisition of syntax. The eighth article is specifically concerned with the acquisition of semantics. The article opens with a discussion of three theories of semantic development before Eve Clark presents her own Semantic Feature Hypothesis. Much of the article concerns the assessment of the evidence which is followed by a consideration of the relationship between semantic and perceptual features in development and the importance of the social dimension.

The Catherine Snow extract presents a social interaction model. As did the Bruner article, she stresses the importance of the relationship between caretaker and child. Catherine Snow suggests a conversational model as the most efficient explanation of the communication between mother and child. She deals with just two infants and their caretakers, emphasising the *reciprocal* nature of communication between mother and child. The conversational model stresses that information is passed in both directions. Much of the extract is concerned with actual examples of speech which are also used to illustrate theoretical points such as the adjacency-pair nature of turn sequences.

The final article in Section One falls broadly into two uneven parts. The first part is very different from most of the material in Section One in that it deals at the specific level of a single system, the acquiring of auxiliary verbs in English. The second part forms a fitting end to the article and to Section One as it examines how different models of language acquisition try to account for the learning of that one system, the auxiliary verb system.

1 HOW DID WE LEARN TO DO IT?

Dennis Fry

Source: Dennis Fry, *Homo Loquens* (Cambridge University Press 1977), pp. 101-24.

If there is one thing that is more astonishing than the ability of the adult human being to talk it is the process by which he learns to do this. Some parts of this process are still very much a sealed book but it is at least possible to describe what the child is doing at various stages in his development of speech even if we do not know exactly how he manages to learn to do it. From the very first moments of his life on earth a baby makes sounds, but for some time they are rather far removed from articulate speech. In something like a year he will probably be at the point where /dada/ will represent the peak of his achievement as a speaker; one more year and he will be coming out with remarks like 'all-gone milk' and after this it seems no time at all before he is capable of saying 'You know, Mummy, this one isn't as nice as the green one Daddy gave me yesterday'. This is a truly remarkable feat of learning and yet it is one that is performed by the vast majority of human beings. Complex operations are involved in dealing with speech and language and the key to the process lies in brain-work, though of course tongue-work and ear-work also play a part. Here, we shall see how much can be said about the ways in which the child's brain develops the requisite capacity, how the memory stores are amassed and how the necessary practice by the tongue and ear is carried out.

In the first few weeks of life most babies are fairly quiet except when they happen to be crying. Any mother can tell you why babies cry: it is because they are uncomfortable or unhappy in some way — they are hungry, or have a pain, or have been suddenly disturbed or need changing. The cry just means that the baby is getting unpleasant sensations of one sort or another and wants something done about it. In a particular baby the cry does not vary a great deal except in its persistence perhaps, but a mother soon learns to recognise the cry of her own child. The crying is important from the point of view of speech because the larynx is already being used to generate sound and because the pattern of breathing for speech is being established. When the baby is quiet, his breathing is a rhythmical 'in-out' but when he begins to cry this is all changed. Sometimes a single cry will go on and on until one wonders how the baby can possibly keep it up without bursting something; then there is a break

17

while he takes in more air, only to start all over again. Already at this early stage it is the air coming from the lungs that is used to produce sound at the larynx, though one will sometimes hear babies also making sound as the air goes in.

It is not very long however before the baby begins to make another kind of sound, one that indicates that life is going rather well and things are particularly pleasant. These sounds of pleasure are the cooings and gurglings which usually come along round about the age of three months and which give so much satisfaction to mummy, making the broken nights and sleepless mornings so well worth while. The breathing pattern for the pleasure sounds is similar to that for the crying but their quality is quite different and in fact the vocal tract is beginning to have more influence on what comes out of the mouth, for the sound of crying is not much modified by its passage through the vocal tract.

In this first period of his life, the baby not only sends out his own sounds of displeasure and pleasure, but he very soon begins to notice some of the sounds that are going on around him. He associates his mother's voice with pleasant things like feeding and bathing and being picked up and after a short time he will respond to the voice itself, especially to the tone of voice, by smiling. This is an important factor because it links all the things which are of interest to the baby with speech and the ordinary mother is quite right in following her instinct to talk to her baby while she is feeding, bathing and dressing him. In this way the child cottons on to the fact that speech is connected in a rather special way with his world and this is most important for the development of speech and language.

The period from about four to nine months is a vital one for speech development because it is then that the baby begins to 'babble'. This is the time when he lies in his cot or his pram, on waking up or before going to sleep, and makes streams of sound of one sort and another, repeating syllables over and over again, stringing them together and in fact 'playing at talking'. You have only to realize that the baby is having fun; he is getting pleasure simply from uttering sounds, without any reference to the world around him. The importance of this babbling activity for speech is partly due to the fact that the child is busy exploring the possibilities of his sound producing apparatus, learning just what can be done with his larynx, his tongue, his soft palate and his lips and practising the actions through continual repetition. In a way it is a bit like the early stages of learning to play the piano: a child will spend hours learning to play five-finger exercises and scales so that later on he may be able to play a Chopin study or a Beethoven sonata. This music may well contain snatches of those same exercises or scales, but the real importance of them is that they lay the foundations of a technique, that is to say habits of movement, which will adapt itself to whatever demands may be made upon it.

The babbling stage is in some ways one of the more mysterious parts of learning to talk because the sounds a baby makes are not closely related to the language spoken around him. English babies in babbling do not confine themselves to sounds that are needed for English, nor do Japanese babies stick to Japanese sounds. They all do a great deal of very general practice which stands them in good stead later on when they do learn the sounds of their mother tongue. The most vital aspect of this practice for speech is that it involves the linking up in the brain of the circuits which produce speech movements and those which control it, the auditory and kin-aesthetic feedbacks. The baby is learning that if he makes his larynx work and at the same time keeps on bringing his lips rhythmically together he will produce the very pleasing sound of 'ba-ba-ba-ba'; he learns the converse too, that if he wants to hear 'ba-ba-ba-ba' he can do so any time by making his larynx work and repeatedly bringing his lips together. The child early becomes very sophisticated about this for you can often catch a baby doing such a sequence in a whisper, which means that he has separated out the effect of the lip movement from the larynx action.

Babbling is an essential stage in speech development then because the child is exploring the possibilities of the talking-box that nature has provided him with, is practising a repertoire of movements, many of which he will need later on and, most important of all, is linking in his brain the circuits concerned with muscle action and feedback control. One of the facts about babbling that is often overlooked is that the baby is certainly not imitating the sounds produced by adult speakers. Listen to a baby babbling for a few minutes and you will be convinced that you would be unable to give a very good imitation of him, so it is not very likely that he is imitating you. As a matter of fact a number of the sounds that he makes will find no place in the English sound system when he comes to learn it. Another indication is that when the baby is truly in the babbling stage, he will not imitate the sounds you produce even if you try specifically to make him do so by hanging over him and repeating the same thing over and over again. If anything happens at all in this situation, it will be that the sound of your voice sets the baby babbling with his own repertoire of sounds, he goes into his own routine.

To speak of the stage a child has reached is only to give a hint as to the general character of the activity he will be most engaged in. Stages in speech development, like those in every other type of learning, merge into each other and cannot be marked off by dates and times. The point at which the child's babbling is frequently triggered off by the sound of an adult voice is however a fairly definite one because it shows that the time is rapidly approaching when the child will begin to get involved with speech as a vehicle for language. Up to this point the baby's activity has had no real connection with language and certainly none with any specific language system. The essence of language lies in its connection with the world outside the speaker and the reference which it makes to that world. The baby's babbling takes place in a private world and no sound or syllable is coupled to some particular aspect of the outside world, so that language, with all the social context it implies, has not yet come into the picture.

Before we begin to explore the stages by which it does so, we may well ask the question why a child should learn to talk at all. The forces which come to bear on the child and persuade him to talk are indeed the social ones which constitute the *raison d'être* of language. They are neatly illustrated by an old story about some parents whose first child turned out to be a rather talkative girl, who was followed at an interval of about two years by a boy. To the dismay of the parents the boy never uttered a word in his first years. The parents did everything they could to find out why this was; the child was obviously bright enough and they were assured that he was not deaf or anything like that. The case was a mystery. Slowly the time passed as the anxious parents saw with growing dismay the passing of his second, third and even fourth birthday with never a word on Peter's part. One morning when the whole family was seated at breakfast, he electrified the rest of them by saying loudly and clearly 'There's no sugar on my cornflakes'. You can imagine the mixture of delight and consternation with which his mother stammered 'But, P-P-Peter, why have you never spoken before?' to which Peter replied, rather huffily, 'Well, everything has been all right up to now!' This sums up very nicely the basic reason why a child learns to talk. It soon becomes apparent to him that the strings of noises which issue from the mouths of adults who inhabit his small world are in some strange way a powerful force which influences what happens in that world and that in fact there is precious little that can happen without the agency of this magical activity. Food and drink appear and they disappear, clothes are put on and they are taken off, delightful things happen and hideous things happen, all preceded by, accompanied by and usually followed by talk, talk, talk. It is little wonder that the baby feels some urge to qualify himself for admission to this powerful club. When it turns out that learning to do it is rather fun anyway, it is not surprising that the overwhelming majority of human beings succeed in converting themselves into *homo loquens* in the space of about five years.

When the baby's babbling is triggered by the sound of the mother's voice this is a sign that speech sounds coming from outside are beginning to have a specific effect on the child and this means in turn that he is getting ready to learn the language system. It serves to illustrate also one of the unvarying principles of speech and language acquisition, namely that everything is learned through the reception of speech before there is any attempt at speech production. This fact is rather hard to digest because all of us, parents, grandparents and everyone else, are naturally hypnotized by what the small child manages to say at any stage and we cannot get over the belief that this is the real indication of his grasp of speech. But anything that the child utters has been recognized long before he makes any attempt to bring it out himself and his mastery of the language system is measured by the differences that he can recognize and distinguish rather than by what he can perform himself. Naturally he will in time learn to produce the things he can recognise but there is a time lag between recognition and production. This principle runs through all stages and all aspects of language learning, whether it be of our mother tongue or of a foreign language. When, for example, as adults we add a new word to our vocabulary, it comes into the passive vocabulary first; we learn to recognize it and then we may later use it ourselves in conversation.

The system of any language is a vastly complicated affair with its various levels, its large memory stores, its statistics, its laws and its routines and one may well wonder where on earth a child can make a start in learning his native language. One has to realize that acquiring one's first or native language is essentially a different matter from learning a foreign language at a later age; it hinges on learning the trick of what language is. It is tempting to think of the child's brain as being ready furnished with an enormous card index or a mammoth set of pigeonholes or file boxes waiting for him to learn the right things to put into each of them. But no language can possibly work like that because the pigeonholes are themselves the language system and there cannot be empty ones; the child has to build the framework as he goes along, starting with a couple of pigeonholes and adding new ones as he needs them, often by dividing an existing one and putting a partition down the middle. When we learn a foreign language, we already know what a language is, even though the knowledge is not very explicit, and so we know that the new language we are going to learn has a certain framework and that we shall have to learn a collection of words, sounds, grammatical and syntactic units and so on. In the brain of the child learning his mother tongue the language system evolves and it is the social pressures from outside that ensure that it evolves in such a way that he can make sense of what people say to him and they can make sense of what he says to them.

Basically there are two parts to the trick of language: the first part is simply that noises stand for things and the second part is that different noises stand for different things. The noises we generally think of as words, so this means that when things are different there will be different words for them. Differences between words are maintained by the operation of the phoneme system, so it is clear that evolving some kind of phoneme system will be among the first steps in learning the trick of language. We speak of a baby's first word and about a small child's learning new words, and rightly so because it is the words that stand for things, but in the early stages these words are essentially the medium through which the phoneme system evolves.

In considering how this comes about we have to bear in mind all the time the two guiding principles of language acquisition, that recognition comes before production and that systems are built up a step at a time. The first language noise a baby recognizes in most cases is the name for the person who is the source of all good things, /mama/, and he does so because this string of sounds is repeatedly uttered in situations where she is obviously involved. The signs that the baby recognizes the word are usually missed because they are so mixed up with the indications that he recognizes the person herself, by turning his head, by smiling and so on, and this is inevitable since most of the time it is mummy herself who is saying her own name. If you watch carefully, however, you can see the word evoking the reaction for some time before the child makes a real attempt to imitate the sound of it himself. At this stage the baby has picked out one morsel of speech and associated it with something quite specific in the world around him and this is the beginning of language.

There is at the same time quite a lot of pressure on the child to produce the word himself; everyone is eagerly awaiting his first word and it is being fed to him frequently in the hope that he will imitate it; in the end he does, much to the satisfaction of all concerned. The first attempts at imitation are distinct from the babbling acitivty for which the sound of adult speech acts only as a trigger and not as a model for imitation. Of course it is no accident that the name the mother gives herself is a simple syllable repeated because she is influenced by the sort of thing that goes on in babbling, where strings of repeated syllables give the child a great deal of pleasure. Imitating /mama/ or something like it can follow on naturally from babbling and once the link between the word and the person is firmly established by recognition, it is not too long before the child reproduces it.

This first word, recognized and then imitated, contains more than is obvious at first sight, more than the principle that the noise stands for the thing. The sequence is made up of a slightly softer sound followed by a slightly louder one and then the whole thing repeated. This embodies both the idea of the syllable and the idea that order is important, for the name he hears is always /mama/ and never by any chance /amam/. We can scarcely talk about a system being involved as yet because there is no question of different noises standing for different things at this stage, but as soon as the baby recognizes a second word as being attached to a different thing, there is a language system in existence in his brain. The second word is most often /dada/ which becomes associated with the rather strange being who tends to come home at the end of the day and perhaps have a jolly five minutes with the baby at the point when mummy is out on her feet, having coped with the little angel for ten hours at a stretch. In order that the new word shall operate successfully it must be consistently distinguished from /mama/. The form of the word is very similar, the rhythm is the same, the loud parts of the syllables are the same, and the only feature that differentiates them is located in the /m/ and the /d/. Since the baby knows which word is which, his brain must have discovered some way of distinguishing /d/ from /m/, in other words it has fastened on to some acoustic cue which will do the job. Although /mama/ is made up to two syllables, the sound is continuous right through the /m/ and the vowel each time, so that there are two little swells of sound, but in /dada/ the sound is interrupted by a short silence, a kind of hiccough. The child's brain has only to pin its attention to this difference between the continuous and the interrupted sound and it will be able to tell infallibly when it hears /mama/ and when it hears /dada/. The child is now operating a language system, one which has not only two words attached to two things, but also three phonemes: /m/, /d/ and /a/. Now phoneme systems will only work as a whole and these three phonemes make a complete system, a mini-system if you like. There are only three pigeonholes and there is something to place in each of them. It is not a case of having forty pigeonholes all ready waiting to be used for different phonemes later on; the child must build the framework as he goes along and at present it consists of just three boxes.

Notice also that his brain has found acoustic cues which are only as complicated as the situation demands.

Let us follow our hypothetical baby a little further and imagine that the third word he recognizes consistently is a name for a grandparent, perhaps /nana/. To do this he must be able to distinguish not only /m/ and /d/ but also /m/ and /n/ and of course /d/ and /n/. The difference between the continuous and the interrupted sound will no longer do the whole job because both /m/ and /n/ are continuous, so some other way has to be found to separate these two sounds. It may be hard to believe but there is good sound evidence that even at this early age babies are capable of noticing differences in second formant transition.[†] When we first hear about this acoustic cue it seems to be an extremely subtle and sophisticated method of distinguishing between sounds, but we have to remember that if we use it as adults it is because we learned to do so as children. There is not much doubt that when the baby recognizes the difference between /mama/ and /nana/ he is relying on the transition cue. In doing so he has expanded his phoneme system by one and there are now four pigeonholes with something to go into each.

The next step might be the addition of a name for the other grandparents, perhaps /baba/ and again the child's brain has a fresh problem. Up till now the interrupted sound always signalled /dada/ but here is a second interrupted sound which must be differentiated because it is attached to a different person. At this point we can see something of the economy of phoneme systems because this small group of two interrupted sounds can be effectively split by the use of the second formant transition cue which already differentiates the two continuous sounds, /m/ and /n/. The brain evolves only the cues that are needed to make the required distinctions and with the system in its present form three cues are enough: the softer-louder cue takes care of the vowel parts of the syllables; the continuous-interrupted cue puts the /m, n/ on one side and the /d, b/ on the other, and then the transition cue separates both /n/ from /m/ and /d/ from /b/. Once more the phoneme system is complete as it stands, with a framework of five pigeonholes for the five phonemes to be distinguished, and it happens that the job can be done with three acoustic cues.

It is important to keep clearly in mind the mechanism by which these developments come about. The first factor is that some person or some thing in the baby's small world takes on a particular interest for him, causing him for the time being to be specially attentive to the word which is associated with it. In order to be sure when this word is said, he has to be able to distinguish it reliably from the other words he already recognizes and his brain sets about the task of finding a cue which is effective. This will quite probably mean that a new phoneme has to be set up, very often by splitting an existing class, as in the case both of continuous sounds and of interrupted ones. So although the child's unconscious purpose is to learn a new word, because of the nature of the language system, he is busy forging for himself an ever expanding phoneme system. We can scarcely follow through step by step the expansion of the system up to the forty-member adult system of English and in any case there is great variation in the way this is done by individual children. The principle, however, is always that which has been illustrated: a phoneme system at every stage complete in itself and determined by the distinctions between words that have to be made. Not every new word recognized calls for a fresh phoneme; it may present existing phonemes in a new order, as is the case for every word learned by an adult, but from time to time a new group of sounds and a new cue become necessary. The child whom we left with the five phoneme system will find the need a little later to notice the hissing sounds which occur in English words; perhaps he gets rather interested in his *shoe.* This hissing sound is a continuous one like /m, n/ but of a very different character so he will pick out the hiss as a fresh kind of sound. But at first all hisses will be the same for him and will form just one class until some new word forces him to split up the hisses, to put a partition in the pigeonhole used for them and to realize that *shoe* and *sock* start off with different hisses, one low-pitched and the other high-pitched. By this kind of process the phoneme framework expands and expands as the child feels the pressure of interest in external things and his brain evolves the acoustic cues needed to make the additional distinctions. By the time the child is about five years old, he will have learned to recognize all the differences involved in the adult system of phonemes, that is in English the forty-odd classes of sound. He cannot yet of course produce in his own speech sounds which adequately embody all these distinctions, but he is now operating with the adult system because he uses it in the reception of speech. Again we have to remember that reception runs ahead of production, that is to say that during the period of language acquisition there is a time lag between the development of recognition and production. One often hears a mother say about her baby at a certain stage 'He understands everything you say to him' and she is implying that he cannot yet say all that he understands; she has noted the time lag between reception and production.

The ability to talk is developing at its own pace all this time, so we will now take a look at what is happening on this side. The baby wants to talk in order to influence events in the world around him and recognition stages are a step in this end. As soon as some progress has been made in speech reception he will try his hand, or his tongue rather, at wielding the magic himself. One might think that with all the practice he put in during the babbling stage this should not give him too much trouble, but in fact it does. The practice was generalized practice which was not linked to a language system and it is an interesting and vital fact that articulations which the baby produced readily in the earlier period cannot simply be called back and pressed into service for the purposes of the phoneme system. Differences in articulation must now be tailored systematically to the demands of the language and this is why prior recognition is so important. The child's aim is to reproduce in his own speech the acoustic cues his brain has evolved for taking in other people's.

In a general sense this is brought about through imitation, mainly of his mother's speech, which is also of course the source of his ability to recognize. Our own speech reaches us in a unique and private version so that when the child imitates there can never be anything like a perfect match between the sounds he hears from other people and the results of his attempts to imitate. What he can do, however, is to try to make sounds in which he detects the acoustic cues he has already learned. This accounts for the lag between reception and production; it takes time for the continually expanding framework of reception to exert its influence on his articulations. He begins with cues that are effective for the distinctions he needs to make and these, from the viewpoint of the complete adult system, are gross distinctions like that between a continuous and an interrupted sound or, at a later stage, between an interrupted and a hissing sound, without any discrimination among the various hissing sounds. When this type of cue is applied to the child's own speech it gives rise to all the childish pronunciations which parents and indeed all the rest of us find so delightful. For some time he will be content to form syllables with almost any kind of interruption, producing sequences like /pudi tat/ for *pussy cat* or /iku gogi/ for *little doggie*. As time goes on the child will be recognizing a wider and wider range of things and will do his best to reproduce them, getting in whatever cues he can; he will tackle things like /bano/ for *piano*, /dohin/ for *dolphin*, /budlozer/ for *bulldozer*, /cocker bisik/ for *chocolate biscuit* and so on. He is doing his best to embody in his own sounds the cues he uses in recognition but obviously what he produces is not all that easy for his listeners to decode. His best audience from every point of view is his mother and there is always a stage when she acts as his interpreter to the rest of the world; but he will not be satisfied for very long if there is only one person whose actions can be influenced by his speech so there is constant pressure on him to modify his pronunciation in order to make what he says easily understood by a wider circle of adults. He can do this by introducing progressively more of the cues his brain has evolved for speech reception. Some distinctions are more difficult for him to manage than others; he may well be halfway through his fifth year before he can articulate very presentable /th/ sounds or a /r/ sound like that of most of the adults around him. Some groups of consonants will give him trouble for quite a long time. For English children the distinction between the initial sounds of *chain* and *train* is a difficult one to achieve. It will probably not have struck you that they are at all alike but if you say the two words in succession, you will notice that the acoustic effect is remarkably similar, the first being just a little higher pitched than the second. Here again the child will have learned to recognize the distinction long before he can produce it and it is interesting that, even when he can pronounce the two sounds, he finds it hard to know when to use one and when to use the other. You may for instance hear a child at this stage say *treeks* for *cheeks, trin* for *chin* and *satrel* for *satchel.* Another confusion that occurs is between /tr/ and /tw/ and this is understandable since for a long time the child has probably been saying /w/ in place of /r/, *wed wabbit* and so on. When he at last succeeds in making the difference, he will still be in doubt when to use each of them and may come out with *trelve* for *twelve, trist* for *twist,* or even rather charmingly 'Trinkle, trinkle little star'.

While the child's pronunciation is shaped mainly by the pressure of the phoneme system, it is at the same time the result of imitation, in normal circumstances of his mother's speech. The phoneme system itself is derived from this model which is responsible also for the more detailed quality of the sounds produced, what is often referred to as the 'accent' of the speaker. In English this is very largely a matter of the quality of the vowel sounds, in which the language system allows a good deal more variation than in the consonants. In determining this aspect of a child's speech, the mother's accent is usually paramount even where it differs from that of most of the other adults who surround the child. A child of a Scottish mother, brought up from birth in London, say, is almost certain to speak with a Scottish accent to some degree. The same influence is strong, too, in deciding characteristics of rhythm and intonation, both the grammatical component of intonation and its use in the expression of emotion. Children begin very early to imitate the tunes of the mother's speech but just as the pronunciation of vowels and consonants is shaped by the need to be understood, so the use of tone and rhythm is modified so as to convey what is intended to a whole circle of adult listeners.

By the time a child is about five years old, then, he has built up by a process of expansion a phoneme system which coincides with that of the adult language around him, he has evolved a set of acoustic cues that enable him to recognize all the necessary distinctions when he is listening to speech, he has applied the knowledge of these cues to his own speech so as to make it intelligible, at least with some degree of good will, to those around him, he has learned to recognize and to produce the appropriate rhythm and intonation patterns and his pronunciation has taken on through imitation most of the features that will characterize his accent. Yet all this has been done by learning new words; one might almost say that these other things are a by-product, though an absolutely essential by-product, of his adding to his vocabulary. In conformity with the general principle, the additions are to his passive vocabulary first, though in these early stages of language acquisition we can be fairly sure that all words will pass from the passive to the active vocabulary. It will be well to consider at this point just what happens as the new words are learned.

For the small child, words are noises which stand for things or people and when he knows only a handful of words, they can stand for only a few items in his world. One of the interesting things that happens is that the area which one word covers for the child changes as time passes; one can say, if you like, that the meaning of the word expands and contracts. A very clear example of this is the word /dada/. When the baby first learns it, it refers to the one person who appears at somewhat lengthy intervals and is so named by mummy. Some weeks later, however, when the child is at the stage of being taken out in the streets by his mother, the meaning of this word expands to include almost any figure in trousers and perhaps a moustache or beard, no matter where or when he appears. The child will then hail loudly any such figure as 'Dada', not without embarrassment to mummy. The meaning of the word will contract again, however, when another word is added to the vocabulary, the word *man*, which is soon seen to refer to the general class and the word /dada/ reverts to its reference to one person only.

Because the world is so full of a number of things, even for a small child, and because he has to build up his store of words bit by bit, this kind of fluctuation in the area of reference of a word goes on continually. One small boy, for instance, learned the word *ladder*, which he pronounced incidentally /ladler/, when the house opposite to his own was being painted. But in a short space of time /ladler/ meant for him a ladder, anything at all propped against the side of a house, any shape such as the back of a garden seat with parallel members and slats across *and* any man in white overalls. Of course it was only a matter of time before the learning of a few additional words would reduce the reference of the word once again until it meant simply – a ladder. For another small boy, at one period, *rain* meant not only wet stuff that fell but also *a reason for not going out*. In perfectly fine weather at midday, when it was too hot to go into the garden, he would go to the door, hold out his hand and say 'Rain', not as a question but as a statement meaning 'we don't go out'.

This brings up another important aspect of the function of words in the early stage of language development. Just as a word can cover a wide area of reference, so it can also function as the equivalent of an adult sentence. This is particularly the case when the child gets to the stage of putting two words together, an important development which we shall be looking at in a moment. For example, when the child says 'Mummy coat' this may simply mean 'That's mummy's coat' but it may also mean 'Where is mummy's coat?' or again 'Mummy should put her coat on so that we can go out'. Even the single word at an earlier stage will have different functions in different situations. /mama/ may at one time mean 'The name of the person I can see is Mama' but on another occasion it may mean 'The hat I'm pointing to belongs to Mama' or it may be the equivalent of the expression 'Mama do it', which the child will use later on. While his language has no explicit grammar, he will use the words he knows with different functions so that adding to his vocabulary is something rather more than just adding to his stock of words. At the age of eighteen months he may be using no more than about twenty words in this way but even three months later the number may have risen to something like two hundred.

Up to this point whatever the child says is basically an imitation of what he hears, though he is making it serve a rather wider range of functions. At about the age of two a great step forward is taken when the child strings two words together, because when this happens his mini-language now has a grammar. Grammar is not to be thought of as the host of complicated rules which we were supposed to learn, not without tears, in our schooldays, rules which we were expected to adhere to when speaking or writing and which we were continually 'breaking'. Real grammar is concerned with what people do when they talk and not with what they *should* do, and it consists of the principles of structure and sequence which apply when any given language is used. As soon as the small child puts two words together in English, he develops a principle, that is effectively a syntax, which controls the order of the words. This is the period when he will use over and over again such expressions as 'Bye-bye Mummy', 'Bye-bye sock', 'Bye-bye boat' and 'All-gone milk', 'All-gone flakes', 'All-gone car', 'All-gone soap' and so on. In all of these the names of different things are combined with a kind of operator word to make what are really sentences in the child language, in which the operator word must come first and then the name. When this principle is established, any new words will appear first in the name class, having of course been learned through recognition. A few very familiar words make up the operators but as time goes on words may pass from the name class into this class. While the child limits his remarks to two-word sequences, he will keep to this basic construction, that is to this syntax.

This stage in language development is extremely interesting because it differs from everything that has gone before. Up to this point the child's sounds and words have been copied from the speech of his mother or of other adults, but here quite suddenly is a development which does not represent a pattern that has been copied. Adults do not spontaneously say things like 'All-gone milk', which do not form part of their language. It is true that mothers may sometimes be concerned about 'teaching the child baby-talk' or they may be reproached by others for doing so. But the boot is entirely on the other foot and it is the baby that teaches mummy baby-talk. When adults use such expressions, they are doing so in imitation of the baby who is now creating his own language and not simply repeating what he hears. This step forward in the use of language represents very much a development in thinking because it means that the child is already grasping the principle which lies behind the use of verbs as well as nouns. From this point onwards, new words learned will eventually fall into different classes because of the different ways in which they will function in the language.

Combinations of an operator word and a name will meet the child's needs for some time but before very long he will extend his technique to include strings of three or four words. Many of his remarks may begin to sound like adult sentences but he will still use only words essential to his meanings and in most cases will keep to his own kind of syntax, producing sequences like 'Where you are?' and 'Mummy biscuits got?' which show clearly that he is evolving for himself the technique of making up sentences and is not just copying strings of words heard from adults.

The ensuing period in the child's life sees what is actually the most spectacular achievement that the child makes in any direction. In the space of about two short years the majority of children progress from remarks like 'Bye-bye sock' to quite complicated sentences on the adult model, things like 'Mummy, I don't think this tractor's as strong as the one Daddy bought me last week'. We take all this as a matter of course and do not realize how miraculous the process is. The child gets hours and hours of practice, virtually all his waking moments, since he is continually surrounded by adult speech. What he does is to infer from the thousands of examples he hears the principles of grammar and syntax which are operating in his native language and it is this that constitutes the most remarkable part of his achievement. With nearly every child there comes a point where language itself becomes intensely interesting and this serves to make his practice still more concentrated. Adults seldom realize that the child who is at the 'Why?' 'What's that?' stage is expressing his curiosity about words rather than things. A mother who has had to reply to the question 'What's that?' by saying 'A bicycle' a hundred times over may be forgiven for thinking her son is passionately interested in bicycles, but the truth is rather that he is learning the word *bicycle* and has to have it repeated many times to make sure he has got it. The same thing holds

Figure 1.1: Successive Stages of Speech and Language Development

The average child does not exist. If he did, he would probably reach the successive stages of speech and language development within the periods suggested in this table.

good with regard to the form of sentences and phrases. The question 'Why?' is an excellent way of hitting the jackpot of variations on a construction. We may imagine the child wants to know why, whereas he is much more keen to check that in reply you can say 'Because it is not so-and-so' or 'Because it is too so-and-so' or 'Because it is not so-and-so' or 'Because it is too so-and-so' or 'Because I haven't so-and-so' and even if he turns up a few 'don't knows', it has been well worth while from his point of view.

Systematic observation of children's speech during this period of language development produces convincing evidence that the child's brain is formulating the principles of the grammar for itself. Just from hearing what adults say the English child will infer, for example, that if something took place in the past you put -*ed* on to the end of words in one particular class, that if you have more than one of a thing, you add -*s* to another class of words, that if some quality is more in one case than in another, you put -*er* on to the word which refers to this quality, and so on. Within a short time the child's brain is stocked with formulations of this kind which he then applies in his own speech. He will apply them quite generally and most of the time this will produce acceptable remarks but sometimes the words which he forms in this way by analogy will not correspond to the usage of the adult language. When he has discovered how to make verbs refer to the past by ending them in -*ed,* he will use forms like *bringed, stranded* and *teached* and similarly he will make plurals such as *mouses* and *scissorses* and comparative forms like *gooder* and *badder.* People are inclined to say that this is because he has not yet learned English grammar, but the reverse is the truth; he does it because he *has* learned English grammar, or rather has inferred its laws for himself since it is clear that he has not heard these forms used by adult speakers.

Examples of many different kinds of formation by analogy can be culled from children's speech, some affecting sentence construction and word formation as can be seen in the two following examples, both of which display a rather charming inventiveness. The first occurred in the speech of a small boy who was heard to exclaim, 'You never do that, never'd you?', thereby showing an essential grasp of a complicated routine for converting a statement with an auxiliary verb into a question. The second concerns a father who, hearing something of a fracas breaking out in another room between an older and a younger daughter, called out loudly 'Deborah, tell Elizabeth not to argue!' What was his surprise, and since he was a linguist his delight too, to hear a childish voice say in authoritative tones 'Elizabeth, don't arg me'. This is an interesting illustration of the child's ability to get the morpheme string appropriately arranged even when not too sure of the content of the words. In the natural course of events, as the child hears more and more adult speech, words like *standed, teached, mouses, gooder* and so on give way to the adult forms, sometimes with explicit help from the parents, and ultimately the child's speech conforms in usage with that of the adults among whom he lives.

The development of grammar and syntax, like that of the phoneme system, takes place through the learning of new words. All of them go first into the passive vocabulary but in the early stages the child needs above all words to use, so that they pass fairly rapidly into his active vocabulary. It often happens that towards the middle of the second year the child concentrates on enlarging his passive vocabulary, which grows very quickly, and comparatively few new words appear in his own speech. During this time a child will usually refuse to repeat a word which he is just learning to recognize; there has to be some time lag before he will even say it aloud, let alone use it spontaneously in his own speech. In the ensuing months there is quite likely to be a marked increase in the number of words he transfers to his active vocabulary.

The words which are entered in our brain dictionary fall into a number of different word classes and three of these, the prepositions, conjunctions and pronouns, have a fixed number of items. During the period of language acquisition we learn the complete list of entries in these classes just as we learn the entire list of bound[†] morphemes and all this material taken together determines the form of what we say as distinct from its content. It is part of the economy of language that the form is regulated by choosing from a finite and restricted number of different elements, while the content is determined by choice from an infinitely greater range of possibilities. Language acquisition would scarcely be a practical proposition were it not for this arrangement; when we learn our mother tongue, we are able to acquire the complete stock of information demanded by the form of a spoken message during the learning period and as our experience and our mental powers increase, we employ these forms to express an ever greater variety of content. Consequently the words which we add to our cortical dictionary throughout life fall into the remaining word classes, nouns, verbs, adjectives and adverbs. Of these the nouns are the most numerous class, with verbs next, with adjectives some way behind and adverbs fewer still. These proportions are reflected in the child's language development. He begins by amassing a comparatively large stock of nouns and only one or two verbs; then about the age of two he will generally enlarge his stock of verbs rather rapidly, though the number will never equal that of the nouns. At this stage he will know a few adjectives, perhaps an adverb or two and one or two interrogative words such as *what* and *where*. It is obvious that mental development and language development go hand in hand and interact very much with each other. The child's grasp of the relations of things in the outside world and his ability to carry out mental operations do a great deal to influence the order in which some word classes grow. A child does not find it easy even to understand the meaning of prepositions, for example, and he therefore does not use them in an early stage of his language learning. At the age of about two he may learn a few, such as *to, in* and *on,* but it will be a long time before he can use words like *under, behind* and *before.* In a similar way he will use the word *and* quite early, but he will be at the stage of putting together complex sentences before he can handle *but, if* and *though.* Up to the age of two or more, a child refers to himself by name and in the third person and therefore pronouns do not appear in his speech until he begins to refer to himself as *me* or *I,* other pronouns coming into his vocabulary later still.

Individual children naturally develop in their own way and at their own pace with respect to speech and language as they do with everything else and the average child remains a figment of the statistical imagination. We may say, as a rough guide to the rate at which vocabulary grows, however, that at two years of age a child may be using about 200 different words; at three this will have risen to about 1000, and at four to something like 2000. An estimate of adult active vocabulary is 4000–5000 words and it may seem strange that the rest of one's life leads to no more than a two-to-one increase. The point is, however, that the 2000 words the child commands comprise the form words, the prepositions, conjunctions and pronouns, and all the commonest nouns and verbs, without which we should not be able to say anything at all, so the twofold increase leaves a considerable margin for the less common words, the technical and specialist vocabularies which characterize the speech of individual adult speakers.

The task of learning our mother tongue, then, is one which we accomplish essentially in the first five years of life. We evolve for ourselves the phoneme system, the acoustic cues for distinguishing sounds, the grammar and the syntax, and we lay the foundations of our personal dictionary. All this is derived from the sound of adult speech by which we are continually surrounded and we copy, mainly from our mothers, our pronunciation, intonation and rhythm. There may be some modifications in the last three in the course of our subsequent experience, but it is extremely difficult to make radical changes in our speech habits, as we all learn when we attempt to acquire a foreign language. Because we devote such an enormous amount of practice to the task, we are able to complete it painlessly and to forget it thereafter but this does not detract from the magnitude of the achievement. Only a few short years separate the bawling baby from the fully paid up member of the club of *homo loquens*. A well-known psychologist once remarked after four full days of discussion of the subject that he still favoured the 'miracle theory' of language acquisition and the more one discovers about speech, the more one is inclined to agree with him.

2 ON COMMUNICATIVE COMPETENCE[1]

Dell Hymes

Source: Excerpts from Dell Hymes, *On Communicative Competence* (University of Pennsylvania Press) 1971.

I

This paper is theoretical. One connotation of 'theoretical' is 'programatic'; a related connotation is that one knows too little about the subject to say something practical. Both connotations apply to this attempt to contribute to the study of the 'language problems of disadvantaged children'. Practical work, however, must have an eye on the current state of theory, for it can be guided or misguided, encouraged or discouraged, by what it takes that state to be. Moreover, the language development of children has particular pertinence just now for theory. The fundamental theme of this paper is that the theoretical and the practical problems converge.

It is not that there exists a body of linguistic theory that practical research can turn to and has only to apply. It is rather that work motivated by practical needs may help build the theory that we need. To a great extent programs to change the language situation of children are an attempt to apply a basic science that does not yet exist. Let me review the present stage of linguistic theory to show why this is so.

Consider a recent statement, one that makes explicit and precise an assumption that has underlain much of modern linguistics (Chomsky, 1965, p. 3):

> Linguistic theory is concerned primarily with an ideal speaker-listener, in a completely homogeneous speech community,[†] who knows its language perfectly and is unaffected by such grammatically irrelevant conditions as memory limitations, distractions, shifts of attention and interest, and errors (random or characteristic) in applying his knowledge of the language in actual performance.

From the standpoint of the children we seek to understand and help, such a statement may seem almost a declaration of irrelevance. All the difficulties that confront the children and ourselves seem swept from view.

One's response to such an indication of the state of linguistic theory might be to ignore fundamental theory and to pick and choose among its products. Models of language structure, after all, can be useful in ways not

36

envisioned in the statements of their authors. Some linguists (e.g., Labov, Rosenbaum, Gleitman) use transformational generative grammar† to study some of the ways in which a speech community is not homogeneous and in which speaker-listeners clearly have differential knowledge of a language. Perhaps, then, one ought simply to disregard how linguists define the scope of 'linguistic' theory. One could point to several available models of language – Trager-Smith-Joos,† tagmemic,† stratificational,† transformational-generative (in its MIT, Pennsylvania, Harvard and other variants), and, in England 'system-structure'† (Halliday and others); remark that there are distinguished scholars using each to analyse English; regret that linguists are unable to agree on the analysis of English; and pick and choose, according to one's problem and local situation, leaving grammarians otherwise to their own devices.

To do so would be a mistake for two reasons: on the one hand, the sort of theoretical perspective quoted above *is* relevant in ways that it is important always to have in mind; on the other hand, there is a body of linguistic data and problems that would be left without theoretical insight, if such a limited conception of linguistic theory was to remain unchallenged.

The special relevance of the theoretical perspective is expressed in its representative anecdote (to use Kenneth Burke's term), the image it puts before our eyes. The image is that of a child, born with the ability to master any language with almost miraculous ease and speed; a child who is not merely moulded by conditioning and reinforcement, but who actively proceeds with the unconscious theoretical interpretation of the speech that comes its way, so that in a few years and with a finite experience, it is master of an infinite ability, that of producing and understanding in principle any and all grammatical sentences of language. The image (or theoretical perspective) expresses the essential equality in children just as human beings. It is noble in that it can inspire one with the belief that even the most dispiriting conditions can be transformed; it is an indispensable weapon against views that would explain the communicative differences among groups of children as inherent, perhaps racial.

The limitations of the perspective appear when the image of the unfolding, mastering, fluent child is set beside the real children in our schools. The theory must seem, if not irrelevant, then at best a doctrine of poignancy: poignant, because of the difference between what one imagines and and what one sees; poignant too, because the theory, so powerful in its own realm, cannot on its terms cope with the difference. To cope with the realities of children as communicating beings requires a theory within which sociocultural factors have an explicit and constitutive role; and neither is the case.

For the perspective associated with transformational generative grammar, the world of linguistic theory has two parts: linguistic *competence* and linguistic *performance*. Linguistic competence is understood as concerned with the tacit knowledge of language structure, that is, knowledge that is commonly not conscious or available for spontaneous report, but necessarily implicit in what the (ideal) speaker-listener can say. The primary task of theory is to provide for an explicit account of such knowledge, especially in relation to the innate structure on which it must depend. It is in terms of such knowledge that one can produce and understand an infinite set of sentences, and that language can be spoken of as 'creative', as *energeia*. Linguistic performance is most explicitly understood as concerned with the processes often termed encoding and decoding.

Such a theory of competence posits ideal objects in abstraction from sociocultural features that might enter into their description. Acquisition of competence is also seen as essentially independent of sociocultural features, requiring only suitable speech in the environment of the child to develop. The theory of performance is the one sector that might have a specific sociocultural content; but while equated with a theory of language use, it is essentially concerned with psychological by-products of the analysis of grammar, not, say, with social interaction. As to a constitutive role for sociocultural features in the acquisition or conduct of performance, the attitude would seem quite negative. Little or nothing is said, and if something was said, one would expect it to be depreciatory. Some aspects of performance are, it is true, seen as having a constructive role (e.g., the cycling rules† that help assign stress properly to sentences), but if the passage quoted at the outset is recalled, however, and if the illustrations of performance phenomena in the chapter from which the passage comes are reviewed, it will be seen that the note struck is persistently one of limitation, if not disability. When the notion of performance is introduced as 'the actual use of language in concrete situations', it is immediately stated that only under the idealization quoted could performance directly reflect competence, and that in actual fact it obviously could not. 'A record of natural speech will show numerous false starts, deviations from rules, changes of plan in mid-course, and so on.' One speaks of primary linguistic data as 'fairly degenerate in quality' (Chomsky, 1965, p.31), or even of linguistic performance as 'adulteration' of ideal competence (Katz, 1967, p. 144). While 'performance' is something of a residual category for the theory, clearly its most salient connotation is that of imperfect manifestation of underlying system.

I do not think the failure to provide an explicit place for sociocultural features to be accidental. The restriction of competence to the notions of a homogeneous community, perfect knowledge, and independence of sociocultural factors does not seem just a simplifying assumption, the sort that any scientific theory must make. If that were so, then some remark to that effect might be made; the need to include a sociocultural dimension might be mentioned; the nature of such inclusion might even be suggested. Nor does the predominant association of performance with imperfection seem accidental. Certainly, any stretch of speech is an imperfect indication of the knowledge that underlies it. For users that share the knowledge, the arrangement might be thought of as efficient. And if one uses one's intuitions as to speech, as well as to grammar, one can see that what to grammar is imperfect, or unaccounted for, may be the artful accomplishment of a social art (Garfinkel, in press), or the patterned, spontaneous evidence of problem solving and conceptual thought (John, 1967, p. 5). These things might be acknowledged, even if not taken up.

It takes the absence of a place for sociocultural factors, and the linking of performance to imperfection, to disclose an ideological aspect to the theoretical standpoint. It is, if I may say so, rather a Garden of Eden view. Human life seems divided between grammatical competence, an ideal innately-derived sort of power, and performance, an exigency rather like the eating of the apple, thrusting the perfect speaker-hearer out into a fallen world. Of this world, where meaning may be won by the sweat of the brow, and communication achieved in labor (cf. Bonhoffer, 1965, p. 365), little is said. The controlling image is of an abstract, isolated individual, almost an unmotivated cognitive mechanism, not, except incidentally, a person in a social world.

Any theoretical stance of course has an ideological aspect, and that aspect of present linguistic theory is not its invention. A major characteristic of modern linguistics has been that it takes structure as primary end in itself, and tends to depreciate use, while not relinquishing any of its claim to the great significance that is attached to language. (Contrast classical antiquity, where structure was a means to use, and the grammarian subordinate to the rhetor.) The result can sometimes seem a very happy one. On the other hand, by narrowing concern to independently and readily structurable data, one can enjoy the prestige of an advanced science; on the other hand, despite ignoring the social dimensions of use, one retains the prestige of dealing with something fundamental to human life.

In this light, Chomsky is quite correct when he writes that his conception of the concern of linguistic theory seems to have been also the position of the founders of modern general linguistics. Certainly if modern structural linguistics is meant, then a major thrust of it has been to define the subject matter of linguistic theory in terms of what it is not. In de Saussure's linguistics, as generally interpreted, *la langue* was the privileged ground of structure, and *la parole* the residual realm of variation (among other things). Chomsky associates his views of competence and performance with the Saussurian conceptions of langue and parole, but sees his own conceptions as superior, going beyond the conception of language as a systematic inventory of items to renewal of the Humboldtian conception of underlying processes. The Chomsky conception is superior, not only in this respect, but also in the very terminology it introduces to mark the difference. 'Competence' and 'performance' much more readily suggest concrete persons, situations, and actions. Indeed, from the standpoint of the classical tradition in structural linguistics, Chomsky's theoretical standpoint is at once its revitalization and its culmination. It carries to its perfection the desire to deal in practice only with what is internal to language, yet to find in that internality what in theory is of the widest or deepest human significance. No modern linguistic theory has spoken more profoundly of either the internal structure or the intrinsic human significance.

This revitalization flowers while around it emerge the sprouts of a conception that before the end of the century may succeed it. If such a succession occurs, it will be because, just as the transformational theory could absorb its predecessors and handle structural relationships beyond their grasp, new relationships, relationships with an ineradicable social component, will become salient that will require a broader theory to absorb and handle them. I shall return to this historical conjecture at the end of this paper. Let me now sketch considerations that motivate a broader theory. And let me do this by first putting forward an additional representative anecdote.

II

As against the ideal speaker-listener, here is Bloomfield's account of one young Menomini he knew (1927, p. 395):

> White Thunder, a man around forty, speaks less English than Menomini, and that is a strong indictment, for his Menomini is atrocious. His vocabulary is small; his inflections are often barbarous; he constructs sentences of a few threadbare models. He may be said to speak no language tolerably. His case is not uncommon among younger men, even when they speak but little English.

Bloomfield goes on to suggest that the commonness of the case is due, in some indirect way, to the impact of the conquering language. In short, there is here *differential competence* within a *heterogeneous speech community*, both undoubtedly shaped by acculturation.[†] (The alternative to a constitutive role for the novel sociocultural factor is to assume that atrocious Menomini was common also before contact. If taken seriously, the assumption would still implicate sociocultural factors). Social life has affected not merely outward performance, but inner competence itself.

Let me now review some other indications of the need to transcend the notions of perfect competence, homogeneous speech community, and independence of sociocultural features.

In her excellent article reviewing recent studies of subcultural differences in language development in the United States, Cazden (1966, p. 190) writes that one thing is clear:

> The findings can be quickly summarized: on all the measures, in all the studies, the upper socio-economic status children, however defined, are more advanced than the lower socio-economic status children.

The differences reviewed by Cazden involve enabling effects for the upper status children just as much as disabling effects for the lower status children. Moreover, given subcultural differences in the patterns and purposes of language use, children of the lower status may actually excel in aspects of communicative competence not observed or measured in the tests summarized. And among the Menomini there were not only young men like White Thunder, but also those like Red Cloud Woman, who

> speaks a beautiful and highly idiomatic Menomini . . . (and) speaks Ojibwa and Potawatomi fluently . . . Linguistically, she would correspond to a highly educated American woman who spoke, say, French and Italian in addition to the very best type of cultivated, idiomatic English. (Bloomfield, 1927, p. 394)

There are tribes of the northeast Amazon among whom the normal scope of linguistic competence is a control of at least four languages, a spurt in active command coming during adolescence, with repertoire and perfection of competence continuing to be augmented throughout life. Here, as in much of our world, the ideally fluent speaker-listener is multilingual. (Even an ideally fluent monolingual of course is master of functional varieties within the one language.)

In this connection it should be noted that fluent members of communities often regard their languages, or functional varieties, as not identical in communicative adequacy. It is not only that one variety is obligatory or preferred for some uses, another for others (as is often the case, say, as between public occasions and personal relationships). Such intuitions reflect experience and self-evaluation as to what one can in fact do with a given variety. This sort of differential competence has nothing to do with 'disadvantage' or deficiency relative to other normal members of the community. All of them may find Kurdish, say, the medium in which most things can best be expressed, but Arabic the better medium for religious truth; users of Berber may find Arabic superior to Berber for all purposes except intimate domestic conversation (Ferguson, 1966).

The combination of community diversity and differential competence makes it necessary not to take the presence in a community of a widespread language, say, Spanish or English, at face value. Just as one puts the gloss of a native word in quotation marks, so as not to imply that the meaning of the word is thereby accurately identified, so one should put the name of a language in quotation marks, until its true status in terms of competence has been determined. (Clearly there is need for a theoretically motivated and empirically tested set of terms by which to characterize the different kinds of competence that may be found.) In an extreme case what counts as 'English' in the code repertoire[†] of a community may be but a few phonologically marked[†] forms (the Iwam of New Guinea). The cases in general constitute a continuum, perhaps a scale, from more restricted to less restricted varieties, somewhat crosscut by adaptation of the same inherited 'English' materials to different purposes and needs. A linguist analysing data from a community on the assumption 'once English, always English' might miss and sadly misrepresent the actual competence supposedly expressed by his grammar.

There is no way within the present view of linguistic competence to distinguish between the abilities of one of the pure speakers of Menomini noted by Bloomfield and those of whom White Thunder was typical. Menomini sentences from either would be referred to a common grammar. Perhaps it can be said that the competence is shared with regard to the recognition and comprehension of speech. While that would be an important (and probably true) fact, it has not been the intention of the theory to distinguish between models of competence for reception and models of competence for production. And insofar as the theory intends to deal with the 'creative' aspect of language, that is, with the ability of a user to devise novel sentences appropriate to situations, it would seem to be a retrenchment, if not more, to claim only to account for a shared ability to *understand* novel sentences produced by others. In some fundamental sense, the competence of the two groups of speakers, in terms of ability to make 'creative' use of Menomini, is clearly distinct. Difference in judgement of acceptability is not in question. There is simply a basic sense in which users of Menomini of the more versatile type have a knowledge (syntactic as well as lexical) that users of White Thunder's type do not. [. . .]

Labov has documented cases of dual competence in reception, but single competence in production, with regard to the ability of lower-class Negro children to interpret sentences in either standard or substandard phonology, while consistently using only substandard phonology in speaking themselves. An interesting converse kind of case is that in which there is a dual competence for production, a sort of 'competence for incompetence' as it were. Thus among the Burundi of East Africa (Albert, 1964) a peasant may command the verbal abilities stressed and valued in the culture but cannot display it in the presence of a herder or other superior. In such cases appropriate behavior is that in which 'their words are haltingly delivered, or run on uncontrolled, their voices are loud, their gestures wild, their figures of speech ungainly, their emotions freely displayed, their words and sentences clumsy'. Clearly the behavior is general to all codes of communication, but it attaches to the grammatical among them.

Such work as Labov's in New York City, and examples such as the Burundi, in which evidence for linguistic competence co-varies with interlocutor, point to the necessity of a social approach even if the goal of description is a single homogeneous code. Indeed, much of the difficulty in determining what is acceptable and intuitively correct in grammatical description arises because social and contextual determinants are not controlled. By making explicit the reference of a description to a single use in a single context, and by testing discrepancies and variations against differences of use and context, the very goal of not dealing with diversity can be achieved – in the limited, and only possible, sense in which it can be achieved. The linguist's own intuitions of underlying knowledge prove difficult to catch and to stabilize for use (and of course are not available for languages or varieties he does not himself know). If analysis is not to be reduced to explication of a corpus, or debauch into subjectivity, then the responses and judgements of members of the community whose language is analysed must be utilized – and not merely informally or *ad hoc,* but in some explicit, systematic way. In particular, since every response is made to some context, control of the dependence of judgements and abilities on context must be gained. It may well be that the two dimensions found by Labov to clarify phonological diversity – social hierarchy of varieties of usage, and range (formal and informal) of 'contextual styles', together with marking for special functions (expressivity, clarity, etc.) will serve for syntactic diversity as well. Certainly some understanding of local criteria of fluency, and conditions affecting it, is needed just insofar as the goal is to approximate an account of ideal fluency in the language in question. In sum, if one analyses the language of a community as if it should be homogeneous, its diversity trips one up around the edges. If one starts with analysis of the diversity, one can isolate the homogeneity that is truly there.

Clearly work with children, and with the place of language in education, requires a theory that can deal with a heterogeneous speech community, differential competence, the constitutive role of socioculture features — that can take into account such phenomena as White Thunder, socio-economic differences, multilingual mastery, relativity of competence in 'Arabic', 'English', etc., expressive values, socially determined perception, contextual styles and shared norms for the evaluation of variables. Those whose work requires such a theory know best how little of its content can now be specified. Two things can be said. First, linguistics needs such a theory too. Concepts that are unquestioningly postulated as basic to linguistics (speaker-listener, speech community, speech act, acceptability, etc.) are, as we see, in fact sociocultural variables, and only when one has moved from their postulation to their analysis can one secure the foundations of linguistic theory itself. Second, the notion of competence may itself provide the key. Such comparative study of the role of language as has been undertaken shows the nature and evaluation of linguistic ability to vary cross-culturally; even what is to count as the same language, or variety, to which competence might be related, depends in part upon social factors (cf. Gumperz, 1964; Hymes, 1968a; Labov, 1966). Given, then, the assumption that the competency of users of language entails abilities and judgements relative to, and interdependent with, sociocultural features, one can see how to extend the notion to allow for this. I shall undertake this, by recasting first the representative anecdote of the child, and then the notions of competence and performance themselves.

III

Recall that one is concerned to explain how a child comes rapidly to be able to produce and understand (in principle) any and all of the grammatical sentences of a language. Consider now a child with just that ability. A child who might produce any sentence whatever — such a child would be likely to be institutionalized: even more so if not only sentences, but also speech or silence was random, unpredictable. For that matter, a person who chooses occasions and sentences suitably, but is master only of fully grammatical sentences, is at best a bit odd. Some occasions call for being appropriately ungrammatical.

We have then to account for the fact that a normal child acquires knowledge of sentences, not only as grammatical, but also as appropriate. He or she acquires competence as to when to speak, when not, and as to what to talk about with whom, when, where, in what manner. In short, a child becomes able to accomplish a repertoire of speech acts, to take part in speech events, and to evaluate their accomplishment by others. This competence, moreover, is integral with attitudes, values, and motivations concerning language, its features and uses, and integral with competence for, and attitudes toward, the interrelation of language with the other code of communicative conduct (cf. Goffman, 1956, p. 477; 1963, p. 335; 1964). The internalization of attitudes towards a language and its uses is particularly important (cf. Labov, 1965, pp. 84-5, on priority of subjective evaluation in social dialect and processes of change), as is internalization of attitudes toward use of language itself (e.g. attentiveness to it) and the relative place that language comes to play in a pattern of mental abilities (cf. Cazden, 1966), and in strategics — what language is considered available, reliable, suitable for, *vis-à-vis* other kinds of code.

The acquisition of such competency is of course fed by social experience, needs, and motives, and issues in action that is itself a renewed source of motives, needs, experience. We break irrevocably with the model that restricts the design of language to one face toward referential meaning, one toward sound, and that defines the organization of language as solely consisting of rules for linking the two. Such a model implies naming to be the sole use of speech, as if languages were never organized to lament, rejoice, beseech, admonish, aphorize, inveigh (Burke, 1966, p. 13), for the many varied forms of persuasion, direction, expression and symbolic play. A model of language must design it with a face toward communicative conduct and social life.

Attention to the social dimension is thus not restricted to occasions on which social factors seem to interfere with or restrict the grammatical. The engagement of language in social life has a positive, productive aspect. There are rules of use without which the rules of grammar would be useless. Just as rules of syntax can control aspects of phonology, and just as semantic rules perhaps control aspects of syntax, so rules of speech acts enter as a controlling factor for linguistic form as a whole. Linguists generally have developed a theory of levels by showing that what is the same on one level of representation has in fact two different statuses, for which a further level must be posited. The seminal example is in Sapir (1925) on phonology, while the major recent examples are in the work of Chomsky and Lamb. A second aspect is that what is different at one level may have in fact the same status at the further level. (Thus the two interpretations of 'He decided on the floor' — the floor as what he decided on/as where he decided — point to a further level at which the sameness of structure is shown.) Just this reasoning requires a level of speech acts. What is grammatically the same sentence may be a statement, a command, or a request; what are grammatically two different sentences may as acts both be requests. One can study the level of speech acts in terms of the conditions under which sentences can be taken as alternative types of act, and in terms of the conditions under which types of act can be realized as alternative types of sentence. And only from the further level of acts can some of the relations among communicative means be seen, e.g. the mutual substitutability of a word and a nod to realize an act of assent, the necessary co-occurence of words and the raising of a hand to realize an oath.

The parallel interpretations of 'he decided on the floor' and 'she gave up on the floor' point to a further level at which the sameness in structure is shown.

Rules of use are not a late grafting. Data from the first years of acquisition of English grammar show children to develop rules for the use of different forms in different situations and an awareness of different acts of speech (Ervin-Tripp, personal communication). Allocation of whole languages to different uses is common for children in multilingual households from the beginning of their acquisition. Competency for use is part of the same developmental matrix as competence for grammar.

The acquisition of competence for use, indeed, can be stated in the same terms as acquisition of competence for grammar. Within the developmental matrix in which knowledge of the sentences of a language is acquired, children also acquire knowledge of a set of ways in which sentences are used. From a finite experience of speech acts and their interdependence with sociocultural features, they develop a general theory of the speaking appropriate in their community, which they employ, like other forms of tacit cultural knowledge (competence) in conducting and interpreting social life (cf. Goodenough, 1957; Searle, 1967). They come to be able to recognize, for example, appropriate and inappropriate interrogative behavior (e.g. among the Araucanians of Chile, that to repeat a question is to insult; among the Tzeltal of Chiapas, Mexico, that a direct question is not properly asked (and to be answered 'nothing'); among the Cahinahua of Brazil, that a direct answer to a first question implies that the answerer has no time to talk, a vague answer that the question will be answered directly the second time, and that talk can continue).

The existence of competency for use may seem obvious, but if its study is to be established, and conducted in relation to current linguistics, then the notions of competence and performance must themselves be critically analysed, and a revised formulation provided.

The chief difficulty of present linguistic theory is that it would seem to require one to identify the study of the phenomena of concern to use here with its category of performance. The theory's category of competence, identified with the criterion of grammaticality, provides no place. Only performance is left, and its associated criterion of acceptability. Indeed, language use is equated with performance: 'the theory of language use — the theory of performance' (Chomsky, 1965, p. 9).

The difficulty with this equation, and the reasons for the making of it, can be explained as follows. First, the clarification of the concept of performance offered by Chomsky (1965, pp. 10-15), as we have seen, omits almost everything of sociocultural significance. The focus of attention is upon questions such as which among grammatical sentences are most likely to be produced, easily understood, less clumsy, in some sense more natural; and such questions are studied initially in relation to formal tree-structures,[†] and properties of these such as nesting,[†] self-embedding,[†] multiple-branching,[†] left-branching, and right-branching. The study of such questions is of interest, but the results are results of the psychology of perception, memory, and the like, not of the domain of cultural patterning and social action. Thus, when one considers what the sociocultural analogues of performance in this sense might be, one sees that these analogues would not include major kinds of judgement and ability with which one must deal in studying the use of language (see below under appropriateness).

Second, the notion of performance, as used in discussion, seems confused between different meanings. In one sense, performance is observable behavior, as when one speaks of determining from the data of performance the underlying system of rules (Chomsky, 1965, p. 4), and of mentalistic linguistics as that linguistics that uses performance as data, along with other data, e.g. those of introspection, for determination of competence (p. 193). The recurrent use of 'actual' implies as much, as when the term is first introduced in the book in question, 'actual performance', and first characterized: 'performance (the actual use of language in concrete situations)' (pp. 3-4). In this sense performance is 'actual', competence underlying. In another sense, performance itself also underlies data, as

when one constructs a performance model, or infers a performative†
device (e.g. a perceptual one) that is to explain data and be tested against
them (p. 15); or as when, in a related sense, one even envisages the possibility of stylistic 'rules of performance' to account for occurring word
orders not accounted for by grammatical theory (p. 127).

When one speaks of performance, then, does one mean the behavioral
data of speech? or all that underlies speech beyond the grammatical? or
both? If the ambiguity is intentional, it is not fruitful; it smacks more of
the residual category and marginal interest.

The difficulty can be put in terms of the two contrasts that usage
manifests:

    1. (underlying) competence v. (actual) performance;
    2. (underlying) grammatical competence v. (underlying) models/rules
of performance.

The first contrast is so salient that the status of the second is left obscure.
In point of fact, I find it impossible to understand what stylistic 'rules of
performance' could be, except a further kind of underlying competence,
but the term is withheld. [. . .]

It remains that the present vision of generative grammar extends only a
little way into the realm of the use of language. To grasp the intuitions and
data pertinent to underlying competence for use requires a sociocultural
standpoint. To develop that standpoint adequately, one must transcend
the present formulation of the dichotomy of competence: performance,
as we have seen, and the associated formulation of the judgements and
abilities of the users of a language as well. To this I now turn.

IV

There are several sectors of communicative competence, of which the
grammatical is one. Put otherwise, there is behavior, and, underlying it,
there are several systems of rules reflected in the judgements and abilities
of those whose messages the behavior manifests. (The question of how
the interrelationships among sectors might be conceived is touched upon
below.) In the linguistic theory under discussion, judgements are said to
be of two kinds: of *grammaticality,* with respect to competence, and of
acceptability, with respect to performance. Each pair of terms is strictly
matched; the critical analysis just given requires analysis of the other. In
particular, the analysis just given requires that explicit distinctions be
made within the notion of 'acceptability' to match the distinctions of
kinds of 'performance', and at the same time, the entire set of terms must

be examined and recast with respect to the communication as a whole.

If an adequate theory of language users and language use is to be developed, it seems that judgements must be recognized to be in fact not of two kinds but of four. And if linguistic theory is to be integrated with theory of communication and culture, this fourfold distinction must be stated in a sufficiently generalized way. I would suggest, then, that for language and for other forms of communication (culture), four questions arise:

1. Whether (and to what degree) something is formally *possible*;
2. Whether (and to what degree) something is *feasible* in virtue of the means of implementation available;
3. Whether (and to what degree) something is *appropriate* (adequate, happy, successful) in relation to a context in which it is used and evaluated;
4. Whether (and to what degree) something is in fact done, actually *performed*, and what its doing entails.

A linguistic illustration: a sentence may be grammatical, awkward, tactful and rare. (One might think of the four as successive subsets; more likely they should be pictured as overlapping circles.)

These questions may be asked from the standpoint of a system *per se,* or from the standpoint of persons. An interest in competence dictates the latter standpoint here. Several observations can be made. There is an important sense in which a normal member of a community has knowledge with respect to all these aspects of the communicative systems available to him. He will interpret or assess the conduct of others and himself in ways that reflect a knowledge of each (possible, feasible, appropriate), done (if so, how often). There is an important sense in which he would be said to have a capability with regard to each. This latter sense, indeed, is one many would understand as included in what would be meant by his competence. Finally, it cannot be assumed that the formal possibilities of a system and individual knowledge are identical; a system may contain possibilities not part of the present knowledge of a user (cf. Wallace, 1961b). Nor can it be assumed that the knowledge acquired by different individuals is identical, despite identity of manifestation and apparent system.

Given these considerations, I think there is not sufficient reason to maintain a terminology at variance with more general usage of 'competence' and 'performance' in the sciences of man, as is the case with the present equations of competence, knowledge, systemic possibility, on the one hand, and of performance, behavior, implementational constraints, appropriateness, on the other. It seems necessary to distinguish these things and to reconsider their relationship, if their investigation is to be insightful and adequate.

I should take *competence* as the most general term for the capabilities of a person. (This choice is in the spirit, if at present against the letter, of the concern in linguistic theory for underlying capability.) Competence is dependent upon both (tacit) *knowledge* and (ability for) *use*. *Knowledge* is distinct, then, both from competence (as its part) and from systemic possibility (to which its relation is an empirical matter.) Notice that Cazden (1967), by utilizing what is in effect systemic possibility as a definition of competence is forced to separate it from what persons can do. The 'competence' underlying a person's behavior is identified as one kind of 'performance' (performance A, actual behavior being performance B). The logic may be inherent in the linguistic theory from which Cazden starts, once one tries to adapt its notion of competence to recognized facts of personal knowledge. The strangely misleading result shows that the original notion cannot be left unchanged.

Knowledge also is to be understood as subtending all four parameters of communication just noted. There is knowledge of each. *Ability for use* also may relate to all four parameters. Certainly it may be the case that individuals differ with regard to ability to use knowledge of each: to interpret, differentiate, etc. The specification of *ability for use* as part of competence allows for the role of noncognitive factors, such as motivation, as partly determining competence. In speaking of competence, it is especially important not to separate cognitive from affective and volitive factors, so far as the impact of theory on educational practice is concerned; but also with regard to research design and explanation (as the work of Labov indicates). Within a comprehensive view of competence, considerations of the sort identified by Goffman (1967, pp. 218-26) must be reckoned with − capacities in interaction such as courage, gameness, gallantry, composure, presence of mind, dignity, stage confidence, capacities which are discussed in some detail by him and, explicitly in at least one case, as kinds of competency (p. 224).

Turning to judgements and intuitions of persons, the most general term for the criterion of such judgements would be acceptable. Quirk (1966) so uses it, and Chomsky himself at one point remarks that 'grammaticalness is only one of the many factors that interact to determine acceptability' (1965, p. 11). (The term is thus freed from its strict pairing with 'performance'.) The sources of acceptability are to be found in the four parameters just noted, and in interrelations among them that are not well understood.

Turning to actual use and actual events, the term *performance* is now free for this meaning, but with several important reminders and provisos. The 'performance models' studied in psycholinguistics are to be taken as models of aspects of ability for use, relative to means of implementation in the brain, although they could now be seen as a distinct, contributory factor in general competence. There seems, indeed, to have been some unconscious shifting between the sense in which one would speak of the performance of a motor, and that in which one would speak of the performance of a person or actor (cf. Goffman, 1959, pp. 17-76, 'Performances') or of a cultural tradition (Singer, 1955; Wolf, 1964, pp. 75-6). Here the performance of a person is not identical with a behavioral record, or with the imperfect or partial realization of individual competence. It takes into account the interaction between competence (knowledge, ability for use), the competence of others, and the cybernetic and emergent properties of events themselves. A performance, as an event, may have properties (patterns and dynamics) not reducible to terms of individual or standardized competence. Sometimes, indeed, these properties are the point (a concert, play, party).

The concept of 'performance' will take on great importance, insofar as the study of communicative competence is seen as an aspect of what from another angle may be called the ethnography of symbolic forms — the study of the variety of genres, narration, dance, drama, song, instrumental music, visual art, that interrelate with speech in the communicative life of a society, and in terms of which the relative importance and meaning of speech and language must be assessed. The recent shift in folklore studies and much of anthropology to the study of these genres in terms of performances with underlying rules (e.g. Abrahams, 1967) can be seen as a reconstruction on an ethnographic basis of the vision expressed in Cassirer's philosophy of symbolic forms. (This reconstruction has a direct application to the communicative competence of children in American cities, where identification and understanding of differences in kinds of forms, abilities, and their evaluation is essential.)

The concept 'performance' will be important also in the light of sociological work such as that of Goffman (cited above), as its concern with general interactional competence helps make precise the particular role of linguistic competence.

In both respects the interrelation of knowledge of distinct codes (verbal: non-verbal) is crucial. In some cases these interrelations will bespeak an additional level of competence (cf., e.g., Sebeok, 1959, pp. 141-2: 'Performance constitutes a concurrently ordered selection from two sets of acoustic signals — in brief, codes — language and music . . .

These are integrated by special rules . . .'). In others, perhaps not, as when the separate cries of vendors and the call to prayer of a muezzin are perceived to fit by an observer of an Arabic city, but with indication of intent or plan.

The nature of research into symbolic forms and interactional competence is already influenced in important part by linguistic study of competence (for some discussion see Hymes, 1968b). Within the view of communicative competence taken here, the influence can be expected to be reciprocal.

Having stated these general recommendations, let me now review relations between the linguistic and other communicative systems, especially in terms of cultural anthropology. I shall consider both terminology and content, using the four questions as a framework.

1. Whether (and to what degree) something is formally possible

This formulation seems to express an essential concern of present linguistic theory for the openness, potentiality, of language, and to generalize it for cultural systems. When systemic possibility is a matter of language, the corresponding term is of course *grammaticality*. Indeed, language is so much the paradigmatic example that one uses 'grammar' and 'grammaticality' by extension for other sytems of formal possibility (recurrent references to a cultural grammar, Kenneth Burke's *A Grammar of Motives*, etc.). For particular systems, such extension may well be the easiest course; it is much easier to say that something is 'grammatical' with respect to the underlying structure of a body of myth, than to say in a new sense that it is 'mythical'. As a general term, one does readily enough speak of 'cultural' in a way analogous to grammatical (Sapir once wrote of 'culturalized behavior'; and it is clear that not all behavior is cultural). We may say, then, that something possible within a formal system is grammatical, cultural, or, on occasion, communicative (cf. Hymes, 1967b). Perhaps one can also say uncultural or uncommunicative, as well as ungrammatical, for the opposite.

2. Whether (and to what degree) something is feasible

The predominant concern here, it will be recalled, has been for psycholinguistic factors such as memory limitation, perceptual device,[†] effects of properties such as nesting, embedding, branching, and the like. Such considerations are not limited to linguistics. A parallel in cultural anthropology is Wallace's hypothesis (1961a, p. 462) that the brain is such that culturally institutionalized folk taxonomies will not contain more than twenty-six entitites and consequently will not require more than six orthogonally related binary dimensions for the definitions of all terms. With regard to the cultural, one would take into account other features of the body and features of the material environment as well. With regard to the communicative, the general importance of the notion of means of implementation available is clear.

As we have seen, question 2 defines one portion of what is lumped together in linguistic theory under the heading of performance, and, correspondingly, acceptability. Clearly a more specific term is needed for what is in question here. No general term has been proposed for this property with regard to cultural behavior as a whole, so far as I know, and *feasible* seems suitable and best for both. Notice, moreover, that the implementational constraints affecting grammar may be largely those that affect the culture as a whole. Certainly with regard to the brain there would seem to be substantial identity.

3. Whether (and to what degree) something is appropriate

As we have seen, appropriateness is hardly brought into view in the linguistic theory under discussion, and is lumped under the heading of performance, and, correspondingly, acceptability. With regard to cultural anthropology, the term *appropriate* has been used (Conklin, Frake, etc.), and has been extended to language (Hymes, 1964, pp. 39-41). 'Appropriateness' seems to suggest readily the required sense of relation to contextual features. (Since any judgement is made in some defining context, it may always involve a factor of appropriateness, so that this dimension must be controlled even in study of purely grammatical competence (cf. Labov, 1966). From a communicative standpoint, judgements of appropriateness may not be assignable to different spheres, as between the linguistic and the cultural; certainly, the spheres of the two will intersect. (One might think of appropriateness with regard to grammar as the context-sensitive rules of sub-categorization and selection to which the base component is subject; there would still be intersection with the cultural.)

Judgement of appropriateness employs a tacit knowledge. Chomsky himself discusses the need to specify situations in mentalistic[†] terms, and refers to proper notions of 'what might be expected from anthropological research' (1965, p. 195, n. 5). Here there would seem to be recognition that an adequate approach to the relation between sentences and situations must be 'mentalistic', entailing a tacit knowledge, and, hence, competence (in the usage of both Chomsky and this paper). But the restriction of competence (knowledge) to the grammatical prevails, so far as explicit development of theory is concerned. By implication, only 'performance' is left. There is no mention of what might contribute to judgement of sentences in relation to situations, nor how such judgements might be analysed. The lack of explicitness here, and the implicit contradiction of a 'mentalistic' account of what must in terms of the theory be a part of 'performance' show again the need to place linguistic theory within a more general sociocultural theory.

4. Whether (and to what degree) something is done

The study of communicative competence cannot restrict itself to occurrences, but it cannot ignore them. Structure cannot be reduced to probabilities of occurrence, but structural change is not independent of them. The capabilities of language users do include some (perhaps unconscious) knowledge of probabilities and shifts in them as indicators of style, response, etc. Something may be possible, feasible, and appropriate and not occur. No general term is perhaps needed here, but the point is needed, especially for work that seeks to change what is done. This category is necessary also to allow for what Harold Garfinkel (in discussion in Bright, 1966, p. 323) explicates as application of the medieval principle, *factum valet*: 'an action otherwise prohibited by rule is to be treated as correct if it happens nevertheless.'

In sum, the goal of a broad theory of competence can be said to be to show the ways in which the systemically possible, the feasible, and the appropriate are linked to produce and interpret actually occurring cultural behavior. [. . .]

V

We spoke first of a child's competence as 'in principle'. Of course no child has perfect knowledge or mastery of the communicative means of his community. In particular, differential competence has itself a developmental history in one's life. The matrix formed in childhood continues to develop and change throughout life with respect both to sentence structures and their uses (Labov, 1965, pp. 77, 91-2; Chomsky, 1965, p. 202) and recall the northeast Amazon situation mentioned earlier. Tanner (1967, p. 21) reports for a group of Indonesians: 'Although the childhood speech patterns . . . foreshadowed those of the adult, they did not determine them . . . For these informants it is the principle of code specialization that is the important characteristic of childhood linguistic experience, not the pattern of code specialization itself. (All are multilingual from childhood.) Not one person interviewed reported a static linguistic history in this respect.' (See now also Carroll, 1968.)

Perhaps one should contrast a 'long' and a 'short' range view of competency, the short range view being interested primarily in understanding innate capacities as unfolded during the first years of life, and the long range view in understanding the continuing socialization and change of competence through life. In any case, here is one major respect in which a theory of competence must go beyond the notion of ideal fluency in a homogeneous community, if it is to be applicable to work with disadvantaged children and with children whose primary language or language variety is different from that of their school; with intent to change or add, one is presupposing the possibility that competence that has unfolded in the natural way can be altered, perhaps drastically so, by new social factors. One is assuming from the outset a confrontation of different systems of competency within the school and community, and focusing on the way in which one affects or can be made to affect the other. One encounters phenomena that pertain not only to the separate structures of languages, but also to what has come to be called *interference* (Weinreich, 1953) between them: problems of the interpretation of manifestations of one system in terms of another.

Since the interference involves features of language and features of use together, one might adopt the phrase suggested by Hayes, and speak of *sociolinguistic interference.* (More generally, one would speak of *communicative interference* to allow for the role of modes of communication other than language; in this section, however, I shall focus on phenomena of language and language *per se.*)

When a child from one developmental matrix enters a situation in which the communicative expectations are defined in terms of another, misperception and misanalysis may occur at every level. As is well known, words may be misunderstood because of differences in phonological systems; sentences may be misunderstood because of difference in grammatical systems; intents, too. and innate abilities, may be misevaluated because of difference of systems for the use of language and for the import of its use (as against other modalities).

With regard to education, I put the matter some years ago in these words (Hymes, 1961, pp. 65-6):

. . . new speech habits and verbal training must be introduced, necessarily by particular sources to particular receivers, using a particular code with messages of particular forms via particular channels, about particular topics and in particular settings — and all this from and to people for whom there already exist definite patternings of linguistic routines, of personality expression via speech, of uses of speech in social situations, of attitudes and conceptions toward speech. It seems reasonable that success in such an education venture will be enhanced by an understanding of this existing structure, because the innovators' efforts will be perceived and judged in terms of it, and innovations which mesh with it will have greater success than those which cross its grain.

The notion of sociolinguistic interference is of the greatest importance for the relationship between theory and practice. First of all, notice that a theory of sociolinguistic interference must begin with heterogeneous situations, whose dimensions are social as well as linguistic. (While a narrow theory seems to cut itself off from such situations, it must of course be utilized in dealing with them. See, for example, Labov and Cohen (1967) on relations between standard and non-standard phonological and syntactic rules in Harlem, and between receptive and productive competence of users of the non-standard vernacular.)

Second, notice that the notion of sociolinguistic interference presupposes the notion of sociolinguistic systems between which interference occurs, and thus helps one see how to draw on a variety of researches that might be overlooked or set aside. (I have in mind for example obstacles to use of research on 'second-language learning' in programs for Negro students because of the offensiveness of the term.) The notions of sociolinguistic interference and system require a conception of an *integrated theory of sociolinguistic description*. Such work as has been done to contribute to such a theory has found it necessary to start, not from the notion of a language, but from the notion of a *variety* or *code*. In particular, such a descriptive theory is forced to recognize that the historically derived status of linguistic resources as related or unrelated languages and dialects, is entirely secondary to their status in actual social relationships. Firstly, recall the need to put language names in quotes (section II). Secondly, the degree of linguistic similarity and distance cannot predict mutual intelligibility, let alone use. Thirdly, from the functional standpoint of a sociolinguistic description, means of quite different scope can be employed in equivalent roles. A striking example is that the marking of intimacy and respect served by shift of second person pronoun in French (*tu* : *vous*) may be served by shift of entire language in Paraguay (Guarani: Spanish). Conversely, what seem equivalent means from the standpoint of languages may have quite different roles, e.g., the elaborated and restricted codes of English studied by Bernstein (1965). In short, we have to break with the tradition of thought which simply equates one language, one culture, and takes a set of functions for granted. In order to deal with the problems faced by disadvantaged children, and with education in much of the world, we have to begin with the conception of the speech habits, or competencies, of a community of population, and regard the place among them of the resources of historically-derived languages as an empirical question. As functioning codes, one may find one language, three languages; dialects widely divergent or divergent by a hair; styles almost mutually incomprehensible, or barely detectable as different by the outsider; the objective linguistic differences are secondary, and do not tell the story. What must be known is the attitude toward the differences, the functional role assigned to them, the use made of them. Only on the basis of such a functionally motivated description can comparable cases be established and valid theory developed.

Now with regard to sociolinguistic interference among school children, much relevant information and theoretical insight can come from the sorts of cases variously labelled 'bilingualism', 'linguistic acculturation', 'dialectology', 'creolization',[†] whatever. The value of an integrated theory of sociolinguistic description to the practical work would be that

1. it would attempt to place studies, diversely labelled, within a common analytical framework; and

2. by placing such information within a common framework, where one can talk about relations among codes, and types of code-switching, and types of interference as between codes, one can make use of the theory while perhaps avoiding connotations that attach to such labels as 'second-language learning', (I say perhaps because of course it is very difficult to avoid unpleasant connotations for any terms used to designate situations that are themselves intrinsically sensitive and objectionable.)

William Stewart's (1965, p. 11, n. 2) suggestion that some code relationships in the United States might be better understood if seen as part of a continuum of cases ranging to the Caribbean and Africa, for example, seems to me from a theoretical standpoint very promising. It is not that most code relationships in the United States are to be taken as involving different languages, but that they do not involve relationships among different codes, and that the fuller series illuminates the part. Stewart has seen through the different labels of dialect, creole, pidgin, language, bilingualism, to a common sociolinguistic dimension. Getting through different labels to the underlying sociolinguistic dimensions is a task in which theory and practice meet.

Let me now single out three interrelated concepts, important to a theory of sociolinguistic description, which have the same property of enabling us to cut across diverse cases and modes of reporting, and to get to basic relationships. One such concept is that of *verbal repertoire*, which Gumperz (1964) has done much to develop. The heterogeneity of speech communities, and the priority of social relationships, is assumed, and the question to be investigated is that of the set of varieties, codes, or subcodes, commanded by an individual, together with the types of switching that occur among them. (More generally, one would assess communicative repertoire.)

A second concept is that of *linguistic routines*, sequential organizations beyond the sentence, either as activities of one person, or as the interaction of two or more. Literary genres provide obvious examples; the organization of other kinds of texts, and of conversation, is getting fresh attention by sociologists, such as Sacks, and sociologically oriented linguists, such as Labov. One special importance of linguistic routines is that they may have the property that the late English philosopher Austin dubbed *performative* (Searle, 1967). That is, the saying does not simply stand for, refer to, some other thing; it is itself the thing in question. To say 'I solemnly vow' is to solemnly vow; it does not name something else that is the act of vowing solemnly. Indeed, in the circumstances no other way to vow solemnly is provided other than to do so by saying that one does so. From this standpoint, then, disability and ability with regard to language involve questions that are not about the relation between language and something else that language might stand for or influence; sometimes such questions are about things that are done linguistically or not at all. (More generally, one would analyse linguistic routines, comprising gesture, paralinguistics, etc. as well.)

A third concept is that of *domains of language behavior*, which Fishman has dealt with insightfully in his impressive work on *Language Loyalty in the United States* (1966, pp. 424-39). Again, the complexity and patterning of use is assumed, and the focus is upon 'the most parsimonious and fruitful designation of the occasions on which one language (variant, dialect, style, etc.) is habitually employed rather than (or in addition to) another' (p. 428). (More generally, one would define domains of communicative behavior.)

Too often, to be sure, the significance of a sociolinguistic feature, such as a code, routine, or term or level of address, is sought by purely distributional means. The feature is traced through the set of contexts in which it can be used without regard to an intervening semantic structure. Such an approach neglects the fact that sociolinguistic features, like linguistic features, are 'signs' in the classical Saussurean sense, comprising both a form and a meaning (*signifiant* and *signifié*). The difference is that one thinks of a typical linguistic sign as comprising a phonological form and a referential meaning (*chien* and the corresponding animal), whereas a sociolingustic sign may comprise with respect to form an entire language, or some organized part of one, while meaning may have to do with an attitude, norm or interaction, or the like. (Recall the Paraguayan case of Spanish/distance: Guarani/closeness (among other dimensions.)) Thus the relation between feature and context is mediated by a semantic paradigm. There is an analogue here to the representation of a lexical element in a language in terms of form (phonological features), meaning (semantic features), and context (features of syntactic selection), or, indeed, to the tripartite semiotic[†] formula of Morris, syntactics, semantics, pragmatics, if these three can be interpreted here as analogous of form, meaning and context.

If the distributional approach neglects semantic structure, there is a common semantic approach that neglects context. It analyses the structure of a set of elements (say, codes, or terms of personal reference) by assuming one normal context. This approach (typical of much componential analysis) is equally unable to account for the range of functions a fluent user of language is able to accomplish (cf. Tyler, 1966). It is true that the value of a feature is defined first of all in relation to a set of normal contexts (settings, participants, personal relationships, topics, or whatever). But given this 'unmarked' (presupposed) usage, an actor is able to insult, flatter, color discourse as comic or elevated, etc., by 'marked' use of the feature (code, routine, level of address, whatever) in other contexts. Given their tacit knowledge of the normal values, hearers can interpret the nature and degree of markedness of the use.

Thus the differences that one may encounter within a community may have to do with:

1. presence or absence of a feature (code, routine, etc.);
2. the semantic value assigned a feature (e.g., English as having the value of distance and hostility among some American Indians);
3. the distribution of the feature among contexts; and
4. the interrelations of these with each other in unmarked and marked usages.

This discussion does not exhaust the concepts and modes of analysis relevant to the sort of theory that is needed. A number of scholars are developing relevant conceptual approaches, notably Bernstein, Fishman, Gumperz, Labov (my own present formulation is indicated in Hymes, 1967a). The three concepts singled out do point up major dimensions: the

60 On Communicative Competence

capacities of persons, the organization of verbal means for socially defined purposes, and the sensitivity of rules to situations. And it is possible to use the three concepts to suggest one practical framework for use in sociolinguistic description [. . .]

Notes

1.   This paper is revised from one presented at the Research Planning Conference on Language Development Among Disadvantaged Children, held under the sponsorship of the Department of Educational Psychology and Guidance, Ferkauf Graduate School, Yeshiva University, June 7-8, 1966. The original paper is included in the report of that conference, issued by the Department of Educational Psychology and Guidance (pp. 1-16). I wish to thank Dr Beryl Bailey and Dr Edmund Gordon of Yeshiva University for inviting me to participate and Dr Courtney Cazden, Dr John Gumperz, Dr Wayne O'Neill and Dr Vera John for their comments at that time.

References

Abrahams, R.D. (1967), 'Patterns of performance in the British West Indies', mimeographed working paper.
Albert, E.M. (1964), 'Rhetoric, logic and poetics in Burundi: culture patterning of speech behavior', in J.J. Gumperz and D. Hymes (eds.), *The Ethnography of Communication, AmA,* vol. 66, no. 6, part 2.
Bernstein, B. (1965), 'A sociolinguistic approach to social learning', in J. Gould (ed.), *Social Science Survey,* Penguin.
Bloomfield, L. (1927), 'Literate and illiterate speech', *Amer. Speech,* vol. 2, pp. 432-9.
Bonhoffer, D. (1965), 'What is meant by "telling the truth"?', *Ethics,* pp. 363-72.
Bright, W. (1966), *Sociolinguistics,* Mouton.
Burke, K. (1966), *Towards a Better Life. Being a Series of Epistles, or Declamations,* University of California Press (first published 1932).
Carroll, J.B. (1968), 'Development of native language skills beyond the early years', in Reed and J.B. Carroll (eds.), *Language Learning,* National Council of Teachers of English.
Cazden, C.B. (1966), 'Subcultural differences in child language: an interdisciplinary review', *Merrill-Palmer Q.,* vol. 12, pp. 185-218.
Cazden, C.B. (1967), 'On individual differences in language competence and performance', *J. Spec. Educ.,* vol. 1, pp. 135-50.
Chomsky, N. (1965), *Aspects of the Theory of Syntax,* MIT Press.
Ferguson, C.A. (1966), 'On sociolinguistically oriented surveys', *Linguistic Reporter,* vol. 8, no. 4, pp. 1-3.
Fishman, J.A. (1966), *Language Loyalty in the United States,* Mouton.
Garfinkel, H. (in press), 'Remarks on ethnomethodology', in J.J. Gumperz and D. Hymes (eds.), *Directions in Sociolinguistics,* Holt, Rinehart & Winston.
Goffman, E. (1956), 'The nature of deference and demeanor', *AmA,* vol. 58, pp. 473-502.
Goffman, E. (1959), *The Presentation of Self in Everyday Life,* Doubleday; Allen Lane, The Penguin Press.

Goffman, E. (1963), *Behavior in Public Places*, Free Press.
Goffman, E. (1964), 'The neglected situation', in J.J. Gumperz and D. Hymes (eds.), *The Ethnography of Communication, AmA*, vol. 66, no. 6, part 2.
Goffman, E. (1967), *Interaction Ritual*, Doubleday.
Goodenough, W.H. (1957), 'Cultural anthropology and linguistics', in P. Garvin (ed.), *Report of the Seventh Annual Round Table Meeting on Languages and Linguistics*, Georgetown University Press.
Gumperz, J.J. (1964), 'Linguistic and social interaction in two communities', in J.J. Gumperz and D. Hymes (eds.), *The Ethnography of Communication, AmA*, vol. 66, no. 6, part 2.
Hymes, D. (1961), 'Functions of speech: an evolutionary approach', in F. Gruber (ed.), *Anthropology and Education*, University of Pennsylvania.
Hymes, D. (1964), 'Directions in (ethno-) linguistic theory', in A.K. Romney and R.G. D'Andrade (eds.), *Transcultural Studies of Cognition*, American Anthropological Association.
Hymes, D. (1967a), 'Models of the interaction of language and social setting', *J. Soc. Iss.*, vol. 23, pp. 8-28.
Hymes, D. (1967b), 'The anthropology of communication', in F. Dance (ed.), *Human Communication Theory: Original Essays*, Holt, Rinehart & Winston.
Hymes, D. (1968a), 'Linguistic problems in defining the concept of the tribe', in J. Helm (ed.), *Proceedings of the 1967 Spring Meeting of the American Ethnological Society*, University of Washington Press.
Hymes, D. (1968b), 'Linguistics – the field', *International Encyclopedia of the Social Sciences*, Macmillan Co.
Hymes, D. (in press), Review of Kenneth Burke, *Language as Symbolic Action, Language*.
John, V. (1967), 'Communicative competence of low-income children: Assumptions and programs', *Report of Language Development Study Group*, Ford Foundation.
Katz, J.J. (1967), 'Recent issues in semantic theory', *Foundations of Language*, vol. 3, pp. 124-94.
Labov, W. (1965), 'Stages in the acquisition of standard English', in R. Shuy (ed.), *Social Dialects and Language Learning*, National Council of Teachers of English.
Labov, W. (1966), *The Social Stratification of English in New York City*, Center for Applied Linguistics.
Labov, W., and Cohen, P. (1967), 'Systematic relations of standard and non-standard rules in the grammar of Negro speakers', paper for Seventh Project Literacy Conference, Cambridge, Mass.
Quirk, R. (1966), 'Acceptability in language', *Proceedings of the University of Newcastle-upon-Tyne Philosophical Society*, vol. 1, no. 7, pp. 79-92.
Sapir, E. (1925), 'Sound patterns in language', *Language*, vol. 1, pp. 37-51.
Searle, J. (1967), 'Human communication theory and the philosophy of language: some remarks', in F. Dance (ed.), *Human Communication Theory*, Holt, Rinehart & Winston.
Sebeok, T. (1959), 'Folksong viewed as code and message', *Anthropos*, vol. 54, pp. 141-53.
Singer, M. (1955), 'The cultural pattern of Indian civilization: a preliminary report of a methodological field study', *Far East. Q.*, vol. 15, pp. 223-36.
Stewart, W. (1965), 'Urban Negro speech: sociolinguistic factors affecting English teaching', in R. Shuy (ed.), *Social Dialects and Language Learning*, National Council of Teachers of English.
Tanner, N. (1967), 'Speech and society among the Indonesian elite: a case study of a multilingual community', *Anthrop. Linguistics*, vol. 9, no. 3, pp. 15-40.
Tyler, S. (1966), 'Context and variation in Koya kinship terminology', *AmA*, vol. 68, pp. 693-707.

Wallace, A.F.C. (1961a), 'On being just complicated enough', *Proceedings of the National Academy of Sciences,* vol. 47, pp. 438-64.
Wallace, A.F.C. (1961b), *Culture and Personality,* Random House.
Weinreich, U. (1953), *Languages in Contact,* Linguistic Circle of New York.
Wolf, E. (1964), *Anthropology,* Prentice-Hall.

3 FROM COMMUNICATION TO LANGUAGE – A PSYCHOLOGICAL PERSPECTIVE[1]

Dedicated to Roman Jakobson on his eightieth birthday

Jerome Bruner

Source: *Cognition,* Vol. 3, 1974-5, pp. 255-87.

Abstract

Any realistic account of language acquisition must take into account the manner in which the child passes from pre-speech communication to the use of language proper. For it can be shown that many of the major organizing features of syntax, semantics, pragmatics,[†] and even phonology have important precursors and prerequisites in the pre-speech communicative acts of infants. Illustrations of such precursors are examined in four different domains: The mother's mode of interpreting the infant's communicative intent; the development of joint referential devices en route to deixis;[†] the child's developing strategy for enlisting aid in joint activity; the transformation of topic-comment organization in pre-speech to predication proper. Finally, the conjecture is explored whether the child's knowledge of the requirements of action and interaction might provide the basis for the initial development of grammar.

Whatever view one takes of research on language acquisition proper – however nativist or empiricist one's bias – one must still come to terms with the role or significance of the child's pre-speech communication system. What is the nature of that system and does its very nature aid the passage from pre-speech communication to language? What makes for linguistic difficulty in answering such questions is that since the child's communication before language is not amenable to conventional grammatical analysis, efforts to trace continuities often seem little more than a hunt for analogies of 'grammar' in early action or gesture. On the psychological side, the difficulty inheres in the tradition of such research – usually to explain away language as 'nothing but' the concatenation of simple conditioning, imitation, or other mysterious simplifications. I shall try in the following pages to show that one can establish continuities between pre-speech communication and language, and do so without recourse to inappropriate reductionism.

The resurgent nativism that followed upon the work of Chomsky

63

(1965) nurtured quite falsely the hope that this first step could be by-passed — although there is nothing in Chomsky's own writing that would lead necessarily to such a conclusion. The reasoning seems to have been that, if language grows from its own roots, it suffices to study the beginnings of language proper if one wishes to understand the nature of its early acquisition. The programme, in effect, was the linguists' programme: Gather a corpus of speech, with due regard for context (unspecified), and subject it to grammatical analysis. Or, to add an experimental dimension, contrive experimental situations to tap the child's capacities for producing and comprehending speech in particular contexts, and draw inferences from the child's responses concerning his underlying linguistic competence.

There can be little doubt that this programme has deeply enriched our understanding of early language and of the course of its early development. The work of Brown (1970, 1973) and his group, of Bloom (1970), of McNeill (1970a, 1970b), of Slobin (1973), of the Edinburgh group (e.g. Donaldson and Wales, 1970) — all attest to the enormous progress of the last decade.

But the early language for which a grammar is written is the end result of psychological processes leading to its acquisition, and to write a grammar of that language at any point in its development is in no sense to explicate the nature of its acquisition. Even if it were literally true (as claimed by Chomsky), that the child, mastering a particular language, initially possesses a tacit knowledge of an alleged universal deep[†] structure of language, we would still have to know how he managed to recognize these universal deep rules as they manifest themselves in the surface[†] structure of a particular language. Even an innate 'language acquisition device' would require a programme to guide such recognition and it would fall to the psychologist to discover the nature of the programme by investigating the alleged recognition process (Chomsky, 1965, p. 27). For Chomsky, the child's problem is 'to determine which of the (humanly) possible languages is that of the community in which he is placed'. If there were no such recognition problems, the child would obviously learn language immediately and perfectly — at least those portions of it to which he were exposed. This is so far from what happens that we generally agree that it is eminently worth studying what might be called the prerequisites necessary for learning a language or for progressing in the mastery of that language. At the most general level, we may say that to master a language a child must acquire a complex set of broadly transferable or generative skills — perceptual, motor, conceptual, social, *and* linguistic — which when appropriately coordinated yield linguistic performances that can be described (though only in a limited sense) by the linguists' rules of grammar. Such rules of grammar may bear no closer resemblance to the psychological laws of language production, comprehension, and use than do the principles of optics bear to the laws of visual perception — in neither case can the one violate the other.

If we are to concentrate upon the prerequisite sensory, motor, conceptual, and social skills whose coordination makes language possible, we must alas abandon in large part the powerful grammar-writing procedures of the developmental linguist. For it no longer suffices to collect a corpus of spoken language for which successive grammars may be written, though these grammars may yield valuable hypotheses about the antecedent psychological processes that brought them into being. Instead one must devise ways of investigating the constituent skills involved in language. And typically one begins well before language begins, following the communicative behavior of particular children until a particular level of linguistic mastery is achieved, testing as well for other, concomitant indices of growth. Not surprisingly, then, there are few such studies available, most still in progress: Trevarthen (1974a, 1974b), Sugarman (1974), Bates, Camaioni and Volterra (1973), Lock (1972), McNeill (1974), Dore (1974, 1975), Urwin (1973), and Burner (1975) though more are starting up.

What is peculiarly difficult in conducting such studies is that their design depends upon more or less explicit decisions concerning what beside language should be studied, decisions derived from hypotheses about the precursors and prerequisites of early language. Typically, in such work, an investigator starts by selecting a 'target' process in later speech and explores its precursors in prelinguistic communication, concentrating upon forms of communication later realized by linguistic means but earlier fulfilled (partially or fully) by gestural or other expression. Studies of this kind explore the continuity between functionally equivalent forms of communication before and after the onset of speech proper. The investigator, for example, may study the prelinguistic devices a child uses for making a *request* or for establishing a *joint referent* before these can be handled through such grammatically appropriate means as interrogatives or demonstratives. Inevitably, such an approach shifts emphasis to functions of language use, to pragmatics and communicative competence (Campbell and Wales, 1970) and away from syntactic competence in the sense employed by Chomsky (1965) and McNeill (1970a, 1970b).

If one pursues this course, one is tempted to look for the 'grammar' inherent in certain forms of social interaction, the emergence of 'proper' grammar then being conceived of as the child gaining insight about how to *express in language* an idea previously held but expressed by other than linguistic means. Both Sugarman (1974) and Bates *et al.* (1973) for example use non-linguistic behavioural indicators to infer the presence in pre-speech behavior of such concepts as *Agent*[†] and *Instrument* (when the child signals an adult to help him do something that he wishes to accomplish). They see these prelinguistic accomplishments as precursors of case-grammatical[†] categories like *Agentive* and *Instrumental* in Fillmore's (1968) sense of case grammar (of which more will be said later).

But this procedure inevitably brings the investigator to the psychological question: What makes it possible for the child to progress, say, from a prelinguistic form of expressing the demonstrative or agentive to a more advanced linguistic form of expression? It is at this point that the second side of this type of research emerges: The search for the constituent skills relevant to linguistic mastery. The commonest practice is to turn to Piaget (e.g., Sinclair, 1969). According to his well-known view, language is facilitated by the development of sensori-motor schemas,[†] that represent the joint outcomes of perception and action. These undergo orderly changes that are nourished (though not shaped) by continued experience in acting on the world. In time, for example, the child comes to separate thought from action in his schemas, and his concepts of objects and events in the world become independent of the actions to be performed on them. Sensori-motor schemas also come with experience to transcend space and time, so that the concept of an object is no longer tied to particular contexts, but becomes somewhat more context-free. The acquisition of language is seen as somehow emerging from these developments. Thus a concept of objects that is independent of action on the object should aid the child in mastering such linguistic distinctions as Action[†] and Object[†] in case grammar or, even Noun Phrase and Verb Phrase in the more usual generative grammar. Bates *et al.*, (1973), for example, attribute prelinguistic progress in signalling imperatives and declaratives to the child's maturing Piagetian sensori-motor schemas, though their basis for doing so is partly by appeal to coincidence between the times of appearance of different forms of signalling and the dates usually cited in Piagetian norms and partly to their presence in the sample studied.

Sugarman does somewhat better in this regard. She notes Piaget's observation (1952) that the child, in organizing a sensori-motor schema, will first go through a phase of dealing separately with particular objects before he is able to subordinate the use of one object to the other, as in using one as a tool for getting the other. She likens this to the process of early skill development which progresses by the combining of skilled routines that have first developed separately (Bruner, 1973). With this as background, she postulates that the child will first go through a stage in which he treats persons and objects independently, developing schemas for each, will then elaborate these, until finally he will combine them into a unified schema: Person-as-agent-to-help-obtain-object. As this schema develops, the child will acquire signalling techniques appropriate to this level of growth. And indeed, her data indicate that the child first addresses himself separately to objects or to the mother, and finally learns to signal the mother to get her help in obtaining an object, with an intermediate stage in which there is elaboration of signalling toward mother and object separately.

My principal concern with the Piagetian approach of these authors and of Sinclair (1969) is that it concentrates almost exclusively on the formal aspects of language at the expense of the functional, the emerging structure of the child's language without due regard for the uses to which language is put in different contexts. It will be clearer in the following pages why I think this is a serious and distorting difficulty. But in general, one can only applaud the aim of such efforts, for they do indeed represent the kind of 'middle way' between extreme nativism that sees no problem because it is all there in advance, and extreme empiricist reductionism that sees no problem because it dismisses what is in fact already there by way of readiness to use language in a particularly structured way.

Whoever studies prelinguistic precursors of language must, I believe, commit himself to what Cromer (1974) has recently called the 'cognition hypothesis'. The cognition hypothesis has two parts to it. The first holds that 'we are able to understand and productively to use particular linguistic structures only when our cognitive abilities enable us to do so' (Cromer, 1974, p. 246). The second holds that when our cognitive abilities allow us to grasp a particular idea, we may still not have grasped the complex rule for expressing it freely but may nonetheless express it in a less complex, if indirect form. He provides as an example the perfect tense and the conceptual idea of completed action: A child who has not yet grasped the perfective device embodied in such sentences as

Have you peeked?

can nonetheless express the same meaning by using the simpler rule of combining a known form with the word *yet,* yielding utterances like,

Did you peek yet?

Presumably, this capacity to express a cognitive insight by means short of the fully realized linguistic rule can be pushed down in age to the point where one asks whether the child is able to use prelinguistic devices for expressing a cognitive insight even before sentential grammar is present in his language.

Both parts of the cognition hypothesis presuppose the doctrine of functional substitutability or at least of continuity. Neither is a doctrine to be facilely accepted. In semantics, substitutability is represented by Bloomfield's (1933) 'fundamental postulate' that in any given speech community one can find formal and semantic equivalents of certain sentences that serve as 'glosses' of each other. The transformational grammarian usually handles these matters by invoking 'a common "underlying" structure for semantically equivalent "surface" syntactic arrangements' (Silverstein, 1975). But while in Cromer's example of the more and less compact versions of the grammatical perfective, one can arguably make the case for a gloss, it becomes progressively more difficult to do so as communicative devices become more separated in ontogenetic time. What is the relationship, for example, between a gestural sign of pointing to an apple and the uttering of the word *apple*? They are plainly not glosses of each other in any formal sense. Yet, one is prepared, if only intuitively, to grant that they may be continuous with each other. We say that the two serve the same function of indicating, or at least *some* aspect of this function. If we make a further separation in time and compare a gestural indication with a simple sentence, *That apple* (whether or not we assume that the existential copula is absent because of a deletion rule), then the gap becomes so great as to seem discontinuous. For example, the predicational form of the more advanced utterance makes it amenable to truth testing, the word *that* already presupposes deictic marking, etc., etc., — none of which is remotely attributable to ostensive† pointing. Yet, again we assume there is *some* continuity. In what does it consist?

I would suggest that continuity can be attributed for two reasons: The first is by a principle of incorporation, that in achieving competence to utter a simple sentential indicative the child necessarily incorporates prior knowledge implied in his mastery of the ostensive indicative. But this is surely a weak form of continuity by incorporation, no stronger than the indubitable claim that an infant must stand before he can take his first step. It is strengthened by two additional considerations, one treated below in examining some bases for attributing continuity, the second being the following. If we can show that the child's prior grasp of ostensive indicating by pointing provides knowledge that permits him to 'crack the code', say, of lexical indicating, that it is in fact a stepping stone in a line of prerequisites leading to the use of a simple sentential form of indicating, then incorporation ceases to be merely logical and becomes psychological. The stronger form would be, then, that lexical indicating occurs if and only if the child has previously grasped a more primitive device of indicating and can be shown to use that device instrumentally in the acquisition of the more advanced form. In a word, for a precursor utterance to become psychologically and linguistically interesting, it must be shown to be an instrumental prerequisite to a more evolved utterance.

A second basis for attributing continuity is provided in a more comprehensive view of the nature of language use within any given culture, a subject too readily overlooked in our headlong pursuit of structural regularities in grammar. Stated at its most banal, it is that speech is meaningful social behavior. But at the same time, it is crucial to bear in mind that articulate phonetic speech is only one of the devices by which meaning is transmitted in such social behavior. Whatever the device employed, 'this functional sign mode always involves some aspect of the context in which the sign occurs' (Silverstein, 1975). This pragmatic aspect of sign use is dependent upon a mastery of cultural conventions and it is the linkage of signs to conventions that assures the 'meaningful' use of any signalling system, language included. It is not surprising that Cohen (1974) has recently lamented that, in applying speech-act theory, it is very difficult to decide where linguistics ends and where the study of 'manners' begins. For, as we shall try to show, many of the conventions that underlie the use of language are learned prior to the onset of articulate phonetic speech. Silverstein (1975), proposing to extend the tradition of pragmatics in the line from Peirce to Jakobson and beyond, puts the matters as follows:

> To say of social behavior that it is meaningful implies necessarily that it is communicative, that is, that the behavior is a complex of signs (sign vehicles) that signal or stand for something in some respect. Such behavioral signs are significant to someone, participants in a communicative event, and such behavior is purposive, that is goal-oriented in the sense of accomplishing (or failing to accomplish) certain ends of communication . . . In general, then, we can say that people are constituted as a society with a certain *culture* to the extent that they share the same means of social communication.

He then goes on to point to various of the properties of communicative events — notably the nature of the relationships that prevail between communicator and recipient. These relationships, interchangeability of roles being one of the most obvious, are highly structured by some subtle mix of human endowment and cultural convention. Silverstein is not concerned directly with the ontogenesis of these role relations, but they lie at the base of the concern of much of what follows in this paper. These are the functioning communicative acts that give shape to the infant's discourse with adults in his immediate environment: referencer and recipient, demander and complier, seeker and finder, task-initiator and accomplice, actor and prohibitor, etc. A close analysis of the first year of an infant's life provides not only a catalogue of the joint 'formats' (see below) in which communicator and recipient habitually find each other, but also provides a vivid record of how roles developed in such formats become conventionalized. The infant is not only learning, as we shall see, what constitutes indicating something to another, or having something indicated to him, but he is also learning how to substitute new means for doing so in order to achieve less uncertain outcomes by the use of more ritualized techniques. When, finally, he reaches a stage at which lexical indicating is psychologically within his reach, he already knows a great deal about the nature of indicative contexts and conventions for dealing with them.

It is in this second sense that continuity becomes of special importance. For if the child, say, already knows (as we shall see) many of the conventions for give-and-take exchanges and how to conduct them by appropriate non-linguistic signalling, he is equipped better to interpret or 'crack the code' of linguistic utterances used as regulators of such exchanges. We too readily overlook the fact, perhaps in celebration of the undoubted generativeness of language, that speech makes its ontogenetic progress in highly familiar contexts that have already been well conventionalized by the infant and his mother (or other caretaker). In this sense, it is not extravagant to say that initial language at least has a pragmatic base structure.

Let one matter, finally, be made abundantly clear. The point of view that has been set forth in this introductory section is in no sense to be interpreted as a rejection of the role of innate predispositions in the acquisition of language. In the opening paragraphs of this section I commented in passing that there is nothing in Chomsky's writings that would in any sense deny the role of prelinguistic precursors of prerequisites in aiding the acquisition of language. Indeed, it would be absurd to imagine that the Chomskean Language Acquisition Device could operate without considerable pre-tuning achieved during the period that precedes the use of articulate phonetic grammatical speech. Chomsky comments (1965, p. 58): 'The real problem is that of developing a hypothesis about initial structure that is sufficiently rich to account for acquisition of language . . .'

Surely, part of that richness is the representation built up of communicative requirements established over the long period of interaction between infant and caretaker. I have argued in this section, and will develop the argument further in what follows, that these representations help the child crack the linguistic code. As I have stated elsewhere (Bruner, 1972), there is a long evolutionary history that has shaped human immaturity and many of the elaborated forms of mother-infant interdependence are sufficiently invariant in our species to make inescapable the conclusion that they are in some crucial measure based on innate predispositions, however much these predispositions require priming by experience. What other forms of innateness must be present for the child to acquire language proper — its grammar and phonology particularly — I cannot debate, though it is worthwhile pointing out that until we discern more clearly the contribution of prelinguistic concepts it is premature to conclude that *innate or even acquired ideas about grammar* are all that operative. Grammar may itself be a product of the evolution of joint action in the species and one does well therefore to examine how the human ontogenesis of joint action contributes to the mastery of that grammar.

The present paper is an attempt to throw some light on some of the persistent problems that are encountered in the study of the transition from pre-speech communication to early language. There are, as this introduction hopefully makes plain, many such problems. I have chosen four of them as illustrative. In a concluding section I shall try to formulate a general conclusion about the role of the three branches of semiotics in such work: Syntax, semantics, and pragmatics (Morris, 1938). The four topics are: (1) The inference of communicative intent, (2) the nature of early reference, (3) the use of language in the regulation of joint action, and (4) the precursors of predication.

Communicative Intentions

Communication, as Silverstein (q.v.) has already noted, presupposes intent or purpose in communicating in the sense that a communication succeeds or fails in its objective. Grammarians usually take intent for granted but one does so at one's peril. To underline the intentionality of language, linguistic philosophers like Austin (1962), Grice (1968), and Searle (1969) have been particularly insistent on drawing the distinction between the performative or illocutionary[†] functions of utterances, judged both by their conventional felicity and their efficacy in achieving desired results, and the locutionary[†] function, to be judged against such criteria as well-formedness or truth value.

But intent in communication is difficult to deal with for a variety of reasons, not the least demanding of which is the morass into which it leads when one tries to establish whether something was *really*, or *consciously* intended. Does a prelinguistic infant *consciously* intend to signal his displeasure or express his delight? To obviate such difficulties, it has become customary to speak of the *functions* that communication or language serve and to determine *how* they do so. This has the virtue, at least, of postponing ultimate questions about 'reality' and 'consciousness' in the hope that they may become more manageable.

Figure 3.1: Analysis of Language Functions

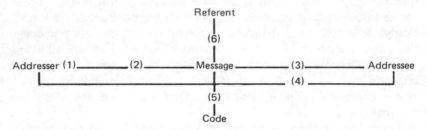

Jakobson (1960) proposes an analysis of language functions based upon the familiar 'information' diagram, functions being noted by numbers. Function 1 is *expressive* and is made up usually of accompaniments to the addresser's feelings. In a primitive sense, its 'success' or 'failure' depends upon innate or early learned recognition routines. In time, the form and the recognition of expressions of state become increasingly conventionalized. Function 2 is *poetic* and involves modes of structuring messages to achieve the illuminative or exhibitive effects of an art form. Again, it comes increasingly to use the conventions and devices of a language community (Gombrich, 1975). Function 3 is *conative* and is concerned with forming messages in such a way as to produce desired behaviour in the addressee. It encompasses the philosopher's illocutionary force. Function 4 is *phatic* and relates to the maintenance of a channel of communication between addresser and addressee. Its conduct too may be governed by standard procedures as represented by permissible pause lengths, etc. Function 5 is *metalinguistic* and it serves to explicate, usually by reference to a code, e.g.

Why do you call it *meta*linguistic?
Oh, because it is talk about talk itself.

Function 6 is *referential* and its use is to make clear the referent of a message by clearing up the context for interpreting an utterance. In the stringent terms of the philosophers of language, we may say that 'If a speaker refers to an object, then he identifies or is able on demand to identify that object for the hearer apart from all other objects' (Searle, (1969), p. 79). But it is usually much sloppier than that in practice, viz.,

What did you mean, in front of the house?
It's right in front of the house, by the wall.

Any linguistic community has, as noted, conventions for dealing with the functions of language. So do sub-communities. Scientists in communication follow conventions of appearing to 'avoid' conative, poetic and expressive functions by the use of meticulous declaratives, passive voice, and words of compact rather than diffuse associate value, etc. The sociologist Garfinkel (1963) notes that in virtually all communities, excessive request for metalinguistic clarification in ordinary discourse is often taken as a sign of hostility or disbelief in one's interlocutor. To be felicitous requires learning a great many such conventions and rituals.

To characterize these conventions Grice (in press) invokes conversational postulates that govern discourse, from which rather loose-fitting maxims are derived — maxims of relevance, of quantity, of quality. Speakers in conversation are expected to stick to the point, to give neither too little nor too much information about context, to speak the truth as they see it. When they depart from these maxims, it is expected that they will do so in a patterned way, with specific intent — irony, humor, or some effort at manipulation. The pre-linguistic child is probably not much under the sway of such maxims. The postulates governing their communication cannot be taken for granted. But we as their tutors in communication very soon learn their speech proclivities and very early try to shape them to those of the adult community. Unfortunately, there are no studies that have investigated the ways in which this is done, although work on social class differences seems to be making a start (Bernstein, 1960; Hess & Shipman, 1965; Schoggen & Schoggen, 1971; Howe, 1975).

Generally (and often unconsciously) adults impute communicative intent to the utterances of infants and children — intent with respect to all the Jakobsonian functions. Indeed, Macfarlane (pers. comm.) in studies of birth 'greeting behavior', finds mothers irresistibly imputing intent to the cries, gestures, expressions, and postures of newborns. And there is often a strikingly moralistic approach to the imputations. Infants are seen to be showing off, to be asking more than their share, to be 'buttering up' mother, to be 'going on too much about it'. Let us postpone for a bit the question whether these inferences about intent are 'correct' or even 'consistent'.

Joanna Ryan (1974) puts the issue of a child's communicative intent and its interpretation by an adult in a useful light. She notes that 'much of what a child utters in the early stages is difficult to understand, if not unintelligible', though the 'child's speech and other vocalizations take place within a context of interaction with adults who are motivated to understand the child's utterances' (p. 199). She continues: 'Many young children experience extensive verbal interchanges with their mothers. During these the mother actively picks up, interprets, comments upon, extends, repeats, and sometimes misinterprets what the child has said,' a point which our own observations would certainly confirm as character- istic of even the three-month-old and his mother. Ryan properly com- plains that the grammarian's emphasis on well-formedness and semantic sense obscures the role of these interpreted exchanges in preparing the child for language use. Not only do mothers interpret the child's gestures and vocalizations in conative terms — what he wants — but also in terms of Grice-like maxims like 'sincerity' ('He's really faking when he makes that sound') and 'consistency' ('Won't you please make up your mind what you want'). Our own observations during the first year of life point to the importance of the creation of what Garvey (1974) has called 'formats', habitual exchanges that provide a basis for interpreting concretely the intent of the communications of the child and of the mother. We shall have more to say in a later section about the nature of such formats and their transformations. It suffices to note here that they serve not only to concre- tize but to socialize and give pattern to the child's communicative intentions as well as providing the adult with a basis for interpreting them.

There is, of course, a great deal of variation in the attitudes of mothers toward their children's communicative intent, variation that produces considerable disparity in the manner in which mothers interact and talk with their young children. Howe (1975) has shown the extent to which middle-class mothers conceive their role toward their infants as being more 'instructive', not only responding more to their infants' efforts to vocalize by speaking in return, but also attempting more often to initiate ex- changes. The working-class mothers in her study were more often *laissez- faire* in their approach. By the time, then, that he is two-and-a-half or three years old, the middle-class child is on average not more *competent* to handle more advanced forms of utterances — propositions of state and of action — but in fact is using such advanced forms more often. For their mothers continued to *interpret* their child's utterances as having to do with state and action (in contrast to propositions of naming only) until the child explicitly replied with such propositional forms. The mother's interpretation of the child's communicative intent is what seemed to keep the verbal interaction going and it keeps going until the child conforms or the mother gives up. While Howe's data begin at 18 months, when holophrases[†] and early two-word utterances were appearing, the same principle can be shown to govern the mother's persistence even when the criterion the mother is applying relates to prelinguistic communicative exchanges.

In interpreting the infant's communicative intent — correctly or incorrectly — the mother has a rich variety of cues to use. So too the child, for if the mother is at all consistent, he gives forth cues that come increasingly to have a predictable consequence as far as her behavior is concerned. In this sense, they are in a transactional situation: their joint behavior determining its own future course. Ryan (1974) adapts a classification of the cues used by the mother prepared originally by John Austin (1962) for the analysis of performative aspects of speech. (1) *Aspects of the utterance* itself including intonation patterns that suggest insistence, pleasure, protest, request, etc. As Ryan puts it, 'what is important is that adults interpret children's use of intonation in a systematic way, thus allowing children to learn what is conventional usage'. Wolff (1969) was one of the first to indicate that the early cries of infants were interpretable by parents. Ricks (1971) has shown even more convincingly that cries of normal babies obtained under controlled conditions (expressing greeting, pleased surprise, request, and frustration) were correctly categorized — although the cries of the parent's own children included in the sample were not reliably identifiable. And Dore (1975) has suggested that intonation contours may be the first carriers of primitive illocutionary force in the child's utterances. (2) *Accompaniments of the utterance* provide a second set of cues for interpretation — 'pointing, searching, playing with specific objects, refusing'. These are evident enough and need no comment here. We shall meet them again in a later section. (3) And finally, *circumstance of the utterance* constitutes the third source of cues, the context of the communicative event. Families of the children in our present study at Oxford typically classify their infants' vocalizations by context; babbling contentedly in his cot on first waking up, calling for attention on waking from the afternoon nap, hunger-fretting before feed time, annoyance at not being able to reach an object, etc. For what it is worth, we have also found distinctive voicing patterns in these calls as early as four months, suggesting that it may not be context alone that is being used as a cue.

When, then, does the infant come to 'intend consciously' to communicate? Early students of prelinguistic communication were given to classifying pre-speech utterances of children into expressive (early cries of discomfort and pleasure), stimulative (producing reactions in others) and representational (Bühler, 1934). The process of going from expressive to stimulative was conceived much as Piaget's (1952) secondary circular reaction for producing or prolonging a desirable state of affairs previously produced inadvertently. Was intent involved in going from the expressive to the stimulative, and could one tell that the trip had been made? That debate does not seem worth a repeat performance, for we surely have no better basis for deciding than did our forbears. Rather, I think we would do better to concentrate instead on the description of particular intention-imputing situations and their outcomes to determine the child's and the mother's course in learning to deal with Jakobson's communicative functions. How indeed do the child and mother cope with the joint reference requirements in communicating? How is the phatic link maintained? How do the child and mother handle misunderstandings and their disambiguation? How do the child and mother express and recognize states of feeling? Is there an early poetic function and what well-turned babbles are rewarded by smiles? Can one discern a systematic trend in the conative devices a child uses to produce desired behavior in his listeners?

If only for methodological reasons, I would propose that we avoid *a priori* arguments about 'conscious intent' and 'when' it is born. For questions whose answers are not in principle recognizable are rarely useful, and it is likely that 'consciousness' and 'intention' are opaque in this way. The issue, rather, is how communicative functions are shaped and how they are fulfilled. In fact, when one examines the development of specific communicative functions, the issue of conscious intent and its dating seems to wither away. An example is provided by one of our own subjects, Jon A., and the development of a signal pattern involving reaching outward bimanually while in a sitting position, hands prone. It had usually been interpreted by the mother as a signal that Jon wanted some familiar, hand-sized object beyond his reach's terminus, and she generally provided him with it, often heightening his anticipation by advancing the object slowly or 'dramatically' toward his hand with an accompanying rising voice pitch. At eight months, one week, Jon used the signal; *M* interpreted it as calling for her hand, since there was no object close by, and performed her 'walking hand' body-game format, with the fingers walking up Jon's front to his chin. He tolerated it, though not entering as exuberantly as usual. That over, Jon then reached out again. *M* interpreted it as request for repetition. He participated even more reluctantly. *M*, on completion, then repeated the game though Jon had not signalled. He averted his gaze and whimpered a little. She repeated again and he was totally turned off. Pause. Then, 27 seconds after Jon first reached out, he reached again, this time pulling M's hands to a position where he could take hold of the ulnar edges and raise himself to a standing position. There was a following sequence of 14 episodes extending for slightly over 9 minutes in which M and Jon played a game of alternating irregularly between the two 'formats' − M's hand either walking on fingers to tickle position, or M's hands in stand-supporting position. Under M's control, it was made into a 'surprise' evoking, alternating format, with her alternative interpretations of his reach gestures being rendered explicit.

In the course of such exchanges, as Ryan (1974) has already noted. 'The child is developing skills that are at least as essential to speaking and understanding language as the mastery of grammar is supposed to be'. Much of that learning is based upon the mother interpreting the child's intent, the child sometimes conforming with the interpretation, sometimes not, but learning, en route, what interpretations his efforts evoke and how these may be modified.

We shall return to these issues in a more general way in the concluding section. Here it suffices to say, with Dore (1974), that any theoretical framework for understanding language development requires a consideration of pragmatics, and a theory of pragmatics must have some way of coping with the communicative intentions of speakers. Dore proposes that communicative intent be defined as the inducement in a listener of the speaker's expectation. In this section, we have looked at intent as being realized in a transactional situation, with mother providing an interpretation to which the infant 'speaker' can conform, dissent, or which he can attempt to modify by correction or persistence. In the following sections we shall deal with more specific communicative intents − referring, regulating joint action and predicating.

Reference

The issues raised in traditional philosophical discussions of reference have often been introduced into the debate by invoking the example of a hypothetical infant learning that a given sound, word, or gesture 'stands for' something in the extralinguistic environment. Though such exercises are logically stimulating − else they would not have continued over the centuries − they are, alas, principally empty or irrelevant in explicating psychologically the infant's real problem in mastering reference. I find myself strongly in agreement with Harrison's (1972) contention that the psychological (and even arguably the philosophical) problem of reference is how the child develops a *set of procedures for constructing a very limited taxonomy* to deal with a limited set of extralinguistic objects with which he traffics jointly with adult members of the linguistic community. What adults do for the child is to teach him or help him to realize how these taxonomic procedures operate in assuring joint reference in relatively well established situations until, finally, the child can go on quite on his own in coping referentially with larger arrays of objects in novel situations. The procedures of reference, I believe, are generative. The issue is how to differentiate among a set of objects, and how to refer precisely to any single one. I am quite prepared to accept Wittgenstein's (1953) demolition of empiricist-associationist[†] theories of naming based on pointing or other forms of ostension on his grounds: That ostension, even with negative feedback, can never specify what it is that a sign refers to in the complex welter of properties that any object necessarily displays. The negative feedback, moreover, is rarely in evidence in the data on language acquisition and when it does occur (e.g., Nelson, 1973), it is usually followed by the child abandoning his effort to use a name to indicate an object. Moreover, associative theories of naming or reference are beleaguered by the presupposition that uttering a sound or making a gesture in the presence of a referent somehow evokes a nascent or innate recognition in the child that the name is associated with some feature of something that is at the focus of the child's attention, so that any concatenation of sign and referent is as likely as any other to be learned, and that is plainly not so. Whatever the reference triangle is (Ogden & Richards, 1923), it is plainly not an isolated bit of mental furniture produced by the linking of a sign, a thought, and a referent. The objective of early reference, rather, is to indicate to another by some reliable means, which among an alternative set of things or states or actions is relevant to the child's line of endeavor. Exactitude is initially a minor issue. 'Efficacy of singling out' is the crucial objective, and the procedures employed are initially quite independent of the particular nature of objects and their defining or essential properties. If what I have boldy asserted here is even arguably so (and for a more carefully reasoned presentation of the same argument, the reader is referred to Harrison's 1972 discussion), then we would do well to avoid falling into the classical empiricist trap of the theory of naming or referring (even Quine's (1960) seductively common sense version of it in *Word and Object*) and look instead at the procedures earliest used by the infant and adult in indicating and differentiating the very limited set of objects with which they traffic.

I shall want to deal with three separate aspects of early reference, and for convenience I shall given them labels. The first we may call *indicating* (if only to avoid the term ostension!), and it refers to gestural, postural and idiosyncratic vocal procedures for bringing a partner's attention to an object or action or state. The second is *deixis* and refers, of course, to the use of spatial, temporal, and interpersonal contextual features of situations as aids in the management of joint reference. The third involves the development of standard lexical items that 'stand for' extralinguistic events in the shared world of infant and caretaker and I shall call the process *naming*. Our task, as already indicated, is to explore the procedures employed in all three of these considerable linguistic accomplishments.

Take indicating first. Studies by Collis and Schaffer (in press), by Kaye (1976), and by Scaife and Bruner (1975) all point to a highly primitive form of indicating early in the child's first year. Collis and Schaffer have shown the extent to which the mother's line of regard follows the infant's, she constantly monitoring and following where the child looks as an important feature of inferring what is at the focus of his attention — better to interpret his demands, to elaborate upon what he is attending to, etc. Kaye has shown the extent to which mothers, asked to teach their child a simple task of taking an object from behind a transparent barrier, actively enlist the child's attention by 'marking' the target object in various ways — touching it, shaking it, etc. Strikingly, such manoeuvres occur far in excess of chance expectancy when the infant *looks away* from the task. In sum, she follows his line of regard, and when it diverges from where the task requires it to be, she uses effective procedures of indicating to reestablish joint attention. The findings of Scaife and Bruner provide the final piece in this picture. Not only, as indicated by Collis and Schaffer (in press), does the mother follow the child's line of regard as an indicator, but in this experiment the infant seems able as early as four months to follow and increasingly does follow an adult's line of regard when it is turned toward a locus removed from the child. We do not yet know what the processes are that bring this accomplishment about, but there are some tantalizing indications of the kinds of factors that are involved and that will have to be unravelled by experiment and close observation. What Scaife and Bruner (1975) have found is that as early as four months in some children and with high frequency by nine months, the infant turns his regard in the same direction as a facing experimenter turns his. To what extent imitation is initially involved is difficult to say, but it can be said that there is no confusion among their young subjects as to which way to turn, though imitation might lead to head turning in either direction. Work is continuing at Oxford on these tangled issues by Scaife and by Churcher, and hopefully a clearer indication of the origins of this behavior will emerge. Qualitative analysis of the responses of Scaife and Bruner's babies seem to suggest that the head turns of the infants are not of a magnitude to match imitatively the degree of head turn by the adult. Yet, it is quite possible that initial imitative turning might lead the child to 'pick up' an interesting object and thereby provide a perceptual reinforcement to the child's head turning. Again, this would very likely depend upon the density and discriminability of targets available to the child who orients in the direction of an adult's gaze. In any case, what we can say at this early juncture is that there is present from a surprisingly early age a mutual system by which joint selective attention between the infant and his caretaker is assured — under the control of the caretaker and/or of the child, eventually managed by joint pickup of relevant directional cues that each provides the other.

Plainly, such devices for assuring a joint focus are insufficient for indicating what feature of a focus of attention is being abstracted — by the mother or by the child. That, of course, is the shortcoming of all ostensive indicating. But it is far more to the point to note not this shortcoming, which in a practical sense seems trivial in terms of what the child is actually doing, but the nature of the accomplishment (whether it be innately primed or somehow learned). What has been mastered is a *procedure* for homing in on the attentional locus of another: Learning where to look in order to be tuned to another's attention. It is a discovery routine and not a naming procedure. It is totally generative within the limited world inhabited by the infant in the sense that it is not limited to looking at oranges or dolls or rattles. It has also equipped the child with a basis for dealing with space that transcends egocentrism, or, in any case, the child's egocentrism does not prevent him from following another's attention. For the child is able to use both a second origin of reference, another's line of regard, as well as various forms of marking or highlighting of objects (as in the Kaye experiment). These accomplishments would surely qualify as precursors of Piagetian decentration,[†] their earlier occurrence being attributable perhaps to the more personal, less object-orientated testing situations used in Oxford. In this sense, these accomplishments guarantee the first bases for spatial, interpersonal deixis.

There is a further procedural accomplishment implied by Kaye's (1976) study of the 'implicit pedagogy' of mothers, their use of 'marking' in indicating an object or event to be attended to. Without going into the details, it is plain that mothers of six-month-olds succeed in getting their infants to attend to and capture the object intended, in spite of the barrier. They not only mark the object, but evoke the action either by a process of tempting — putting the object nearer and at the edge of the barrier — or by modelling the behavior themselves. The marking involves a combination of 'highlighting' features and exaggerating the structure of acts to be performed. They do both in a manner that is highly contingent on the child's state, his attentional deployment, and his line of activity.[2]

We may now profitably introduce the concept of 'natural categories' so interestingly expounded in a recent series of papers by Rosch (1974). She argues that in development, categories of objects are built on the basis of a common sharing of 'motor programs' and of those perceptual features required for their execution. In this sense, they are 'practical' objects that are marked by features of use and their structuring into equivalence classes is based upon that use. In this sense, jointly managed activities provide an essential contextual basis for parent indicating to child and child to parent. As Nelson (1973) notes, categories of use are the first to develop and the childish definition 'a hole to dig' is to be taken as something more than quaint. But what is apparent is that indicating in either direction − child to mother or mother to child − occurs in situations where *both* are involved jointly in the act of digging or of reaching or of knocking down. The indicating that is used by each is based on the joint knowledge of the course of these actions and initially takes the form of exaggerating or 'marking' some phase of the action as a signal (often accompanied by ancillary vocalization and gesture, as in the child indicating a target of reaching by exaggerating the reach toward an object and making an 'effort' or 'fretting' vocalization, or by the mother shaking or vocally marking by *'C'mon'* a proffered object). Note again that the procedure is independent of the conventional defining properties of the objects involved and relates instead to the programme of use.

Generative procedures for indicating undergo three striking changes over time: *Decontextualization, conventionalization,* and increased *economy*. Decontextualization involves the development of indicating strategies that are not so closely linked to the specific action patterns in which they are embedded. Rather than indicating by exaggerating a feature of the reach (like extension) and fretting, the child now uses a more peremptory reach toward the object. This manoeuvre appears to signal more the child's line of regard and less the next step in his line of activity. *The extended hand becomes an external pointer for noting line of regard rather than direction of activity*. It is probably this crucial fact that leads to an increase in economy in indicating. For by eight months, and often earlier in 'comfortably familiar' joint action formats, the child holds his hand out toward the object in a non-grasping directional gesture. By a year, when he is presented pictures on the page of a book, he rarely 'grasps' at the picture, but touches it, and eventually touches it only with the index finger.

With respect to conventionalization, its basis is somewhat problematic. Its origin may be in the phenomenon of visual 'cross checking' between mother and infant: Each looking at the other *en face* while in the process of indicating (present from the start for the mother, but increasingly evident for the child after six months in our own observations as well as in those by Sugarman, 1974, and by Bates *et al.*, 1973). They appear to be seeking agreement on a referent. The term conventionalization may, perhaps, be inappropriately grandiose for such a minimal sign. I use it nonetheless to indicate that mother and child seem increasingly in the second half of the first year to be checking whether their gesturing or marking is 'getting through' to the other, as if there were mutual recognition of a correct way to signal.

It is after all of this prior learning that holophrastic 'naming' comes into the picture. Again, it seems highly unlikely that naming is what in fact is at issue. For as I have argued in a previous paper (1975), and as Bloom (1973), Greenfield and Smith (in press) and others, I think, abundantly illustrated, the child's holophrases are grammatically contextualized in a Fillmore-like (1968) case form that highlights some aspect of who is doing what with what object toward whom in whose possession and in what locution and often what instrumentality: Agent, Object, Recipient of Action, Location,[†] Possession,[†] Instrument. And it is not surprising, as Eve Clark (1973) has pointed out, that from a sheerly referential point of view, the child's usage is highly overgeneralized, since he is still grouping objects and actions in terms of function rather than properties — a point well made in Greenfield's (1973) paper on 'Who is Dada?' In this sense, the emphasis is upon a rough taxonomic procedure rather than exactitude of response.

Equipped with such useful and generative procedural rules, the child may then get on with the Augustinian business of learning to refer — but in no sense can it be taken as claimed by St Augustine (cf. Wittgenstein, 1953) as learning language through naming *ab initio*. For if the child now fails to be able to discern the properties to which orange or rattle or Dada refer, he has an extensive repertory of procedures available for disambiguation — though, to echo Wittgenstein's critique again, there is no set of ostension procedures that can ever *uniquely* determine reference or meaning.

We may now turn to the issue of *deixis* and its development. Recall that from the fourth month there is already some basis for spatial deixis in the line-of-regard following of mother and infant and, probably, this implies some appreciation of deixis of person — at least the recognition that it is *another's* line of regard being followed. Much of the 'reality of discourse' depends upon the establishment of what Benveniste (1971) calls a locution-dependent I/You concept. Adult speech would be impossible without it and Lyons (1974) has argued that reference is dependent for its growth upon it to deal not only with the shifters *I* and *You* but with spatial and temporal indicators like *here* and *there, now* and *later,* etc. Benveniste's point is worth quoting (1971, pp. 217-8):

> Between *I* and a noun referring to a lexical notion, there are not only the greatly varying formal differences that the morphological and syntactic structure of particular languages imposes; there are also others that result from the very process of linguistic utterance and which are of a more general and more basic nature. The utterance containing *I* belongs to that level or type of language which Charles Morris calls pragmatic, which includes, with the signs, those who make use of them. A linguistic text of great length — a scientific treatise, for example — can be imagined in which *I* and *you* would not appear a single time; conversely, it would be difficult to conceive of a short spoken text in which they were not employed. But the other signs of a language are distributed indifferently between these two types of texts. Besides this condition of use, which is itself distinctive, we shall call attention to a fundamental and moreover obvious property of *I* and *you* in the referential organization of linguistic signs. Each instance of use of a noun is referred to a fixed and 'objective' notion, capable of remaining potential or of being actualized in a particular object and always identical with the mental image it awakens. But the instances of the use of *I* do not constitute a class of reference since there is no 'object' definable as *I* to which these instances can refer in identical fashion. Each *I* has its own reference and corresponds each time to a unique being who is set up as such.
>
> What then is the reality to which *I* or *you* refers? It is solely a 'reality of discourse', and this is a very strange thing. *I* cannot be defined except in terms of 'locution', not in terms of objects as a nominal sign is. *I* signifies 'the person who is uttering the present instance of the discourse containing *I*'. This instance is unique by definition and has validity only in its uniqueness. If I perceive two successive instances of discourse containing *I*, uttered in the same voice, nothing guarantees to me that one of them is not a reported discourse, a quotation in which *I* could be imputed to another. It is thus necessary to stress this point: *I* can only be identified by the instance of discourse that contains it and by that alone. It has no

value except in the instance in which it is produced. But in the same way it is also as an instance of form that *I* must be taken; the form of *I* has no linguistic existence except in the act of speaking in which it is uttered. There is thus a combined double instance in this process: the instance of *I* as referent and the instance of discourse containing *I* as the referee. The definition can now be stated precisely as: *I* is 'the individual who utters the present instance of discourse containing the linguistic instance *I*'. Consequently, by introducing the situation of 'address', we obtain a symmetrical definition for *you* as the 'individual spoken to in the present instance of discourse containing the linguistic instance *you*'. These definitions refer to *I* and *you* as a category of language and are related to their position in language. We are not considering the specific forms of this category within given languages, and it matters little whether these forms must figure explicitly in the discourse or may remain implicit in it.

This constant and necessary reference to the instance of discourse constitutes the feature that unites to *I/you* a series of 'indicators' which, from their form and their systematic capacity, belong to different classes, some being pronouns, other adverbs, and still others, adverbial locutions.

If we can interpret Benveniste as implying psychologically that a grasp of reciprocal roles in discourse is the essential prerequisite for deixis of person, place, and time, then some very interesting questions arise about the development of reference. For one thing, the Benveniste hypothesis places pragmatics – the relation of language to those who are speaking it – at the heart of the problem of reference.

Again, the beginnings of a locution-dependent reciprocal concept emerges in action well before it is ever used in formal language. Established and reversible role relationships obviously provide a primitive base for later linguistic deixis. The universal prelinguistic game of 'Peekaboo' is a striking example (Bruner and Sherwood, in press; Greenfield, 1972) of such reversible role structures, bound as it is by rule constraints with respect to who is the recipient and who the agent of coverings and uncoverings and how these may be reversed. Give-and-take routines, early established between mother and infant, again with reversibility of roles, and often marked by distinctive vocalizations for marking the giving and the receipt of an object (Bruner, 1975) provide another example. In such games, once developed, the child looks mother directly in the eye for a signal at crucial pauses in the play, as if to calibrate his intended actions with hers and to check which one is playing which role. In the first year of life, then, the child is mastering a convention — checking procedure not unlike that of adults — indeed, even using eye-to-eye contact for determining intent, readiness, and whose 'turn' it is (Argyle & Ingham, 1972).

But there is a big step from 'behavioral' to 'linguistic' deixis. In the latter, the context is contained in the message, in the former in the behavioral field of the speakers. Are there any small steps that help the child scale the heights from extralinguistic to intralinguistic deixis?

Perhaps one such step is through early phonological marking. One of the children we are studying showed at six months a difference in range of pitch for vocalizations accompanying the manipulation of objects in hand and those accompanying his interactions with his mother. Vocal 'comments' or babblings while manipulating objects were higher pitched than those accompanying exchanges with the mother. The mother was observed to look back to the child when the pitch of his vocalization dropped, to check whether he had redirected his attention toward her, though pitch difference did not develop as a systematic calling device to which the child and mother had recourse. The same child used a sharper onset of voicing when reaching toward out-of-reach objects than when taking one in hand that was within easy reach, a distinction akin to Lyons' (1974) second-order deictic marker, proximal/non-proximal. When the child did use sharper onset voicing the mother responded by moving an out-of-reach object toward him. It may well be, to be sure, that the sharper onset was an accompaniment of the effort of reaching for the more distant object — and in this sense be 'expressive' — but the fact remains that the distinction provided a *vocal* cue to the mother as to topic of the child's attention. We cannot know whether the child 'deliberately' used the distinction for signalling purposes, but the mother responded as if it were deliberate and he continued to use such signalling in appropriate situations. In one other instance with the same child, again at six months, he was observed to use a distinctive vocalization that soon was able to produce a particular act by the mother. The situation was the familiar one in which mother 'looms' an object toward the child, the termination of the looming being to touch the object to the child's chest or hand or forehead. It is a standard body game play 'format' for this child-mother pair. The child responded to looming with a pharyngeal fricative, shifting to velar stop,[†] and terminating with the achromatic[†] vowel, *aah*. When the mother delayed looming, the child used this call. If mother delayed too long, the vocalization shifted to a fretting call. This signalling was observed over two observational sessions separated by three weeks.

Kaplan and Kaplan (1971) have set out a plausible case for such phonological marking as a beginning of a semantic referential system that may precede or operate independently of syntax. Cromer's (1974) admirably concise summary of the Kaplans' position will serve:

> (They) propose that the child's semantic position develops out of the early distinctions present in his communication system. They feel that with adequate data one will be able to identify a set of semantic features and chart the developmental order of their emergence. For example, when the infant makes the early distinction between human and non-human sounds, the Kaplans suggest the feature '± human' has become operative. When the infant differentiates himself from others, as observable in the effect of delayed auditory feedback on crying (i.e., indicating that the infant can distinguish between his own voice and other sounds), he is credited with the feature '± ego'. As the child develops his knowledge of object properties he adds such features as '± existence' and '± presence'. Other later acquisitions would include '± agent', '± past' and the like. These semantic features would place constraints on the child's language acquisition.

May not such devices provide the beginnings of the idea of vocally marking different positions of play in the relation between mother and child? I am all too aware that such instances do not provide a proper 'tracing' of the course from behavioral to linguistic deixis, yet I would urge that an effort be made to examine the small steps that might, in combination, provide the big insight that must be involved in learning to handle the classical deictic 'shifters' — those expressions whose interpretation varies as a function of which member of a pair uttered them, ranging from *you* and *me* to *in front of* and *behind*. We shall pursue this matter further in the following section.

With respect to naming proper, finally, there is ample evidence that well before language, the *idea* of the word or label as an instrument of reference becomes firmly fixed. Indeed, Nelson's (1973) study of language acquisition indicates that one of the two 'styles' of language acquisition is referential — exercises in labeling being at the center of certain mother-infant verbal interactions. (The other style, expressive, will be considered in the following section.) It takes the form, prior to word *production,* of playing: 'Where's your nose', or 'Show me your eyes'. Thus the *concept* of a label must be a very early feature of language competence. Indeed, it too may have a deictic element as evidenced by the very common phenomenon of labeling both the infant's mouth, eyes, nose, etc., *and* the infant then indicating the mother's corresponding parts.

How early a start the lexical concept or label may get is indicated in some recent work by Ricks (1971). He distinguishes at eleven to eighteen months three classes of vocalization: Babble sounds with no evident referent, 'dada' words with a loose referent, and 'label' words. He lists seven properties of the last of these (like 'bow-wow') : They are not found in babbling, they are used only in the presence of a particular object or event, they are not modified toward conventionality but rather are adopted by the parents, they are frequently generalized and over-generalized (Clark, 1973), the expression of the 'word' is often accompanied by excitement, mention of the label word alerts the child to searching and also leads the child to repetition of the word. Ricks' data start at eleven months. By eighteen or twenty months, some children have even introduced a word that stands for 'label-lacking' objects as with Matthew in Greenfield, *et al.*, (1972) who uses 'Umh' for unknowns and Bloom's (1970) Allison whose 'wid ə' is even more ambiguous.

We know very little about the onset of labeling as an instrument of reference. It seems highly likely that, at least later and possibly earlier as well, it is related to IQ, for after three or four, the single best indicator of a child's measurable intelligence is the size of his vocabulary (Raven, 1948). Surely, if we are to understand the origins of and the later elaboration of reference, we shall have to explore more fully the kinds of phenomena reported by Ricks as they begin to manifest themselves in the first year of life. They may be a natural outgrowth of the phonological labels mentioned earlier or may indeed be an elaborated and later accompaniment to mutual pointing and joint gaze direction. All of these phenomena point to the early existence of means for managing joint reference. Yet none of them moves very far along the line toward discourse-sensitive, deictically dependent reference of the kind so carefully described by Benveniste. We turn next to a form of development that may explicate the early phases of such reference.

Language and Joint Action

As we have already noted, emphasis upon linguistic competence can easily distort the study of acquisition toward or preoccupation with syntax. Joanna Ryan's critique (1974, p. 185) is doubtless correct: 'Recent psycholinguistic work has neglected the earliest, presyntactic stages of language development, concentrating exclusively on the details of the child's later mastery of grammar. This approach can be characterized as exclusively cognitive, in the sense that it regards language as something to be studied as the *object* of the child's knowledge, and ignores all the other skills that determine actual language use. This neglect of what has come to be known as "communicative competence" (Campbell & Wales, 1970) is not only serious in itself, but has also led to a distorted view of the child's grammatical abilities.'

Perhaps the best antidote to syntactic preoccupation is to examine closely how the infant masters the task of communicating to others his needs, wishes, and objectives in order to assure either assistance or joint action. It is this that constitutes the beginnings of the more elaborated speech acts that are developed to 'get things done with words'. Rejecting as incomplete Chomsky's definition of the task of linguistics as the specification of rules that relate sound and meanings, Searle (1975) comments: 'I don't think that his picture is false, so much as it is extremely misleading and misleading in ways which have unfortunate consequences for research. A more accurate picture seems to me this. The purpose of language is communication. The unit of human communication in language is the speech act, of the type called illocutionary act. The problem (or at least an important problem) of the theory of language is to describe how we get from the sounds to the illocutionary acts. What, so to speak, has to be added to the noises that come out of my mouth in order that their production should be a performance of the act of asking a question, or making a statement, or giving an order, etc.?' To the beginning of this process we turn now.

From the start, the child is well equipped with communicative routines in what we shall call the *demand mode*, many derived from innate patterns of expressing discomfort. By the third or fourth month of their baby's life, most mothers claim to be able to distinguish forms of satisfaction expressed by vocalization. The demand cries almost always include pain or physical discomfort, hunger, demand for social interaction, and fatigue-frustration. Whether these cries have a universal phonological pattern or are idiosyncratic is not clear. Alan Leslie and Christopher Pratt at Oxford are currently carrying out analyses of changes that occur in such cries recorded in the child's familiar home setting.

'Pleasure' vocalizations usually include 'chatting' upon awakening and then playing by oneself and also the gurgling accompanying 'happy' interactions with a familiar caretaker. We can say little about these as yet save that they are recognizable to the mother and do not sound 'troubled' to the naive listener. Characteristically, 'trouble' demand cries, on the other hand, are insistent, with no pauses in anticipation of response, are 'wide spectrum' in their distribution of energy across a range of audible frequencies, and if unattended are followed by uncontrolled scream-crying. In practice, they are usually responded to, with the effect of establishing an expectancy of response. When such expectancy is established, at least three changes occur, marking the beginning of what I call a *request mode*. One major change is moderation in the wide-band intensity and 'insistence' of initial calling. Its wide band spectrum is reduced. A second change is condensation of the call to a more limited time span with a pause in anticipation of response. If the response is not forthcoming, the infant reverts to the demand mode. There also ensues an increasing 'stylization' of initial calling with each infant developing a more recognizable 'signature' call. Studies of crying and fretting (e.g., Sander *et al.*, 1970; Ainsworth, 1975) point to the important role of a consistent caretaker in effecting this transition from demand to request.

There next appears a distinctive *exchange mode*. It begins with indicating a demand for an object gesturally and often with vocal accompaniment. By 8-10 months, the child not only calls for and receives an object, but hands it back, calling again, receiving it, and handing it back again. As noted in the discussion of deixis, he reverses roles with himself first as recipient of action, then as agent. Indeed, exchange may make an even earlier appearance at the gestural level for as early as 2 weeks of age, an infant will imitate facial and manual gestures (Moore and Meltzoff, 1975). If the child's imitation of the mother is then imitated in turn by the mother, the rate of the child's responding with matching gesture can be raised (Rheingold, Gewirtz, and Ross, 1959). Meltzoff (pers. comm.) has preliminary results indicating, moreover, that if the mother responds to the child's imitative gesture with a non-matching one, the child will either start imitating that gesture or will stop and may show distress or gaze aversion. It is difficult to say whether this early gestural exchange has any role in supporting the later exchange patterns first described, for the later pattern involves tasks with objects rather than directly inter-personal ones.

The exchange mode is gradually transformed into what we may call a *reciprocal mode*. Interactions are now organized around a *task* that possesses *exteriority, constraint,* and *division of labor.* The two participants enter upon a task with reciprocal, though non-identical, roles. It may involve nothing more complex than the mother holding steady the ever-present toy pillar box into which different shapes can be inserted. Elsewhere (Wood, Ross, and Bruner, in press) we have referred to this as 'scaffolding' activity by the mother on the child's behalf. In time, and with the development of anticipatory schemas, the child's conception of the task is elaborated. He may now hold up a form to his mother's view before placing it in the pillar box. The mother may hand him one to put in. He may hand her one to insert. Much intermittent eye-to-eye checking and vocalizing accompanies these variations. The task is gradually being structured into reciprocating roles, the roles defined into rounds, each composed of turns, often with turns interchangeable (Garvey, 1974). The *task* and its constitutents have become the objects of joint attention. Betimes, more complex tasks emerge and task formats are combined, with a strong quality of play and pleasure. But however playful, the striking thing about such task formats is that they are rule bound and constraining.

The progress from demand to request to exchange to reciprocity during the first year is, I believe, of central importance to the development of speech acts (or, more properly, communicative acts) and, as well, to the establishment of a ground work for the later grasping of case in language. An unexpected source of information about the elaboration of communicative acts comes from Ainsworth and Bell's study of mother-infant pairs (1974). They report that as 'crying and fretting' — what we could call the demand mode — recedes, more subtle forms of communicating increase, and those children who persist in the demand mode are slow in developing communicatively. More directly relevant are contextualized observations of my own (Bruner, 1975) and of Edwards (1975).

The first example is from the Oxford corpus: Ann had learned between 8 and 10 months to play a well modulated exchange game involving the handing back and forth of objects. When, at 13 months, the game was well organized, Ann picked up her mother's receiving *Thank you*. She used it both when giving and when receiving an object. After two weeks the expression dropped out of the giving position, nothing at first taking its place, but remained in the receiving position. Meanwhile, the demand demonstrative *Look* was appearing in Ann's lexicon, used in referential situations, as when looking at pictures in a book. At the end of the thirteenth month, *Look* was transposed as well into the position at which Ann handed her mother an object. *Look* was later replaced by *There* in the giving-taking format.

I would interpret Ann's performance in terms of Searle's (1975) earlier quoted comment on how we go 'from sound to illocutionary force'. Initially, she accompanies *both* roles in the exchange format by a single expression, in recognition of the compact of exchange. In time, each role is appropriately and conventionally accompanied by differentiated vocalizations, one of them borrowed from a demonstrative speech act (*Look*), but shortly replaced by one more appropriate to the act of bestowal. One is reminded of Cohen's (1974) discussion of 'markers' used for characterizing such semantic force properties as imperative, optative, interrogative, exclamatory, or performative. He goes on to raise the issue of whether there might not also be markers used for differentiating the uses to which performatives are put: Indicating explicitness/implicitness, noting intention/inadvertence, whether a verdict, commitment, or promise is being made, etc. One has the impression in examining protocols that something of this order is occurring, and in the present case, the final shift on the 'giving' end from *Look* to *There* is a subtle recognition by Ann that exchange and demonstration involve different accompanying performatives.

The second example illustrates a somewhat different point: That a joint-action format provides, as already noted, an opportunity for the child to master major elements of case grammar as it relates to specific and familiar action formats. Edwards (1975) shows how a child's knowledge of a 'prohibitive' format — having to do with objects she was not to touch — provided an opportunity for her to develop grammatical concepts. Initially, she used the simple negative *No* to characterize situations in which she was not to touch an object. This was followed, in comparable formats, by the introduction of possession, *Yours* or *Mine* for objects she was forbidden to touch or play with. Still later, a verb form was inserted into the format — *Leave it* for what was prohibited. And finally, again in the same format type, the adjectival form appeared: *Hot* or *sharp* for the object that was prohibited. Edwards' Alice was learning not only grammar, but learning it as an adjunct to social situations whose structure she was having to learn *and* to manage. The case variants were all embodiments of a self-directed imperative — to keep clear of the object in question.

We turn next to predication and its prelinguistic precursors and prerequisites.

Predication

Looked at in its linguistic sense, 'predication involves affirming or asserting something of or about the subject of a proposition' (Wall, 1974, p. 9). It might seem then somewhat jejune to inquire about the precursors or even the prerequisites for predication in the prelinguistic child, for surely he can in no sense be thought to be dealing in propositions. What has made the issue of pre-propositional predication a persistent and interesting one, however, was the early insistence of DeLaguna (1927) that the single words of holophrastic speech could profitably be treated as compacted sentence forms, and that single words could be conceived within that framework as comments upon extralinguistic topics inferent in the contexts in which the child found himself. The primitive topic, then, was implicit rather than explicit. This interpretation of early one-word utterances persisted in the literature — cited principally in general reviews of language development — until picked up again in McNeill's (1970a, 1970b) work, and then further developed by Bloom (1973) and more recently in a rather widely circulated manuscript by Greenfield and Smith (in press) who were specifically concerned with interpreting the run-up in early speech development from single word utterances to the patterns that are found when M.L.U.'s approach two morphs.[†] Like DeLaguna, these investigators were interested in the manner in which the 'unmentioned' topic finally found its way into explicitness to be represented by a nominal or other grammatically interpretable form that could carry language development beyond dependence on unspecified context – DeLaguna's famous claim that language development could be conceived as a process of decontextualization.[3]

McNeill (1970a, 1970b) carried the argument one step further. Arguing from the existence of the predicational postpositions in Japanese, *ga* and *wa*, indicating respectively extrinsic and intrinsic predicates, the latter being habitual or essential and the former temporary or transitory, he proposed that initial predication with unmentioned topic could be conceived of as the intrinsic form, while extrinsic predication was more of the *ga* type. In Japanese, the postpositions could be noted by the contrast: 'The dog-wa has hair', versus 'The dog-ga is on the chair'. He found that for both Japanese and English speaking children, early sentences contained about twice as many intrinsic as extrinsic predications, and that subject noun phrase topics that referred to the speaker were particularly rare. This led him to conclude that 'holophrastic utterances consist largely, if not exclusively, of intrinsic predicates . . . Children would add subjects to predicates . . . when the predicates become extrinsic. Such an event appears to happen first when the children are 18 to 24 months old' (1970b, p. 1093). To this interesting finding (or contention) should be added two others. Quite counter-intuitively, Wall (1968) found that the mean length of dialogue between children and parents was *shorter* than dialogues between the same children and strangers. Chafe (1970) had, meanwhile, urged that one must make the contrast between 'new' information and 'old' or shared information, that the two are handled grammatically in different ways. Wall (1974, pp. 232-3) makes the point 'It seemed possible that the difference in utterance length might well be explained on the basis of presence or absence of shared information between participants in the conversations. That is, it is necessary for relative strangers to state explicitly whatever it may be that they are trying to communicate verbally for efficient information transfer, whereas among friends and close associates remarks are often greatly abbreviated with little or no resulting loss of information transferred.' Vygotsky (1962, p. 139) has made the same point (en route to presenting his argument that the nature of inner speech is condensed predication, with topical subject left implicit): 'Now let us imagine that several people are waiting for a bus. No one will say, on seeing the bus approach, "The bus for which we are waiting is coming". The sentence is likely to be an abbreviated "Coming", or some such expression, because the subject is plain from the situation.' And, indeed, in Wall's (1974) study too, her 18-to 30-month-olds conformed to the rule in an interesting way. She compares the number of constituents in sentences given in response to a question (where the topic, of course, is shared in advance) and sentences spoken spontaneously. Just half of the spontaneous sentences contained two or more constituents, but only 18 percent of those in reply to a topic-setting question.

We may now, in the light of the foregoing, consider afresh the significance of established, mutual-action formats discussed in the preceding section. They constitute the implicit or shared topics on which comments can be made by the child without having to be mentioned. These are the implicit topics about which comments can be made. And as these formats become differentiated into reversible or complementary roles during the growth of exchange and reciprocal modes, implicit topics become that much more contextualized in the action that adult and child share. I used the three terms, division of labor, exteriority, and constraint to characterize the nature of the shared action formats that developed during the onset of the reciprocal mode — terms borrowed, of course, from Durkheim's (1933) characterization of the requisite properties of social norms — to specify the manner in which formats seemed to take on a shared existence binding the two partners in discourse. And it is this development that is, in my view, crucial to the course of prelinguistic predicational activity to which we now turn — particularly to the development of intrinsic predication in McNeill's (1970b) sense.

What, we may first ask, are the forms of 'comment' that can be made prelinguistically (or pre-propositionally) on such shared topics as the joint action patterns described in the preceding section? Before we can answer this question, we must first consider the function of predication in a communicative act. Its functions are three in number: (a) To specify something about a topic that is explicit or implicit, (b) to do so in such a way that topic and comment can be rendered separable (e.g. *John is a boy* and *John has a hat*), and, (c) to specify something in a way that is subject to truth testing or, more simply, negation. I do not know whether prelinguistic 'comments' (in forms we shall consider) upon implicit topics fulfill all three of these functions, and I should prefer to leave out of consideration the last of these, (since it is now just in the process of being studied by Roy Pea in our laboratory), to treat the second rather lightly, and to concentrate principally upon the first function.

The first and perhaps simplest form of comment is, I think, giving indication that a topic is being shared in joint action, and it is principally revealed in the child's management of gaze direction. Typically in our own protocols, the child when involved in a transaction over some object or activity, looks up at some juncture and makes eye-to-eye contact with the mother, often smiling as well. The topic is the joint activity, the comment is the establishment of 'intersubjective' sharing in connection with that activity, after which the activity goes on. A good example is provided in the account of glance management in an exchange game reported by Bruner (1975). The 'comment' consists of noting whether both partners are 'with it', engaged in the game. Similarly, when one of our mothers uses a toy such as a clown that disappears inside a cone, when the clown has disappeared and then reappeared, the child will usually then turn from the clown to the mother for gaze contact. I would interpret this 'joining' as an act of reasserting the joint action, a primitive version of the 'inter-personal concept' in respect of which Benveniste (1971) was cited in a previous section.

This form of confirming comment is supplemented and extended at around the ninth month by the emergence of a form of vocalization we have dubbed 'proclamative'. It occurs at two points during joint action sequences: First, at a point where the infant is about to undertake his part of a jointly attended action, seemingly as an accompaniment to intention; second, when the act is complete. The vocalized babbling may be co-incident with the child looking back at the mother or may precede it. The vocalization, in short, appears to be initiating or completive with respect to an act embedded in a jointly attended task. In this sense, it may be considered as a 'candidate-comment' on an implicit topic. In time, the pattern becomes further elaborated, and the child may not only vocalize in these positions and make gaze contact, but also hold up an implicated object to show the mother, as when picking up a brick and placing it on a pile.

Elsewhere I have commented on the fact that attentional deployment as revealed in eye movement records (Bruner, 1975; Mackworth and Bruner, 1970) may itself predispose to topic-comment structures in the very organization of information processing. For typically, large saccades† that move attention to a sharply defined focus in the visual field are followed by smaller inspection saccades that play around features of this focus. Heywood and Coles in our laboratory are now exploring this feature of early attention, and while it is too early to say anything defini-tive about the onset of these focus-inspecting eye-movement patterns, their stabilization might surely be thought of as a further predisposing factor to topic-comment communication — linguistically or prelinguistically.

Finally a word about the separability of topic and comment achieved in predication. It is by now a common observation that the child's play with objects takes one of two forms (a point also noted for chimpanzees by Köhler, 1926, and commented upon by Bruner, 1972, 1973). An *object* is successively placed into as many different action-patterns as the child can manage: A ball is successively mouthed, squeezed, banged on the table, thrown down, called for, etc. Or an *action* is fitted to as many different objects as it will accommodate: Successively a cup is banged, then a spoon, then a doll, then any other loose object to hand. These play patterns, while in no sense direct precursors of propositional predicating, are nonetheless striking examples of separation and variation of comments on topics, with either the object serving as topic and actions-upon-it as comments, or the action serving as organizing topic and a variety of fitting objects as comments. Typical of the play of both higher apes and children (Loizos, 1967), this focus-variation pattern should not be overlooked as a factor that predisposes action, attention, and eventually language to the pattern that at the propositional level we call predicational.

In conclusion, I find myself in strong agreement with Lyons (1966, p. 131) when he comments:

> By the time the child arrives at the age of eighteen months or so, he is already in possession of the ability to distinguish 'things' and 'properties' in the 'situations' in which he is learning and uses language. And this ability seems to me quite adequate as a basis for the learning of the principal deep-structure relationship between lexical items (the subject-predicate relationship), provided that the child is presented with a sufficient amount of 'primary linguistic data' in real 'situations' of language use.

Before he reaches eighteen months, indeed during the second half of his first year, he is well on the way toward conceptual mastery of these concepts in the extralinguistic sphere.

Conclusion

The developmental psychology of language is currently in a rather confused state. The initial optimism that grew out of Chomsky's formulation of a generative-transformational grammar has not been sustained by the torrent of work that it provoked. His was a powerful idea, one that will want a revisit after other aspects of language acquisition become clearer.

The central notion – that the child in some sense 'has a knowledge' of the rules of language and that he is attempting to generate from this knowledge hypotheses about a local language – while boldly suggestive, is plainly insufficient.

Principally as a result of the studies of Brown (1973) and his students, it has become increasingly apparent that language acquisition is enormously aided by the child's prelinguistic grasp of concepts and meanings that make it easier for him to penetrate grammatical rules. In a closely reasoned and provocative paper published in 1972, Macnamara formulated the case well, arguing that syntactic rules are discovered by the child with the aid of meaning. His view was that the child roughly determined the referent of principal lexical items in a sentence and then used previously acquired knowledge of these referents to decode the grammar of the sentence. Sinclair's (e.g. 1969) work too has alerted the psycholinguist to the link between development and the child's emerging, extralinguistic knowledge of the world. And Bloom's most recent work has also dealt a strong blow in favor of the early semantic origins of single-word utterances. She concludes that 'children develop certain conceptual representations of regularly recurring experiences, and then learn whatever words conveniently code such conceptual notions' (1973, p. 113). The effect of this recent work has been to put the semantic element back into the developmental picture and make more attractive such ideas as Fillmore's (1968) semantically relevant case categories.

But neither the syntactic nor the semantic approach to language acquisition takes sufficiently into account what the child is trying to do by communicating. As linguistic philosophers remind us, utterances are used for different ends and use is a powerful determinant of rule structures. The brunt of my argument has been that one cannot understand the transition from prelinguistic to linguistic communication without taking into account the uses of communication as speech acts. I have, accordingly, placed greater emphasis on the importance of pragmatics in this transition – the directive function of speech through which speakers affect the behavior of others in trying to carry out their intentions. I find myself in sympathy with Dore's effort (1975) to understand the process whereby 'primitive forces' or 'orectic intentions'† are gradually conventionalized and 'grammaticalized' so that they can be reformed into communications with illocutionary force. I am not dismayed at all by Jonathan Cohen's (1974) warning that the conventionalizations by which illocutionary force is achieved are often, strictly, extralinguistic 'manners', for perhaps, as Silverstein (1975) suggests, there is not so sharp a boundary between social convention and grammatical devices. Dore's account of how illocutionary skill is augmented by the acquisition of such 'grammaticalizing devices' is interesting. He defines a primitive speech act 'as a rudimentary referring expression plus a primitive illocutionary force' (such as requesting, answering, etc.) so that the child 'communicates *what* it is he means or wants' through referential tricks and, through prosodic pattern initially and then by other means, '*that* he intends or wants something'. How the child gets from the primitive to the grammaticalized is left to rather mysterious processes like 'emergence' and 'grammaticalization' that may do no more than paper over the discontinuous course of language acquisition with some new rods. Yet, my sympathies are with Dore's effort to examine how the requirement of 'getting different things done with words' constantly alerts the child to appropriate devices and conventions and, in an evolutionary sense, may even have equipped him with special sensitivities for picking these up. Yet, for all that, I hope I have not seemed to deny that syntactic and semantic precursors can also be explored fruitfully: Grammar-like principles underlying reference, predication, privileges of occurrence, etc. But if there is one point that deserves emphasis, whether one is searching for syntactic, semantic, or pragmatic precursors of early language, it is that language acquisition occurs in the context of an 'action dialogue' in which joint action is being undertaken by infant and adult. The joint enterprise sets the deictic limits that govern joint reference, determines the need for a referential taxonomy, establishes the need for signalling intent, and provides a context for the development of explicit predication. The evolution of language itself, notably its universal structures, probably reflects the requirements of joint action and it is probably because of that evolutionary history that its use is mastered with such relative ease, though its theoretical explication still eludes us.

Notes

1.   This research was supported by a grant from the Social Science Research Council of Great Britain, and parts of this paper have been presented at the Universities of Stirling and London and at the University College of Swansea. I am particularly grateful for criticism to Mr Churcher, Mr Leslie, Dr Scaife, Ms Caudill, and Ms Garton of Oxford, as well as to Dr Richard Cromer, Dr Elisabeth Bates and Susan Sugarman. I gratefully dedicate this paper to Professor Roman Jakobson in honor of his eightieth birthday.
2.   For a fuller account of earlier implicit pedagogies concerned with such 'marking', see Wood, Ross, and Bruner (in press).
3.   With respect to the issue of the sentential or predicational status of the holophrase – still a very lively theoretical issue – the reader is referred to Bloom (1973), whose conclusions will be taken up in the final section, and Dore (1975) who reviews the arguments for and against sentential status for the holophrase and

ends by opting for the view that holophrases represent a first step along the hard path from primitive force to grammaticalized illocutionary force, a path one traverses by successive mastery of grammaticalizing devices such as using word order, intonation, etc. in the spirit of Harrison (1972).

References

Ainsworth, Mary D. Salter (1975) Social development in the first year of life: maternal influences on infant-mother attachment. Paper presented in Geoffrey Vickers Lecture, London. (Unpublished)

Ainsworth, Mary D. Salter and Bell, Sylvia M. (1974) Mother-infant interaction and the development of competence. In K. Connolly and J.S. Bruner (eds.), *The Growth of Competence*. London and New York, Academic Press.

Argyle, M., and Ingham, R. (1972) Gaze, mutual gaze and proximity. *Semiotica*, Vol. IV, (1) 32-49.

Austin, J.L. (1962) *How To Do Things with Words*, Oxford, Oxford University Press.

Bates, Elizabeth, Camaioni, L., and Volterra, V. (1973) The acquisition of performatives prior to speech. Technical Report No. 129, Consiglio Nazionale delle Ricerche, Rome.

Benveniste, F. (1971) *Problems in General Linguistics*. (Translated by M.E. Meek) Coral Gables, Florida, University of Miami Press.

Bernstein, B. (1960) Language and social class. *Brit. J. Sociol.*, 11, 271-276.

Bloom, Lois (1970) *Language Development: Form and Function in Emerging Grammars*. Cambridge, Mass., M.I.T. Press.

Bloom, Lois (1973) *One Word at a Time: The Use of Single Word Utterances Before Syntax*. The Hague, Mouton.

Bloomfield, L. (1933) *Language*. New York, Holt.

Brown, R. (1970) *Psycholinguistics*. New York, The Free Press.

Brown, R. (1973) *A First Language: The Early Stages*. Cambridge, Mass., Harvard University Press.

Bruner, J.S. (1972) The nature and uses of immaturity. *Amer. Psychol.*, 27, (8), 1-22.

Bruner, J.S. (1973) Organisation of early skilled action. *Child Devel.*, 44, 1-11.

Bruner, J.S. (1975) The ontogenesis of speech acts. *J. child Lang.*, 2 (1) 1-19.

Bruner, J.S. and Sherwood, Virginia (in press) Early rule structure: the case of peekaboo. In J.S. Bruner, A. Jolly and K. Sylva (eds.), *Play: Its Role in Evolution and Development*. London, Penguin.

Bühler, K. (1934) *Sprachtheorie: die Dartstellungsfunktion der Sprache*. Jena, Fischer.

Campbell, R., and Wales, R. (1970) The study of language acquisition. In J. Lyons (ed.), *New Horizons in Linguistics*. London, Penguin.

Chafe, W.L. (1970) *Meaning and the Structure of Language*. Chicago, University of Chicago Press.

Chomsky, N. (1965) *Aspects of the Theory of Syntax*. Cambridge, Mass., M.I.T. Press.

Clark, Eve (1973) What's in a word: on the child's acquisition of semantics in his first language. In T.E. Moore (ed.), *Cognitive Development and the Acquisition of Language*. New York, Academic Press.

Cohen, J. (1974) Speech acts. In T.A. Sebeok (ed.), *Current Trends in Linguistics*, vol. 12: Linguistics and the Adjacent Arts and Sciences. The Hague, Mouton.

Collis, G.M., and Schaffer, H.R. (in press) Synchronisation of visual attention in mother-infant pairs. *J. child Psychol. Psych.*, 16.

Cromer, R.F. (1974) The development of language and cognition: the cognition hypothesis. In B. Foss (ed.), *New Perspectives in Child Development*. London, Penguin Education Series.

DeLaguna, Grace (1927) *Speech: Its Function and Development*. New Haven, Connecticut, Yale University Press.

Donaldson, Margaret, and Wales, R. (1970) On the acquisition of some relational terms. In J.R. Hayes (ed.), *Cognition and the Development of Language*. New York, Wiley and Sons.

Dore, J. (1974) Communicative intentions and the pragmatics of language development. Unpublished paper.

Dore, J. (1975) Holophrases, speech acts, and language universals. *J. child. Lang.*, 2 (1), 21-40.

Durkheim, E. (1933) *The Division of Labor*, Glencoe, Illinois, The Free Press.

Edwards, D. (1975) Constraints on action: a source of early meanings in child language. Based on 'The three sources of a child's first meanings', delivered at the Symposium on Language and Social Context, University of Stirling, 10-11 January.

Fillmore, C.J. (1968) The case for case. In E. Bach and E.T. Harmes (eds.), *Universals in Linguistic Theory*. New York, Holt, Rinehart and Winston.

Garfinkel, H. (1963) Trust and stable actions. In O.J. Harvey (ed.), *Motivation and Social Interaction*. New York, Ronald.

Garvey, Catherine (1974) Some properties of social play. *Merrill-Palmer Q.*, 20 (3), 164-80.

Gombrich, F. (1975) Mirror and map: theories of pictorial representation. *Philosophical Transactions of the Royal Society. (Biol. Sci.)*, Vol. 270, No. 903, 119-49.

Greenfield, Patricia M. (1972) Playing peekaboo with a four-month-old: a study of the role of speech and nonspeech sounds in the formulation of a visual schema. *J. Psychol.*, 82, 287-98.

Greenfield, Patricia M. (1973) Who is 'Dada'? . . . some aspects of the semantic and phonological development of a child's first words. *Lang. and Speech*, 16, (1), 34-43.

Greenfield, Patricia M., Bruner, J.S., and May, M. (1972) *Early Words* (A Film). New York, Wiley.

Greenfield, Patricia M., and Smith, J.H. (in press) *Language Beyond Syntax: The Development of Semantic Structure*. New York, Academic Press.

Grice, H.P. (1968) Utterer's meaning, sentence-meaning and word-meaning. *Found. Lang.*, 4, 1-18.

Grice, H.P. (in press) Logic and conversation. The William James Lectures, Harvard University, 1967-8. In P. Cole and J. Morgan (eds.), *Syntax and Semantics*, Vol. 3, Speech Acts. London and New York, Academic Press.

Harrison, B. (1972) *Meaning and Structure*. New York and London, Harper and Row.

Hess, R.D. and Shipman, Virginia (1965) Early experience and the socialisation of cognitive modes in children. *Child Devel.*, 36, 869-86.

Howe, Christine (1975) The nature and origin of social class — differences in the propositions expressed by young children. Unpublished Ph.D. thesis, University of Cambridge.

Jakobson, R. (1960) Linguistics and poetics. In T.A. Sebeok (ed.), *Style in Language*. Cambridge, Mass., M.I.T. Press.

Kaplan, F., and Kaplan, G. (1971) The pre-linguistic child. In J. Eliot (ed.), *Human Development and Cognitive Processes*. New York: Holt, Rinehart and Winston.

Kaye, K. (1976) Infants' effects upon their mothers' teaching strategies. In J.C. Glidewell (ed.), *The Social Context of Learning and Development*. New York, Gardiner Press.

Köhler, W. (1926) *The Mentality of Apes*. New York, Harcourt, Brace.

Lock, A. (1972) From out of nowhere? Proceedings of the International Symposium on First Language Acquisition, University of Ottawa Press.

Loizos, E. (1967) Play behaviour in higher primates: a review. In D. Morris (ed.), *Primate Ethology*. London, Weidenfeld & Nicolson.

Lyons, J. (1966) General discussion to D. McNeill's paper, The creation of language. In J. Lyons and R. Wales (eds.), *Psycholinguistic Papers*. Edinburgh, Edinburgh University Press.

Lyons, J. (1974) Deixis as the source of reference. Unpublished paper.

Macfarlane, A. (1975) Personal communication.

Mackworth, N.H., and Bruner, J.S. (1970) How adults and children search and recognise pictures. *Hum. Devel.*, 13, (3), 149-77.

Macnamara, J. (1972) Cognitive basis of language learning in infants. *Psychol. Rev.*, 79, (1) 1-13.

McNeill, D. (1970a) *The Acquisition of Language: The Study of Developmental Psycholinguistics*. New York, Harper and Row.

McNeill, D. (1970b) The development of language. In P.H. Mussen (ed.), *Carmichael's Manual of Child Psychology*, 3rd ed. Vol. 1. New York, Wiley.

McNeill, D. (1974) Semiotic extension. Paper presented at the Loyola Symposium on Cognition, 30 April, Chicago, Illinois.

Meltzoff, A.N. (1975) Personal communication.

Moore, M.K., and Meltzoff, A.N. (1975) Neonate imitation: a test of existence and mechanism. Paper delivered at the Society for Research in Child Development meeting, Denver, Colorado, April.

Morris, C.W. (1938) *Foundations of the Theory of Signs*. Chicago.

Nelson, Katherine (1973) Structure and strategy in learning to talk. *Soc. Res. Child Devel. Mono.*, 38, Nos. 1-2, Serial No. 149.

Ogden, J.C., and Richards, I.A. (1923) *The Meaning of Meaning*. New York, Harcourt Brace Jovanovich, Inc.

Piaget, J. (1952) *The Origins of Intelligence in Children*. (1st ed., 1936). New York, International Universities Press.

Quine, W.V.O. (1960) *Word and Object*. Cambridge, Mass., M.I.T. Press.

Raven, J.C. (1948) The comparative assessment of intellectual ability. *British J. Psychol.*, 39-40, 12-19.

Rheingold, H.L., Gewirtz, J., & Ross, H. (1959) Social conditioning of vocalisations in the infant. *J. comp. Physiol. Psychol.*, 52, 68-73.

Ricks, D.M. (1971) The beginnings of vocal communication in infants and autistic children. Unpublished doctorate of medicine thesis, University of London.

Rosch, Eleanor (1974) Basic level objects in natural categories. Paper presented at the Psychonomic Society, Boston, November.

Ryan, Joanna (1974) Early language development. In M.P.M. Richards (ed.), *The Integration of the Child into a Social World*. Cambridge, Cambridge University Press.

Sander, L.W., Stechler, G., Burns, P. and Julia, H. (1970) Early mother-infant interaction and 24-hour patterns of activity and sleep. *J. Amer. Acad. Child Psych.*, 9, 103-23.

Scaife, M. and Bruner, J.S. (1975) The capacity for joint visual attention in the infant. *Nature*, 253, No. 5489, 265-6.

Schoggen, M. and Schoggen, P. (1971) Environmental forces in the home lives of three-year-old children in three population subgroups. D.A.R.C.E.E. Papers and Reports, Vol. 5, No. 2, (John Kennedy Center for Research on Education and Human Development, George Peabody College, Nashville, Tenn.).

Searle, J.R. (1969) *Speech Acts: An Essay in the Philosophy of Language*. Cambridge: Cambridge University Press.

Searle, J.R. (1975) Speech acts and recent linguistics. Paper read at the Conference on Developmental Psycholinguistics and Communication Disorders, New York Academy of Sciences, January 24-25.

Silverstein, M. (1975) Shifters, linguistic categories and cultural description. Unpublished manuscript.

Sinclair-de Zwart, Hermine (1969) Developmental psycholinguistics. In D. Elkind and J.H. Flavell (eds.), *Studies in Cognitive Growth: Essays in Honour of Jean Piaget.* New York, Oxford University Press.

Slobin, D. (1973) Prerequisites for the development of grammar. In C.A. Ferguson and D. Slobin (eds.), *Studies of Child Language Development.* New York, Holt, Rinehart and Winston.

Sugarman, Susan (1974) A sequence for communicative development in the prelanguage child. Unpublished paper.

Trevarthen, C. (1974a) Conversations with a two-month-old. *New Scientist,* 62, (896), 230-5.

Trevarthen, C. (1974b) Infant responses to objects and persons. Paper presented at the Spring 1974 meeting of the British Psychological Society, Bangor.

Urwin, Catherine (1973) The development of a blind baby. Unpublished manuscript presented at Edinburgh University.

Vygotsky, L. (1962) *Thought and Language.* Cambridge, Mass., M.I.T. Press.

Wall, Carol (1968) Linguistic interaction of children with different alters. Unpublished paper, University of California, Davis.

Wall, Carol (1974) *Predication: A Study of its Development.* The Hague, Mouton.

Wittgenstein, L. (1953) *Philosophical Investigations.* New York: Macmillan.

Wolff, P.H. (1969) The natural history of crying and other vocalisations in early infancy. In B.M. Foss (ed.), *Determinants of Infant Behavior,* Vol. 4, London, Methuen.

Wood, D., Bruner, J.S. & Ross, Gail (in press) The role of tutoring in problem solving. *J. Child Psychol. Psych.*

4 THE STRENGTHS OF THE WEAK FORM OF THE COGNITION HYPOTHESIS FOR LANGUAGE ACQUISITION

Richard Cromer

Source: specially written for this volume. Copyright © 1978 The Open University.

The major problems one faces in outlining the cognition hypothesis of language acquisition is that it is not entirely true — or rather, like any hypothesis, it was originally put forward in a particular historical context and consequently emphasises certain issues at the expense of considering other important issues. Essentially, the cognition hypothesis states that the course of first language acquisition is determined by the developing cognitive processes in the young child. Both the pace of acquisition and the types of linguistic forms and even lexical items which are used by the child are constrained by the cognitive processes which determine what the child is capable of understanding. A weak form of the cognition hypothesis asserts that while this is basically true, the child must also possess certain abilities which enable him to encode[†] these cognitions into specifically linguistic forms, and that the linguistic system is a system in its own right which must be studied if language acquisition is to be understood. In order to understand why the cognition hypothesis was put forward in the way it was, and to try to correct some misleading emphases that position seemed to imply, it may be useful to give a brief and rather personal sketch of the relatively recent background of language studies, for only a few years ago a nearly opposite point of view prevailed.

The Historical Background

In the 1920s and 1930s, Edward Sapir and Benjamin Lee Whorf separately put forward the view that the language one speaks determines important aspects of the thoughts one is able to have about what we think of as the 'real world'; or to put it more accurately, 'reality' is a construction, and a major determinant of this constructive process is the language that one speaks. As Whorf put it (1952), individuals cut up and organise the spread and flow of events because of the language that they speak and not because nature is naturally segmented in a particular way which everyone can readily observe. Linguistic differences mean that different speakers objectify reality in differing ways. Speakers of most European languages, for example, are said to treat the flow of time as if it were an objective

102

entity, like a ribbon with spaces marked off denoting past, present, and future. According to Whorf this is due to the structure of these languages which requires the encoding of verb forms into tenses. By contrast, the Hopi Indian language of North America has no tenses for its verbs. Furthermore, it has no words, grammatical constructions, or expressions that refer directly to what we call time. The consequences of this linguistic difference have been summarised by Stuart Chase in his foreword to the selected writings of Whorf (edited by Carroll, 1956), and a short quotation from that summary will help to make clear more exactly what the Sapir-Whorf claim is:

> 'The light flashed', we say in English. Something has to be there to make the flash; 'light' is the subject, 'flash' the predicate. The trend of modern physics, however, with its emphasis on the *field*, is away from subject-predicate propositions. Thus a Hopi Indian is the better physicist when he says Reh-pi — 'flash' — one word for the whole performance, no subject, no predicate, no time element. We frequently read into nature ghostly entities which flash and perform other miracles. Do we supply them because some of our verbs require substantives in front of them?
>
> The thoughts of a Hopi about events always include *both* space and time, for neither is found alone in his world view. Thus his language gets along adequately without tenses for its verb, and permits him to think habitually in terms of space-time. Properly to understand Einstein's relativity a Westerner must abandon his spoken tongue and take to the language of calculus. But a Hopi, Wharf implies, has a sort of calculus built into him.

The Sapir-Whorf hypothesis makes the claim, then, that various aspects of the language we speak and of which we are not normally aware, restrict our view of the world. Or as Chase worded it, 'The structure of the language one habitually uses influences the manner in which one understands his environment. The picture of the universe shifts from tongue to tongue'.

There is very little experimental work bearing on this claim, and the few experiments that have been reported have been primarily concerned with lexical items such as colour terms, rather than on the structure of language *per se*. It seems reasonable to suppose that language influences thought, but does it totally determine thought in the way that the Sapir-Whorf hypothesis appeared to claim? Roger Brown (1956) argued that it is possible to translate concepts expressed in one language into another. In one language certain concepts may be easily codable and thereby easily used; in another language, however, these same concepts may require long phrases, circumlocutions and awkward forms, but they nevertheless can be expressed. The Hopi language may lend itself to relativistic concepts, but speakers of European languages can come to understand these concepts even though their syntactic structures do not easily lead them to comprehend reality in this way. Brown talked about these differences in terms of 'codability'. The more easily codable a concept was in a language, the more likely a speaker would be to use it. This 'weaker' form of the Sapir-Whorf hypothesis held, then, that languages do not determine thinking; they only predispose people to think in particular ways. Again, it seems reasonable to suppose that language will have some such effect, and I will mention some experimental work on this topic nearer the end of this paper.

During this same period, there were not many studies on the acquisition of language. The prevailing view, however, was based on a direct extension of behaviourist[†] principles of learning any behaviour, — principles which were very popular at the time. According to some theorists, stimuli became associated with responses by means of reinforcement. Other theorists claimed that such associations were built up merely by the occurrence of stimuli and responses in temporal contiguity. Whatever the precise principles invoked to explain the connections, the emphasis was on associations between elements. The behaviourist position was applied both to associations between a child's intentions and the language that he heard and to the connections among the words forming a grammatical utterance. The reinforcement view was applied to language acquisition by Skinner in his book *Verbal Behavior* (1957). On both theoretical and on empirical grounds, reinforcement theory has been found to be wholly inadequate to deal with the language acquisition process. Chomsky (1959) in a review of Skinner's book gave a number of compelling reasons why an associationistic viewpoint was inadequate to explain both the structure of language and its acquisition by children. In the 1960s, observational, and later, experimental studies of young children acquiring language also failed to provide evidence to support the typical 'learning theory' principles as applied to the acquisition of language. These studies showed that the young infant was far from a passive organism bombarded by linguistic stimuli with which he formed associations. The reader who is interested in both the theoretical reasoning and empirical evidence against behaviourist theories of language acquisition can find excellent reviews by Bellugi (1967, 1971), Bever, Fodor, and Weksel (1965a, 1965b), Brown, Cazden and Bellugi-Klima (1969), Chomsky (1959), Ervin-Tripp (1966), McNeill (1966, 1970a, 1970b), Miller and McNeill (1969), Sachs (1971), and

Slobin (1971), amongst others. A non-reinforcement position, that associations are built up by mere contiguity of stimuli and responses, suffers from many of the same defects of the reinforcement view, and is similarly unsupported by empirical research on children acquiring language. But we will also see that many modern theorists who hold the 'strong form' of the cognition hypothesis to be outlined below, have drifted into formulations concerning language acquisition not unlike this contiguous association theory. We will also see that the 'weak form' of that cognition hypothesis attempts to correct that misapplication.

The atmosphere in the 1960s, then, was pervaded by the conflict between the more traditional behaviourist accounts of language and language acquisition in terms of associations, and the theoretical papers and experimental studies which were casting doubt on these views. What ensued was a number of sometimes acrimonious exchanges between the supporters of those two positions. The early studies of language in children at that time centred on the emerging structure of the linguistic system. This structure was studied in terms of grammatical categories based on such syntactic properties as word order and structural inflections (e.g. Bellugi, 1967; Braine, 1963a, 1963b; Brown and Bellugi, 1964; Brown, Cazden and Bellugi-Klima, 1969; Brown and Fraser, 1964; and Brown and Hanlon, 1970). However, little attention was yet paid to the developing cognitive processes of young children and their effect on language acquisition. It is true that Piaget had been publishing work on cognitive development for some 40 years at that time, but it must be recalled that his influence on psychology in English-speaking countries was very slight until the early 1960s, and on the language acquisition studies at that time his influence was negligible. His work on the language and thought of the child (1926) was concerned with the functions of language, the relation between egocentric and internalised speech,[†] understanding between children, questions asked by children, and the like, and except for a few pages on the 'collective monologues'[†] of children aged four and five, was devoted entirely to older children of at least six years of age. By contrast, the child language studies of the 1960s were interested in the first structured language at and shortly after the stage of forming two-word uttterances — about 1½ to 2 years of age — and Piaget's book on language was not seen as directly relevant to those concerns. Similarly, Vygotsky's important book, *Thought and Language*, originally published in 1934, was not translated into English until 1962. Vygotsky proposed that language and thought had separate roots which were evidenced in what he called pre-intellectual speech and in prelinguistic thought. At a certain point these separate processes became linked and thought became verbal and speech rational. After this point, however, Vygotsky claimed that the nature of processes changed so that thought development was determined by language. Again, what was emphasised was the tremendous influence that language had on the thought processes. Soviet work on thought and language developed along lines emphasising the priority of language-based processes, and theories were put forward that centred on notions such as the 'second signalling system' and the directive function of speech (see, for example, Luria, 1959).

In summary, then, the main concern in the early 1960s of those looking at child language was with the acquisition of syntactic forms. However, in the late 1960s, perhaps under the influence of the 'discovery' of Piaget by psychologists in English-speaking countries, the atmosphere began to change. In 1966 and 1967, while making a study of the acquisition of time concepts by children during their acquisition of language (Cromer, 1968) I noted several curious things about the acquisition process which led me to propose that certain aspects of grammatical acquisition depended crucially on developing cognitive processes. Similarly, Lois Bloom (1970) studied the acquisition of language in three children by focusing on the meanings they attempted to express and the situational contexts in which their utterances were made. These studies will be reviewed below in a section devoted to the point of view that cognitive processes determine language acquisition. The movement in the 1970s, then, has been toward understanding language acquisition in terms of its cognitive underpinnings and has increasingly focused on the semantic or meaningful aspect of language. For example, Ervin-Tripp (1971) and Macnamara (1972) suggested that language could never be learned unless the meanings were obvious to the child when he heard the sentences expressing them. In other words, the child cannot discover syntactic structures without the aid of meaning. Other studies have been increasingly devoted to the development of the semantic component of language both at the structural level and in terms of the acquisition of single word meanings (e.g. Bloom, 1973; Bowerman, 1973; Clark, 1971, 1972; Donaldson and Balfour, 1968; and Donaldson and Wales, 1970).

By the late 1960s, linguists had already shifted much of their interests from syntax itself, considered in isolation, to the semantic aspects of language. Fillmore (1968) for example, put forward a case theory of grammar in which underlying meanings play a primary role. McCawley (1968) suggested a directly semantic deep structure. Some of the views which were in opposition to Chomsky's concentration on syntax came to be known broadly as 'generative semantics' (see, for example, Lakoff, 1971; McCawley, 1971a, 1971b, 1973; and a collection of reprinted articles edited by Seuren, 1974). The interpretation by psychologists of some of these changes in emphasis have led to at least two major problems, however. First, there has been a tendency to interpret 'semantics' as being synonymous with the broader cognitive sense of 'meaning'. The claim by some linguists that syntax is generated from a semantic base, i.e., that the meaning component plays an essential part in the generation of syntactic structures, has been treated by some psychologists as if this constituted a cognitive and not a linguistic theory. I have even heard one prominent psychologist exclaim, 'Well, at last we can forget about linguistics and go back to doing psychology'. This is misguided. The word 'semantics' is not identical to thought or to meaning in the broader sense. Semantics is concerned specifically with the representation of meaning in language.

The second problem is the growing belief that all of language acquisition can be explained solely in terms of developing cognitive categories or in terms of thoughts, intentions, pragmatic relations, and the like. This really constitutes the strong form of the cognition hypothesis, and I will argue that such a view is inadequate.

In the remainder of this article, then, these two main problems of current concern with semantics and cognition will be addressed. First, I will present a descriptive diagram representing some structures, processes, and operations in order to clarify the issues and the terminology to be used. In a subsequent section, I will turn to the cognition hypothesis of language acquisition itself. Some studies will be reviewed that illustrate how cognitive structures, cognitive operations, and cognitions (thoughts) affect the language acquisition process. As has been indicated, if no other factors are taken into account, a claim that language acquisition depends solely on these types of cognitive underpinnings constitutes the strong form of the cognition hypothesis. It may be that Piaget's claims could be seen in this light. As a corrective to this view, some examples from linguistics and psycholinguistics will be given in support of the claim that language itself constitutes a system that must be understood and which has its own genetic roots. Language acquisition cannot be understood in isolation from these more purely linguistic processes. A position incorporating both cognitive and more purely linguistic processes is what I called the weak form of the cognition hypothesis. I mentioned earlier the necessity of noting the historical context of any theory. At the time I coined these phrases, I was attempting to parallel the Sapir-Whorf hypothesis which held the opposite point of view and which was still in vogue. It may be recalled that the Sapir-Whorf hypothesis held that language determined thought. Its weak form allowed thought processes to have a separate existence independent of language. The weak form of the Sapir-Whorf hypothesis held that language did not determine thought, but merely influenced it by predisposing speakers of various languages to think in differing ways. The opposite point of view — the cognition hypothesis — similarly had to be stated in a weak form. Cognitive processes by themselves are necessary but not sufficient to explain language acquisition. Purely linguistic factors must also be taken into account.

In order to focus attention on the change from a concentration solely on language to a newer viewpoint which emphasised the effects of cognitive processes on language acquisition (either in its strong or weak form) I placed the two alternatives in stark contrast. Schlesinger (1977) has rightly pointed out the need to see both cognitive and more purely linguistic processes as interactive during the acquisition of language. Having first reviewed the work on the contrasting processes of cognition and language as relatively autonomous processes, I will briefly outline some of the ways these two processes interact, for certainly Schlesinger's view is the more accurate in describing the true growth of language competence by children in actual day-to-day situations. Like studies of genetic versus environmental factors on behaviour, both processes can be studied or focused on in their own right. Nor is it merely the case that 'both positions are true'. Rather, the two processes interact in ways which change the significance of either. Nevertheless, each process has its own laws and determinants, and the value of treating them as distinct at some level is greatest when either process is impaired in some way.

A Descriptive Diagram and Some Terminology

It is misleading to treat the cognitive underpinnings of language as if they constitute some definite entity. Instead, it may be more useful to separate the various components of cognition. I have divided these into three types: cognitive structures and processes, cognitive operations, and cognitions. These types are not, in fact, clearly distinct, and this division is meant merely to focus attention on various cognitive constituents that can be explored. Cognitive structures and processes are meant to include a number of basic underlying capacities such as short-term memory, auditory processing mechanisms,[†] production span capacities,[†] and the like. It will be noted that these are certainly not strictly structural entities. On the other hand, they resemble structures in the sense that they constitute a number of basic cognitive mechanisms which can be impaired with serious consequences for language acquisition (and cognitive functioning in general). By contrast, the next type, cognitive operations, is somewhat less basic and includes abilities and operations which act on the output of

Figure 4.1: Structures and Operations Relevant to Language

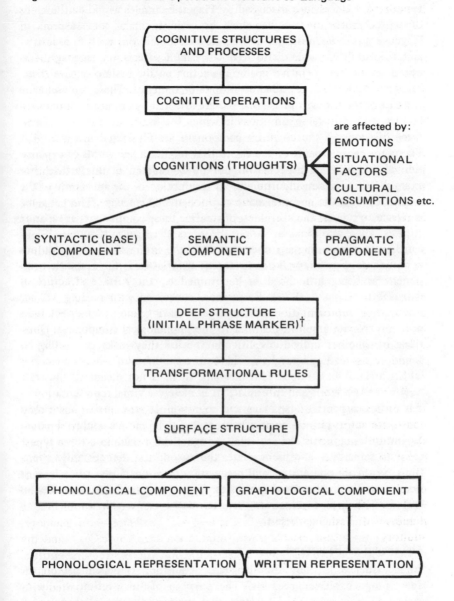

(Round boxes basically represent structures; square boxes denote rules and operations linking the structural levels.)

the more basic cognitive structures and processes. Here would be included the operations discussed by Piaget. Examples would be the kinds of sensori-motor operations which are said to make some aspects of language structure possible, as well as later operations such as identity[†] and reversibility[†] which also have important effects on language. The outcomes of the cognitive operations acting on the basic cognitive structures and processes are called cognitions or thoughts. These represent the content of the thought processes, and are affected by emotions, situational factors, and cultural assumptions in which the individual partakes. These three divisions of the cognitive component are illustrated in Figure 4.1. There are other aspects of the figure that require a few words of explanation although those aspects will not be considered in this article. For example, the diagram incorporates an assumption of the autonomy of the syntactic, semantic and pragmatic components of language. There is some evidence to suggest the usefulness of treating these components as separate entities when one looks at various disorders of language (Cromer, 1974). Furthermore, the diagram does not show the interaction of the various components. For example, some recent theories treat the semantic component as being influenced or determined by the surface structure of language (Chomsky, 1976). Researchers concerned with reading will see the written representation of language as having important direct links not only to the graphological but to the phonological component. Questions of whether individuals differ in the use they make of reading by sound versus reading by sight would require a number of cross-connections which are not illustrated. This diagram, then, is not meant to illustrate how processes work and interrelate; it is merely a visual representation of the various aspects of language and cognition. It attempts to make clear the different types of cognitive processes that can be included under 'cognition'; highlights the fact that thoughts and meanings are not identical with semantics; and incorporates the assumption that semantic operations, syntactic operations, and pragmatic operations are at some level at least partially independent processes. The concern of the remainder of this article will be to illustrate the interrelations among the various cognitive levels and language itself.

The Cognition Hypothesis

What evidence is there that language acquisition is dependent on the developing cognitive processes? The purpose of this section will be to review some experimental evidence that supports the notion that various cognitive factors strongly influence the course of first language acquisition. A few examples will be given that illustrate the contribution of the different levels of cognition as outlined above. These descriptions will necessarily be short and selective; some of the arguments are developed more fully and additional experimental evidence given in Cromer (1974, 1976).

Evidence for the Effect of Cognitive Structures and Processes on Language Acquisition

The effect of various cognitive structures on language acquisition can be most easily seen in studies either of normal children in different developmental periods or of children who suffer from varying cognitive deficits. Menyuk (1964, 1969) studied a number of children who had been diagnosed as using 'infantile language'. These children were aged between 3:0 and 5:11. Menyuk hypothesised that a deficit of short-term memory might be responsible for their language difficulties. She studied the spontaneous utterances of these children and also their responses in an imitation task, the latter task also being administered to normal-speaking children. The analysis of spontaneous productions revealed that these children were not really using less mature language forms as compared to normal-speaking children of the same chronological age.[†] Rather, their language structures were different from those used by young normal children, and this was true throughout the age range. Their language, then, was deviant and not 'infantile'. In the imitation task, this deviant language group showed striking differences from normal children. The imitations by the normal children were constrained by syntactic structure, not the length of the sentence to be imitated. Thus, normal children as young as three years of age were able accurately to imitate some sequences up to nine words long. The correlation between sentence length and the inability to imitate sentences was at chance level (0.04). By contrast, the imitations of the language deviant group were determined by length rather than by syntax. The correlation for these children between length and inability to imitate was 0.53. An analysis of the mistakes made by these children also showed that sentence length was an important factor. The ends of the sentences were most frequently repeated while initial portions of the sentence were often omitted. In addition, Menyuk noted that these children showed strong evidence of impaired auditory memory in that even strings[†] as short as three to five morphemes in length gave rise to omissions and modifications. Menyuk speculated that if a child is able to keep in memory no more than two or three morphemes, a linguistic analysis of the incoming language data would be severely impaired. The result would be the production of utterances which would not only be impoverished and limited, but possibly even based on hypotheses and rules concerning language that differ from those rules generated by normal children. This leads to deviant language forms being produced.

A similar hypothesis concerning short-term memory limitations and their effects on language was put forward by Graham (1968, 1974; Graham and Gulliford, 1968). He was studying the language of educationally subnormal children. He related both comprehension and repetition scores to short-term memory measured by random words and digits, and found that these scores increased regularly with increasing short-term memory. The grammatical form of a sentence also played a part in that sentences of the same length but of varying grammatical complexity resulted in performance differences. Interpreting syntactic differences as involving differing amounts of computation, Graham concluded that children failed to process sentences which made demands on short-term memory that were beyond their capacity.

Another type of developing capacity which has important consequences for language is what might be called a 'productive span capacity'. It may be that young children have some limitation on the length of utterances they can produce, even though they understand the grammatical relationships involved. Bloom (1970) has made a very convincing case for just this type of cognitive limitation by making a careful analysis of sequences of utterances made by children and the situational contexts in which they occurred. For example, over a short period of time and within the same situational context in which she was playing with a toy car, Kathryn, a child Bloom was recording, produced:

Kathryn under bridge.
Kathryn ə make ə under bridge.
Make ə more under bridge.
Make ə car under bridge.

Now in the actual situation, Kathryn herself was not under the bridge. Bloom claims that the only way one can account for the relationship between 'Kathryn' and 'bridge' in the first utterance is through the assumption that the child was employing some sort of reduction transformation — that is, using a rule whereby some sentence elements were omitted in order to shorten the over-all length of the utterance. The child deleted certain categories during the series of utterances while expanding or adding others. Thus, in the later utterances in this sequence, categories of action and object represented by 'make' and 'car' were added while the subject, 'Kathryn' was deleted. Incidentally, Bloom does not interpret this production limitation to be based on sentence length *per se*. Rather, she feels it is a cognitive limitation in handling structured complexity and would be measured in terms of the number of syntactic operations required.

Reseachers investigating the problems of aphasic children — children in whom the normal growth of language function has failed but whose problem is not attributable to deafness, mental deficiency, motor disability, or severe personality disorder — have proposed a number of structural or process deficits to account for their lack of language. For example, Efron (1963) observed that some adult aphasic patients who had suffered brain damage were seriously impaired in their ability to judge which of two sounds occurred first unless they were separated by a gap far in excess of that needed by normals to make this same judgement. This notion of a sequencing or temporal ordering deficit has been extended to 'aphasoid children' by Lowe and Campbell (1965). They found that their language-impaired group required over ten times the length of interval between two sounds that normal children required in order to specify which came first (350 msec. for the aphasoid children compared with only 30 msec. by the normal children on average). Most researchers experimenting with sequencing problems in aphasic children interpret that deficit as being responsible for their lack of or poor performance in language. Tallal and Piercy, however, in a series of experiments demonstrating sequential ordering deficits in aphasic children (1973a, 1973b, 1974, 1975) included conditions which led them to conclude that the language impairment in these children is not due to a sequencing inability as such. Rather, their experiments seem to indicate that the deficit involves the rate of auditory processing. In other words, these children may have some cognitive structure or processing deficit which evidences itself in lowered speed of auditory processing, and this results in difficulties in discriminating speech sounds.

It would certainly seem reasonable to suppose that children must have normal, intact cognitive structures in order to acquire language. Thus, if they suffer from deficits in short-term memory, sequencing ability, or auditory processing they may be prevented from acquiring normal language. In addition, the cognitive structures of normal children change during the course of early development. Such processes as short-term memory and production span capacity increase with age. If these processes constrain the complexity of grammatical forms that can be acquired either in comprehension or production, then there is evidence for the cognitive hypothesis of language acquisition at least for this type or level of cognitive ability. There is also evidence that the next 'level', cognitive operations, also affects the language acquisition process.

Evidence for the Effect of Cognitive Operations on Language Acquisition

Much of the impetus for studies on cognitive operations underlying language acquistion comes from the Piagetian school. It is claimed, for example, that the child must possess certain types of cognitive schemata even to begin comprehending and producing language. These early schemata are built up during the sensori-motor period (i.e., from birth to about 18 to 24 months of age) and have certain structural properties which make language acquisition possible. Sinclair (1971) has best summarised the effects of the sensori-motor schemata and the corresponding linguistic abilities to which they give rise. For example, the child's emerging ability to put things in spatial and temporal order manifests itself linguistically in the stringing together of linguistic elements. The child's newly acquired ability to classify actions (i.e., to use an entire category of objects for the same action, or to apply an entire category of action schemata to one object) allows, as its linguistic counterpart, the categorisation of linguistic elements into major categories such as noun phrase and verb phrase. The ability to relate objects and actions to one another provides the basis for functional grammatical relations like 'subject of' and 'object of'. The achievement of the ability to embed action schemata into one another is said to allow for linguistic embedding in which phrase markers can be inserted into other phrase markers as is found in centre-embedded† structures and relative clauses. In other words, the structure of language is said to be dependent on and make use of the cognitive schemata which are developed during the sensori-motor interactions of the infant.

Greenfield, Nelson and Saltzman (1972) studied some of the action strategies used by infants in putting together cups in a seriated or nested arrangement, and attempted logically to relate these strategies to particular grammatical constructions. For example, an advanced strategy used by three-year-olds, but not by younger children, was dubbed the sub-assembly method of putting the cups together. It consisted of taking a previously constructed structure of two or more cups and moving it as a unit into or onto another cup or cup structure. In essence, this method consists of a first cup (actor) entering (action) a second cup (acted-upon object) which itself (now becoming a subject) enters (action) a third cup (acted-upon object). This kind of action would parallel the kinds of relations found in relative clause sentences like 'The dog chased the cat that caught the mouse', where the acted-upon object of the first clause (the cat) is the subject of the second clause. Although sentences of this type are not within a child's competence until several years later, the Greenfield *et al.* argument is that the same cognitive abilities underlie and are responsible for both the action structures and the linguistic structures.

In later experiments, this hypothesis has been extended to more complex principles of object construction and their possible relations to language, including the ability to deal with interruptedness, role change of the entities involved and hierarchical tree structures (Goodson and Greenfield, 1975; Greenfield and Schneider, 1977).

The view that language depends on developing cognitive structures is reinforced by studies at later ages of childhood. Sinclair-de-Zwart (1969), for example, has investigated the effect on both language structure and terminology of what Piaget calls 'operational thinking',[†] as evidenced in the well-known conservation[†] experiment. Still other aspects of operational thinking are emphasised by Inhelder (1969) who reported a study that she and Sinclair made of linguistic descriptions of a series of sticks arranged in order of increasing size. The various stages in the ability of children to build such a seriated structure were paralleled by their verbal descriptions of the material. For example, their youngest children, who failed in the seriation task, used only two descriptive terms to describe the sticks, 'long' and 'short'. Older children used three descriptive terms. Still older children, who were on the verge of achieving seriation ability, used comparative terms and were able to describe the sticks in one direction as in saying 'short, longer, longer, longer . . .' as they indicated the sticks increasing in size. However, when asked to describe the sticks again beginning at the other end, they were unable to do so. They couldn't label a stick they had just referred to as 'longer' as being 'shorter'. Non-operational children who are unable to solve the seriation problem are said by Piaget not to have yet mastered the operation of reversibility. Evidently this lack of reversibility extends to verbal descriptions as well.

Ferreiro and Sinclair (1971) made a study of another aspect of reversibility and its relation to language. In this experiment children watched two events occur in a particular order and were asked to describe the actions, but to talk about the second event first. For example, in one situation, a girl doll washed a boy doll and then the boy doll went upstairs. In order to comply with the instructions of the task an adult might say, 'The boy doll went upstairs after the girl washed him'. Ferreiro and Sinclair found that children of about 4½ years of age were unable to comply with the instructions. They either reported the events in the actual order of occurrence, or, if they inverted them as instructed, merely omitted any temporal indicators as in 'He went upstairs and she washed him'. Older child who were, however, also non-operational (about 5½ years of age) were often able to follow the task instructions, but were unable to use linguistic temporal indicators correctly to indicate what had truly occurred. They used a variety of techniques to solve their problem: some children simply inverted the order of occurrence in their descriptions, as in 'The boy went to the top of the stairs and afterwards the girl cleaned him'. Others inverted the actions ('He goes downstairs again and the girl washes his arms'), and still other children went so far as to attribute the actions to the opposite actors ('The boy goes and washes her face and then it's her that goes upstairs'). The children clearly knew, however, which event had been carried out by whom and which had occurred first, as revealed in questioning by Ferreiro and Sinclair, but they were unable to encode these linguistically. According to Ferreiro and Sinclair, this linguistic inability was due to the lack of reversible cognitive operations in these pre-operational stage children.

In some studies I made of the development of temporal reference (Cromer, 1968), I also noted the inability of children to reverse temporal indicators before about 4½ or 5 years of age. In fact, a number of aspects of time reference in general began to emerge at about that age, or shortly thereafter. I attributed the incipient use of several of these time categories not to cognitive abilities like reversibility which appear in the operational stage child, but to earlier aspects of cognition related to Piaget's concept of egocentrism. In studying egocentrism, Piaget had been primarily concerned with spatial egocentrism — that is, the inability to conceptualise an array from another person's perspective. He studied this with his well-known three mountain experiment in which a child had to indicate the positions of three cardboard mountains of different sizes not as seen from his own side of the display table, but 'as seen' by dolls placed at various points around the display. The child had to indicate the doll's view by pointing to the correct picture from ten differing views of the display, or by constructing from cardboard the three mountains as seen by the doll. In another condition, children were shown a single picture and had to indicate the correct position of the doll in order for it to see the mountains in that way. Piaget's findings (Piaget and Inhelder, 1948) were reported in terms of a series of developmental stages, but it appears that the first sign of the ability to decenter in this spatial task was shortly after five years of age. It was just about this age that the children whose language and meanings I studied began to refer to various aspects of time which appear to require *temporal* decentering. These included the ability to form grammatical constructions in which the order of mention, linguistically, no longer matched the order of real time occurrence, the expression of hypothetical events, and the expression of timeless events, amongst others. These categories are explained in detail with examples from the language of children in Cromer, (1968, 1974, 1976) where it is claimed that the ability to express these and several other types of linguistic structures depend on the developing cognitive ability of the child to decenter his viewpoint from that of the speaker in the present so as to refer to events from other points in time. What was especially interesting in the developmental data was that language structures which are comparatively simple linguistically but which require decentering, were not used by young children. Slobin (1966) had made a similar observation in children acquiring Russian. For example, grammatically speaking, the form for expressing hypothetical statements in Russian is exceedingly simple. Its emergence in Russian-speaking children, however, is quite late.

It might be argued that some of these grammatical forms which are acquired late may be structurally simple but rarely used by adults, and that the late acquisition of these forms by children is due to frequency considerations. However, further confirmation that what accounts for their acquisition instead is underlying cognitive development comes from an analysis of the very *words* children use that are related to these time concepts. It was found that whole categories of time words began to be used by the child at the same point in development when he first began using grammatical constructions to express these same concepts. This was true in spite of the fact that many of these time words had been used by the parents in their conversation to their children for years before the child began spontaneously to use them. In other words, it appears that certain cognitions are necessary for the acquisition of both words and grammatical structures.

In the case of temporal concepts, the claim was made that acquisition was not a piecemeal addition of various aspects of time. Rather, the child developed certain cognitive operations — in this case the ability to decenter — which then allowed the acquisition of a number of concepts. An experiment analogous to Piaget's three mountain problem but in which children had to decenter to other points in a time sequence (Cromer, 1971) confirmed that children did not begin to decenter temporally until after age 4:11. Furthermore, this ability to decenter did not depend on particular linguistic structures. Rather, children showed a global ability to decenter. Various linguistic structures influenced whether the child's decentered responses were correct or incorrect, but younger children gave no decentered responses at all. In other words, it appears that the cognitive ability to decenter first develops; then that ability begins to manifest itself in the comprehension and production of structures dependent on it.

It has been argued that the aspects of time which were considered, depended upon the development of broader cognitive operations in order to be acquired, and that they therefore were developed as cognitions and thoughts at about the same age. Other cognitions, in spite of depending at some level on the cognitive operations of which a person is capable, may however develop in a more piecemeal fashion. In the next section, a few examples of these and their effect on the acquisition of particular linguistic structures helps further to demonstrate how language processes are dependent on underlying cognitions.

Evidence for the Effect of Cognitions (Thoughts) on Language Acquisition

The well-known studies by Roger Brown have traced both the development of grammar and the expression of meaning in three children, Adam, Eve, and Sarah (Brown, 1973) over several years during their acquisition of language. At the beginning of their earliest stage of language acquisition, which Brown defined in terms of the mean length of their utterances rather than by age, the three children used verbs in their unmarked, generic form. That is, the verb did not have any inflectional endings attached to it. Nevertheless, the parents attributed four types of meanings to these verbs, depending on the situation and context in which the child's utterance occurred. One of these was the *imperative*, as when a child said 'Get book' in what appeared to be a kind of command. A second meaning was reference to the *past*. When, for example, a book had just been dropped, the child might say, 'Book drop, Mommy'. The third meaning ascribed to the child was that of *intention* or *predication*. For example, one child said 'Mommy read' (pronounced as if 'reed') when the mother was getting ready to read to the child. Finally, there was the expression of what is called *present temporary duration*, where an adult speaker would use a progressive form such as 'The fish is swimming'. The child's unmarked form was merely 'Fish swim'.

During this early stage of language acquisition, the children began to modify their verbs in three ways. They began using some past tense forms — either a regular form like 'dropped', or an irregular form such as 'fell'. A second way they began to modify the verb was to use it along with a semi-auxiliary such as 'gonna', 'wanna', or 'hafta'. The meaning of these is characterised by Brown as being mainly that of expressing some kind of intentionality or imminence, a kind of immediate future about the child's own intentions or of actions about to occur. Utterances which express these kinds of meaning, based on situational cues included 'I wanna go' and 'It's gonna fall'. The third modification of the verb by these young children was the beginning of the use of the progressive form — but without the auxiliary. Thus, a child might say 'He swimming', providing the *-ing* but omitting the auxiliary *is*. What is very startling about these acquisitions is that they encode three of the four meanings the child

has been credited by adults as expressing in his first unmarked verbs —
immediate past, intention or predication, and present temporary duration.
What is more, the fourth meaning, the imperative, has no inflectional
marker in English, but Brown noted that the children began using the
word 'please' at just this time along with the other three markers. It
appears, then, that the first grammatical distinctions that a child makes
with his verbs express exactly the kinds of meanings the adults around him
have been attributing to his unmarked verbs, that is, those meanings he has
been credited with trying to express just prior to the acquisition of those
linguistic forms.

There are a number of other examples where the child apparently
begins to express particular meanings just before acquiring the linguistic
means for their proper expression. Both Bloom (1970) and Brown (1973)
present evidence from children acquiring language clearly showing that
children used the concept of possession before acquiring the 's grammatical inflection. In one case, reported by Brown, Eve went round the
room pointing and appropriately saying 'That Eve nose; that Mommy nose
right there; that Papa nose right there'. There is even evidence that the
very first words that a child uses are not imitations but inventions for what
he wants to communicate (Ricks, 1972; see Cromer, 1974 for a summary
of Ricks' results).

Note, in all these examples, how far we have come from the Sapir-
Whorf hypothesis. That hypothesis had claimed that it was the structure
of the language that one spoke that determined the categories or manner
of thoughts one could have. Instead, we now find evidence for the very
opposite point of view. It appears that the kinds of thoughts or cognitions
one has determine what aspects of language one will acquire during language acquisition. Thus, the cognition hypothesis of language acquisition
claims that the developing structures and processes, cognitive operations,
and the actual cognitions which emerge, constrain or determine the
grammatical and semantic acquisitions of which the child is capable.
Language does not determine cognition; cognition determines language
development.

There are, however, several major problems with this view. First, while
it is very useful to show that language development is constrained by the
various cognitive properties which have been discussed, nothing has been
said concerning how language is actually acquired. It is all very well to say
that children will not normally imitate language which encodes things
they do not understand and that they will only spontaneously acquire and
actively use language which expresses cognitions of which they are
capable; but how are these cognitions specifically encoded in a linguistic

system? In other words, it is one thing to claim that certain cognitive abilities are *necessary* in order for certain aspects of language acquisition to occur, but is is quite a different matter to claim that they are *sufficient*. This distinction can be made clearer if one considers examples where language processes are impaired. There are some children who have difficulty acquiring linguistic structures but who are otherwise intellectually normal (developmentally aphasic children). Since they possess sensori-motor intelligence, and those over seven years of age, operational intelligence, what prevents them from acquiring language? What about adults suffering from some sort of traumatic aphasia and who as a consequence losing certain grammatical and semantic abilities (but not the cognitions or thoughts underlying them)? Furthermore, what about unimpaired adults learning a foreign language? Since they have presumably passed through all the developmental stages and possess all the necessary cognitive equipment, what prevents them from easily acquiring in the second language hierarchically complex forms, embedded structures, structures with interrupted sequences, and the like?

The naïve assumption by many who hold a view similar to the strong form of the cognition hypothesis is that children develop certain cognitions or meanings. They then merely note in the adult speech around them how these meanings are expressed. What this constitutes is really nothing more than the old theory of associations, slightly 'updated' by the modification of adding a developmental factor. As the child develops certain meanings he forms associations between these meanings and the ways they are encoded in the language he hears about him. The main problems with such a neat theory are that it doesn't work and it is not supported by the data from real children acquiring language.

There are a number of important arguments from a theoretical perspective concerning why an association theory of language acquisition is inadequate. Such arguments can be found in Chomsky (1959), McNeill (1970a, 1970b), and Miller and McNeill (1969) to name only a few, and these arguments will not be reviewed here. However, the next section will give a few examples actually observed in children of the development of particular linguistic forms which show that associations do not adequately explain the course of acquisition of language by the child. The examples also serve as a second criticism of the strong form of the cognition hypothesis. Not only can one question whether cognitive principles are sufficient to explain language acquisition, but one can extend the argument by claiming that language has its own roots and its own developmental principles which still remain to be explained.

Purely Linguistic Processes and the Weak Form of the Cognition Hypothesis

Having cognitive meanings does not tell one how to encode those meanings in language, as anyone learning a foreign language is well aware. The problem, however, is even more complex than merely trying to provide some explanation of a direct relation between thoughts and the linguistic forms in which they are expressed. In looking at children acquiring language, researchers have found that children express meanings in ways which are not found in the adult models around them. Furthermore, the means of expression change over the course of development, and not always in ways which developing cognitive capacities, such as increased memory span, can explain. A few short examples will serve to illustrate the problem.

It is a common observation by parents that children express their intentions in a primitive way compared to the structures of adult language. Many people will recognise how familiar sentences like 'No wipe finger', and 'Not fit' sound when attributed to the very young child first expressing negation. Ursula Bellugi (1967) made a careful study of the linguistic forms used to express negation by young children as they acquired language. She indeed found that at the first stage, the child merely attached a negative morpheme such as 'no' or 'not' to the beginning of utterances, thus giving rise to expressions like the two just quoted above. Notice that children are not imitating the adult forms they hear around them. Adult utterances for the two examples are likely to be something along the lines of 'Don't wipe your finger . . .' and 'It doesn't fit', but the child, at this initial stage in the expression of negation merely prefixes 'no' or 'not' to his affirmative utterances. At a second stage, Bellugi observed that children used the negative in five grammatical settings, but that these were unrelated to one another. For example, 'don't', 'can't' and 'why not' occurred as vocabulary items, so that non-adult utterances like 'Why not cracker can't talk?' were observed to occur. At a third stage, however, the child had begun to use auxiliary transformations in his speech. At this stage, the negative was truly attached to the auxiliary verb. The former vocabulary items like 'don't' and 'can't' dropped out and these forms were derived by transforming the auxiliary and a negative element. Thus, sentences like 'Why not cracker can't talk?' no longer occurred. The reasons why changes such as these take place are still unknown. Notice, however, that explanations that children change their systems in order to improve their competence in communications are unconvincing. Parents responded to the primitive forms in the earliest stages as expressing negative intent. On the other hand, one might argue that the changes occur due to developing cognitive structures and processes allowing longer sequences and a greater number of linguistic operations. This will, of course, be true of some developing structures. But there are other structures where such an explanation would seem difficult to entertain. For example, Bellugi (Bellugi-Klima, 1969; Bellugi, 1971) traced the progression of self-reference by children through several stages, and it is difficult to see how cognitive principles can explain that progression.

At the earliest stage of self-reference, the child used his name instead of a pronoun no matter where in the sentence it occurred. This led to the child producing sentences such as:

Adam home.
Pick Adam up.
Like Adam book shelf.

In a second stage, he began to use the pronoun 'I' for his name if it occurred in the first position in the sentence, and the pronoun 'me' for any other position in the sentence. When he used 'I', he occasionally produced both the pronoun and his name together, so he produced sentences at this stage like:

I like drink it.
I making coffee.
I Adam driving.
I Adam do that.

In this same, second stage, the production of 'me' for self-reference in all sentence positions other than the first position, resulted in some sentences which sounded very adult-like:

One for me.
Wake me up.
Why laughing at me?

But this same strategy also led the child to produce a number of regularly patterned errors, i.e., productions explained by the rule he was using which deviated from sentences allowable in adult grammar. These included:

Why me spilled it?
What me doing?

Again, it should be noted that these regular 'errors' are not likely to be imitations; the child is not merely matching the adult model and learning language by associating his intent to refer to himself with the ways this is done by adults around him.

At a third stage, the child changed his rules again. He now produced 'I' for his name if it served a nominative function in the sentence, and used 'me' if it served an object function, regardless of sentence position:

That what I do.
Can I put them on when I go outside?
You watch me be busy.
You want me help you?

These initial stages in the development of self-reference (there are further stages which include acquisitions of possessive pronouns like 'mine' and reflexive pronouns like 'myself') are enough to illustrate the problem. The child develops his grammar in a regular and systematic manner. These productions can be described by certain rules than can account for the discrepancies between what the child produces and the adult models around him. These stages change over time and in ways that do not always match more closely the adult models. And most importantly, note that these changes are not based on meaning or reference. In these examples, reference has remained the same – reference to self. Furthermore, it is difficult to see how limitations of cognitive structures and processes could be responsible for the earlier rules. Utterances at the second stage like 'Why me spilled it?' and 'What me doing?' do not appear to be cognitively simpler in structure than 'Why I spilled it?' and 'What I doing?' which conceivably could have been produced by the child at that stage but were not. In other words, neither meaning nor a simple measure of cognitive complexity, such as the number of elements, is sufficient to account for developmental changes of the type found in the expression of self-reference. Many examples from other linguistic structures could be given. For example, in my own work with the acquisition of forms which allow the child to identify who the actual actor is in sentences like 'The wolf is *glad* to bite' and 'The wolf is *fun* to bite', when the child is provided with wolf and duck hand puppets, it was noted that children do not consistently answer in an adult manner until after the age of ten years. When children aged four through to nine years interpret 'The wolf is *fun* (*hard, tasty,* etc.) to bite' as if the wolf is doing the biting, it is not because they do not know the meaning of the words 'fun', 'hard' and 'tasty'. What they lack is some specific knowledge about the structures which allow these items and the related transformations in which they can be used – a set of purely linguistic principles (see review in Cromer, 1975).

In some cases the specifically linguistic processes that affect language acquisition may be phonological, not syntactic. In Geneva, Annette Karmiloff-Smith has designed a number of ingenious experiments for teasing out the variable involved in the child's acquisition of gender endings in French (Karmiloff-Smith, 1976). She used 30 nonsense words which were assigned to various pictures. These words had typically masculine, feminine, or neutral endings (phonological cues). They were sometime used in sentences where they were or were not in agreement with the gender of the article (syntactic cues). And there were conditions in which the sex of the person was or was not consistent with the noun suffix (semantic cues). All questions put to the child used forms in which gender was not audibly gender-marked, so that the child had to provide some marking in the form that he used as his answer. Karmiloff-Smith found that young children (about four years of age) primarily based their productions on a very powerful system of phonological rules. The answers they gave were based on the consistency of phonological changes of word endings. Neither syntactic cues (gender of article) nor semantic cues (sex of the person in the drawings) determined gender agreement. In more recent work, Karmiloff-Smith (1977) has provided evidence that for the child, language is an object of attention itself. She has argued that language is treated by the child in a manner similar to physical objects to be sorted, classified, etc. Indeed, the very language system itself may in turn affect cognitive understanding.

The examples given in this section indicate that there is more to language acquisition than merely matching cognitions and thoughts to their expression in the adult language. Theoretically, such a view can be shown not to be adequate in explaining language structure. Practically, child language studies have shown that the child's acquisitions do not follow such an associative pattern. Language is a system in its own right and there are aspects of its acquisition which differ from the acquisition of other cognitive processes. It is not acquired by laws of learning which resemble those hypothesised for the learning of other behavior. On the other hand, language is not learned in a vacuum. The first half of this paper has been spent in outlining how cognitive processes of various types constrain acquisition of language structures during the course of development. These cognitive underpinnings were said to be necessary but not sufficient to explain language acquisition. A full explanation requires the introduction of some specifically linguistic principles and processes. This is what is meant, then, by the weak form of the cognition hypothesis. Cognitive development predisposes the child to encode certain meanings; how these are actually encoded in language depends on both underlying cognitive processes and specifically linguistic ones. The specifically linguistic processes are still little understood.

A Note on the Interaction of Language and Cognition

In the introduction to this paper, mention was made that although it is possible to treat language and cognition as separate entities, one very important aspect of development in general is their constant interaction (see, for example, Schlesinger, 1977). The cognition hypothesis has mainly emphasised the contribution of cognitive processes in general to language acquisition, and the weak form of this hypothesis allows for some specifically linguistic processes to play a part as well. But important effects also occur in the other direction. Language processes can have important consequences for developing cognitions. For example, Vygotsky (1962), although he pointed out the separate roots of language and thought, claimed that the nature of development changed when thought became verbal. Thought development becomes determined by language, that is, by the linguistic tools of thought and by the socio-cultural experience of the child as mediated by language and language concepts.

Karmiloff-Smith (1976) has proposed that linguistic structure itself can influence conceptual processes. That is, she argues that the child is as obsessed with similarities in his linguistic environment as in his physical environment. She points out that the consistent treatment of certain words or word classes may lead to broader concepts. For example, articles occur before objects ('*an* elephant') and before actions ('*an* event'). This commonality, she argues, allows for the child to go beyond the existing conceptual distinction between objects and actions, to see that an action can be treated as an object.

Nelson (1974) has also argued that language plays an important part in concept development. For example, naming may draw a child's attention to objects, relationships, and instances that share common attributes, thereby causing him to look for an underlying relation that will form the basis for a concept. Several years ago, the Soviet psychologist A.A. Liublinskaya (1957) conducted several experimental studies on the effect language had on the perceptual organisation and consequent problem-solving behaviour in young children. The children were required to sort butterflies on the basis of the patterns on their wings. In order to do this, they had to abstract pattern from wing colour. Children in the experimental group were given verbal labels such as 'spots', 'stripes' and 'nets' in order to fix the patterns, while children in a control group were not given any verbal labels. When the patterns were given names, even the youngest children in the experimental group began to turn their attention away from colour and to compare patterns which were different in colour. By contrast, even the oldest children in the control group with no labels could barely distinguish the patterns. They made many mistakes and did not understand their own rare correct solutions. Liublinskaya reports that not one child in the control group could explain his choice. When asked, 'How did you know that this was the butterfly to choose?', these children would reply, 'I just knew', 'I had a good look', etc. So language may direct attention to certain aspects of a perceptual situation. This in turn will aid in particular problem-solving tasks, as in the example of sorting butterflies by wing patterns. In other words, the weak form of the Sapir-Whorf hypothesis is also true: language may not determine our thoughts but it predisposes us to think in certain ways.

Conclusion

In returning to a consideration of the weak form of the cognition hypothesis, we can note two reservations which have been discussed in this paper. First, as has been pointed out in the previous section, an interaction exists between language and thought. Second, the weak form of the cognition hypothesis, even with a recognition of the interaction of cognitive and linguistic processes, is nevertheless only a partial hypothesis of language acquisition. In the introduction, I said that stating the hypothesis in the particular form in which I did was due to the particular historical context — i.e., the set of beliefs prevailing at the time it was put forward. For the same reasons, any hypothesis is inaccurate in that it emphasises certain details and neglects others. As a theory of language acquisition, the weak form of the cognition hypothesis is necessarily still only part of the story. I have focused on the acquisition of the grammatical aspects, the syntax, of language, a process that is still mysterious and unexplained. I have tried to point to some of the ways that process may interact with various types of cognitive processes (structures, operations, and thoughts). A full theory of language will, of course, have to deal with a great many other issues: the kinds of presuppositions, cultural assumptions, situational factors, and emotions that affect not only thoughts, but various aspects of the syntactic, semantic and pragmatic components of language. There will have to be detailed investigations into the semantic component of language, studies of how language is used in the pragmatic sense, and studies of the various functions that language serves. Perhaps we are not yet ready for grand theories of language acquisition. To build a wall, you must first have a few bricks.

References

Bellugi, U. 'The acquisition of the system of negation in children's speech', unpublished doctoral dissertation, Harvard University, 1967.

Bellugi, U., 'Simplification in children's language', in R. Huxley and E. Ingram (eds.), *Language acquisition: models and methods.* Academic Press, London and New York, 1971, p. 95-119.

Bellugi-Klima, U., 'Language acquisition', paper presented at the Wenner-Gren Foundation for Anthropological Research in the symposium on Cognitive Studies and Artificial Intelligence Research, Chicago, 1969.

Bever, T.G., Fodor, J.A., & Weksel, W., 'Is linguistics empirical?' *Psychological Review*, 72, 1965a, pp. 493-500.

Bever, T.G., Fodor, J.A., & Weksel, W., 'Theoretical notes on the acquisition of syntax: A critique of "context generalization" ', *Psychological Review*, 72, 1965b, pp. 467-82.

Bloom, L., *Language development: Form and function in emerging grammars*, MIT Press, Cambridge, Massachusetts, 1970.

Bloom, L., *One word at a time*, Mouton, The Hague, 1973.

Bowerman, M., *Early syntactic development*, Cambridge University Press, Cambridge, 1973.

Braine, M.D.S., 'On learning the grammatical order of words', *Psychological Review*, 70, 1963a, pp. 323-48.

Braine, M.D.S., 'The ontogeny of English phrase structure: The first phase', *Language*, 39, 1963b, pp. 1-13.

Brown, R., 'Language and categories', in J.S. Bruner, J.J. Goodnow, and G.A. Austin (eds.), *A study of thinking*, John Wiley and Sons, New York, 1956, pp, 247-312.

Brown, R., *A first language*, Harvard University Press, Cambridge, Massachusetts, 1973.

Brown, R., & Bellugi, U., 'Three processes in the child's acquisition of syntax', *Harvard Educational Review*, 34, 1964, pp. 133-51.

Brown, R., Cazden, C., & Bellugi-Klima, U., 'The child's grammar from I to III', in J.P. Hill (ed.), *Minnesota Symposia on Child Psychology*, vol. 2. The University of Minnesota Press, Minneapolis, 1968, pp. 28-73.

Brown, R., & Fraser, C., 'The acquisition of syntax', in U. Bellugi and R. Brown (eds.), 'The acquisition of language', *Monographs of the Society for Research in Child Development*, 29, 1964, pp. 43-79.

Brown, R., & Hanlon, C., 'Derivational complexity and the order of acquisition in child speech', in J.R. Hayes (ed.), *Cognition and the development of language*, John Wiley and Sons, New York, 1970, pp. 11-53.

Carroll, J.B. (ed.), *Language, thought and reality: selected writing of Benjamin Lee Whorf*, MIT Press and John Wiley and Sons, New York, 1956.

Chomsky, N., 'A review of B.F. Skinner's verbal behavior', *Language*, 35, 1959, pp. 26-58.

Chomsky, N. *Reflections on language*, Maurice Temple Smith, Ltd., London, 1976.

Clark, E.V., 'On the acquisition of the meaning of *before* and *after*', *Journal of Verbal Learning and Verbal Behavior*, 10, 1971, pp. 266-75.

Clark, E.V., 'On the child's acquisition of antonyms in two semantic fields', *Journal of Verbal Learning and Verbal Behavior*, 11, 1972, pp. 750-8.

Cromer, R.F., 'The development of temporal reference during the acquisition of language', unpublished doctoral dissertation, Harvard University, 1968.

Cromer, R.F., 'The development of the ability to decenter in time', *British Journal of Psychology*, 62, 1971, pp. 353-65.

Cromer, R.F., 'The development of language and cognition: The cognition hypothesis', in B. Foss (ed.), *New perspectives in child development*, Penguin Books, Harmondsworth, Middlesex, 1974, pp. 184-252.

128   *The Strengths of the Weak Form*

Cromer, R.F., 'Are subnormals linguistic adults?', in N. O'Connor (ed.), *Language, cognitive deficits, and retardation,* Butterworths, London, 1975, pp. 169-87.
Cromer, R.F., 'The cognitive hypothesis of language acquisition and its implications for child language deficiency', in D.M. Morehead and A.E. Morehead (eds.), *Normal and deficient child language,* University Park Press, Baltimore, Maryland, 1976, pp. 283-333.
Donaldson, M., & Balfour, G., 'Less is more: A study of language comprehension in children', *British Journal of Psychology,* 59, 1968, pp. 461-72.
Donaldson, M., & Wales, R.J., 'On the acquisition of some relational terms', in J.R. Hayes (ed.), *Cognition and the development of language,* John Wiley and Sons, New York, 1970, pp. 235-68.
Efron, R. 'Temporal perception, aphasia, and déjà vu', *Brain,* 86, 1963, pp. 403-24.
Ervin-Tripp, S., 'Language development', in M. Hoffman and L. Hoffman (eds.), *Review of child development research,* vol. 2. University of Michigan Press, Ann Arbor, Michigan, 1966, pp. 55-105.
Ervin-Tripp, S., 'An overview of theories of grammatical development', in D.I. Slobin (ed.), *The ontogenesis of grammar: a theoretical symposium,* Academic Press, New York, 1971, pp. 189-223.
Ferreiro, E., & Sinclair, H. 'Temporal relations in language', *International Journal of Psychology,* 6, 1971, pp. 39-47.
Fillmore, C.J., 'The case for case', in E. Bach and R.T. Harms (eds.), *Universals in linguistic theory,* Holt, Rinehart, & Winston, New York, 1968, pp. 1-88.
Goodson, B.D., & Greenfield, P.M., 'The search for structural principles in children's manipulative play: A parallel with linguistic development', *Child Development,* 46, 1975, pp. 734-46.
Graham, N.C., 'Short term memory and syntactic structure in educationally subnormal children', *Language and Speech,* 11, 1968, pp. 209-19.
Graham, N.C., 'Response strategies in the partial comprehension of sentences', *Language and Speech,* 17, 1974, pp. 205-21.
Graham, N.C., & Gulliford, R.A., 'A psychological approach to the language deficiencies of educationally subnormal children', *Educational Review,* 20, 1968, pp. 136-45.
Greenfield, P.M., Nelson, K., & Slatzman, E., 'The development of rulebound strategies for manipulating seriated cups: A parellel between action and grammar', *Cognitive Psychology,* 3, 1972, pp. 291-310.
Greenfield, P.M., & Schneider, L., 'Building a tree structure: The development of hierarchical complexity and interrupted strategies in children's construction activity', *Developmental Psychology,* 13, 1977, pp. 299-313.
Inhelder, B., 'Memory and intelligence in the child', in D. Elkind and J.H. Flavell (eds.), *Studies in cognitive development,* Oxford University Press, New York, 1969, pp. 337-64.
Karmiloff-Smith, A., 'The interplay between syntax, semantics, and phonology in language acquisition processes', paper presented at the Stirling Conference on the Psychology of Language, Stirling, Scotland, June, 1976.
Karmiloff-Smith, A., 'The child's construction of a system of plurifunctional markers', in M. Bullowa (chair), *Language development,* Symposium presented at the biennial conference of the International Society for the Study of Behavioural Development, Pavia, Italy, September, 1977.
Lakoff, G., 'Presupposition and relative well-formedness', in D.D. Steinberg and L.A. Jakobovits (eds.), *Semantics,* Cambridge University Press, Cambridge, 1971, pp. 329-40.
Liublinskaya, A.A., 'The development of children's speech and thought', in B. Simon (ed.), *Psychology in the Soviet Union,* Routledge and Kegan Paul, London, 1957, pp. 197-204.

Lowe, A.D., & Campbell, R.A., 'Temporal discrimination in aphasoid and normal children', *Journal of Speech and Hearing Research,* 8, 1965, pp. 313-14.

Luria, A.R., 'The directive function of speech in development and dissolution: Part I: Development of the directive function of speech in early childhood', *Word,* 15, 1959, pp. 341-52.

Macnamara, J., 'Cognitive basis of language learning in infants', *Psychological Review,* 79, 1972, pp. 1-13.

McCawley, J.D., 'The role of semantics in a grammar', in E. Bach, and R.T. Harms (eds.), *Universals in linguistic theory,* Holt, Rinehart and Winston, New York, 1968, pp. 124-69.

McCawley, J.D., 'Meaning and the description of languages', in J.F. Rosenberg and C. Travis (eds.), *Readings in the philosophy of language,* Prentice-Hall, Englewood Cliffs, New Jersey, 1971a, pp. 533-48.

McCawley, J.D., 'Where do noun phrases come from?', in D.D. Steinberg and L.A. Jakobovits (eds.), *Semantics,* Cambridge University Press, London, 1971b, pp. 217-31.

McCawley, J.D., 'A review of Noam A. Chomsky, Studies on semantics in generative grammar', paper reproduced by the Indiana University Linguistics Club, 1973.

McNeill, D., 'Developmental psycholinguistics', in F. Smith and G.A. Miller (eds.), *The genesis of language,* MIT Press, Cambridge, Massachusetts, 1966, pp. 15-84.

McNeill, D., *The acquisition of language,* Harper and Row, New York, 1970a.

McNeill, D., 'The development of language', in P.H. Mussen (ed.), *Carmichael's manual of child psychology,* vol. 1, John Wiley and Sons, New York, 1970b, pp. 1061-1161.

Menyuk, P., 'Comparison of grammar of children with functionally deviant and normal speech', *Journal of Speech and Hearing Research,* 7, 1964, pp. 109-21.

Menyuk, P. *Sentences children use,* MIT Press, Cambridge, 1969.

Miller, G.A., & McNeill, D., 'Psycholinguistics', in G. Lindzey and E. Aronson (eds.), *The handbook of social psychology,* 2nd edition, vol. 3, Addison-Wesley, Reading, Massachusetts, 1969, pp. 666-794.

Nelson, K., 'Concept, word, and sentence: Interrelations in acquisition and development', *Psychological Review,* 81, 1974, pp. 267-85.

Piaget, J., *The language and thought of the child,* Harcourt, Brace, New York, 1926.

Piaget, J., & Inhelder, B., *The child's conception of space,* Routledge and Kegan Paul, London, 1956, (originally published in 1948).

Ricks, D.M., 'The beginnings of vocal communication in infants and autistic children', unpublished doctorate of medicine thesis, University of London, 1972.

Sachs, J., 'The status of developmental studies of language', in J. Eliot (ed.), *Human development and cognitive processes,* Holt, Rinehart, and Winston, New York, 1971, pp. 381-94.

Schlesinger, I.M., 'The role of cognitive development and linguistic input in language acquisition', *Journal of Child Language,* 4, 1977, pp. 153-69.

Seuren, P.A.M. (ed.), *Semantic syntax,* Oxford University Press, London, 1974.

Sinclair-de Zwart, H., 'Developmental psycholinguistics', in D. Elkind and J.H. Flavell (eds.), *Studies in cognitive development,* Oxford University Press, New York, 1969, pp. 315-336.

Sinclair, H., 'Sensori-motor action patterns as a condition for the acquisition of syntax', in R. Huxley and E. Ingram (eds.), *Language acquisition: Models and methods,* Academic Press, London and New York, 1971, pp. 121-30.

Skinner, B.F., *Verbal behavior,* Appleton-Century-Crofts, Inc., New York, 1957.

Slobin, D.I., 'The acquisition of Russian as a native language', in F. Smith and G.A. Miller (eds.), *The genesis of language,* MIT Press, Cambridge, Massachusetts, 1966, pp. 129-48.

Slobin, D.I. (ed.), *The ontogenesis of grammar: A theoretical symposium,* Academic

Press, New York, 1971.

Tallal, P., & Piercy, M., 'Defects of non-verbal auditory perception in children with developmental aphasia', *Nature*, 16 Feb., 241, 1973a, pp. 468-9.

Tallal, P., & Piercy, M., 'Developmental aphasia: Impaired rate of non-verbal processing as a function of sensory modality', *Neuropsychologia*, 11, 1973b, pp. 389-98.

Tallal, P., & Piercy, M., 'Developmental aphasia: Rate of auditory processing and selective impairment of consonant perception', *Neuropsychologia*, 12, 1974, pp. 83-93.

Tallal, P., & Piercy, M., 'Developmental aphasia: The perception of brief vowels and extended stop consonants', *Neuropsychologia*, 13, 1975, pp. 69-74.

Vygotsky, L.S., *Thought and language*, MIT Press, Cambridge, Massachusetts, and John Wiley and Sons, New York, 1962, (originally published in 1934).

Whorf, B.L., *Collected papers on metalinguistics*, Department of State, Foreign Service Institute, Washington D.C., 1952.

5 LANGUAGE ACQUISITION AND COGNITIVE DEVELOPMENT

Hermine Sinclair-de Zwart

Source: Timothy E. Moore (ed.), *Cognitive Development and the Development of Language* (Academic Press, London 1973) pp. 9-25.

Lately, much has been written about the relationship between linguists' grammars and interiorized or mental grammars;[†] what used to be called the problem of the psychological reality of linguistic theory is now usually rephrased in terms of relations or links between different models. Generative grammar can certainly qualify as a model — but what should we compare it with? Nothing resembling a psychological language model has as yet been constructed, and though the heuristic value of generative grammar has been amply demonstrated, its use for the discovery of the constructive mechanisms through which humans learn and use their language appears more doubtful.

The Genevan position as regards the relationship between linguistic theory and the study of the way the (epistemic) speaker-listener understands and produces utterances is parallel to the position Piaget has adopted on logic and cognitive psychology. Logic is an axiomatization of reasoning and is a purely formal discipline. Starting from axioms, theorems are derived in a mechanical, deductive manner. There is, however, a corresponding experimental science, which should not be confused with the formal discipline, and that is the psychology of thinking. The two have indeed often been confused — Aristotle intended to describe thought as the reflection of logical laws, with the proviso that this only concerned true thought, by contrast with everyday thought, which is subject to many social, emotional, and other error-inducing influences.

According to Piaget, the relationship between logic and the corresponding experimental science, cognitive psychology, has to be seen in the following manner, to quote Piaget (1967):

Formal logic does not have to appeal to psychology, since factual questions have no place in a hypothetico-deductive[†] theory: inversely, it would be just as absurd to invoke formal logic for the purpose of deciding an experimental question — as for instance the question of the mechanisms of intelligence. However, in so far as psychology aims at analyzing the final states of equilibrium attained by thought, there

131

is, not a parallelism, but a correspondence between experimental knowledge and logic, as there is a correspondence between a schema and the reality it represents. Each question which arises in one of the two disciplines corresponds to a question in the other, though neither their methods nor their solutions are interchangeable. [p. 37]

Since mathematics and logic have become tools in linguistics, and especially since linguists have tried to axiomatize their procedures, a similar confusion to the one Piaget noticed in the case of German *Denkpsychologie* has arisen in linguistics and psycholinguistics. It is probably no coincidence that the distinction between true thought which was considered to be a direct reflection of logic, and thought in general reminds us of the distinction between competence and performance in its first formulation, when performance was regarded as the debased expression of competence. The necessity pointed out by Piaget, to distinguish clearly axiomatization and experimental science, has since then also been felt in psycholinguistics. A second necessity, also pointed out by Piaget, and, in fact, taken by him as a prerequisite for our understanding of cognitive functioning, especially from an epistemological point of view, is the following: Different axiomatizations can be evaluated as to their resemblance to what he calls dynamic or living thought; and most importantly, certain axiomatizations will show greater resemblance to the way cognitive structures are elaborated in development than others. To understand structures at their various levels of equilibrium it is necessary to know how they have been formed.

Chomsky (1965) distinguishes two levels of adequacy for grammars: The first level, that of descriptive adequacy, is reached when the grammar correctly describes its object, namely the linguistic intuition — the tacit competence — of the native, adult speaker.

The much deeper and hence much more rarely attainable level of explanatory adequacy is reached when the grammar is justified on internal grounds. The problem of internal justification — of explanatory adequacy — is essentially the problem of constructing a theory of language acquisition, an account of the specific innate abilities that make this achievement possible. [p. 26-7]

Except for the word *innate*, there is nothing here with which Piaget would not agree. I think that too much rather vacuous discussion has been devoted to this innate issue. *Pace* Washoe, only human babies learn to talk, only human babies become mathematicians, bakers, and candlestick makers. In that sense, obviously, language and many other abilities as well are innate.

In the case of intelligence, Piaget has shown conclusively that it is possible to follow the slow construction of cognitive structures from birth to formal logic, and that no sudden emergence of preformed logical concepts takes place. This view does not mean that therefore learning takes place in a passive, associative sense, according to what the environment imposes upon a child. Quite the contrary, this development obeys internal laws, and though interaction with people and things is a necessary condition, concepts are formed in the same way by children all over the world, despite very different environmental influences. It has been said that the strict nativist position is a philosophical lazy Susan — that may be so, but as regards linguistic theory it makes matters more difficult, not easier. Chomsky (1965) says:

> A theory of linguistic structure that aims for explanatory adequacy incorporates an account of linguistic universals, and it attributes tacit knowledge of these universals to the child . . . The important question is: what are the initial assumptions concerning the nature of language that the child brings to language learning and how detailed and specific is the innate schema that gradually becomes more explicit and differentiated as the child learns the language? [p. 27]

It would seem to be an impossibly difficult task to make hypotheses about *innate* schemata; also, until neurology provides precise data, the nativist idea seems to put the burden of finding explanatory hypotheses of the nature of human language on linguistics rather than on psychology — and one may well ask if this is an efficient division of labor. Since the child has to be taken into account, developmental psychology seems to be better suited for this purpose. Moreover, it seems easier, and much more hopeful, to suppose that the child brings to the task of acquiring his mother tongue a set of universal cognitive structures which have been built up during the first year of life and which provide enough assumptions about the nature of human language to enable the child to begin to join the talking community at about the age of 1½. In this sense one could indeed, to quote Slobin (1971), take Piaget as a handbook for psycholinguistic development. Hopefully, such a point of view would also make it possible to explain *how* the child's initial assumptions become more and more explicit and differentiated, while agreeing that, up to the period when children everywhere seem to produce utterances that are remarkably alike in structure, there is little question of learning taking place on the basis of presented linguistic data through some kind of inductive generalization. Up to this point, then, we may assume that we are dealing with utterances which are made possible through the assumptions children everywhere make about the nature of human language. These universal linguistic assumptions and the acquisitions they make possible would be reflections of the universal cognitive structures acquired by that age, just as what Piaget calls the structure of sensorimotor intelligence is a reflection of these same general cognitive structures. McNeill (1970) supposes the existence of basic, language-definitional universals – strong linguistic universals – which reflect a specific linguistic ability and may not be a reflection of a cognitive ability at all. I find it impossible to admit that language might not be a cognitive ability; and I find it equally difficult to admit another interpretation of the same statement, that is the idea (also proposed by Vygotsky) that language stems from totally different roots from those of sensorimotor intelligence, and that preverbal intelligence and preintelligent speech only join at the period of the first utterances which are comprehensible for the adult speaker. This view introduces a dichotomy which is not backed up by any facts, and which leaves the beginnings of language shrouded in mystery. Quite to the contrary, I suppose that the closest link between language and intelligent activity dealing with reality is to be found during the earliest period of language learning, and that therefore Piaget's analyses of cognitive structures will be of the greatest use when one deals with the question of the basic hypotheses about the nature of human language.

As soon as children start producing utterances of more than three elements, matters become immensely more complex, and at that point some kind of inductive procedure has to be supposed to account for the appearance of forms and structures belonging to the grammar of one specific language. Clearly, inductive ability is also something that develops; and therefore Piaget can once again give some indications as to the interpretation to be given to the progressive acquisitions children make in the grammar of their mother tongue. But equally clearly, this will depend on many other factors as well, perhaps mainly on the complexity of the language in question as regards the expression of certain grammatical relations. Piaget sees the construction of cognitive operations as following structurally defined stages and as a universal phenomenon. Their progression toward a state of equilibrium is functionally determined by the necessary character of these operations, in the sense that to be internally consistent they cannot be different from what they are. No such necessary and universal character is attached to the morpho-syntactical rules of specific languages, and therefore we cannot expect either universality or clearly defined structural stages; in fact we expect them less and less as language learning proceeds. For the same reason we expect less and less correspondence with the development of intellectual operations, and the occasions to use Piaget for explanatory hypotheses will be correspondingly fewer. However, even in this later period, say from 3 or 4 to 10 and beyond, it is sometimes possible to find in Piaget's theory an interpretation of the difficulties children have with a certain sentence pattern, whereas a pattern that to the adult seems identical or very similar is easily understood and correctly used much earlier. An example from Geneva is the slow elaboration of time relationships studied by Ferreiro (1971), and studied for English by E. Clark (1971), with remarkably similar results in both languages. It seems important that evidence of such relatively late and laborious constructions is accumulating; other examples are to be found in C. Chomsky (1969). It is conceivable that the corresponding phenomenon (i.e., the early correct appearance of certain patterns), can be interpreted by features of the cognitive apprehension young children have of certain situations which give rise to what can be called natural patterns. It should be emphasized that this remark does not refer to so-called iconic characteristics of the situation but to the child's cognitive interpretation which can be quite different from the adult's.

Piaget's theory of cognitive development could therefore be used: first, to help us attain explanatory adequacy by trying to define the child's initial set of linguistic universals, and second, to study from a cognitive point of view the unexpected difficulties which arise later in development.

It is, of course, quite impossible to sketch Piaget's theory in a few paragraphs. However, as regards our first problem, the initial set of linguistic universals, a few remarks will suffice; after discussion of one of our experiments, some further elaboration will follow. The second problem has been dealt with at some length by Ferreiro (1971).

Piaget qualifies his epistemological theory as interactionist and biological. Knowledge is acquired through the subject's action upon, and interaction with, people and things. Action patterns become established, extended, combined with others, and differentiated under the influence of internal regulatory mechanisms; later, they become interiorized (i.e., mentally representable), and organized into grouplike structures. Acting upon environment, rather than copying it or talking about it, is the source of knowledge. Language is only one way among others to represent knowledge. Representation in general does not appear until the end of the sensorimotor period (around the age of 1½) when direct-acting-on-objects has become organized in a first grouplike structure: A move from *a* to *b* (e.g., when the child goes from one point to another himself, or when he moves objects, or when he observes other people moving) can be retraced to find the starting point *a*; it can also be composed of two different moves: from *a* to *x*, and *x* to *b*. Simultaneously and in close connection with this action structure, objects acquire what Piaget calls permanence; that is to say, no longer does the child act as if they have ceased to exist when they disappear from his field of action, but he knows that he can find them again, even if they are successively hidden in different places (as long as he has seen the moves) by using the action structure described above. This achievement is the result of a long development about which we will have more to say later on: it is the culmination of sensorimotor, practical intelligence and at the same time the beginning of representational intelligence. Representation has several forms — symbolic play, mental images, imitation, drawing — and in some of them objects and events are symbolized by something else; it is likely that this is only possible when objects have acquired a certain identity of their own, and no longer exist only when the child acts upon them. To be able to symbolize in play a car by a pebble, one has to know, to a certain extent, both cars and pebbles. To progress, intelligence now has to go beyond the *hic et nunc*: to do this, representation is necessary for recapitulation and anticipation.

Between 2 and 6 years of age Piaget analyzes what is in many respects a reconstruction of sensorimotor intelligence on a different, i.e., representational, level. Slowly, action patterns become interiorized, leading to the system of concrete operations[†] and their invariants. The interiorization leads to reversibility — the capacity to undo mentally what has been done, and therefore to be able to conserve quantities: or the capacity to understand that if one finds out that one stick is shorter than another, the latter is inevitably longer than the former. The development of the preoperational period is subject to certain laws which determine what Piaget calls its semilogical character, comparable to the one-way mappings of set theory.[†]

Similarly, knowledge of objects, their properties, and their behavior develops — moving toward more and more specificity. In a way, the development of logic and that of knowledge of the physical world are contrastive and complementary: A logical structure is more powerful when it becomes more general and less linked to a particular content, whereas understanding of object properties is more powerful when it becomes more specific and differentiated. We are tempted to think that syntactic structures and lexicon follow similar opposite and complementary directions, with here, too, a close link between the two so that new acquisitions in either lead to new acquisitions in the other. However, in the rest of this paper the emphasis will be mainly on syntactic structures.

Among the many questions that can be asked about basic linguistic capacity, the following has recently been discussed in several papers: What is the status of the basic grammatical relations subject-of, main-verb-of, object-of, etc., which in many languages are expressed by the order of the words in surface structure, and presumably, also in base[†] structure (cf. Hayes, 1970). Greenberg (1961) has shown that in most languages the subject precedes the object, and that of the three possible orders where this is so (SVO; SOV; VSO), SVO and SOV are the most frequent. The fact that in some languages the order is relatively free does not seem highly relevant, since even in those languages a basic SVO or SOV order is always preferred whenever a sentence would be ambiguous (as for instance in the case of neuters in Latin, for which nominative and accusative have the same form). It has been supposed by Jakobson (1961) and N. Chomsky (1965, p. 225) that the explanation for the quasi-universality of this order of the elements in the base is to be sought in iconic factors. As Watt (1970) puts it: 'Here of course the presumption is that our attention tends to be seized first by the "subject" of an action being perceived and being put into language – and only secondarily by the "object", if any or perhaps only secondarily by what (in the VP) is to be predicated [p. 65].' Though I cannot agree that the explanation lies in any iconic factors or in a supposedly fundamental characteristic of perception, it does seem plausible that some universal psychological factor is involved. I will come back to this question later on, but for the moment, I suppose that the order of the elements in the base as an expression of grammatical relationships is one of the structures that, for very young children, belongs to their expectancies about the nature of 'language', or at least, that this hypothesis gets instilled very early in language learning.

It has often been said that in the very first two- and three-word utterances, children already use word order consistently to express relations. However, many counterexamples can be found in French publications (Bloch, 1924). We find just as often *maman partie* as *partie maman*; or *cassée poupée* as *poupée cassée*. What is more, we find children apparently trying out different kinds of word order, saying e.g., *couper cheveux papa*; *cheveux couper papa*; *papa couper cheveux*. We also noticed such unusual word order when we asked 3-year-olds to describe some simple events (acted out in front of them with toys). For instance when a monkey knocked a teddy bear down, a 3;2 child said first: '*Il fait tomber le nounours*' ('He makes the bear fall'); but when the experimenter asked 'Yes, that's right, who did it?' the child answered: '*Il a tombé le singe le nounours*' ('He made fall the monkey the bear'): VSO. During the same session this child said, when the cat caressed the pig: '*Il a caressé le cochon le chat*': VOS. Another child said, when the girl doll caressed the dog:

'*le chien a caressé la fille*': OVS. From 3½ onward, the only departure from the SVO order seems to be *il* + VOS: '*Il a poussé les oiseaux le cochon*'. This pattern persists in French in colloquial adult language, but is avoided when ambiguity would result. 'He's mowing the lawn, John' is frequent; 'He met Peter, John' is not.

The problem of linguistic universals has to do with competence, and competence, of course, has to do with our intuitions about language. Since adults' utterances do not necessarily correspond to their intuitions about language, there is no reason to suppose that children's utterances correspond to their intuitions. However, the existence of word order that deviates from SVO or SOV, both in three-word utterances without any grammatical markers, and in the utterances of 3-year-olds which already incorporate pronouns and some inflections, made us wonder about the universality and about the fundamental nature of the SVO order.

We decided on an experiment of the type 'let's see what happens' — and we presented children from 2;6 to 7 with childlike utterances of the type: *cheveux couper papa*. We simply pronounced either two nouns and a verb in the infinitive,[1] or two verbs and a noun (in different orders and with different types of verbs and nouns), and asked the children to guess, and to show us with toys, what we could mean; adding, for the older children, that we were not speaking good French, that what we said was not quite right, but that we wanted them to guess. We hoped that in this way the children might use their set of basic assumptions about language to guess the meaning. We wondered whether they would use word order, and if so, in what way; or whether they would act randomly.

We chose five different three-word combinations, and presented each one in the six possible orders (30 items in all, presented in random succession). A first group consisted of the permutations of girl-push-boy: two animate nouns (N) and a verb (V), where no pragmatic considerations suggest one particular SVO construction. These six permutations are:

NVN: boy-push-girl; girl-push-boy
NNV: boy-girl-push; girl-boy-push
VNN: push-boy-girl; push-girl-boy

The second series consists of the permutations of boy-open-box, where pragmatic considerations suggest one particular solution. A third series is car-roll-truck; the verb *rouler* or *avancer* was chosen because it can be both transitive and intransitive. A fourth series is: pig-horse-leave, two animate nouns and an intransitive verb, and the last group: bear-shout-jump, one noun and two intransitive verbs (we had a toy bear who made a noise when pressed). Our subjects are divided into four age groups: 2; 10–4, 4–5, 5–6, and 6–7. For the moment we have 15 to 20 subjects per group (Sinclair & Brockart, 1972).

Before discussing the results, I would like to point out that the six possible orders of patient, agent and action can be obtained through transformations in surface structure in the following manner, where P = patient, A = Agent, V = action.

AVP: *Le garçon pousse la fille.*
        The boy pushes the girl.
VAP: *Poussée par le garçon, la fille . . .*
        Pushed by the boy, the girl . . .
APV: *C'est par le garçon que la fille est poussée.*
        It's by the boy the girl is pushed.
PAV: *C'est la fille que le garçon pousse.*
        It's the girl the boy pushes.
VPA: *Poussant la fille, le garçon . . .*
        Pushing the girl, the boy . . .
PVA: *La fille est poussée par le garçon.*
        The girl is pushed by the boy.

We are starting to study these surface structures as well, and we hope to be able to use the results of the first experiment to interpret the way children of different age-groups understand these sentences.

The main results of the first experiment, the only one to be discussed here, may be described as follows. The actions for the two series with verbs that are intransitive from the adult point of view (pig-horse-leave, and bear-cry-jump) and the series with 'roll' (which was almost always taken in its intransitive sense) differ from the series boy-push-girl and boy-open-box in three ways:

(*a*) Though in general we had little difficulty in making the children understand what we wanted them to do, these intransitive items were the easiest, especially for the youngest subjects. They did not hesitate, they did not stop and think as they did for the others. One of them expressed this clearly: when boy-box-open followed horse-pig-leave he said, 'The other one was easier'.

(*b*) The solutions given to the two transitive-verb series changed from age-group to age-group, whereas no change in behavior with age was noticed for the intransitive items, apart from a tendency on the part of the youngest group to use only one of the animals or to act only one of the verbs mentioned.

(c)   For the intransitive series, the subjects almost always gave the same solution in all six items, whatever the order in which the words were presented; whereas in the transitive series, and especially in boy-push-girl, solutions were consistently different according to the order of the words.

The most interesting series were therefore boy-push-girl and boy-open-box, and these are the only items I will discuss. To start with boy-push-girl, we had foreseen only two solutions: Either the boy pushing the girl or the girl pushing the boy, and we supposed that at least the younger subjects would choose one of these solutions randomly. Our first surprise was that this was not true at all; and an analysis per subject of solutions for all items shows astonishing consistency, so that we have to suppose that the children used quite specific strategies. These strategies changed with age, and the following pattern emerges.

In Group 1 (2;10–4) two types of action account for about two thirds of all solutions: (a) the verb *push* is understood in an intransitive sense, and the child makes the boy and the girl walk on the table and says *They are walking, they go ahead* — something like *they push on*. One child thought for a long time, chose this solution and then said: *You should have said: 'They walk!'* (b) the child himself performs the action of pushing on the boy and the girl and says, *I push them down*. Evidently, it was sometimes difficult to distinguish these two types, but most of the time the children's remarks and behavior made the distinction clear.

These two strategies disappear in the older age-groups, but not at the same time for the different word order patterns. For NVN or VNN the intransitive solution (SSV$_{intr}$) has disappeared in Group 2, and the solution in which the child (C) acts upon both nouns – (C)VOO – disappears in Group 3; but for NNV, the intransitive solution only disappears in Group 3, and the solution in which the child acts on both nouns only in Group 4.

Two other strategies appear when the children start decoding this series of either 'the boy pushes the girl' or 'the girl pushes the boy'. One of these is the establishment of a link between the verb and the noun which is nearest to it as an agent-action relationship; and the other is the establishment of a link between the verb and the noun nearest to it as an action-patient relationship. In the case of VNN the first strategy (for push-boy-girl) results in the boy pushing the girl (and, results correspondingly, for push-girl-boy, in the girl pushing the boy). The second strategy gives the opposite solution, that is to say: push-boy-girl = 'the girl pushes the boy'. VNN is either decoded as VSO or as VOS. In the NNV series the two strategies again give different solutions: SOV or OSV. The establishment

Table 5.1: Percentage of (C)VOO[a] and SSV$_{intr}$ [b] Solutions as a Function of Age[c]

Presentation order	Age group	Solution	
		(C)VOO	SSV$_{intr}$
VNN	1	18	41
	2	23	3.5
	3	0	7
	4	12.5	0
NVN	1	18	50
	2	20	4
	3	3.5	3.5
	4	4	0
NNV	1	16	59
	2	31	21
	3	23.5	3.5
	4	8.5	0

[a] Child himself acts on both nouns.
[b] The two nouns are made to perform an 'intransitive' action.
[c] See text for explanation.

of the verb-object link may be a little later than the verb-subject link; it is mainly for subjects of Group 3 that the two strategies seem to be in conflict. It is to be noted that in the case of VNN, the strategy of taking the noun immediately following the verb as its object runs counter to a later strategy, which seems preponderant in Group 4, namely that of considering the relative position of the two Ns and choosing the first as the subject, whereas in the case of NNV the verb-object link concurs with that of choosing the first of the two Ns as the subject.

For the NVN series the developmental trend is quite clear: This is of course the only series that corresponds to the normal SVO order in French. As soon as the two primitive strategies have been eliminated NVN = SVO becomes the preponderant solution, already at 65 per cent in Group 2 and at 92 per cent in Group 4. However, for the youngest group this solution represents only 37 per cent of answers, the others belonging to one of the two primitive strategies. Solutions whereby NVN is decoded as OVS are extremely rare. In this series it is impossible to distinguish between the subject-verb link, the verb-object link, and the N_1 = subject, N_2 = object solution; all three result in NVN = SVO.

It is noticeable that in all three combinations the developmental tendency is clearly directed towards the solution: first noun is subject,

Table 5.2. Types and Percentages of Solutions[a] as a Function of Age

Presentation order	Age group	Solution	
		VSO	VOS
VNN	1	23	18
	2	60	13
	3	52	41
	4	66	21
		SVO	OSV
NVN	1	37	0
	2	65	11
	3	80	13
	4	92	4
		SOV	OSV
NNV	1	4	21
	2	31	17
	3	46	26
	4	52	39

[a] Solutions other than those reported in Table 5.1.

second noun is object, whatever the place of the verb (cf. Bever, 1970).

Before giving some tentative interpretations of the results, a few points have to be made about the series boy-open-box. We expected that almost all children would decode all six permutations (boy-open-box, boy-box-open, open-boy-box, etc.) as 'the boy opens the box'. The expectation was not at all confirmed. In the first place, these items, especially if box preceded boy gave rise to between 10 and 20 per cent refusals — which never happened with the other items. Second, here, too, we saw the primitive solution of the child himself acting; that is to say, leaving the doll out and opening the box himself (or herself). Partly, this may just be due to a manipulatory difficulty. More interestingly, in all cases where box preceded boy, and especially in box-open-boy, some children took the box, poked at the boy, lifted up his jacket and said something like: *The box can't really do it, it pricks him*. Percentages of the 'box opens the boy' solution for Groups 1–4 were: 11, 12.5, 20, and 36, respectively. The 6-year-olds seem to be particularly convinced formalists and choose this remarkably antipragmatic solution to our riddle; at that age the SVO pattern seem to be so firmly established that a good proportion of our subjects prefer the most improbable solution.

Our tentative conclusion regarding the building up of the subject-object-verb relationship runs somewhat as follows. We suppose that by our technique the children are put into a position of listening to a language of which they know certain words but not the syntactical rules. We suppose that their initial set of hypotheses about the structure of human language is again set in motion and leads them to choose certain solutions.

At first there are two possibilities: Either the child considers all three-word combinations as describing an event in which he himself takes no part, in which case he supposes names of animals or persons to be the agent to whom is ascribed an action expressed by the verb. Alternatively, he supposes the utterance to describe an action in which he himself takes part, and in that case it is he himself who performs the action on the persons or objects mentioned. His initial pattern for the understanding of an utterance would thus be either subject-predicate and predicate-subject, with no preference for a fixed order, or verb-object and object-verb, again without a fixed order; and in the latter case the subject is not mentioned and is taken to be himself.

Subsequently, these two patterns get combined to form the trilogy SVO; the subject-verb link becoming an ordered pair first, and whatever is left is taken to be the object, as a sort of extension of the subject-predicate construction. A little later, the verb-object link becomes firmly established to form the verb phrase which can be combined with the noun phrase. This results either in SVO, or in SOV, Greenberg's two most likely candidates for the universal base. In both, the subject precedes the object, and the VP node, i.e., the link between object and verb, remains unbroken. In arboreal presentation:

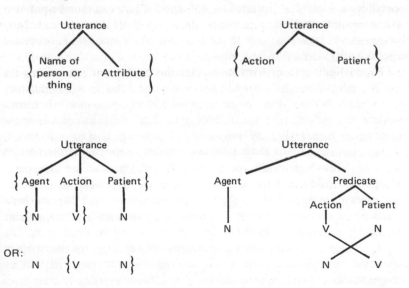

The developmental phase presented here is preceded by the holophrastic period, during which, as I have argued elsewhere, there is no differentiation between subject and predicate or between topic and comment. The above diagrams can be taken to represent either the analysis the child makes of a heard utterance or the child's own production, i.e., the way he combines the elements at his disposal into a surface structure.

To continue speculating, we can now ask how far this supposed construction of the basic grammatical relations corresponds to Piaget's structural analysis of the basic patterns of intelligence. During the sensorimotor period, and starting from reflex activity, the baby extends his action patterns to an ever greater number of objects (sucking his fingers, his toys, etc.) and acquires new action patterns on the basis of already existing ones (e.g., when he tries to grasp an object hanging from his cot, he may accidentally set it in motion so that it swings; this spectacle being interesting, he will then repeat the action of making objects swing). At the same time his actions become differentiated because the properties of the objects acted upon demand certain adjustments and modifications (e.g., he cannot grasp a corner of his blanket in the same way as he grasps his mother's finger). Though all things and persons are only seen in relation to his own actions and desires, the coordination of several patterns and their differentiation will bring knowledge about the objects themselves. The child discovers, for example, that certain things when shaken produce a noise, and links this action both to listening and to looking. New objects, looked at, listened to, and acted upon, can then be put into two categories: those that make a noise and those that do not. New discoveries will be made when the baby intentionally starts shaking objects to see whether they make a noise.

The establishment of ever more complex action patterns leads to a bipolar construction of knowledge: On the one hand coordinations are established between the action patterns themselves, and on the other hand between the action patterns and objects. The child introduces some organization into reality by assembling, separating, putting on top of, putting into, etc.; at the same time he discovers properties of the objects themselves. However, the properties of things and persons are discovered through the child's activity, and not through his submission to them. At first, objects are not heavy or sharp in the adult sense, but they are 'hard to lift', 'hurting', etc.; and they have these properties mainly at the moment the child is in contact with them. Only gradually will the child change his view of reality so that he himself is not the only agent or the only person concerned; he realizes that he is only one agent among many (first, other persons and later, objects, are understood as acting on other objects).

The earliest spontaneous utterances can be interpreted in this conceptual framework. As Piaget (1949) has remarked, the first holophrastic utterances can be seen as an expression of actual or possible action patterns, partly desubjectivized, but mainly referring to the subject himself. For example, when a 1;6-year-old girl says *vaou* when she sees a dog from the balcony, this *vaou* will be extended to animals that resemble dogs, but also to everything she can see from the same viewpoint: a horse, a baby in a pram, when seen from the balcony are called *vaou*. *Panana* (from grandpapa) is said whenever she wants somebody, not necessarily her grandfather, to do something her grandfather used to do with her. In general one can say that these holophrases accompany in the present an action done by the child or interesting to the child; or they express a desire for an action the child wants to perform or to have performed immediately by someone else. It is only a little later that these *jugements d'action* get supplemented by *jugements de constatation*; that is, descriptions of past events or of properties of objects or persons (again, obviously, properties important to the child). *Fille méchante, poupée cassée, papa parti* belong in this category. It is probably no coincidence that among the very first universal utterances the indication of disappearance and apparition is so frequent; one of the first permanent properties of objects is their very existence.

Following this analysis, we might interpret the linguistic patterns as follows: at first the child expresses a (possible) action pattern related to himself, in which agent, action and eventual patient are inextricably entwined. Second, he either expresses the result of an action done by somebody else (but not the action-object link in that case), or an action he performs or is going to perform himself. In this way, the capacity for representing reality follows at a later stage the same evolution which took place when the child was still dealing directly with reality without representation. The first direct-action differentiations — i.e., between the subject's own action and the object acted upon on the one hand, and the child himself as an agent and some other person or object as agent — give rise to the first grammatical functions of subject-predicate and object-action. It is to be emphasized that in this analysis the SVO structure is established through and around the verb. That there is no question of rule N_1 = S becoming established on its own, as it were, is further confirmed by the fact that when we present only two nouns, and nothing else, no action follows — either the child does nothing at all and asks, *et puis quoi?* or he takes the two objects named. The order in which we present these nouns makes no difference. Some spontaneous utterances are apparent contradictions to this hypothesis. Utterances such as *maman café* look like a concatenation of subject-object in certain circumstances. But since we suppose that at this level word-classes have not yet been established *café* may very well represent an action-pattern: coffee-drinking. In other cases such utterances are no more than a juxtaposition of two holophrases; and in more advanced examples the same combination is a noun-modifier pattern: *mommy's coffee*. Just as action-patterns lead to first groupings of objects (pushable, suckable, shakeable, etc.) the first patterns of grammatical relations lead to categorizations: nounlike words, verblike words, modifiers, etc.

From this point of view, during the second year of life the child's fundamental assumptions about the nature of human language would become established and would develop in the following manner. To leave aside many important points that need clarification, and to attempt no more than a first approximate sketch: once the child has made the link between a series of sounds pronounced by the adult and an event, and singles out a short combination (how and why is a mystery), he assumes that these sounds express the action-pattern aspect of the event, and he will use the same series (in better and better phonetic approximation) whenever there is, in his view, a recurrence of the action pattern. Just as he has made differentiations in his own former direct dealings with reality, he will then notice that the utterances he hears are composed of different parts — for instance, having singled out *aplu* (all gone) from utterances such as *il n'y a plus de gateau* and having used it in the manner described, he will now assume that the part of the utterance which until now was left out of account has a certain relation to the other part — a relation of subject to predicate (that is, a description of an interesting state or property of an object or a person) or a relation of action-patient (that is, the expression of an action being, or to be performed by or in the interest of the child himself). Both assumptions then get combined into the expectation of a three-constituent structure, without as yet any established order, and with only the beginnings of word-categorization. At this point the child can express the distinction (which has already been well-established in his direct dealings with reality) between himself as an acting and desiring person and other actors or desirers. Finally, this combination gives rise to the coordination of Agent + Action (+ Patient), and again, the new structural pattern goes together with more refined categorizations; at this point we might suppose that the pattern NP + VP (with the VP composed of either only a predicate, or a verb and a noun) is established concurrently with the functional relationship SV_{intr}, SVO, or SOV.

This long piece of speculation is based on two important Piagetian postulates. (1) Very general cognitive structures composed of systems of actions are established during the first 2 years of life; these systems constitute the basis for many different types of cognitive structures, as much for the construction of logico-mathematical knowledge as for knowledge of the physical world and for the understanding and use of linguistic structures. (2) Higher-level knowledge involves a reconstruction of already acquired concepts and patterns, and thus shows a formation process isomorphic to that by which earlier knowledge was acquired.

Clearly, this explanatory interpretation of the universal base is very different from the justification by some sort of iconic factor quoted above. In the first place, our interpretation supposes this universal base to be constructed, and not to be innate; in the second place, it supposes this construction to be based on the way the child acts on reality, and changes it by his action, instead of basing it upon a perceptive constant, which implies a more passive, copylike apprehension of reality. The universal base is a result of universal cognitive activity, not of a tendency whereby our attention tends to be seized first by the subject of an action. Moreover, our adult experience, cognitive and perceptive as well as linguistic, surely contradicts this hypothesis; in particular, linguistic transformations allow us to topicalize or to emphasize any one of the three components, (Action, Agent, or Patient) according to our apprehension of the event to be described. Young children do this too, first by using a rather free order of the three elements, and later by using substitutions, deletions and permutations which result in grammatically not-quite-acceptable sentences such as quoted earlier.

It would seem that to take Piaget as a handbook for developmental psycholinguistics is not a simple task. It implies rather involved, and (to many, maybe) rather devious, reasoning. A direct transposition of his theory of cognitive development is impossible. Moreover, until recently, Piaget concentrated on logico-mathematical knowledge, and his studies of the development of physical concepts such as force, movement, etc. are as yet little known outside Geneva. These recent studies show that there are close links between knowledge in one field and that in another, but they also show that what were initially described as universal cognitive structures are more properly considered as symptoms (in the field of logical thinking) of even more general structures which also underlie concepts of causality, time, etc., where they may acquire rather different forms. Piaget (Ferreiro, 1971, Preface) himself has suggested the possible application of these ideas to language acquisition: Linguistic structures may well be yet another symptom of the very general, universal cognitive structures.

Notes

1.   For verbs in *-er,* the infinitive has the same spoken forms as the past participle and the polite or plural imperative. This is not the case with verbs in *-ir,* which we also used.

References

Bever, T.G. The cognitive basis for linguistic structures. In J.R. Hayes (ed.), *Cognition and the development of language.* New York: Wiley, 1970, pp. 279-362.

Bloch, O. La phrase dans le langage de l'enfant. *Journal de Psychologie Normale et Pathologique,* 1924, XXI.

Chomsky, C.S. *The acquisition of syntax in children from 5 to 10.* Cambridge, Massachusetts: MIT Press, 1969.

Chomsky, N. *Aspects of the theory of syntax.* Cambridge, Massachusetts: MIT Press, 1965.

Clark, E.V. On the acquisition of the meaning of "before" and "after". *Journal of Verbal Learning and Verbal Behavior,* 1971, 10, 266-275.

Ferreiro, E. *Les relations temporelles dans le langage de l'enfant.* Geneva: Droz, 1971.

Greenberg, J. *Universals of language.* Cambridge, Massachusetts: MIT Press, 1961.

Hayes, J.R. (ed.), *Cognition and the development of language.* New York, Wiley, 1970.

Jakobson, R. Implication of language universals for linguistics. In J. Greenberg (ed.), *Universals of language.* Cambridge, Massachusetts: MIT Press, 1961.

McNeill, D. *The acquisition of language.* New York: Harper, 1970.

Piaget, J. *La formation du symbole.* Neuchatel: Delachaux et Niestle, 1949.

Piaget, J. *La psychologie de l'intelligence,* 3rd ed. Paris: A. Colin, 1967.

Sinclair, H. & Bronckart, J.P. SVO – A linguistic universal. *Journal of Experimental Child Psychology,* 1972, 14, 329-348.

Slobin, D. Suggested universals in the ontogenesis of grammar. Paper presented at the Conference on Developmental Psycholinguistics, Buffalo, August, 1971.

Watt, W. On two hypotheses concerning psycholinguistics. In J.R. Hayes (ed.), *Cognition and the development of language.* New York: Wiley, 1970.

6 THE ACQUISITION OF LANGUAGE

David McNeill

Source: David McNeill, *The Acquisition of Language*, Harper and Row 1970, pp. 70-5 and pp. 155-64.

Linguistic Universals

According to a traditional view, language is a systematic relation between sound and meaning. In a transformational grammar this view is embodied in the distinction between underlying and surface structures. The underlying structure is associated with meaning or content and the surface structure with sound or expression. Underlying and surface structures are in general different from each other, but they stand in specific relations described by the transformations of the language, as is discussed later in this extract. One inherent aspect of any sentence is therefore the existence of an abstract underlying structure. Fluent speakers have gained knowledge of these structures. They have done so even though they have never encountered such information in the form of examples, stimuli, or anything else. Moreover, children make use of the information of the underlying structure very early in the acquisition of language. From the first moment of speech, children have the ability to communicate grammatical relations in a manner understandable to adults. We can easily overlook what an astonishing fact this is, but it means that the most abstract part of language is the first to appear in development.

To develop the connection with the theory of grammar let us put the problem in a semiformal way. Consider the 'Language Acquisition Device' discussed by Chomsky (1957, 1965), which we can call LAD for short (alternatively, a Language Acquisition System, or LAS – the feminine form). LAD or LAS receives a certain corpus of utterances. Many of these utterances are grammatical sentences in the language to which LAD is exposed. The corpus may be large, but it is not unlimited in size. Assume that it contains the number of utterances overheard by a typical 2-year-old child.

Given such a corpus, LAD is so constructed that it can develop a theory of the regularities that underly the speech to which it has been exposed. The theory is LAD's grammatical competence, its knowledge of the language. LAD now becomes able to go far beyond the corpus with which it began. It can distinguish the infinitely many grammatical sentences in its language from the infinitely many nongrammatical alternatives.

The situation may be diagrammed as follows:

Corpus ⟶ ┌─────┐ ⟶ Grammatical competence
　　　　　　│ LAD │
　　　　　　└─────┘

Clearly, the problem of understanding how LAD, given a corpus, develops grammatical competence requires understanding of LAD's internal structure.

It is useful to distinguish two major components of LAD. One is a set of procedures for operating on a corpus — for example, conducting a distributional analysis, or using 'inference rules',† for finding transformations of certain kinds (Fodor, 1966). The other is a body of *linguistic information* — for example, that all sentences include noun and verb phrases, or that sentences exist. It is conceivable that LAD contains only one of these components. LAD might contain a set of procedures for discovering a grammar or it might contain a set of assumptions about the form of grammar or, of course, it might contain both.

Whatever LAD contains, however, must be universally applicable. For LAD must be able to acquire any language; it will not include anything that makes some languages unlearnable. That is because no actual language, which must be acquired and is not ordinarily taught, can drift away from LAD's internal structure. Thus LAD could contain information and procedures bearing on the general form of language, but could contain nothing that is inconsistent with any particular language. The following remarks are directed to the possibility that LAD contains universal linguistic information; almost nothing has been done to examine the possibility that LAD contains universal procedures of analysis.

LAD is, of course, a fiction. The purpose in considering it is to discuss real children, not abstract ones. We can accomplish this because LAD and children present the same problem. LAD is faced with a corpus of utterances, from which it develops a grammar on the basis of some kind of internal structure. So do children. We can readily posit that children and LAD arrive at the same grammar from the same corpus, and stipulate that children and LAD therefore have the same internal structure, at least within the limits that different children may be said to have the same internal structure. Accordingly, a theory about LAD is *ipso facto* a theory about children.

The description of linguistic universals is included in the theory of universal grammar. As opposed to the grammar of a single language, the theory of grammar is a description of the general form of human language

(Chomsky, 1965; Katz, 1966). The purpose is to state the universal conditions that the grammars describing individual languages must meet. Our theory of language acquisition will be that the theory of grammar and its universal constraints describes the internal structure of LAD and, thus, of children.

What are the universals mentioned in the theory of grammar, which we now presume to be a reflection of children's linguistic capacities? Some are phonological. Every language, for example, employs consonants and vowels, syllabic structure, and a handful of distinctive features (Jakobson and Halle, 1956; Halle, 1964). In the case of syntax, every language utilizes the same basic grammatical categories, arranged in the same way — sentences, noun phrases, verb phrases, etc. Every language utilizes the same grammatical relations among these categories — subject and predicate, verb and object, etc. All of these are characteristics of the abstract underlying structure of sentences.

The transformations of a language, on the other hand, present much more idiosyncracy. For example, in English the underlying and surface structures of auxiliary verbs are related by permuting the order of verbs and affixes as is discussed later in this extract. This transformation appears in French also (Ruwet, 1966), and possibly elsewhere, but is not universal. Transformational idiosyncracy arises from the way a few universal transformational types are exploited. Permutation, for example, is a universal transformational relation. It is used in a unique way in English and French. Other universal relations are deletion[†] and addition,[†] there are perhaps only a half dozen varieties of universal transformations.

We can collect these several considerations into a theory of language acquisition. Important aspects of the deep structure of sentences are described by universals; most transformations are idiosyncratic uses of universal transformational types. Assuming that linguistic theory describes linguistic abilities, we can say that the abstractions of the underlying structure reflect children's linguistic capacities, and are *made* abstract by children discovering the transformations of their language (McNeill, 1966). One can say that children begin speaking underlying structure directly. The existence of abstract underlying structure, far from being problematical for this theory, is a trivial consequence of it.

The process of language acquisition (McNeill, 1970) fits the above view closely. The grammatical relations of the holophrastic period already define a basic part of the abstract underlying structure of sentences. This structure is therefore present at an early point in development. What changes is the child's method of expressing the underlying structure of sentences in speech. First single words convey underlying structures, then simple P-O or appositional combinations, then more complex combinations. There is a constant elaboration of the relation between the underlying and surface structures of sentences, i.e., a constant elaboration of the transformational structure.

Grammars can differ greatly in complexity. How can this difference in complexity be reconciled with the theory that language acquisition consists of learning transformation?

The answer lies in recognizing the distinction between the structural change of a transformation and its structural index.[†] All the complexity in one grammar may exist to meet the structural indices of the transformations that it contains but another grammar may not. There may be few or no new grammatical relations in the first grammar. Thus we can conclude that most, if not all, of the changes in the underlying structure of sentences between a first and second grammar are induced by the transformations being acquired.

Cognition and Language

The term 'language and cognition' with 'language' first, describes the influence of language on thought. It is a topic with a rich history (cf. Chomsky, 1966; Whorf, 1956; Bruner, Olver, and Greenfield, 1966). Our concern in this section is with the opposite topic, with the word 'cognition' first: in what manner does the structure of thought influence the structure of language?

The question is not whether the acquisition of language depends on specific abilities. We accept the theory of grammar as a description of such abilities. The question concerns the origin of linguistic abilities, whether they come into language from cognition or are the result of a special linguistic capacity. It is easy to demonstrate that the content of speech is determined by intellectual development. John Stuart Mill, whose speech included the writing of a history of Rome at age six, lived in a cultured setting, had an IQ estimated to be in the 200's, and was the beneficiary (or victim) of the advanced ideas of his father about education. However, the problem of cognition and language has nothing to do with content, and Mill's precocity had nothing to do with the influence of his thought on his language. The question of cognition and language rather has to do with structure, and in this respect Mill was not unusually precocious.

Among the early arrivals in child language are the grammatical categories of noun and verb. Where do they come from? One hypothesis would be that they are the reflection, in language, of the final step in the development of sensory-motor intelligence (Piaget, 1952). During the first 18 months of life a baby develops the idea that physical objects have an independent existence. A very young baby believes that he can create and annihilate things since they are an extension of his acts. An 18-month-old child accepts the existence of things that are separate from himself. The separation implies a distinction between objects and actions, and this distinction now appears in speech as the distinction between nouns and verbs.

This argument was given by Sinclair-de Zwart (1968) in what probably is the only existing paper on cognition and language. It explains a structural arrangement in child language by reference to a universal of intellectual development. All children pass through the sensory-motor period and all therefore have nouns and verbs. Other scholars have argued that the universal features of child language can be explained along similar lines. Schlesinger (in press) has issued a strong call for such explanations and Slobin (1966) has hinted that he would like them too. It is impressive for Sinclair-de Zwart's hypothesis that the chronology is correct. Nouns and verbs are present in child speech when words are first combined into sentences, roughly at 18 months, which also is when the sensory-motor period comes to a close. The hypothesis is plausible and appears to have empirical support, but let us look at it more closely.

In principle, one can distinguish between two different kinds of linguistic universals.

1. A *weak linguistic universal* is the reflection in language of a universal cognitive ability. The cognitive universal is a necessary *and* sufficient cause of the weak linguistic universal.

2. A *strong linguistic universal* is a reflection of a specific linguistic ability and may not be a reflection of a cognitive ability at all. The cognitive universal, if it has anything to do with the linguistic one, is a necessary but *not* a sufficient cause of the strong linguistic universal. It is not sufficient because a linguistic ability is necessary as well.

The empirical content of this distinction is purely psychological. Linguistics has nothing to do with it and linguistic theory gives no hint of the cause of linguistic universals. More surprisingly, parallels of form or function — as between action-object and verb-noun — and the synchronic development of such parallels of form or function also do not establish causation. Such observations cannot separate the two kinds of linguistic universals described above. Any parallel and synchronization are consistent equally with linguistic universals being strong or weak. We would expect that, if linguistic abilities evolved to express thought, strong linguistic universals would be parallel to cognitive universals. And if a strong universal depends on meeting two necessary conditions, one cognitive and one linguistic, the strong universal could not appear in language until both conditions were met.

Thus, neither parallel form nor developmental synchrony unambiguously bears on the weak-strong distinction. Sinclair-de Zwart's hypothesis must be evaluated on other grounds. To see how the weak-strong distinction can be approached, consider an observation reported by Braine (1970). He taught his 2-year-old daughter two new words, one the name of a kitchen appliance (*niss*) and the other the name of the act of walking with the fingers (*seb*). Neither word was used by an adult in any grammatical context. The child used both words appropriately — *niss* as a noun and *seb* as a verb — as in *more niss* and *seb Teddy*. In addition, however, she used *seb* as a noun but never used *niss* as a verb. There were sentences like *more seb* and *this seb* but none like *niss vegetables*. Braine observed a similar asymmetry in his daughter's use of newly acquired Hebrew verbs and nouns, the verbs being used as nouns but not the nouns as verbs. These observations are significant for the strong-weak distinction. Evidently the syntactic classification of a noun does not depend on an association of a word with an object. *Seb* was the name of an action but was used productively as a noun. On the other hand, the name of an object was not used as a verb. One might tentatively conclude, therefore, that the syntactic category of noun is a *strong* universal and the category of verb is *weak*. Association with action alone is necessary and sufficient to establish a verb but some further syntactic property defines a noun.

The appearance of [+NP] as the central unmarked lexical feature of the P-O distinction can be explained if nouns are strong universals and verbs weak. The specifically linguistic definition necessary for nouns would have just such as effect. The advantage for nouns as holophrastic words (they have the widest scope of all grammatical classes since they occur in every grammatical relation) is also consistent with nouns being strong universals. The situation is not as neat as we might wish, however, for association with an object may also be sufficient for a word to become a noun. Braine's observations are ambiguous on this point. Perhaps we must further subdivide linguistic universals into weak, strong, and 'erratic' types. An erratic universal has two sufficient causes and therefore no necessary ones. Either the cognitive category of an object or a linguistic ability can cause a word to become a noun.

Aside from these observations, no investigation has been carried out that bears on the causes of linguistic universals. There are not yet empirical grounds for classifying linguistic universals as strong, weak, or erratic. Such claims as Schlesinger's, that linguistic structures are '. . . determined by the innate *cognitive* capacity of the child' (Schlesinger, in press), or

Sinclair-de Zwart's, that 'linguistic universals exist precisely because thought structures are universal', (Sinclair-de Zwart, 1968), are premature. Also, they are unnecessarily sweeping, as there is no reason to suppose that all linguistic universals are of one kind — weak, strong, or erratic. Far more probably, language is a mixture of the three.

The question of whether thought affects language cannot therefore be answered in general or in advance. A vacuum exists precisely where speculation, which abhors a vacuum, would most like to enter — into the explanation of children's linguistic abilities. Nonetheless, the biological uniqueness of the human ability to express grammatical relations suggests that some part of this ability is specifically linguistic and results in strong or, at least, in erratic linguistic universals.

TRANSFORMATIONS AND THE NOTIONS OF UNDERLYING (DEEP) AND SURFACE STRUCTURE

In a general way, language can be described as a system whereby sound and meaning are related to each other. That sound and meaning are separate and so need relating is evident from paraphrase, where the same meaning is expressed in different patterns of sound (*the man pursued the woman* and *the woman was pursued by the man*) and from ambiguity, where the same pattern of sound has different meanings (*outgoing tuna*). Between sound and meaning stands *syntax*. The relation between sound and meaning is therefore understood to the degree that the syntax of a language is understood. In this section we shall examine what is known of this relation.

Rationalist philosophers have argued since the seventeenth century that sentences have an inner and an outer aspect, the first connected with thought and the second with sound (Chomsky, 1966). The kind of evidence that leads to this conclusion, and hence to the phenomenon of concern here, is given in Table 6.1 (after Miller and McNeill, 1968). The three sentences on the left of Table 6.1 all have the same superficial form. They start with a pronoun *they*, followed by *are*, followed by a progressive form, followed by a plural noun. Despite this superficial identity, however, there are clear differences in structure among these three sentences. To understand the differences we will eventually need the notions of a transformation rule and of deep and surface structure.

Sentence (a) differs from sentences (b) and (c) in several fairly obvious ways. One difference is that the two kinds of sentences accept pauses in different places. With sentence (a) one might say *they . . . are buying . . . glasses*, but probably not *they . . . are . . . buying glasses*. It is the opposite with sentences (b) and (c). One could say *they . . . are . . . drinking*

Table 6.1: Sentences Showing Differences in Underlying (Deep) and Surface Structure

	Sentences	Paraphrases	Nonparaphrases
(a)	They are buying glasses		
(b)	They are drinking glasses	They are glasses to use for drinking	They are glasses that drink
(c)	They are drinking companions	They are companions that drink	They are companions to use for drinking

companions or *they . . . are . . . drinking glasses*, but not *they . . . are drinking . . . companions* or *they . . . are drinking . . . glasses*, unless the reference was to cannibalism or suicide. A second difference is in the proper location of articles. We have *they are buying the glasses* but not *they are the buying glasses*. We have *they are the drinking companions* but not *they are drinking the companions*.

The location of pauses in a sentence is fixed by its phrase structure. Pauses tend to go around constituents, not inside them. The location of articles is likewise determined by phrase structure. They go before NPs only. We can thus summarize the differences between sentence (a) and sentences (b) and (c) by saying that they have different phrase structures. In particular, the progressive form in sentence (a) is associated with the verb *are*, whereas in (b) and (c) it has moved over to the plural noun. The essential parts of the three phrase markers are as follows: *(they) (are buying) (glasses)*, *(they) (are) (drinking companions)*, and *(they) (are) (drinking glasses)*.

Sentence (a) and sentences (b) and (c) are distinguished in their *surface structure*. The difference, as we have seen, has to do with the distribution of pauses and the location of articles. Surface structure also is intimately connected with stress and intonation (Chomsky and Halle, 1968). In general, the surface structure of a sentence has to do with phonology — with one of the two aspects of language that need to be related by syntax.

Let us now look more carefully at sentences (b) and (c). They accept pauses in the same way, they take articles at the same places, they are accordingly bracketed in the same way, and, indeed, they have the same surface structure. But it is clear that they are not structurally identical throughout. They differ in a way that is important to meaning, the other aspect of language that is to be related by syntax. That they differ in meaning can be seen in the paraphrases and nonparaphrases of the two sentences in Table 6.1. Sentence (b) means 'they are glasses to use for drinking' and (c) means 'they are companions that drink'. Exchanging the form of the paraphrase between (b) and (c) leads to a nonparaphrase. Sentence (b) does not mean 'they are glasses that drink' any more than sentence (c) means 'they are companions to use for drinking'. Despite the identity of surface form, (b) and (c) differ importantly in underlying form. We shall say that they differ in *underlying* or *deep structure*, saving until later a more precise definition of what this means. First, however, let us note two implications that follow from the fact that (b) and (c) have the same surface structure but different underlying structures.

One is that the *relation* between underlying and surface structure must be different in the two sentences. The statement of this relation is assigned a special place in a grammar. It is done by the *rules of transformation*, and it is these rules, together with the underlying and surface structure of sentences, that embody the connection between sound and meaning in a language. The reader will have realized, of course, that in a statistical sense sentences (b) and (c) are freakish. The vast majority of sentences that have different underlying structures and different transformations also have different surface structures. Sentences (b) and (c) happen not to, but for this very reason conveniently illustrate what is true of all sentences. Every sentence, however simple, has some kind of underlying structure related to some kind of surface structure by means of certain transformations. The substance of grammar consists of making explicit these three terms.

The second implication of the difference in paraphrase between sentences (b) and (c) is that the underlying and surface structures of sentences are not identical. This is evidently true of at least one of the sentences, (b) or (c). In fact it is true of all sentences. Transformations provide enormous flexibility in developing surface structures from underlying structures and this advantage has been pressed by language in even the most elementary sentence types (an example with simple declaratives is given below). Thus, the underlying structure of every sentence is abstract in the sense given above. The underlying structure, the part connected with meaning, is not present in the overt form of any sentence. The acquisition of linguistic abstractions is a universal phenomenon — it is a basic fact about the development of language and on its success rests the emergence of all adult grammar. It would be impossible to understand sentences (b) and (c) correctly if this were not so.

All these concepts — underlying structure, surface structure, linguistic abstraction, and the way transformations tie them together — can best be seen in an example. The one we shall use is borrowed from Miller and McNeill (1968) and is based on Chomsky (1957). Consider the following sentences:

He walks	(present singular)
They walk	(present plural)
He walked	(past singular)
They walked	(past plural)

These four sentences mark two distinctions: number (singular and plural) and tense (present and past). Number is marked both in the form of the pronoun and in the inflection of the present-tense verb. Tense is marked in the inflection of the verb. Let us focus on the verbs, for it is here that a transformation becomes involved.

There are three verb suffixes: *-s*, *-ϕ* (which means null, but is a suffix all the same), and *-ed*. They encode information of a certain type, viz., the form of the verbal auxiliary, so we might suppose that this information can be expressed by a rewriting† rule. If we label the genus part of the rule C, then we can use the following context-sensitive rule:

$$C \longrightarrow \begin{cases} \text{-}s \text{ in the context NP}_{\text{sing}} \\ \text{-}\phi \text{ in the context NP}_{\text{pl}} \\ \text{-}ed \end{cases}$$

and summarize all four of the sentences above by a single schema, NP + V-C.

Let us now complicate the sentences slightly by incorporating an auxiliary verb, *be*, and see what happens.

He is walking
They are walking
He was walking
They were walking

The first thing to note is that using a form of *be* adds *-ing* to the following main verb. C, for its part, has moved forward. It is no longer attached to the main verb but to the auxiliary, and we have *be-s* (pronounced *is*), *be-ϕ* (pronounced *are*), and *be-ed* (pronounced *was* or *were*, number being marked on past-tense verbs in this case, a detail we can ignore). The schema for these sentences therefore is NP + *be*-C + V-*ing*.

Next consider the effect of adding a different auxiliary verb, a form of *have*, to the original sentences. Doing so, we obtain:

He has walked
They have walked
He had walked
They had walked

The main verb again takes a suffix, this time *-ed*, and C again moves forward to the auxiliary. It is the same therefore as when *be* is the auxiliary, except that different pronunciation rules are involved (*have-s* is *has*, *have-ϕ* is *have*, *have-ed* is *had*) and the main-verb suffix is *-ed* instead of *-ing*. Indicating these changes, we obtain the schema NP + *have*-C + V-*ed* for the use of *have* as an auxiliary.

The two auxiliaries can, of course, be combined, as in these sentences:

He has been walking
They have been walking
He had been walking
They had been walking

Both auxiliaries have the effects already demonstrated. *Be* adds the suffix *-ing* to the following verb and *have* adds a 'past' suffix to *be*. (In this case it is *be-en*, another difference in detail that we can ignore.) C also follows its usual pattern, for it is still attached to the first auxiliary verb. The schema therefore is NP + *have*-C + *be-en* + V-*ing*.

These sentences can be complicated still further by adding one of the modal auxiliaries. Modals are the words *will, can, may, shall, must*. Let us add *will*:

He will have been walking
They will have been walking
He would have been walking
They would have been walking

C has moved forward again, attached now to the modal. *Have* still adds a 'past' inflection to the following *be*, and *be* still adds *-ing* to the following main verb. The schema thus is NP + M-C + *have* + *be-en* + V-*ing*, where M stands for 'modal'.

It is evident from these examples that C always appears with the first member of an auxiliary construction, no matter how long this construction is. The location of C is a fact known to all speakers of English — *he will had been walking* obviously is not the way to indicate past tense in an auxiliary construction. Part of an English speaker's competence thus has C at the start of a verb phrase. Another part involves the contingency between *have* as an auxiliary and a following 'past' inflection, as well as the contingency between *be* as an auxiliary and the following *-ing*. Let us try to represent these facts about competence by constructing a rule that meets the following two conditions: (1) the true order of elements is maintained, and (2) elements contingent on one another are placed together. Doing so will lead to a simple solution.

Meeting the first condition requires placing C first, then M, then *have*, and finally *be*.[1] Since C appears in every sentence our rule must make it obligatory. The remaining constituents are optional, however, so we write them with parentheses. Let us call the whole construction 'Auxiliary', abbreviate it 'Aux', and put down the following rule:

Aux ⟶ C (M) (*have*) (*be*)

The following main verb (V) is omitted from this rule because it is introduced along with Aux by the PredP rule, which is now enlarged to read:

PredP ⟶ Aux V (NP)

The Aux rule is still incomplete, since it does not yet meet the second condition. The contingencies to be represented are that *have* goes with *-en* (or *-ed*) and *be* goes with *-ing*, so we write these elements together and thereby produce the following:

Aux ⟶ C (M) (*have-en*) (*be-ing*)

after which there will always be a V.

We now have all but one of the rules necessary to generate the examples given above. The missing one, a transformation, will be provided shortly. However, in order to see the need for the transformation and to appreciate the role it plays in representing the structure of these sentences, we should first see the result of producing sentences without it. The structural relations to be expressed by the transformation will be those not expressed by the rules already developed. If we have done our job well the division between the two kinds of rules, the transformation and the phrase-structure rules, will correspond to a real division between two kinds of structural information within sentences.

Figure 6.1: Underlying Structure of *they would have been walking*

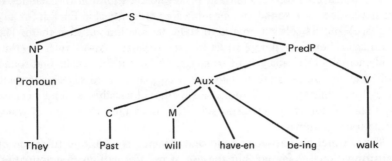

Figure 6.1 contains a phrase-marker generated by the phrase-structure rules presented in the preceding paragraphs. Note that the order of elements at the bottom of the phrase-marker is *they* + Past + *will* + *have* + *en* + *be* + *ing* + *walk*. This string and its associated structure is the underlying structure of *they would have been walking*. The surface structure is a specific instance of the last schema given above — *they* + *will-Past* + *have* + *be-en* + *walk-ing*. The deep structure thus differs from the surface structure in the order of suffixes and verbs. It is abstract in the sense used here since the deep-structure arrangement never appears overtly. It is important to realize, nonetheless, that the deep structure in Figure 6.1 reflects actual linguistic knowledge — the information summarized by C *is* always first in a predicate phrase, *have* and *-en do* always appear together, just as *be* and *-ing* always do.

The deep structure must therefore be transformed in order to obtain the surface structure. The transformation is simple: Wherever the sequence affix-verb appears in the underlying structure, change the order to verb-affix (Chomsky, 1957). If the reader applies this transformation he will find the surface structure of *they would have been walking* rolling out quite automatically.

There remains one important point. Note that the linguistic information expressed by the phrase-structure rules in generating *they would have been walking* is fundamentally different from the information expressed by the transformation rule. Which is to say that the distinction between the two is linguistically meaningful. The former rules define such matters as the genus-species relations within the sentence (e.g., *they* is an NP), establish the basic order of elements (e.g., C is first in the PredP), and indicate what the elements are (e.g., *have-en* is an element). Information of this kind is essential for obtaining the meaning of the sentence. The relations just mentioned, among others, are exactly what we understand of *they would have been walking.*

The transformation, in contrast, makes no contribution to meaning. It exists only because sound and meaning are not identical in English (or any language) and its sole purpose is to state the relation between them. The distinction between phrase-structure and transformation rules is thus fundamental to the analysis of language. Without it the insight that sound and meaning are separate in language would be lost; to suggest, as some have done, that transformations are methodologically unsound because they lead to arbitrary linguistic solutions, is to miss the point of transformational grammar.

The distinction between sound and meaning is a basic justification of transformational grammar, but the use of transformations in grammatical analysis is supported by other arguments as well. One is economy. If we dispense with transformations and try to generate sentences with phrase-structure rules alone the result becomes unnecessarily complex. The sentences given above, for example, require eight different and independent phrase-structure rules, one for each combination of auxiliary verb and C, instead of the single phrase-structure rule required when a transformation is allowed. Without the transformation, we would need at least the following rules: $Aux_1 \longrightarrow$ V-C, $Aux_2 \longrightarrow$ *be*-C + V-*ing*, $Aux_3 \longrightarrow$ *have*-C + V-*ed*, $Aux_4 \longrightarrow$ *have*-C + *be-en* + V-*ing*, $Aux_5 \longrightarrow$ M-C + V, $Aux_6 \longrightarrow$ M-C + *be* + V-*ing*, $Aux_7 \longrightarrow$ M-C + *have* + V-*ed*, and $Aux_8 \longrightarrow$ M-C + *have* + *be-en* + V-*ing*. Note that these rules cannot be collapsed onto one another by means of the parentheses notation used before. The changing location of C prevents it. This phrase-structure version of the auxiliary therefore not only overlooks valid linguistic generalizations − such as the fact that C always appears first in the auxiliary, or that there *is* an auxiliary, or that -*ing* depends on *be* and not on V − but it is also cumbersome. Relative economy is always an argument in support of one theoretical interpretation over another and using it in the present case inclines the balance toward a transformational solution.

The argument of economy has special significance in the context of language acquisition. We prefer to think of children doing the simpler thing, whatever that might be. In the case of linguistic development, the simpler thing is to acquire a transformational grammar instead of a phrase-structure grammar.

The suffix-transformation used in generating the English auxiliary verb is one rule within a vast and intricate network of transformations making up the language. Passive sentences, negation, questions of various kinds, conjunctions, apposition of nouns and adjectives, and many other

Figure 6.2: Underlying Structure of *the ostrich that was terrified by the zebra that the hunter shot stuck its head in the sand*

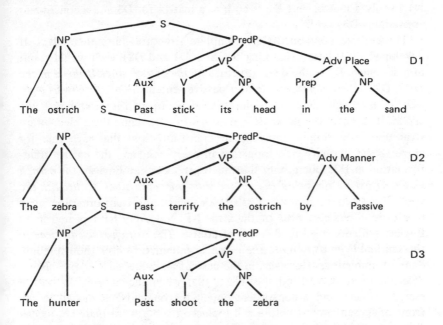

grammatical devices all depend on transformations.

There is one set of transformations of special significance, and this section will conclude with a discussion of them.

In developing the underlying structure of any sentence it is possible to include, along with other underlying morphemes, the element S, thus calling for the insertion of *another* underlying structure at that point. That sentence, in turn, may also have an S in it, calling for the insertion of yet another underlying structure, and so forth. The result makes infinite productivity possible through recursion.[†] There are definite restrictions on where such embeddings may take place. Figure 6.2 shows a succession of underlying structures, each with another embedded within it.

Figure 6.2 is the result of applying phrase-structure rules alone and represents the underlying structure of (*the ostrich* (*that was terrified by the zebra* (*that the hunter shot*)) *stuck its head in the sand*), a sentence with two relative clauses. English employs several transformations to develop this surface structure from the deep structure in Figure 6.2. In discussing them, we shall use terminology suggested by Lees (1960), and call the structure containing S the *matrix* and the S contained the *constituent*.

Thus, D3 in Figure 6.2 is the constituent of the matrix D2, and both are the constituent of the matrix D1. In Figure 6.2, D3 is only a constituent, D1 is only a matrix, but D2 is both — a matrix for D3 and a constituent (containing D3) for D1.

These three components are complete structures unto themselves. If developed in isolation (ignoring the S in D1 and D2), each would result in a sentence. D1 is the deep structure of *the ostrich stuck its head in the sand*; D2 is the deep structure of a passive sentence, *the ostrich was terrified by the zebra*, and D3 is the deep structure of *the hunter shot the zebra*. It is obvious that more is required in combining these elementary structures than simply applying the transformations that each calls for alone — the auxiliary transformation in every case, and the passive transformation in D2. Doing only this much produces non-English: *the ostrich was terrified by the zebra the hunter shot the zebra stuck its head in the sand*. To avoid such a word salad, an embedding transformation must delete double occurrences of the same NP. Not every NP repeated in an English sentence need be deleted, of course. *The ostrich stuck its head in the sand and the ostrich ate the worm* is grammatical even though redundant or ambiguous. However, in the case of an embedded relative clause, deletion must occur, and the rule is that when the same NP is both a matrix subject and a constituent object the object-NP is moved to the front of its sentence structure and replaced by the word *that*. Let us call this operation the deletion transformation. In the case of Figure 6.2, it produces *the ostrich that the zebra that the hunter Past + shoot Past + terrify by + Passive Past + stuck its head in the sand*. Applying the auxiliary transformation to this structure wherever called for (e.g., *Past + shoot* becomes *shot*) and the passive transformation to D2, the surface structure of which Figure 6.2 is the underlying structure rolls out. (Actually, such 'singulary' transformations as the affix transformation and the passive transformation are applied, when called for, to the most deeply embedded S first, then to the next most deeply embedded S, and so on up to the top, before the embedding transformations are applied. Cf. Chomsky, 1965, for a discussion of such transformational cycles.)

Again notice that a natural distinction exists between the information contained in the transformation and the information contained in the underlying structure. As before, the latter has to do with meaning and the former with the relation between sound and meaning. When one understands a relative clause he grasps the fact that there are two or more underlying structures, one inserted in the other, with the deletions described by the transformation *not* performed. Obtaining the meaning of *the ostrich that was terrified by the zebra that the hunter shot stuck its head in the sand* depends on knowing that the first *that* means *ostrich* and the second *zebra*, which is to disregard both deletions in the semantic interpretation of the sentence.

There remains one point. If transformations are correctly stated in a grammar they apply automatically whenever the proper conditions exist in the deep structure. In other words, transformations are obligatory (Chomsky, 1965; Katz & Postal, 1964). The specification of the 'proper' condition is done by the *structural index* of a transformation and setting it down is an important part of writing a transformational rule. Should the structural index be wrong, a transformation will relate wrong underlying and surface structures, even though the operations described in the transformation are themselves correct when the circumstances are appropriate. To supplement the rules already mentioned, then, we must add that the auxiliary transformation applies to any occurrence of affix + V, the passive transformation to any occurrence of NP_1 Aux V . . . NP_2 . . . *by* + Passive (the subscripts indicating that the two NPs must be different and the dots indicating that other unspecified material can be inserted), and the relative-clause transformation to any case where the matrix-subject and the constituent-object are the same NP. The structural index is clearly part of grammatical knowledge. Applying the relative-clause transformation to underlying structures where the subject- and object-NPs are different results in a sentence that expresses the wrong meaning. If, for example, the deep structures of *the ostrich stuck its head in the sand* and *the ostrich ate the worm* are connected by the relative-clause transformation, meaning shifts and the result becomes something out of Alice in Wonderland — *the ostrich stuck its head in the sand that ate the worm*. Since violation of the structural index of a transformation leads to an inappropriate expression of meaning, it is evident that the structural index is a part of the relation between meaning and sound.

Notes

1.   It is not clear precisely how the connection should be developed between this ordered structure and more abstract unordered structures (McNeill, 1970, Chapter 5). The whole question of ordering in the underlying structure is quite obscure and unsettled.

References

Braine, M.D.S. The acquisition of language in infant and child. In Carroll Reed (ed.), *The learning of language: Essays in honor of David H. Russell*. New York: Appleton-Century-Crofts, 1970.
Bruner, J.S., Olver, Rose, and Greenfield, Patricia M. *Studies in cognitive growth*.

New York: Wiley, 1966.

Chomsky, N.A. *Syntactic structures.* The Hague: Mouton, 1957.

Chomsky, N.A. *Aspects of the theory of syntax.* Cambridge, Mass.: MIT Press, 1965.

Chomsky, N.A., and Halle, M. Some controversial questions in phonological theory. *J. Ling.,* 1966, 2, 97-138.

Fodor, J.A. How to learn to talk: Some simple ways. In F. Smith and G.A. Miller (eds.), *The genesis of language: a psycholinguistic approach.* Cambridge, Mass.: MIT Press, 1966, pp. 105-23.

Halle, M. On the basis of phonology. In J.A. Fodor and J.J. Katz (eds.), *The structure of language.* Englewood Cliffs, N.J.: Prentice-Hall, 1964, pp. 324-33.

Jakobson, R., and Halle, M. *Fundamentals of language.* The Hague: Mouton, 1956.

Katz, J.J. *The philosophy of language.* New York: Harper & Row, 1966.

Katz, J.J. and Postal, P. *An integrated theory of linguistic descriptions.* Cambridge, Mass.: MIT Press, 1964.

Lees, R.B. *The grammar of English nominalizations.* Indiana Univ. Publ. in Anthro. and Ling., Memoir 12, 1960.

McNeill, D. The creation of language by children. In J. Lyons and R. Wales (eds.), *Psycholinguistics papers.* Edinburgh: Edinburgh Univ. Press, 1966, pp. 99-114.

McNeill, D. *The acquisition of language.* London: Harper and Row, 1970.

Miller, G.A. and McNeill, D. Psycholinguistics. In G. Lindzey and E. Aaronson (eds.), *Handbook of social psychology,* Vol. 3. Reading, Mass.: Addison-Wesley, 1968, pp. 666-794.

Piaget, J. *The origins of intelligence in children.* New York: International University Press, 1952.

Ruwet, N. La constituent 'auxillaire' en française moderne. *Language,* 1966, 4, 105-22.

Schlesinger, I.M. Production of utterance and language acquisition. In D.I. Slobin (ed.), *The ontogenesis of grammar: Facts and theories.* New York: Academic Press, in press.

Sinclair-de Zwart, Hermine. Sensorimotor action schemes as a condition of the acquisition of syntax. Unpubl. paper, University of Geneva, 1968.

Slobin, D.I. Comments on "Developmental psycholinguistics". In F. Smith and G.A. Miller (eds.), *The genesis of language: A psycholinguistic approach.* Cambridge, Mass.: MIT Press, 1966, pp. 85-92.

Whorf, B.L. *Language, thought, and reality.* New York: Wiley, and Cambridge, Mass.: MIT Press, 1956.

7 TELEGRAPHIC SPEECH

Roger Brown

Source: Roger Brown, *A First Language*, (Penguin Books 1976), pp. 98-115.

Words in a telegram cost money, and so that is reason to be brief, to say nothing not essential. If the full message were: 'My car has broken down and I have lost my wallet; send money to me at the American Express in Paris,' the telegram would be: 'Car broken down; wallet lost; send money American Express Paris'. The telegram omits ten words: *my, has, and, I, have, my, to, me, at, the, in.* These words are pronouns, prepositions, articles, conjunctions and auxiliary verbs. The words retained are nouns and verbs. The adult user of English when he writes a telegram operates under a constraint on length and the child when he first begins to make sentences also operates under some kind of a constraint that limits length. The curious fact is that the sentences the child makes are like adult telegrams in that they are largely made up of nouns and verbs (with a few adjectives and adverbs) and in that they generally do not use prepositions, conjunctions, articles or auxiliary verbs.

Early characterizations

Brown and Fraser in 1963 described an experiment in which six children, between two and three years old, were asked to imitate thirteen simple English sentences. The results appear in Table 7.1. Brown and Fraser point out that the younger children tended to preserve nouns, verbs, adjectives and pronouns, and to omit articles, prepositions, copular *be* and auxiliary verbs. They also omitted inflections: *showed* becomes *show, goes* becomes *go, books* becomes *book*. Adult telegrams, incidentally, do not omit inflections, since these bound morphemes are not 'charged' as words and are obligatory in English grammar. With increasing age the children in Table 7.1 retain more and more of the words that are at first omitted.

Brown and Fraser point out that the results may be rather effectively summarized in terms of the distinction some linguists make between 'contentive' words and 'functors'. Contentives are the nouns, verbs and adjectives and some, but not all, make concrete reference to persons, objects, actions and qualities. The word classes, or 'parts of speech', involved have very many members and readily admit new members. Functors are forms that do not, in any simple way, make reference. They mark grammatical

167

Table 7.1: Imitations of Spoken Sentences[a]

	Model Sentence	Eve, 25½ months	Adam, 28½	Helen, 30	Ian, 31½	Jimmy, 32	June, 35½
1.	I showed you the book.	I show book.	(I show) book.	C	I show you the book.	C	Show you the book.
2.	I am very tall.	(My) tall.	I (very) tall.	I very tall.	I'm very tall.	Very tall.	I very tall.
3.	It goes in a big box.	Big box.	Big box.	In big box.	It goes in the box.	C	C
4.	Read the book.	Read book.	Read book.	—	Read (a) book.	Read a book.	C
5.	I am drawing a dog.	Drawing dog.	I draw dog.	I drawing dog.	Dog.	C	C
6.	I will read the book.	Read book.	I will read book.	I read the book.	I read the book.	C	C
7.	I can see a cow.	See cow.	I want see cow.	C	Cow.	C	C
8.	I will not do that again.	Do again.	I will that again.	I do that.	I again.	C	C
9.	I do not want an apple.	I do apple.	I do a apple.	—	I do not want apple.	I don't want a apple.	I don't want apple.
10.	Do I like to read books?	To read book?	I read books?	I read books?	I read book?	C	C
11.	Is it a car?	't car?	Is it car?	Car?	That a car?	Is it car?	C
12.	Where does it go?	Where go?	Go?	Does it go?	Where do it go?	Where do it go?	C
13.	Where shall I go?	Go?	—	—	C	C	C

Source: Brown and Fraser, 1963.

[a] ( ) indicates uncertain transcription;
— indicates no intelligible imitation was obtained;
C indicates imitation was correct.

structures and carry subtle modulatory meanings. The word classes or parts of speech involved (inflections, auxiliary verbs, articles, prepositions and conjunctions) all have few members and do not readily admit new members.

Table 7.2 from Brown and Fraser (1963) shows that, in the imitations of the six children studied, functors were more often omitted than contentives. Pronouns, it may be noticed, occupy a kind of intermediate position with respect to the proportion of the time they are omitted, and that is a fact to which we shall return.

The imitations of Table 7.2 have one further important property in common: they preserve the word order of the model. This is an aspect of the performance that is so familiar and somehow reasonable that one does not at once recognize it as an empirical outcome rather than as a natural necessity. But of course it is not a necessity, the outcome could have been otherwise. Words might, for example, have been said back in the reverse of their original order, the most recent first.

Finally, Brown and Fraser note that the telegraphic characterization fits the spontaneous sentences of the children they studied as well as it fits their imitations:

> For the striking fact about the utterances of the younger children, when they are approached from the vantage point of adult grammar, is that they are almost all classifiable as grammatical sentences from which certain morphemes have been omitted. You may have noticed that while Eve's sentences are not grammatically 'complete' they are somehow intelligible as abbreviated or telegraphic versions of familiar constructions. 'Mummy hair' and 'Daddy car' seem only to omit the possessive inflection. Both 'Chair broken' and 'That horsie' become acceptable copular sentences if we leave the word order intact and fill in *is* and *a* or *the*. [p. 188]

It was even the case that the mean length of utterance (MLU) calculated for spontaneous sentences closely corresponded with the MLU calculated for sentences produced as imitations.

In 1964 Brown and Bellugi reported on the early sentences of two of the children in their longitudinal study: Adam and Eve. With respect to both imitations and spontaneous sentences they fully confirm the 'telegraphic' characterization. There is a limit of length, contentives are produced and functors are not, normal word order is preserved. The authors speculate about possible reasons for these characteristics. The limit of length cannot be explained by immediate memory span, since it is the

Table 7.2: Percentages Correctly Imitated of Morphemes in Various Syntactic Classes[a]

Syntactic class	Correctly imitated
Classes having few members in English	
Inflections	44
Pronouns	72
Articles	39
Modal auxiliaries	56
Copular verbs	33
Classes having many members in English	
Nouns	100
Adjectives	92
Main verbs	85

Source: Brown and Fraser, 1963.

[a] Using tests for differences between two percentages, the percentage correct in each of the classes with many members is significantly greater than the percentage correct in any of the classes with few members ($p < 0.001$, 2-tailed test).

same for spontaneous sentences which have no antecedent models as it is for imitations. Neither is it a matter of the number of words in long-term memory since Adam and Eve at Stage 1[†] knew, at least, several hundred words. Presumably the real limitation involves the complexity, in grammatical or semantic terms, of the sentences that can be processed, a complexity reflected in sentence length.

The fact that the child's first sentences preserve normal word order partially accounts for the ability of an adult to 'understand' these sentences and so to feel that he is in communication with the child. Brown and Bellugi note that: 'It is conceivable that the child "intends" the meanings coded by his word order and that, when he preserves the order of an adult sentence, he does so because he wants to say what the order says. It is also possible that he preserves word order just because his brain works that way and that he has no comprehension of the semantic contrasts involved' (p. 137). In English declarative[†] sentences, order will distinguish subject from object, modifier from head,[†] subject from locative, possessor from possessed even when such structure signs as the possessive inflection, the copular verb and prepositions are missing.

Brown and Fraser and also Brown and Bellugi opened their discussions of telegraphic speech with reference to imitation and then went on to say that the child's spontaneous sentences seemed to be telegraphic in just the same way as his imitations. When there is a model sentence the retention of contentives and loss of functors is established by comparison with the model. How can one demonstrate that functors are 'missing' from spontaneous sentences which have no models? In certain contexts particular functors are obligatory. For example, when a transitive verb is followed by a count[†] noun (*see ball*) an article is obligatory, and if it is absent it may be said to be missing. When a cardinal number greater than one modifies a count noun (e.g. *two ball*) the noun requires a plural inflection. For eleven contexts of this type I have calculated the percentages of functors missing in the sentences of Adam, Eve and Sarah at I and the results are: Adam, 94 per cent, Eve, 87 per cent; Sarah, 84 per cent. So the tendency to omit functors is a strong one. At Level V for the three children the percentages of obligatory functors missing are: Adam, 26 per cent; Eve, 33 per cent; and Sarah, 21 per cent. Between I and V great progress occurs in the direction of standard English with respect to obligatory functors though even at V the children have some distance to go.

In terms of gross percentages functors seem to enter child speech by a long gradual process. However, these gross percentages sum across a number of very different grammatical features: definite and nondefinite articles, progressive aspect,[†] past tense, plural number and so forth. Each of these has an individual course of development, and at any given point of time there is great variation among them in the levels attained. At V, for instance, locative prepositions are almost always present in obligatory contexts whereas the auxiliary verb *be*, obligatory with the progressive, is still missing. In short, the functors are not one story but many. These stories are the focus of Stage II. (Brown, 1976.)

Confirming Evidence

Simply as a descriptive characterization of a fairly rough sort 'telegraphic speech' is apt for Stage I, and seems very generally to be so. It is confirmed repeatedly by the data from the studies listed in Brown (1976 Tables 9 and 10) as well as by general statements the authors make. Leopold (1949), for instance, writes of Hildegard: 'The preposition was omitted from all adverbial phrases' (p. 59) and 'Articles were not used at all during the first two years' (p. 64). Miller and Ervin (1964) wrote of their children: 'It is often striking that one can provide a translation of children's utterances into adult utterances by the addition of function words and inflectional affixes. It appears that the children select the stressed utterance segments, which usually carry the most information' (p. 13). Bloom (1970) writes to the same effect about all her children in Stage I. Braine (1963) does not call special attention to it but the data he has published for Gregory, Andrew and Steven mostly lack articles, copulas, prepositions, plural and third-person inflections.

The aptness of the telegraphic characterization for Stage I speech goes far beyond English and, insofar as the topic is raised, seems to be universal for the studies we are considering. Bowerman (1973), for instance, has calculated the percentage of functors present in obligatory contexts for Seppo 1, Seppo II and Rina I, and they are 3.1 per cent, 8.2 per cent and 9.5 per cent. Rydin (1971) has done the same for Swedish and obtained the higher value of 39 per cent, but she reports that almost all of these are the definite article with other functors almost invariably absent. Concerning the early Hebrew of Gil and Gila, Bar-Adon (1971) writes: 'Even our few examples show clearly that during his speech at this stage, the child employs only the principal elements: he retains the major part of the "content words" or "contentives" especially nouns and verbs and some adjectives, but tends to omit "function words" or "functors", especially prepositions, adverbs, conjunctions, determiners, certain inflection suffixes, etc'. (p. 47). Grégoire's summarizing is: 'L'enfant choisissant les mots capitaux dans les phrases "imitées" et faisant tomber les autres . . .' (1937, p. 84). Chao (1951) makes piecemeal observations which suggest the telegraphic quality: 'Subordination is mostly in the same word order as in SM [Standard Mandarin] but the subordinative particle *de* is not used' (p. 36). Slobin (1966) after studying Gvozdev's data for Zhenya writes: 'Child grammar begins with unmarked forms' (p. 134). Korean has no articles, copula or number inflection but its case-marking postpositions were almost all absent from Susin's speech until well after Stage I. Blount's Stage I Luo children lacked the plural inflection on nouns and had no tense or aspect auxiliaries with their verbs. Kernan's Samoan children used nouns without articles and formed the possessive without an obligatory particle (rather like the English preposition *of*).

Contradiction

Park, in his study (1970) of the acquisition of German, finds contradictory results. He did a small imitation experiment with Ulrike at her one-word stage presenting two- or three-word models like *Mein Teddy, Ein Brötchen* and *Heike ist da.* He found, contrary to the findings of Brown and Bellugi (1964) and Ervin (1964), that functors like *mein* and *ein* and *da* were just as likely to be imitated as were contentives like *Teddy, Brötchen* and *Heike.* Furthermore, in Park's tabulated two-word utterances from his children, one finds numerous occurrences of such functors as *das, ein, hier, mehr, ander* and *da*. Park also calls attention to the fact that the sometimes separable[†] verb prefixes like *ab, an, auf, mit, um, weg* and *zu* were often used in Stage I speech apparently as the names of actions in place of full verbs. Park's own conclusion about telgraphic speech is: 'Apparently, functors do not operate in the same manner in American and German children' (p. 6).

At first sight Park's paper suggests the breakdown, just in the case of German, of a description of Stage I speech, otherwise universally apt. In fact, however, his data are not so very different from data reported by other investigators. After all, no one found functors invariably absent from Stage I, only usually so. What is different about the German study is the stance Park takes up. Most of us, especially students of English, have taken the position that Stage I speech is, in the main, telegraphic and have tried to explain away the exceptions in one way or another. Park, in not committing himself to the maintenance of the generalization, turns us back to the data of the other studies to see what the *exceptions* to the rule have been like.

In the Brown and Fraser imitation data of Table 7.2, you may remember that pronouns were correctly imitated 72 per cent of the time, which made them quite different from inflections, articles and the like. In fact, just about all studies of Stage I American English do find frequent occurrence of the personal pronouns *I, you, me* and *my* as well as the demonstrative pronouns *this* and *that*. What is special about pronouns among English functors? All kinds of things. They can, for instance, function in what Brown (1976) has called major semantic roles as agent, patient, benefactor† and so forth. In syntactic terms they function in major syntactic relations as subject, object and modifier. They do not express what Brown (1976) has called modulations† of meaning as do English articles and inflections for plurality and person. In addition the pronouns are full syllables as the inflections are not, and they may receive one of the heavier stresses as the inflections may not. Which is to say there is more 'phonetic substance'† to the pronouns than to the inflections and so perhaps greater perceptual salience. That is not the end of the special qualities of the pronouns but it is enough for the moment. The way in which they are not peculiar among functors is that pronouns, like other kinds of functors, are small, closed grammatical classes.

The child Susan, studied by Miller and Ervin, made such heavy use of the words *off* and *on* that Miller and Ervin classified these terms as, what Braine (1963) called, 'terminal pivots'. They seemed privileged to follow any noun or verb in a two-word utterance. Braine's child, Andrew, also used *off* as a terminal pivot. Now, if these words *off* and *on* derive from the adult prepositions of the same form then it is odd that the children should use them in terminal position. Adults use the prepositions in prepositional phrases like *on the floor* and *off the table*. The likelihood is that

Susan's and Andrew's *off* and *on* were derived from particles which belong to certain verbs. Forms like *take off* and *put on* as in *take it off* and *put it on* are to be regarded as separable verbs, as verbs in two physically discontinuous parts. They are, in fact, just like such separable German verbs as *aufmachen, mitnehmen, anfassen, anziehen* and very many others. And Park's observation that particles like *ab, an, auf, mit* and so on occur in Stage I speech is not really at variance with the American studies. Examples like *Boat off* and *Water off* (Braine, 1963) in the American studies suggest that English particles sometimes function as Park suggests that German particles do in Stage I children: as the names of actions, replacing the full verbs to which they belong. As such, particles figure in basic semantic and syntactic relations. What else is special about them? Like pronouns they probably have more perceptual salience than do inflections and articles. They are full syllables, and they can take heavy stress as in *Take that off!* They can also occur in terminal position which may be perceptually favoured.

What of Park's *mehr, ander, hier* and *da*? They all have parallels in American studies. In fact *more, 'nother, here* and *there* are among the words most reliably found in Stage I English. *Here* and *there* have two functions: they may operate like demonstrative pronouns in naming utterances (e.g., *Here book*) or as 'pro-locatives', which can stand in for 'understood' locative nouns much as pronouns can stand in for understood noun subjects and objects. In either case *here* and *there* play major semantic roles (for example, locative) and enter into major syntactic relations. They are also, of course, full syllables which can be stressed and can occur either initially or finally. *More* and *'nother* do not play any of the semantic roles listed by Brown (1976) but they do play an additional role we shall find universal in Stage I speech. They comment on or request the *recurrence* of a referent. In this role they are, from the syntactic point of view, modifiers in the basic relation 'modifier-noun'. And once again these forms are at least one syllable long and can be stressed.

This review of the major 'exceptions' to the telegraphic characterization of Stage I English, exceptions which have been on record from the beginning of the contemporary interest in child speech, shows that Park's data for German are not really out of line with the data for English. There are also 'exceptions' in all the studies of other languages but we are not able to describe all their properties in the language in question and so cannot be sure that they are consistent with the German and American data. Still they seem to be so. Blount, for instance, notes that while his Stage I children failed to use inflections for plurality, tense or aspect they did use inflections for subject, object and possession. McNeill notes that Izanami used the Japanese subject postposition *ga* often and correctly. Kernan notes the frequent occurrence in Stage I Samoan of *itda*, which may be translated as *there is*, and of *manta*, close to *more*, and of *upda*, close to *no* or *no more*.

From Categorical Description to Functional Relations

Let me say what I think Park's stance and the re-examination of familiar exceptions do to the characterization of Stage I speech as 'telegraphic'. They move us from a rather sterile description in terms of the linguistic category functor to the study of functional relations between variables characterizing functors and several kinds of Stage I performance. The outcome of this kind of functional examination will be a more complicated and refined sense of the 'telegraphic' character of Stage I speech. What has become evident is that the category of functors, or, as they are called in Stage II, 'grammatical morphemes', is a category which in American English is defined by the partial convergence of a large number of characteristics or variables. Some, at least, of these variables affect the probability that a given form will occur in Stage I speech. The 'exceptions' are simply those words that do not have enough of the determinants working against them. For a time developmental psycholinguists have tried to treat functors as a category defined by the nearly perfect conjunction of a set of variables and to make the functor-less, telegraphic description stick by selectively attending now to one and now to another of these variables. It has not been difficult for me, for instance, to forget the fact that pronouns and prolocatives are small closed classes just as surely as inflections, articles and auxiliary verbs.

What must happen is that the category 'functor' must undergo fission into a set of variables having different values for different forms and different values in different languages for comparable forms. What the study of languages other than English does, of course, is to change the correlations among variables and so help to force us to think not in terms of a class but of variables. Thus, Luo uses verb inflections where English uses prepositions and word order. German *ein* is not only an article like English *a* but also a pronoun cognate with *one*.

What are some of the properties or attributes which converge imperfectly on the category 'functor' in American English? For Hocket (1958) who actually used the term, and Gleason (1961) whose term 'function word' seems to mean the same thing, the core characteristics are: (1) the relatively small size of classes like articles, prepositions, pronouns and the like, compared to nouns, verbs and adjectives; (2) their relatively fixed membership. English does not readily admit new functors as it does nouns or verbs, and the native speaker commonly learns all the functors in his pre-school years but learns new nouns, verbs and adjectives throughout his lifetime. These two are the invariable characteristics. There are also characteristics applicable to some but not all. I will not attempt to exhaust these here, since Stage II (Brown, 1976) is entirely focused on the acquisition of the English functors or grammatical morphemes but simply try to show that one functor is by no means the same as another.

Consider frequency first. It is obvious that most functors are more frequent than most individual nouns and verbs. Their frequencies are also more stable from sample to sample than are the frequencies of content words, since they are more independent of the topic of conversation. It is, perhaps, an indication of the minor role that frequency plays as a determinant of order of acquisition that it is just these high-frequency forms that are largely missing from Stage I speech. Still some lower limit of frequency is obviously essential to enable the form to be stored in long-term memory, its semantic ascertained and the rules of its usage discovered. Brown (1976, Table 52) gives frequencies for some of the major functors in samples of 713 utterances each from the parents of Adam, Eve and Sarah. While the forms almost all have reasonably high frequency there is enormous variation among them in actual level. There are, for example, between 150 and 200 articles in each sample but 25 fewer instances of the regular third person present indicative inflection and none at all of the functors that enter into the formation of the full passive in English. Here, then, is ample variation on one independent[†] variable within the class of functors to help account for the variations one finds in their appearance in Stage I speech.

Consider next perceptual salience, which like high frequency should favour acquisition. Probably salience involves several things: perhaps amount of phonetic substance, susceptibility to heavy stress and high pitch, and the possibility of occurring in utterance-final position, which there is some indication (Blasdell and Jensen, 1970) that children favour in imitation. Inflections like the plural and possessive on the noun and the regular past on the verb are not even full syllables in English. In German, on the other hand, some of these are syllabic, as in the *-en* of *Sie haben das Buch*. Words like *here, there, this, that, I, you* and *more* are all full syllables, as are the German equivalents. On this variable also, then, there is ample variation within the class of functors to account for the variation in performance from form to form within Stage I children, and on equivalent forms between children learning different languages.

Consider the semantics of the functors. There is, in the first place, the distinction between forms which can function in major semantic roles or

relations like the personal and demonstrative pr
locatives *here* and *there*, and forms like articles, inflec
tense and aspect, which only modulate basic meaning
modulating forms, whether bound, like the inflections,
articles, never occur as total utterances, and it is inconcei
should, since their meanings are not separable from the m
relations. Then there is the matter of redundancy as opposed ....na-
tiveness. The third person present indicative inflection in ...glish is
perfectly redundant or predictable if the subject is expressed. The copula,
before it is inflected for tense, and the possessive inflection [-s], between
a proper noun and the name of some possession (as in *Adam's chair*) are
almost perfectly predictable. Probably redundancy militates against acquisition of a functor, and the information-redundancy variable need not
come out the same, even for cognate forms in closely related languages
like German and English let alone in somewhat analogous forms in unrelated languages.

Then there is the variable: conditioning of the functors by verbal
context. Except for the progressive -*ing* English regular inflections have
three phonetic shapes (allomorphs) which vary with the phonological
properties of the stem. That should make them harder to learn. There is
also conditioning by the class membership of the noun or verb stem and,
in English as in German and other languages, there are numerous 'irregular'
classes. It is obviously hard to get these straight since children learning
English say things like *digged* and *swimmed* well into their school years.
There is even lexical conditioning in which the inflection is peculiar to
just one stem (*ox* – *oxen*). There is conditioning by semantic role or
case: *I* is nominative, *me* is accusative, *my* is possessive. Some or all of
these varieties of verbal context conditioning probably affect ease of
acquisition of a functor. English functors are obviously greatly different
from one another on this variable, and so are cognate forms between
related languages.

In Table 7.3 I have taken some of the variables described above, treated
them as binary rather than continuous, and assigned plus to the value
assumed to facilitate acquisition and minus to the value assumed to
operate against acquisition. This is a very rough, impressionistic table, and
its only point is to show that words like *I, me, my, this, that, here, there*
and so forth, which are regularly found in Stage I speech in both German
and English, constitute a very different class from inflections, articles, the
copula and so on, which are seldom found in Stage I.

Guesses about the effects of independent variables are only guesses but
fortunately we are beginning to get experimental studies. One of these

7.3: Some Properties of Functors (small closed grammatical classes) with examples from English

Functor	Freq. High +[a] Low −	Syllabic + Not −	Semantic (syntactic) Role + Modulation −	Info. + Red. +	Not Phon. Cond. + Cond. −	Not Gramm. Cond. + Cond. −
Pl. -s	+	−	−	±	−	−
Poss. -s	−	−	+	−	−	+
-ing	+	+	−	+	+	−
-ed	−	−	−	±	−	−
Past irreg.	+	+	−	±	+	−
-s pres. ind.	−	−	−	±	−	−
Copula	+	±	−	±	−	−
Articles	+	+	−	±	−	−
Here, there	+	+	+	+	+	+
This, that	+	+	+	+	+	+
I, me, my	+	+	+	+	+	+
More, 'nother	+	+	+	+	+	−
Particles	+	+	+	+	+	−

[a] Plus indicates value of the variable presumed to facilitate acquisition; minus the value presumed to operate against acquisition.
Abbreviations:
Freq. High − Frequency over 50 tokens in 713 utterances.
Info. − Information. Not guessable from verbal context.
Red. − Redundant. Guessable from verbal context.
Phon. Cond. − Phonetically conditioned as the several allomorphs of plurality are by the terminal sound on the stem.
Gramm. Cond. − Grammatically conditioned as in the case of *I, me, my.*

(Blasdell and Jensen, 1970) is concerned with two aspects of perceptual salience: stress and word position. In English sentences these are hard to separate, and so the study employs strings of nonsense syllables such as:

tud   gop   nʌk   pim*
mʌp   kit   pod*   tok

The asterisk indicates the syllable receiving primary stress. Across the full set of twelve four-syllable strings primary and intermediate stress were equally distributed in all possible combinations with respect to serial position. The two variables were thus independent. Stress was defined as it is normally in English by increases of both pitch and intensity. The subjects were children between the ages of twenty-eight and thirty-nine months (probably well beyond Stage I), and what they were asked to do was to imitate each string as fully as possible. It was first established in a screening procedure that all the children taking part would have their imitative capacities overloaded by the model strings. Four nonsense syllables, though all were well-formed in terms of English phonology, are of course much more difficult than four words. The authors found, in this experiment, that both primary stress and terminal position favoured reproduction of the syllable by the children, and so these variables have the effect they seem to have in naturalistic samples where imitations also often occur.

Two experiments by Scholes (1969, 1970) make it clear that, while stress and terminal position evidently favour immediate reproduction of nonsense words in strings which children may or may not process as sentences, perceptual salience is certainly not the only class of variable likely to be important in producing telegraphic speech. Scholes used real English words, contentives as well as functors, in some of his experimental conditions. The importance of stress, among factors probably affecting perceptual salience, was minimized by making up strings and sentences by splicing tapes of 'citation style'† readings of individual words, functors being given as prominent a stress as contentives. Of course inflections would still have gone unstressed. Schole's child subjects were probably all well beyond Stage I, since the age range was generally from three to five years. It is worth recording, as a matter of incidental interest, that when the model sentences employed real English functors the errors of children even in this age range were primarily deletion errors and that functors were deleted about three times as often as contentives. This outcome is consistent with what is learned in Stage II (Brown, 1976) about the long-drawn-out process of acquiring full control of English functors.

What is particularly interesting in the 1970 paper is the suggestion the data make that the semantic roles of the functors are important determinants of imitation. I cannot take this idea very far because I do not have the full lists of sentences or detailed data. However, Scholes included both well-formed meaningful sentences (*My cat liked his milk*) and anomalous sentences (*My cat drove his milk*) and ill-ordered sentences (*Cat milk his my liked*). What is particularly interesting is that, across sentences generally, the differential deletion of functors and contentives only occurred in significant degree in the well-formed sentences. Furthermore, in sentences composed partially of nonsense words and partially of real words, the nonsense accompanied by real contentives was more likely to be deleted than the nonsense accompanied by real functors. Scholes asks:

'Could the child be equating importance with some semantic notion like propositional nucleus? Perhaps he could. If the semantic cohesion of the string is destroyed, the differential relation also disappears' (p. 169). Scholes suggests of the child: 'So long as he can assign a reading to the string, he will delete the functors' (p. 170). What all this suggests to me, though the data are not detailed enough to prove the point, is that contentives and *certain* functors (like *his* or *my*) will be preserved in imitation because of the semantic roles or relations they play so long as these roles or relations can be made out. When the contentives are nonsense or when all English strings are anomalous or ill-ordered the semantic factor that distinguishes most contentives from most functors is neutralized.

The Blasdell and Jensen and Scholes studies are important not only because they put some experimental force behind guesses about variables but also because, by using imitation, they point to a second necessary change in how we deal with the telegraphic aspect of Stage I speech: it is necessary to differentiate the dependent variable. The simple sounding of a functor, whether in imitation or in a spontaneous utterance, is a very different thing from full semantic and grammatical control. Practically all students of child speech have recognized the necessity of making some distinctions on the performance side.

Hildegard, Leopold's daughter, before she was twenty-four months old, said both *piece of toast* and *drink of water*. The author notes that these phrases contained the only preposition heard before twenty-four months and that the phrases were completely rigid in form; there were no such variants as *piece of your toast* or *drink of cold water*. Therefore, Leopold suggests, the phrases were probably simply long words for Hildegard, words having no internal structure.

Sarah at I and Kathryn at I both used *that's* in ostensive sentences, and Susan used *this-a* and *have-a*, and Adam used *get-a* and, just beyond I, Adam used *it's*. It is certain that some, at least, of these are simply segmentation errors such that the child has mistakenly incorporated into a word as a terminal phoneme some functor that very commonly follows it without pause or other juncture sign. So long as the child uses his 'word' in contexts which require the two morphemes one cannot detect the segmentation error. Utterances like *its book* and *this a book* and *I go get it,* since they are well-formed are unrevealing. However, Susan said *this-a Bonnie pants* and *have-a pants*, and Adam in I said *Mommy get it ladder* and in later samples he said *it's go* and *it's went*. In all these cases the seeming functor is out of place. Such over-extensions[†] are explained if we suppose that the seeming functors are simply incorporated into the antecedent words, that the functors are really word-final sounds (see Brown,

1976.)

Grégoire describing the development of articles in Charles and Edmond notes that before twenty-four months they were usually absent but that an occasional noun seemed to be preceded by *un, une* or *la*. He rejects the notion that these really are the articles in question, neither the masculine-feminine gender distinctions nor the definite-nondefinite distinction is consistently observed. Grégoire's (1937) judgement is that in this early phrase 'L'article semble appartenir au mot' (p. 194).

Eric in II used *blocks* and *hats* and five other nouns which seemed to be inflected for plural number. He apparently did not over-extend these forms to produce such utterances as *a blocks* or *this hats*. Nevertheless, Bloom judges that the nouns are not really inflected, for the reason that none of the 'plural' nouns ever occurred in the singular. In the absence of a singular-plural contrast the probability is that the seven nouns in question were simply learned as words in a form having terminal sibilants; possibly because parents happened usually to use these nouns in a plural sense.

A number of the children in Brown (1976, Table 9, e.g., Gia I, Eric I, Eve I) sometimes produced a mid-vowel sound (the schwa) that one might take for an article or a preposition if it occurred before a noun. However, both Bloom and I, looking at the detailed distributional evidence, are of the opinion that these schwas are not functors at all but simply phonetic extensions of certain words.

What all these examples show is that on the performance side one has in addition to total absence and full control what might be called 'pre-fabricated routines', which to the casual listener may seem to include one or another functor. On careful examination, however, they prove to be rigidly limited in distribution or semantically inappropriate and so distinguishable from full control. Full control has been given a reasonable operational definition in Stage II (Brown, 1976), and the story of its development for a set of English functors is told there.

In place, then, of the description of Stage I speech as 'telegraphic' in lacking what linguists have called 'functors' we now have a very large number of independent variables which assign quite different descriptions to different functors and also several dependent performance variables including, at least: (1) total absence; (2) occasional presence in routines; (3) full control. The functional relations between the two sets of variables are in process of being worked out.

Slobin (1971), drawing upon his considerable knowledge of the course of acquisition in different languages, has postulated some very likely 'operating principles', which amount to postulations about the effects of various values of the independent variables. For example:

Operating principle A: Pay attention to the ends of words (p. 335).
Operating principle C: Pay attention to the order of words and morphemes (p. 348).
Operating principle E: Underlying semantic relations should be marked
overtly and clearly (p. 346).

And he offers many others, most of them plausible on his evidence. These
are principles on which he suggests that children everywhere operate in
processing adult language. Slobin goes on to develop their consequences
in terms of features of child speech that should be universal.

I think the dependent variable Slobin has in mind is always full control.
If we think of other performance outcomes and of combinations of values
of the independent variables that apply to functors then we may guess at a
new characterization of the telegraphic character of Stage I speech. It
would go something like this:

1. If functor x has some minimal frequency, high perceptual salience,
is unconditioned by verbal context and expresses a basic semantic role
rather than a modulation, then it will be fully controlled in Stage I (used
freely and correctly).

2. If functor x has high frequency and high perceptual salience then
whether conditioned or not, and whatever its semantic role, it will occur
in Stage I but only in prefabricated routines.

3. If functor x has low frequency and low perceptual salience and is
verbally conditioned and expressive of a semantic modulation then it will
be completely absent from Stage I.

What has become of the characterization of Stage I speech as 'telegraphic'? I think it remains valid if we understand 'telegraphic' not as the
total absence of words from small closed grammatical classes but rather
in the sense of the three propositions above. What seems to be clearly
lacking in Stage I in all the studies we have reviewed is full semantic and
grammatical control of those functors that encode semantic modulations
rather than basic semantic relations.

Competence and Performance

A team of investigators at the University of Pennsylvania, Shipley, Smith
and Gleitman (1969) has asked the interesting question: Is the Stage I
child's 'competence' as telegraphic as his performance? By competence
they mean grammatical knowledge, and they quite correctly argue that
samples of performance constitute only an imperfect set of clues to
competence. The Pennsylvania team has thought of an experimental
method for obtaining some clues that go beyond spontaneous speech

production. It is a method that inquires into the child's response to utterances of various kinds. They worked with eleven children between eighteen and thirty-three months old whom they divided into three groups in order of increasing grammatical maturity: holophrastic, telegraphic and mature. The children were assigned to one group or another on the basis of median length of utterance (*median*, not *mean*). The median is a measure of central tendency less sensitive to extreme values than the mean and, since distributions of utterance lengths are skewed to the right at this age, medians should run somewhat lower than means. The median values for the holophrastic group were 1.06–1.16; for the telegraphic group 1.40–1.85; for the mature group 2.50–3.50. On the basis of these values we can identify the groups in our own terms: holophrastic as 'early Stage I'; telegraphic as 'later Stage I'; and mature as 'beyond Stage I'. We may disregard the last of these groups and consider only the results for 'early' and 'late' Stage I.

The mothers of the children directed to them mild imperatives of three types: well-formed or verb-functor-noun imperatives like *Give me the ball*; telegraphic or verb-noun imperatives like *Give ball*; and holophrastic or noun imperatives like *Ball!* The nouns in the commands were familiar terms like *horn, ball* and *drum*. The verbs were either ones normally associated with the nouns (*Throw ball, Blow horn, Bang drum*) or else such general terms as *find, give* and *show*. Obedience to any of these commands, even to the noun alone, would seem to entail, at a minimum, touching or looking at the object named. Of course, for some of the verbs, full compliance would require more but as a common, minimally appropriate response to the whole range of commands the Pennsylvania researchers decided to use touching or looking. The question was whether the child would most often respond in this minimally comprehending way to a command having the same form as his own speech or to a command at another level. The result: early Stage I children responded best to holophrastic or telegraphic commands, the kind they themselves most often produced. However, later Stage I children responded best to the mature command with functors included which would not have been their own most usual way of speaking. Shipley, Smith and Gleitman take this result to be evidence that telegraphic (or later Stage I) children have a competence that extends beyond their performance, and so the investigators judge that conclusions drawn from production data alone must underestimate the real level of grammatical knowledge.

It is necessary to ask what kind of knowledge has been demonstrated. Knowledge of the meanings of the functors or of their grammatical roles has not been demonstrated. The sentences did not include contrasts like

Give me the ball, Give him the ball or *Give me the ball, Give me a ball*, and so the sentences could not test for understanding of the functors. The kind of knowledge the results suggest to me is knowledge that the sentences with functors sound more 'natural' or 'usual' coming from mother than does a telegraphic sentence. The only thing that need actually be processed in the sentence in order to give rise to a response of touching or looking is the object noun *ball* or *horn* or whatever. Probably the telegraphic or holophrastic imperative from mother was sufficiently odd to give the child pause and interfere with his response. It is not apparent that this is more competence or knowledge than is manifested in the performance of the late Stage I child. As we have seen the child at this time probably does control certain 'functors' (e.g., *me, here, there*), whereas others (e.g., articles, copula, inflections) are not controlled until long after Stage I. These latter, however, do occasionally seem to be 'heard' in Stage I speech simply because they belong to the child's pronunciation of certain unanalysed and routine phrases. If we grant that the Stage I child may be aware of the usual presence of 'article sounds' in the pronunciation of familiar nouns like *ball* and *horn* even though, as Stage II shows (Brown, 1976), he is far from controlling the articles themselves, then the data of Shipley and others are not surprising and do not demonstrate that 'competence' assessed by their method is greater than the competence attributed to the child on the basis of his own speech performance.

The discussion of Brown and Fraser (1963), and also of Brown and Bellugi (1964), because they started with the telegraphic properties of imitations, might seem to imply that child speech at I is no more than a repertoire of memorized sentences 'cut down' from adult originals. The authors did not intend to suggest this, and both papers actually discuss the process of rule induction which makes the child's speech productive. Nevertheless, the characterization of speech as telegraphic, even in the much more complicated sense we have given it here, does not in its own right provide for productivity for the construction of new sentences; it is a purely descriptive characterization. In 1963, the same year that Brown and Fraser published, Martin Braine characterized the beginnings of syntax in terms of a few simple productive rules, rules corresponding to none in the adult grammar.

References

Bar-Adon, Aaron, 'Primary Syntactic Structures in Hebrew Child Language', in Aaron Bar-Adon and Werner F. Leopold (eds.), *Child Language: A Book of Readings*, Englewood Cliffs, NJ: Prentice-Hall, 1971, pp. 433-72.

Blandell, Richard, and Paul Jensen, 'Stress and Word Position as Determinants of Imitation in First-Language Learners', *Journal of Speech and Hearing Research* (1970), 13: pp. 193-202.

Bloom, Lois, *Language Development: Form and Function in Emerging Grammars*, Cambridge, Mass.: MIT Press, 1970.

Bowerman, Melissa, *Early Syntactic Development: A Cross-linguistic Study with Special Reference to Finnish*, Cambridge, England: Cambridge University Press, 1973.

Braine, Martin D.S., 'The Ontogeny of English Phrase Structure: The First Phase', *Language* (1963), 39: pp. 1-14.

Brown, Roger, *A First Language*, Harmondsworth: Penguin Books, 1976.

Brown, Roger, and Ursula Bellugi, 'Three Processes in the Acquisition of Syntax', *Harvard Educational Review* (1964) 34: pp. 133-51.

Brown, Roger, and Colin Fraser, 'The Acquisition of Syntax', in Charles N. Cofer and Barbara Musgrave (eds.), *Verbal Behaviour and Learning: Problems and Processes*, New York: McGraw-Hill, 1963, pp. 158-201.

Chao, Yuen R, 'The Cantian Idiolect: An Analysis of the Chinese Spoken by a Twenty-Eight-Months-Old Child', in W.J. Fishel (ed.), *Semitic and Oriental Studies*, University of California Publications in Semitic Philology, XI. Berkeley and Los Angeles: University of California Press, 1951.

Ervin, Susan M., 'Imitation and Structural Change in Children's Language', in Eric H. Lenneberg (ed.), *New Directions in the Study of Language*, Cambridge, Mass.: MIT Press, 1964, pp. 163-89.

Gleason, Henry A., Jr., *An Introduction to Descriptive Linguistics*, rev. ed., New York: Holt, Rinehart & Winston, 1961.

Grégoire, Antoine, *L'Apprentissage du Langage: Les Deux Premières Années*, Paris: Librairie E. Droz, 1937.

Hockett, Charles F., *A Course in Modern Linguistics*, New York: MacMillan, 1958.

Leopold, Werner F., *Speech Development of a Bilingual Child: A Linguist's Record*, Vol. III, *Grammar and General Problems in the First Two Years*, Evanston, Ill.: Northwestern University Press, 1949.

Miller, Wick, and Susan Ervin, 'The Development of Grammar in Child Language', in Ursula Bellugi and Roger Brown (eds.), *The Acquisition of Language*, monographs of the Society for Research in Child Development (1964) 29, pp. 9-34.

Park, Tschang-Zin, 'The Acquisition of German Syntax', unpublished paper, University of Bern, Switzerland, Psychological Institute, 1970.

Rydin, Ingegard, 'A Swedish Child in the Beginning of Syntactic Development and Some Cross-Linguistic Comparisons', unpublished paper, 1971, on file with Roger Brown, Harvard University, Cambridge, Mass.

Scholes, Robert J., 'The Role of Grammaticality in the Imitation of Word Strings by Children and Adults', *Journal of Verbal Learning and Verbal Behavior* (1969), 8: pp. 225-8.

Scholes, Robert J., 'On Functors and Contentives in Children's Imitations of Word Strings', *Journal of Verbal Learning and Verbal Behavior* (1970), 9: pp. 167-70.

Shipley, Elizabeth F., Carlota S. Smith and Lila R. Gleitman, 'A Study of the Acquisition of Language: Free Responses to Commands', *Language* (1969), 45: pp. 322-42.

Slobin, Dan I., 'The Acquisition of Russian as a Native Language', in Frank Smith and George A. Miller (eds.), *The Genesis of Language*, Cambridge, Mass.: MIT Press, 1966, pp. 129-48.

Slobin, Dan I., 'Developmental Psycholinguistics', in William Orr Dingwall (ed.), *A Survey of Linguistic Science*, College Park, Maryland: William Orr Dingwall, Linguistics Program, University of Maryland, 1971, pp. 279-410.

8 WHAT'S IN A WORD? ON THE CHILD'S ACQUISITION OF SEMANTICS IN HIS FIRST LANGUAGE[1]

Eve Clark

Source: Timothy E. Moore (ed.), *Cognitive Development and the Development of Language*, Academic Press, 1973, pp. 65-110.

Introduction[2]

Any hypothesis about the development of semantic knowledge in first language acquisition has to deal eventually with many different issues, but the central question is: what meaning has the child attached to a particular phonological sequence, and how does the child's meaning for this word develop into the adult meaning? Because the answer to this general question is crucial to any theory about the acquisition of the semantic knowledge, this paper will explore the following topics: What sort of lexicon does the child have in the very early stages of language acquisition? What form does the child's semantic knowledge take, and does it differ from the adult's? How is the child's knowledge structured and how does its structure change over time to resemble more closely the adult model?

Although there has been a considerable resurgence of interest in the topic of language acquisition over the last decade, most recent research has centered on the acquisition of the syntactic structure of language. Little attention, by comparison, has been paid to the acquisition of semantics.

The work that has been done on semantics has been concerned principally with the semantic functions of words within the context of an utterance. Slobin (1970), for instance, classified early two-word utterances on the basis of the semantic function of the utterance, e.g., whether it expressed need, possession, location, etc. He found singular resemblances in the types of two-word utterances used by children speaking a number of different languages; his examples were drawn from data on the acquisition of English, Finnish, German, Luo, Russian, and Samoan. Brown (in press) has also done some very detailed functional semantic analysis, concentrating mainly on the acquisition of morphology in the early stages of acquiring English. In his analysis, he pointed out that semantic distinctions that are already known to the child must underlie the introduction of new morphological markers.

The approach to semantics considered by Slobin and Brown is quite different from the one to be pursued here. Their approach is essentially concerned with the *semantic functions* of words in utterances, while the present one will be concerned with a different issue, one basic to language acquisition as a whole. That is the issue of how words are used to *refer to* or represent external objects and events appropriately, from the earliest stages in acquisition on.

In this paper I shall propose a general hypothesis about the acquisition of semantic knowledge by the child and shall present linguistic data on the referential use of language from various stages of language acquisition in support of the hypothesis. In the first part, I shall consider three hypotheses that have recently been entertained by some psychologists and linguists. I shall then present the Semantic Feature Hypothesis on acquisition and relate it to the earlier proposals. In the next section, I shall consider evidence from the early referential use of words by children from a number of different linguistic backgrounds, as well as some data on the later acquisition of word meanings. For these data as a whole, I shall show how the phenomenon of *overextension* provides strong support for the Semantic Feature Hypothesis. In the third section, I will relate semantic features or components of meaning to other developmental phenomena such as perception in discussing the possible sources for semantic features. I shall conclude by stressing the importance of semantics for language acquisition as a whole.

Theories of Semantic Development

Three previous proposals about semantic development will be described in this section. The first is McNeill's (1970) hypothesis about the nature of the child's lexicon in the earliest stages (implicit grammatical relations) as well as the later possibilities for the reorganization of the lexicon as it goes from a sententially based store to a word-based store. This hypothesis will be referred to as the Grammatical Relations Hypothesis. The second proposal to be considered is Anglin's (1970) Generalization Hypothesis about the growth of word meaning as judged from evidence of children's overt knowledge of form class for words in isolation rather than in sentential contexts. The third proposal is in a sense more speculative but some of its assumptions will, I suspect, eventually prove to be essential to a unified theory of first-language acquisition. This hypothesis, proposed by Postal (1966) and Bïerwisch (1967, 1970a) will be referred to as the Universal Primitives Hypothesis. Following the discussion of these three proposals, I shall describe the hypothesis of the present paper, the Semantic Feature Hypothesis.

The Grammatical Relations Hypothesis

McNeill (1970) proposed that when the child begins learning his language, he has some form of sentence-meaning dictionary in which each lexical entry is tagged with all the grammatical relations that are used (implicitly) at the one-word stage. Because of the need to store information about the underlying (innate) grammatical relations, McNeill claims that the child does not have semantic features at this stage since they would be too great a burden on memory. However, in stating his assumption about the primacy of grammatical relations in the earliest stages of language acquisition, McNeill seems to have ignored the issue of what the child knows about the referential use of words, and how or where this knowledge about reference is stored. Notice that such knowledge of the referential properties has logically to precede knowledge of any grammatical constraints on word use (i.e., what are grammatical relations and what are not). In other words, the child has to know at least something of what a word *means* before he can use it grammatically (cf. further Bloom, in press; Bowerman, 1970, 1973).

Later on, as soon as the child begins to use rules for sentence construction (presumably, then, as soon as the first two-word utterances appear in the child's speech), he begins to reorganize his dictionary, according to McNeill, on a word-meaning basis rather than on a sentence-meaning one. This is because it is now more economical given the number of items to be stored. At this point, McNeill considers two possibilities for the growth of the child's reorganized lexicon (1970, pp. 116f.). His first proposal is that the child's lexicon develops 'horizontally'. This means that only some of the semantic features associated with a word need enter the dictionary when the word itself does. As a result, the child could have words in his vocabulary that had different overall semantic properties to the *same* words in the speech of older children or adults. The child could then proceed to complete the dictionary entries for words horizontally, by the gradual addition of features to each entry. While this seems to be an inherently reasonable proposal, McNeill does not go on at this point to discuss which features might appear first in the lexical items entering the dictionary, nor whether there might be any order of acquisition for semantic features in general. Another omission is any discussion of the nature of the semantic features: Where do they come from? Do they suddenly appear just when the child is about to reorganize his lexicon to accommodate word entries? McNeill appears simply to assume that the features are the same somehow as the adult's features.

The alternative to the horizontal model of dictionary organization is what McNeill calls 'vertical' development of the lexicon (he does not choose between the two in his book). By vertical development, he appears to mean that all the semantic features of a word enter the child's dictionary at the same time (when the word itself does), but at first the dictionary entries are 'separated' from each other. In other words, the same semantic features are not necessarily recognized as being the same in different entries within the lexicon. This form of organization, though, would seem for one thing to entail that words would then have to have the same semantic properties for young children as for adults. (It will be shown, however, that such an assumption is not supported by the data.) Under this proposal, semantic development would seem to consist simply of collecting separate occurrences of the same features into some sort of unified group or schema. It is unclear what form the organization of such a lexicon would take developmentally, beyond one's being able to list a gradual increase in the number of vocabulary items used by the child.

Although McNeill cites some data in support of each of the above proposals, the weakness of both lies in the fact that all of the evidence discussed in their favor comes from children older than 6 or 7 years of age. Nonetheless, it is obvious that children much younger than this, indeed from the age of 2 or 2½ upward, must already know a great deal about the semantics of their language in order to (a) communicate with others with considerable success, and (b) use many of the syntactic rules of their language appropriately.

The Generalization Hypothesis

Anglin (1970) proposed that semantic development follows a generalization process in which the child's ability to see semantic relations between the names of objects (words), for example, goes from the concrete to the abstract, where the abstract relations are also the more general ones (i.e., they include larger categories). Anglin (1970, p. 53) attaches this generalization process directly to the lexical level of language and appears to equate the acquisition of more general, superordinate, lexical items with the acquisition of general (abstract) superordinate concepts. At the earlier stages of acquisition, then, he claims that the young child is only aware of the specific, concrete relations between words; as the child's semantic knowledge increases with age, he comes to make generalizations over larger and larger (more abstract) categories. These generalizations are expressed through the use of superordinate lexical items. For example, at an early stage a child might learn the words *rose, tulip, oak,* and *elm*, at the next stage he will group these words into pairs, each with a superordinate lexical item: *flowers* and *trees*. These words in turn could eventually be grouped as *plants*, then ultimately as *living entities*.

In support of his generalization hypothesis, Anglin presented data from a variety of tasks, most of which asked about explicit knowledge of form-class membership (a syntactic rather than a semantic property). He was concerned with the relations among some twenty words in the context of sorting tasks, free recall,[†] structured recall,[†] and a sentence-frame completion[†] task. The words he used were arbitrarily selected from the semantic point of view in that he chose them largely on the basis of whether one could in any way group words sharing the same form-class membership on at least one superordinate dimension. For example, the six nouns used were *boy*, *girl* (children), *horse* (all three are animate or all are mammals), *flower* (all four are living), *chair* (all five are material objects), and *idea* (all six are entities, or all six are nouns).

The superordinate, more abstract or more general, relations between such words, then, are ones which can be named by use of a word (usually a superordinate) or phrase in English. Anglin was much more concerned with the lexical items as wholes, though, than with any potential components of meaning. Thus, his final definition of a feature (which he equates with a word) is fairly far removed both from the term used in perception (Gibson, 1969) and from any recent linguistic definition, viz., '. . . a feature is a complex verbal concept rich in properties just as a word is' (Anglin, 1970, p. 95). Overall, his data simply showed that children learn explicit notions of form class (that is, for words divorced from their sentential contexts) fairly late, up to two or three years after such notions are first broached in school. Anglin claimed that such knowledge of form class is semantic development. However, his theory, which runs counter to much of the data in the literature, is quite unable to account for the fact that children can use words appropriately in sentential contexts at an age when they are unable to say anything about form class.

As in the case of the supporting evidence cited by McNeill for his two proposals *vis-à-vis* the structure of the child's lexicon, Anglin's data too were all collected from children aged 9;0 years and older. He practically ignores the fact that younger children must have some semantic knowledge in order to use their language.

In formulating the Generalization Hypothesis, Anglin said nothing about the nature of lexical entries in the child's dictionary at any stage. It is therefore difficult to compare his hypothesis with McNeill's, beyond pointing out that both McNeill and Anglin, probably because of their concentration on syntactic notions and grammatical relations in language acquisition, assumed that semantic structure develops both later and more slowly than syntactic knowledge of the language. They both presented data from children of 6 years and older, yet the fact remains that younger children can and do use language in a meaningful way. Even if certain aspects of semantic knowledge were not acquired until the age of 6 or 7, much of it – including some knowledge about reference – must be acquired earlier on.

The Universal Primitives Hypothesis

Beginning from a rather different standpoint, Postal (1966) has recently suggested that underlying all languages is a set of universal semantic primitives, together with rules for the combination of primitives into lexical items. Languages differ from each other principally in the rules of combination used to go from the semantic primitives to the lexical items. These primitives would be equivalent or even identical to the semantic components of componential analysis,[†] to Hjelmslev's minimum units of content[†] or to Katz and Fodor's (1963) semantic markers.[†] Furthermore, Postal (1966) pointed out that:

> . . . each of these primitives bears a fixed relation to the universe which is determined by the biological structure of the organism. Thus the relation between the semantic primitives and their combinations which are part of the combinatorial structure of language and the word is not learned but innate. What must be learned is only the relations between fixed sets of semantic primitives and sets of phonological and syntactic properties [p. 179, fn. 10].

This view of universal semantics has been spelled out in more detail by Bierwisch, who pointed out (1967) that 'the idea of innate basic elements of semantic structure does not entail a biological determination of concepts or meanings in a given language, but only of their ultimate components' (1967, p. 4). In other words, the child would not have to learn the components themselves since they would be innate in the sense that they are biologically given through the structure of the human organism (cf., e.g., H. Clark, 1973). Postal, however, oversimplified somewhat in claiming that *all* that had to be learned was 'the relations between fixed sets of semantic primitives and sets of phonological and syntactic properties'. The child acquiring his first language has undoubtedly got to do this, but he has to learn first which combinations of primitives have lexical exponents in his language, and which do not.

Bierwisch (1970a) has put the Universal Primitives Hypothesis position most clearly and succinctly in a recent article on semantics. He further elaborates the idea of innate semantic primitives or components of meaning, and their relation to external physical attributes of objects and events:

It seems natural to assume that these [semantic] components represent categories or principles according to which real and fictitious, perceived and imagined situations and objects are structured and classified. The semantic features do not represent, however, external physical properties, but rather the psychological conditions according to which human beings process their physical and social environment. Thus they are not symbols for physical properties and relations outside the human organism, but rather for the internal mechanisms by means of which such phenomena are perceived and conceptualized. This then leads to the extremely far-reaching, though plausible, hypothesis that all semantic structures might finally be reduced to components representing the basic dispositions of the cognitive and perceptual structure of the human organism. According to this hypothesis, semantic features cannot be different from language to language, but are rather part of the general human capacity for language, forming a universal inventory used in particular ways by individual languages [pp. 181-2].

This suggests that Bierwisch would have to claim that there is a common interpretive format into which all percepts are translated, where the components used in interpreting any sort of input to the human organism, whether linguistic or no, *are* the semantic primitives, or at least are isomorphic in some significant way with these semantic primitives. The extension of the Univeral Primitives Hypothesis to account for first-language acquisition would then ultimately have to relate the development of semantic knowledge to general perceptual and cognitive development. That there is a close relation between language and cognitive development has often been assumed, but few attempts have been made so far to investigate the nature of this relationship (cf., e.g., Sinclair-de Zwart, 1967; Slobin, 1971).

The Universal Primitives Hypothesis is, as Bierwisch points out, a very plausible one and it has important implications for a developmental theory; at the same time it is extremely difficult either to verify or to disprove, since we still have little idea how to identify the primitives, much less any notion of what form the rules for their combination into the appropriate lexical items would take within a particular language. It is possible that some of the work being done within generative semantics (e.g., Lakoff, 1970a, b, 1971; McCawley, 1968; Postal, 1970) may eventually provide solutions to such problems.

The Present Hypothesis: Semantic Feature Acquisition

The hypothesis to be presented and tested here is concerned with what the child learns about the meanings of words as he goes through the process of acquiring his first language. Since the child's knowledge, in general, is greatly restricted in comparison to the adult's, this will affect his language development as well as his other behaviors. The Semantic Feature Hypothesis states that when the child first begins to use identifiable words, he does not know their full (adult) meaning: He only has partial entries for them in his lexicon, such that these partial entries correspond in some way to some of the features or components of meaning that would be present in the entries for the same words in the adult's lexicon. Thus, the child will begin by identifying the meaning of a word with only one or two features rather than with the whole combination of meaning components or features (*qua* Postal) that are used criterially by the adult. The acquisition of semantic knowledge, then, will consist of adding more features of meaning to the lexical entry of the word until the child's combination of features in the entry for that word corresponds to the adult's. The hypothesis therefore assumes that the child's use and interpretation of words may differ considerably from the adult's in the early stages of the language-acquisition process, but, over time, will come to correspond to the adult model.

Although the child does not know the full meaning of some word, there is nothing to tell him this fact and he will, therefore, use the word. As soon as he has attached some feature(s) of meaning to it, it simply has that meaning for him. The child will use those one or two features criterially in deciding when to apply the word and when not. Since he has only a partial characterization of the word's meaning set up, his referential categories may often differ considerably from the adult's for the same words. The child will make referential errors because he does not know the combinations of features that will allow him to delimit his categories differently. The principal difference between child and adult categories at this stage will be that the child's are generally larger since he will use only one or two features criterially instead of a whole combination of features.

For example, let us suppose that the child has learned the word *dog* (or *doggie*); however, he only uses one feature to characterize the meaning of this word, so the set of objects that he will put into the category named *dog* will be larger than the set in the adult category. For instance, he might have characterized the word *dog* as meaning *four-legged*; the sets of objects referred to as *dog*, therefore, might include cows, sheep, zebras, llamas, dogs and anything else that is four-legged. This feature, four-leggedness, is clearly inadequate to specify the meaning of the word *dog* in such a way that the child's category will coincide with the adult's (unless the only four-legged creatures the child sees are dogs). However, with the addition of other features, the child will gradually narrow down this initially very general meaning of *dog* until it means what the adult means. This narrowing-down process will presumably run concurrently with the introduction of new words into the child's vocabulary that take over parts of the overextended semantic domain. To continue with the same example as an illustration, if the child next acquires the word *zebra*, he must add something to the feature *four-legged* to keep the meaning of this word distinct from that of *dog*; he might add any of the following features: *hoofs*, *mane*, *striped*. For the word *cow*, further specifications might include the sound made (*mooing*), or other features of shape like *horns* or *udders*. At the same time, the child will probably add to the lexical entry for *dog* things like *sound: barking, size: relatively small* (in comparison to cows, zebras and llamas), etc. These combinations of features are then used criterially, and eventually come to delimit the adult categories.

Let us now consider the child who has arrived at a more advanced stage: many of his dictionary entries are practically complete. However, there are other words or word pairs in his language that are very closely related in meaning, and therefore have a large number of semantic features in common. For example, the pair of words *more* and *less* both refer to quantity but *more* is unmarked (Greenberg, 1966) and positive: It refers to an amount that is positive with respect to some standard on a scale, whereas *less* refers to an amount that is negative with respect to some standard. The dimensional adjectives in English are similarly related: Both *high* and *low*, for example, refer to a single dimension, both specify that the dimension is a vertical one, but *high* refers to a positive distance along the dimension while *low* is negative in the same way as *less*. Thus, if the child learned a feature like + Amount first in learning the meanings of *more* and *less*, the meanings of these two words could well be confused. It would not be until the child learned the contrasting values of polarity — that *more* was positive and *less* negative — that this pair of antonyms would be interpreted correctly. Similarly, there might be a stage in acquisition at which the meanings of *high* and *low* would be confused by the child, for the same reason.

Another area in which words share a number of semantic features in common is where there is an overlap in meaning: One word may refer to a subset of objects that may be included within a category covered by another word. An example of this sort of relationship is the overlap between the words *brother* and *boy*. All brothers are boys, but not all boys are brothers. The word *brother*, in fact, singles out a subset of the category named by the word *boy*. It is predicted in this instance that the child will confuse the more specific term (*brother*) with the more general one (*boy*) until he learns the other semantic features needed in the entry for *brother*.

Thus, if two words are opposites and their meanings differ simply by one feature (or by the value on a feature within a binary system), or if they share a number of features in common, but one word has some additional, more specific, features in its entry as well, then they are likely to be regarded at some point as having the same meaning. Later, of course, the child will learn the contrasting values on a feature or the more specific features that differentiate between the meanings of such closely related words.

So far, in outlining the present hypothesis, no real attempt has been made to define what is meant by *feature* or *component of meaning*. One of the basic assumptions of the theory clearly is that the meanings of words can be broken down into some combination of units of meaning smaller than that represented by the word. These units may be talked about in many ways, and have been variously called features, components, minimal units of content, semantic markers, etc. These units have generally reflected some of the notational constraints imposed on the form and scope of the semantic theory being proposed (cf., e.g., Bierwisch, 1969, 1970b). No theoretical issues will be raised here, although I will use a binary type of notation to represent the child's semantic knowledge about particular sets of words. This notation does not imply any theoretical commitment to binary features, and will simply be used for clarity's sake in presenting the data.

The main question, though, remains: What is a feature? And its corollary: Does the child use the same features as the adult? In an ideal world where we knew what the universal semantic primitives were, we could assume these would be used by both child and adult. However, we are not in a position at present, theoretically or empirically, to (a) identify the set of universal semantic primitives postulated by Postal and Bierwisch, or (b) claim that these primitives are what the child uses when he first attaches some meaning to a word. The present theory will simply make the following, testable, assumption: (a) the first semantic features that the child uses are liable to be derived from the encoding of his percepts, and (b) at a later stage, as the child learns more about the structure of his language as a whole, he will learn which percept-derived features play a particular linguistic role (e.g., *animacy*) and which are relatively redundant within a set or combination of features. Since the adult also uses perceptually derived information, many of the semantic features used by the adult are also used by the child. The main differences will lie in the fact that the child has to learn the rules of combination for each lexical item.

One further point to be stressed in the present discussion of semantic features is the relation between the child's perception of objects and events and his learning to use words to encode a particular meaning. The fact that the child may begin by simply attaching the feature or component of meaning *four-legged* to the word *dog* says nothing about the child's perception of different objects or of the differences between objects. A child can clearly see the differences between dogs, cows, and horses, but there is no *a priori* reason for the child to respect either adult or biological taxonomies when he first begins to learn the meaning of a word. In the example of *dog* being taken to mean something like *four-legged*, the child simply sees that all these animals (cows, dogs, and horses) have the appropriate perceived characteristic for this word to be applied. He will therefore include all three adult categories under *dog* (= *four-legged*) until he adds further specifications or features of meaning to the word that will lead him to reduce the size of his category to something nearer the adult one. The growth of lexical entries for word meanings, therefore, makes no claims about what the child actually perceives, only about the sorts of meaning that he will attach to a word in the very early stages of language acquisition.

Besides considering the source of the child's earliest semantic features (perceptual attributes and their encoding), the present hypothesis is also concerned with whether some kinds of semantic features are learned before others: Does the child learn features that are general or specific to the meaning of a word first? The Semantic Feature Hypothesis would predict that it is the more general semantic features that will be acquired earliest. This claim is concomitant with the predictions made earlier about the confusion of antonyms and of words that overlap in meaning. It also follows from the prediction that children will overextend (by adult standards) many words in such a way that their categories will be delimited differently from the adult's. Furthermore, on the basis of some recent experimental work, it would appear that if the features which, combined, make up the meaning of a word are related to each other hierarchically, then the order of acquisition is top-down, i.e., the top feature, being the most general in the definition of the word, is acquired first with the other features being acquired in the order of their hierarchical dependence. For example, in the acquisition of the meanings of *before* and *after*, children first learn that both words have to do with time: + Time: next they learn that these words refer to sequence rather than to simultaneity of some sort: − Simultaneous. The feature − Simultaneous carries with it a specification of ordering in the sequence: + Prior. This combination of features

(+ Time, − Simultaneous, + Prior) characterizes the meaning of *before* but not that of *after*. The last feature that children learn is − Prior, i.e., that *after* is in fact the opposite of *before* (E. Clark, 1971a).

Finally, it is essential to point out that the features for each word separately have to be learned in the acquisition of the word itself. Therefore, the acquisition of a feature or even of a combination of features in one context (one word) does not imply, for example, that the child will immediately recognize synonyms. He has to find out first that the new word does, in fact, contain the same combination of semantic features (though it may have different syntactic properties). For example, in acquiring the meanings of various time-related words, children learn what *first* means before they learn what *before* means; and, in learning the meaning of *before*, children add the features in turn to this new lexical item. However, the combination of features (+ Time, − Simultaneous, + Prior) is one they already know because they know what the word *first* means.

How is the present theory related to those discussed earlier? First, it is clear that a number of assumptions in the present theory are related to the Postal and Bierwisch formulations. For instance, that there is a universal set of semantic primitives, although we do not yet have a good way of identifying them; and that semantic knowledge is closely related to the human organism's interpretation of perceptual inputs.

Superficially, the present hypothesis also appears to draw on one of McNeill's proposals about the structure of the child's lexicon − that lexical entries are completed horizontally. However, McNeill said nothing about the nature of the semantic features used by the child after the purported reorganization from a sentential store with grammatical relations to a lexical store with semantic features of words. In contrast, the present theory makes specific proposals about the earliest semantic features used, and assumes that the child stores semantic information about the words he has from the earlier stages on. McNeill also does not say anything about the order of acquisition of semantic features with respect to individual words, whereas the present theory claims that there is an order of acquisition in which the more general features are acquired first. The later addition of more specific features is what eventually distinguishes between several words which share the same general feature(s). This form of semantic development will automatically result in what McNeill called horizontal completion of the dictionary entries in the child's lexicon.

Lastly, how is the present theory related to Anglin's Generalization Hypothesis? The direction for the development of semantic knowledge proposed by Anglin was specific to general. Anglin took words as his units rather than anything smaller, but even at the word level the Generalization Hypothesis cannot adequately account for the vocabulary data (cf. Brown, 1958) since children do not invariably acquire subordinate terms, e.g., *oak*, *elm*, before they acquire superordinate ones, e.g., *tree*. The present hypothesis, in considering features of meaning below the level of the word, predicts that general features will be acquired first, and only later (as the child learns more about the meaning of the word) does the child gradually add the specific features that differentiate the meaning of one word from another.

From the description of the Semantic Feature Hypothesis, it is clear that the areas most likely to yield information about the child's semantic structures in the early stages of language acquisition are the referential use of words, the use of opposites and the use of overlapping terms. Since the theory predicts that the meanings of many (and maybe all) words are not equivalent for the young child and the adult, how can we detect this lack of correspondence? First of all, if the child uses only one or two features criterially in the application of a word, then there should be evidence of overextension in his speech — the establishment of categories that do not correspond to adult ones. The term extension will be used to refer to the child's use of a word once it has entered his vocabulary. Some uses will appear to be appropriate and others not. It is the inappropriate ones that will be referred to as overextensions. By considering the actual categories that result from an overextension, one should be able to infer which features the child has used criterially. The domain of each set of over-extensions can be treated as a semantic field, and the changes in its structure (either because of more overextensions or because of the later narrowing-down of the word's meaning) can be studied over time. One should, then, be able to work back from the structure at a particular stage to the criterial features that would have to have been used in order to produce such a structure within the semantic field.

The phenomenon of overextension and its subsequent elimination (with the narrowing-down of categories) as the child learns more about the word's meaning will allow (a) the investigation of criterial features used by the child, and (b) more detailed proposals about which semantic features are known to the child. In the next section, I shall present data on several kinds of overextension in the child's use and comprehension of words in various naturalistic and experimental settings. These data provide a pre-liminary test of the present hypothesis.

The Evidence

In this section, I shall discuss data from the following sources: first, the use of words by very young children as reported in the many nineteenth and twentieth century diary studies; secondly, some work on various relational terms carried out more recently by Donaldson and Balfour (1968), Donaldson and Wales (1970), and E. Clark (1971a), with 3- to 5-year-old children; and lastly, some work with school-age children on verbs by C. Chomsky (1969), and on complex relational nouns by Piaget (1928).

Overextension in Early Speech

The first form of overextension to be described is one that is widely reported in the diaries kept on the early speech of children from a number of different language backgrounds. The accounts of this phenomenon are remarkably alike and consistently report similar findings. As a result, overextension appears to be language-dependent (at least at this early stage in acquisition), and is probably universal in the language acquisition process. Among the sources for the present data, for example, are: Ament (1899): German; Chamberlain and Chamberlain (1904): English; Guillaume (1927b): French; Idelberger (1903): German; Kenyereś (1926): Hungarian; Imedadze (1960): Georgian, Russian; Leopold (1939, 1949a): English, German; Luria and Yudovich (1959): Russian; Moore (1896): English; Pavlovitch (1920): French, Serbian; Rasmussen (1922): Danish; Shvachkin (1948): Russian; Taine (1877): French; Tauble (cited by Preyer, 1889): Estonian; etc.

The general characteristics of the diary data are the following:

(1)   The studies consulted all reported overextension within approximately the same age-range, generally between 1;1 and 2;6 years. The period in which this phenomenon is noticed lasts for up to a year for each child, but the overextension of a particular word rarely lasts much more than 8 months, and may take place only very briefly.

(2)   The more detailed studies relate overextensions in the child's speech to vocabulary growth. They point out that there seems to be a sudden increase in the child's vocabulary, usually combined with intensive questioning activity of the *what('s) that?* variety, which often marks the end of this early form of overextension.

(3)   The reports suggest that generally only some words in the child's vocabulary are noticeably overextended. Others appear to be used in a manner consistent with adult criteria from the moment of their introduction into the child's speech.[3] I use the word *appear* advisedly, since there are undoubtedly many occasions on which an adult simply does not notice whether the child used an overextension or not. The adult's report

will depend very heavily upon the context in which the child uses a word: an overextension has to be noticeable and therefore has to occur in contexts in which it cannot be put down as a reference to some other appropriate object that is in the same vicinity, and so on.

(4)   Finally, the features that are used criterially in the overextensions of words appear to be derived predominantly from the perceptual input to the child — whether the percepts come from visual, tactile, olfactory, or auditory sources. Thus, the majority of overextensions reported in these data appear to be based on the perceived similarities between the objects or events that are included referentially within a single category. The principal criterial characteristics can be classified into several categories such as *movement, shape, size, sound, taste,* and *texture*. The categories are clearly derived from the child's perception of the properties of the objects around him.

Examples of these early overextensions are given in Tables 8.1 to 8.7. The examples have been grouped according to the type of feature that appears to underlie the overextension. Table 8.1, for instance, contains examples in which the child appears to have attached the meaning *movement* to the vocabulary items in question. The main kinds of feature (shape, size, sound, etc.) used in the overextensions are illustrated in Tables 8.1 to 8.6, in which the perceptual source of the criterial feature(s) is generally quite clear. In Table 8.2, for example, one can infer immediately from the overextensions which shape is being used criterially. For many small children, the category of *small round objects* crops up very frequently (cf. the examples cited from Chamberlain and Chamberlain, 1904). Another category based on shape that appears quite often is *square container*; Lewis (1951) reports a rather different category for which the criterial feature was a set of parallel, upright bars — a category which resulted from the child's overextension of the word used for the bars of his cot.

While the large majority of overextensions fit into the categories illustrated in Tables 8.1 to 8.6, there is a residual group of overextensions in which the words used usually seem to refer to actions rather than to objects. A few examples are listed in Table 8.7. The perceptual basis for these overextensions with verbal force cannot be as readily identified with one or two perceived attributes of the situation. Nevertheless, there are some obvious similarities between the contexts in which these overextensions occurred.

The headings for Tables 8.1 to 8.6 give a somewhat oversimplified picture of the perceptual categories that the child appears to use in

Table 8.1: Some Overextensions Related to Movement[a]

Source	Lexical item	First referent	Extensions and overextensions in order of occurrence
Kenyereš (1926)	titi	animals	> (pictures of animals) > (things that move
Leopold (1949a)	sch	sound of train	> (all moving machines)

[a] Overextensions will be indicated by > where the following object — in parentheses — was given the same name. The probable source of the child's phonological form in the parents' speech is indicated by <.

Table 8.2: Some Overextensions Related to Shape

Chamberlain & Chamberlain (1904)	moo i	moon	> (cakes) > (round marks on window) > (writing on window and in books) > (round shapes in books) > (tooling on leather book covers) > (round postmarks) > (letter O)
Grégoire (1937)	wawa	dog	> (small white sheep)

Table 8.3: Some Overextensions Related to Size

Kenyereš (1926)	baba	baby	> (adults in pictures) > (pictures in books)
Moore (1896)	fly	fly	> (specks of dirt) > (dust) > (all small insects) > (his own toes) > (crumbs of bread) > (a toad)

Table 8.4: Some Overextensions Related to Sound

Leopold (1949a)	sch	noise of train	> (music) > (noise of any movement) > (wheels) > (balls)
Pavlovitch (1920)	koko	cockerel's crowing	> (tunes played on the violin) > (tunes played on the piano) > (tunes on an accordian) > (tunes on a phonograph) > (all music) > (merry-go-round)

Table 8.5: Some Overextensions Related to Taste

Source	Lexical item	First referent	Extensions and overextensions in order of occurrence
Leopold (1949a)	cake	candy	$>$(cakes)
Leopold (1949a)	candy	candy	$>$(cherries) $>$(anything sweet)

Table 8.6: Some Overextensions Related to Texture

Source	Lexical item	First referent	Extensions and overextensions in order of occurrence
Grégoire (1949)	sizo ($<$ sciseaux)	scissors	$>$(all metal objects)
Idleberger (1903)	bow-bow	dog	$>$(toy dog) $>$(fur piece with animal head) $>$(other fur pieces without heads)

Table 8.7: A Few Early Overextensions Involving Actions Rather Than Objects

Source	Lexical item	First referent	Extensions and overextensions in order of occurrence
Guillaume (1927b)	our ($<$ ouvrir) 'open'	in relation to father's door	$>$(in relation to piece of fruit-peel) $>$(in relation to box) $>$(in relation to pea pod) $>$(in relation to shoes that needed to be unlaced)
Preyer (1889)	atta (= all gone)	departures	$>$(opening or closing of doors) $>$(raising box lid) $>$(any disappearance of object from sight)

overextensions. In fact, in some instances, more than one kind of feature may be involved in a series of overextensions: For example, shape and size are not always separable, and sound often accompanies movement. Furthermore, inspection of the data reveals examples in which two features may be playing a criterial role, but it is unclear whether one is dominant or whether they are being used as a criterial combination. Two features seem to alternate in dominance, giving rise to some overextensions on the basis of shape, for example, and then, after a switch, giving rise to others on the basis of sound or texture, etc.[4] Most of the examples presented, though, are reasonably unambiguous with respect to the type of criterial feature used, even if the actual feature itself cannot always be identified in these data with absolute certainty.

The six classes of overextension in Tables 8.1 to 8.6 cover all the kinds of overextension found in relation to objects. Although the overextensions are clearly based on perceived features of different objects, there is one surprising omission among these features: the attribute of *color* does not appear criterially at all. Its insignificance in comparison to other physical attributes has been pointed out, for instance, by Pavlovitch (1920): 'Toutefois il faut indiquer que la couleur comme élément constituitif ne joue qu'un rôle minime [p. 116] '. Pavlovitch also found that taste was less used than the other classes of perceptual attributes as a basis for over-extension. This accords with the literature as a whole which contains comparatively fewer overextensions in this class (Table 8.5). The most important perceptually derived criteria for overextensions are based on movement, shape, size, and sound (cf. Tables 8.1 to 8.4).[5]

Once the child gets past this main period of overextensions, how does he begin to narrow down the meaning of overextended terms? The present hypothesis claims that the child will gradually add more specific features to the word as new words are introduced to take over subparts of a seman-tic domain. The addition of other features to the word combined with the introduction of new words will require the further differentiation of quasi-synonyms, and a considerable restructuring of the semantic domains of overextensions. This, unfortunately, is where a major weakness of the diary literature becomes apparent. Although so many observers duly reported the first appearance and the types of overextensions used, only a few provide any form of systematic documentation on their disappear-ance. In many studies, one has to rely on the reports of new vocabulary acquisitions in order to infer that the domain of a particular overextension has been restricted to something nearer the domain of the adult lexical item. Only two diaries give fairly clear accounts of some of the restructur-ing due to the narrowing-down of meanings: Pavlovitch (1920) and Leopold (1949a).

The narrowing-down or restructuring process that goes on provides data that can be used to find out which (criterial) features are being added by the child as the meaning of a word becomes more specific. One way of analyzing both the overextensions and the narrowing-down processes is to treat the domain of any one word as a semantic field[†] (Lyons, 1968: Ohman, 1953). As an example, I have taken data from several studies and presented it in composite form in Table 8.8 to illustrate some of the possible changes in a semantic field.

Notice that at Stage I the child acquires *bow-wow* which is used to refer to dogs (semantic field or domain). No records give enough detail for us to know whether this is a distinct stage or whether, given the oppor-tunity, overextensions begin immediately a word has been acquired. At

Table 8.8. A Sample Instance of Overextension and Restructuring[a]

	Word	Semantic domain	Possible criterial feature(s)
Stage I	bow-wow	dog(s)	shape
Stage II	bow-wow	dogs, cows, horses, sheep, cats	shape
Stage III	(a) bow-wow[b]	dogs, cats, horses, sheep	
	(b) moo	cows	sound, (horns?)[c]
Stage IV	(a) bow-wow	dogs, cats, sheep	
	(b) moo	cows	sound
	(c) gee-gee	horses	size, (tail/mane?)
Stage V	(a) bow-wow/doggie	cats, dogs	size
	(b) moo	cows	
	(c) gee-gee/horsie	horses	
	(d) baa	sheep	sound
Stage VI	(a) doggie	dogs	
	(b) moo	cows	
	(c) gee-gee/horsie	horses	
	(d) baa lamb	sheep	
	(e) kitty	cats	shape, sound

[a] Cf., e.g., data in Ament (1899), Grégoire (1937), Leopold (1948), Lewis (1957), Perez (1892) and Shvachkin (1948).
[b] There may be some overlap in the use of the two words if *new* animals are seen at this point.
[c] Size may be an important factor: e.g. Shvachkin (1948) found that *vava* was used for dogs and *mu* for cows and big dogs.

the second stage, *bow-wow* has been overextended to cover a domain comprising dogs, cats, cows, horses, and sheep. As soon as the child adds other words to his vocabulary, though – words that also apply to subparts of this domain – he will have to add other features of meaning to the entry for the new word so as to keep their meanings apart. Thus, at Stage III, the addition of the word *moo*, which then takes over only the subset of cows from the domain of *bow-bow*, suggests that the entry for *moo* must contain something like a feature denoting the particular sound made by this subclass or else additional features of shape such as *horns* or *udders* besides the original feature of shape, *four-legged*. At the next stage when *gee-gee* is introduced and takes over the subclass of horses from *bow-bow*, one could infer that either the entry for *gee-gee*, like that for *moo*, has added to it additional features based on shape or sound, or else that the entry for *bow-bow* has had added to it a feature of size restricting its application to relatively small members of the category (i.e., cats, dogs, and sheep) leaving horses to be covered by the new term *gee-gee*. Or, alternatively, both entries (*bow-bow* and *gee-gee*) have such features added to them at the same time. With the introduction of *baa* (Stage V) for sheep, the entries for the lexical items have to be restricted or specified still further: besides shape and size, the entry for *baa* might contain a feature coding the sound this type of animal makes or the texture of its coat. Finally, at the last stage in narrowing down the original (over-extended) domain of the word *bow-bow* (or *doggie* which replaces the baby word), the child adds the lexical item *kitty* which results in a sub-division of the dogs-cats class into two separate categories. Since over-extensions are rarely reported once a domain has been restricted, one might propose that by this stage, the child has analyzed and coded particular configurations of perceptual features, and it is now the configurations of features that are used criterially in deciding on appropriate instances. However, the use of a configuration rather than isolated features does not necessarily mean that the lexical entry for a particular word is complete, but simply that the child has by now coded what appears to be the relevant set of attributes used to identify a certain set of objects or events. These perceptually based configurations are often represented in a shorthand form of notation as something like + Canine or + Bovine in the adult lexicon.

This example of overextension followed by narrowing-down is to some small degree fictitious although sequences of many of the stages are actually reported for the child in the diaries referenced. However, the details of the criterial features are largely speculative, and new detailed studies of the phenomenon of overextension are needed for a more careful investigation of the exact criterial features used at this stage by the young child.

What form has the restructuring been reported to take in those diaries that do discuss this phenomenon as well as overextension? Pavlovitch (1920) refers to this restructuring as 'restriction du sens', and suggests that it occurs because of the acquisition of new words by the child. It must also occur as a result of parental prompting: *That's not a dog; it's a cow*, and so on. Pavlovitch gives a number of quite detailed examples of the narrowing-down process, describing how new words take over parts of a domain resulting from overextension, just as in the partly hypothetical example presented above. One of the domains he described in detail is that of the word *bébé* which was first widely extended and then gradually narrowed down. The narrowing-down process is schematized in Table 8.9. The different stages that Pavlovitch describes are very similar in kind to those in the example given in Table 8.8. He also lists the changes in a

Table 8.9: The Restructuring of a Semantic Domain[a]

	Word(s)	Semantic domain
Stage I	bébé	reflection of self in mirror; photo of self; all photos; all pictures; books with pictures; all books
Stage II	(a) bébé	reflection to self in mirror; photo of self; all pictures; books with pictures
	(b) deda (grandfather)	all photos
Stage III	(a) bébé	reflection of self in mirror; photo of self; books with pictures; all books
	(b) deda	all photos
	(c) ka'ta (karta = card)	all pictures of landscapes, views
Stage IV	(a) bébé	reflection of self in mirror; photo of self
	(b) deda	all photos
	(c) ka'ta	all pictures (not of people)
	(d) kiga (book)	all books
Stage V	(a) bébé	self; small children in pictures
	(b) deda	photos
	(c) ka'ta	pictures
	(d) kiga	books
	(e) slika (reflection)	reflections in mirror
	(f) duda (Douchau, own name)	photo of self

[a] Data from Pavlovitch (1920).

number of other domains in which he had previously observed over-extensions.

Leopold (1949a) also reports on a number of restructured domains that resulted from the breaking-down of a large domain into several smaller ones. One example which he presented in some detail (p. 134) is that involving the words *sch* and *auto*, which for a short time were used as synonyms in some contexts. *Sch* was the first of the two words to appear in the child's speech (1;0) and was used initially to refer to the sound of trains, extended to music, and then extended (1;4) to any moving object (e.g., cars, trains, a chair pushed across the floor). After this, *sch* was extended to anything that could move but it was not necessary for the objects to be in motion, e.g., pictures of cars and carriages, a toy wheelbarrow. At 1;8, *sch* was replaced by *auto* which had been synonymous with *sch* in referring to cars and pictures of cars since 1;5. At the same time, the word *ride* was introduced and seemed to take over the idea of moving, while *choo-choo* began to share part of the domain of *sch* with *auto*. *Auto* by 1;8 was simply used to refer to cars, and *choo-choo* took over the rest of the domain of *sch*. being applied to all complicated instruments, then to trains, then to machinery (1;9), to airplanes and a wheelbarrow (1;10), and to a streetcar (1;11). At this point, the three words *train, wheelbarrow,* and *airplane* were acquired, and each took over the appropriate part of the domain of *choo-choo*. The latter word was then abandoned, except for occasional use in *choo-choo train.*

It is clear from these examples in Pavlovitch (1920) and in Leopold (1949a) that we can tentatively identify some of the features that the child uses in overextending and then narrowing down the domain referred to by a particular word. It is also clear from the examples summarized in Tables 8.1 to 8.7 that the initial overextensions are based on some of the perceived characteristics of the objects around the child. Equally, the child uses a complex of such characteristics or features when he narrows down the referential application of a word to the appropriate (adult) domain. Among the questions that these data raise are: How many 'correct' instances of an object does the child have to see, and hear named, before he picks out a criterial feature to use in applying the word in other contexts? And, is there any way of finding out whether each new word in the child's vocabulary goes through a brief period of referring only to 'correct' instances before being overextended? The lack of detail in many of the diaries prevents us from answering these questions at the moment. New studies, paying far more attention to the context of each utterance will have to be undertaken before we can identify the exact features used, for example, or any order in the use of perceptually derived features.

Relational Terms†

The second type of overextension to be discussed is much less obvious to the observer, and is possibly never noticed in the context of spontaneous utterances by the child. The phenomenon only comes to light when one begins to study the child's comprehension of certain word pairs, such as *more-less, big-wee* (small), *tall-short, before-after,* and so on, which are closely related in meaning. In each instance, the meaning of one of the pair is extended to cover both words. Without specific contexts which will distinguish between understanding and misunderstanding of an instruction that contains a particular word, this form of overextension will not be noticed. The studies to be described, therefore, have dealt mainly with comprehension rather than production.

The children who took part in these studies were slightly older than those using the first form of overextension that was discussed. Several of the comprehension studies were done with fifteen children whose ages ranged from 3;5 to 4;1 years; the same children were also given some follow-up tasks six months after the first experiments (cf. Donaldson &

Table 8.10: More and Less[a]

A.	Question	Yes	No[b]	Same	Total
	Does one have more?	65	3	1	69
	Does one have less?	55	0	0	55

[a] Based on Donaldson and Balfour (1968, p. 464).
[b] Subsequently changed to "Yes".

B.	Question	Correct choice	Incorrect choice	No choice	Total
	Which one has more?	63	5	1	69
	Which one has less?	15	40	0	55

Balfour, 1968; Donaldson & Wales, 1970; Wales & Campbell, 1970). Another experiment studied forty children between the ages of 3;0 and 5;0 years in a cross-sectional study of meaning acquisition (E. Clark, 1971a). The data from each of these studies will be described in turn.

Less is More. The first research that found evidence of this second form of overextension was done by Donaldson and Balfour (1968). In their study, they looked at how 3-year-old children interpreted the relational terms *more* and *less.* The stimuli used were two cardboard apple trees on which one could hang up to six apples. Beginning from situations in which the trees either had the same or different numbers of apples on them, the experimenter asked various questions about the state of the trees ('Does one tree have more/less apples on it than the other?') and also asked the children to alter certain states ('Make this tree so that it has more/less apples . . .', etc.). The most consistent and surprising finding was that the majority of the children gave no indication that they could differentiate the word *less* from the word *more.* Questions that contained the word *less* were answered in exactly the same way as those with the word *more.*

The general pattern of the children's responses is shown in Table 8.10. When asked whether one tree had more or one had less apples on it than the other, the children nearly always responded affirmatively. Then, when asked to point out which tree had more on it, 91% of the responses were correct. However, when asked to point out which tree had less on it, 72.7% of the responses were wrong. Thus, on 40 of the trials in which children had previously judged that one tree had less on it, they subsequently chose as the one with less the one that actually had more. All the questions asked by the experimenter produced the same results: *less* was treated as if it were synonymous with the word *more*. In addition, the children showed no signs of hesitation over giving the word *less* the interpretation of *more*. Donaldson and Balfour (1968) point out that the children responded to *less* as if they knew that it referred to quantity: 'What seems to occur is that 'less' is understood to refer to quantity but . . . . it remains largely undifferentiated from 'more' as the consistently dominant interpretation for the undifferentiated pair' (p. 468).

Another way of stating their conclusion is to say that the meaning of *more* has been overextended to cover the word *less* as well, and this results in *less* being interpreted as the synonym rather than as the antonym of the word *more*.

What relations are there between these acquisition data and the semantic components that make up the meanings of these relational terms? In his discussion of the Donaldson and Wales (1970) paper, H. Clark (1970a) related some of their data to the relevant linguistic analyses. He pointed out that many of the words that Donaldson and Wales had studied were what are called unmarked-marked pairs. The unmarked member of the pair can be used nominally (i.e., naming a dimension, as in *The man is six feet tall*) and contrastively (where it means 'taller than average', as in *The man is tall*). The marked term, on the other hand, can only be used contrastively (*The man is short*) and cannot be used simply to refer to height (**The man is six feet short*). The nominal *tall* has to precede contrastive *tall* and contrastive *short* since the dimension itself has to be there before one can talk about greater or lesser extent along that dimension. For the set of dimensional adjective pairs in English (and in many other languages), it is always the unmarked term that denotes physical extent along the dimension.

These linguistic facts were then used in positing a particular developmental sequence in the acquisition of the terms *more* and *less*: First, the child uses *more* and *less* in the nominal noncomparative sense only. Next, since the nominal term refers to extension rather than to lack of extension, the child will use both *more* and *less* to refer to the extended end of the scale, and finally, he will distinguish *less* from *more* and use it contrastively to apply to the less extended end of the scale.

At the first stage, therefore, *more* is simply taken to mean 'amount' or 'a quantity of', and its comparative nature is not understood. (This interpretation of *more* accords very well with many of the diary accounts of the early use of this word.) While this nominal interpretation of both words would explain why *more* and *less* were treated as synonyms, it does not account for why *more* and *less* both mean 'more'. As H. Clark points out, one has to make one assumption at this point: that the notion 'having extent' is always best exemplified by the object with the *most* extent. Thus, the child asked to point out which tree has *more* or *less* apples on it will indicate the one with more, because it best exemplifies a tree with *some* [quantity, amount] apples on it. At the last stage, *more* and *less* will be used comparatively in their contrastive sense, and *less* is then differentiated from *more*.

These stages can be summarized using a feature notation where first of all the meaning attached to the words *more* and *less* can be represented as + Amount. Next, where extent is the best exemplar of amount, the child's entry for *more* has added to it the feature + Polar; but since the child knows that *less* also 'means' + Amount, he will assume it too contains the feature + Polar. Finally, in the last stage of the acquisition of these meanings, the child learns that *less* refers to the other end of the scale, and thus contrasts in meaning with *more*: *less* is − Polar.

Same and Different. In another study carried out with the same group of children, Donaldson and Wales (1970) looked at instructions which used the words *same* and *different* in a sorting task. The task involved either everyday objects such as toothbrushes, eggcups, etc. (I and II) or else formal geometric shapes (III and IV). Within each of these classes, form and color were either coincident (I and III) or not (II and IV). The experimenter in the task asked children to give him an object that was either 'the same in some way' or 'different in some way' from the item he picked. The results of this task are equally striking: The children nearly all picked objects that were the same both when asked to choose one that was the same and when asked to choose one that was different (see Table 8.11).

In effect, the word *different* was interpreted as though it meant *same*. Here, then, is another example of the meaning of one of a pair of antonyms being overextended to cover the other term. Both *same* and *different* meant 'same' to these children.

Dimensional Adjectives. Besides the pairs *more-less* and *same-different*, Donaldson and Wales (1970) also reported some preliminary studies of children's comprehension and use of several pairs of dimensional adjectives. The comprehension task involved the use of comparative and superlative forms. The adjective pairs were *big-wee* (small), *long-short*, *thick-thin*, *high-low*, *tall-short*, and *fat-thin*. (Except for the last pair − *fat-thin* − these dimensional adjectives consist of unmarked-marked pairs.)

In the comprehension task, the children had to point first to the

Table 8.11: Same and Different[a]

Instruction	Choice same	Choice different	'There isn't one'	No response	Total
Tasks I and III					
One that's the same	28	0	2	0	30
One that's different	25	5	0	0	30
Tasks II and IV					
One that's the same	28	0	2	0	30
One that's different	24	2	3	1	30

[a] Based on Donaldson and Wales (1970, p. 244).

biggest and to the wee-est of the objects, and then to one that was bigger or wee-er than a standard among the stimuli. They responded correctly more often when the adjective belonged to the positive-pole set (i.e., the unmarked adjectives together with *fat* according to the Donaldson and Wales definition) than when it belonged to the negative-pole set. This difference was much larger in the case of the superlative forms than in that of the comparative forms used in the instructions. Furthermore, from the data presented in Wales and Campbell (1970), it is clear that the children did much better overall when the superlative forms were derived from the pair *big-wee* (100% correct) than on any other pair of adjectives in the instructions (cf. Wales & Campbell, 1970, p. 379).

Although Wales and Campbell discuss the quasi-superordinate status of the pair *big-wee* in relation to the other pairs of dimensional adjectives (e.g., *big* can be substituted in most contexts for the positive-pole terms, and *wee* for the negative-pole ones), they do not explicitly relate these facts to the data they present. However, that there is a close relation between the pair *big-small* and the other dimensional adjectives can be seen both from their data and from some data I recently collected from 4-year-olds on opposites (E. Clark, 1972). In this study, I found that *big* was treated as a synonym for many of the unmarked adjectives, while *small* or *little* was substituted in the same way for the corresponding marked members of each adjective pair. For example, *big* was given as the opposite of *small, short, thin, low, young,* and *shallow* (ranked by frequency) while *small* or *little* were given as the opposite to *big, high, tall, long, wide, thick,* and *old* (ranked by frequency). These data support the interpretation that the meaning of *big* at first extends over the meanings of the unmarked dimensional terms like *long, high, tall, wide,* and only later does the child learn to apply the other dimensional adjectives to more specific areas of the semantic domain. *Small (little, wee)* likewise, for a time, acts as the cover term for the marked members of the dimensional adjective pairs.

In a production task[†] used to elicit the same dimensional terms, Wales and Campbell (1970) found that the adjective *big* was the most frequently used by the children (aged 3;5 to 4;1); this finding was repeated in the posttests on the same children (mean age of 4;8) where 46.2% of all the positive-pole adjective responses used the word *big*, versus an average of 25.2% for all the other positive-pole adjectives combined (see Wales & Campbell, 1970, p. 393). Combining the pretest and posttest data on the unmarked versus the marked adjectives used by these children (i.e., omitting the data on pairs like *fat-thin*), unmarked adjectives were used an average of 68.5 times, while marked adjectives were used only an average of 29.5 times. These data show that children have a strong preference for using unmarked rather than marked dimensional terms in their descriptions. One reason for this (that will require further research) could be that they do not yet understand many of the marked terms.

Another experiment designed to explore the child's knowledge of unmarked-marked pairs somewhat further was recently carried out by Tashiro (1971). Tashiro used a picture-identification task to look at the child's interpretations of the noncomparative forms of some pairs of dimensional adjectives. Overall, she found that the pair *big-little* was significantly better understood by the children (average age 3;4) than the other pairs of dimensional terms. Furthermore, the unmarked members of the pairs were significantly better understood than their marked counterparts. Tashiro argues that these results support an order of acquisition going from the more general concept to the more specific ones, i.e., from *big* to the more specific *tall, long, wide*, etc. The children in this study also appeared to comprehend *tall* better than *high*, and found *thick* and *wide* the most difficult of the unmarked dimensional adjectives used (see also E. Clark, 1972).

The data on dimensional terms can also be represented in terms of components of meaning known by the child at different stages in the acquisition process. *Big* is substituted for other unmarked dimensional terms because it is specified (like them) as + Dimension(3) and + Polar, but the child at this stage has not yet worked out how many dimensions are necessarily presupposed by the other terms such as *long* and *tall*. He has yet to differentiate between the dimensional properties of linearity, surface, and volume. While *big* simply applies to three dimensions, *tall* is more complex since it supposes that all three dimensions are present, and then talks about one specific dimension: + Vertical. The child appears to learn first the feature of dimensionality, then, later on, he specifies further what kind of dimensionality he is talking about; for instance, whether the dimension is + Vertical as in *tall* or *high*, or − Vertical as in *long, deep, far*, etc. (cf. further discussion of the properties of different dimensional terms in H. Clark, 1973). In addition to this, the child also has to learn that these pairs contrast in meaning: One member of the pair is unmarked and can be used nominally as well as contrastively, while the other, marked, adjective is only used contrastively. Where the children did much better on the unmarked terms than the marked, it looks as though they are still at the second stage, or else in transition to the third stage, where H. Clark (1970a) posited that both members of an adjective pair will be treated as if they refer simply to the 'most extent'. In other words, both are treated as if they contain the feature + Polar: they have not quite reached the stage where the unmarked adjective + Polar is in contrast with its opposite, which is eventually specified as − Polar.

To summarize, these data provide considerable evidence that the pair *big-small* is overextended to cover the domain of the other more specialized dimensional terms such as *tall-short, high-low, wide-narrow, long-short*, etc. Moreover, within each of these subordinate pairs of terms, there is a certain amount of evidence that the unmarked member of each pair is at first easier to understand than the marked member. It seems more than probable that further investigation with younger children might reveal an overextension phenomenon among these pairs of adjectives also that would be comparable to the data on *more-less* and *same-different*.

Before and After. Lastly, I shall present some of the data from E. Clark (1971a) on the acquisition of the meanings of the relational conjunctions *before* and *after*. Unlike many of the terms studied by Donaldson and Wales (1970), the pair *before* and *after* are not unmarked and marked, respectively, by linguistic criteria, but can be characterized as positive and negative (cf. E. Clark, 1971a). In this study, I used both an elicitation task designed to find out when children would spontaneously use the words *before* and *after* to encode temporal relations, and a comprehension task to find out what they understood of the meaning of the two words at different stages in the acquisition process.

After an analysis by age of the results, the children were sorted into groups representing different stages on the basis of the error pattern in their data (see Table 8.12). At the first stage in the comprehension task, children did not understand either word and simply used a strategy based on order of mention: The event mentioned first was treated as the first event in the sequence. Therefore instructions with a *before*-clause in initial position ($before_1$) and with an *after*-clause in second position ($after_2$) were consistently wrong. At Stage II, *before* was generally correct;

Table 8.12: Percentage Errors by Comprehension Stage for Each Construction (E. Clark, 1971a)

Comprehension stage	N^a	$Before_1$	$Before_2$	$After_1$	$After_2$
I	21	80	4	10	83
IIa	7	4	4	0	89
IIb	3	25	8	75	92
III	8	9	0	0	6

[a] One *S* from the youngest age-group was unclassifiable.

after in IIa was still dealt with by using an order-of-mention strategy, but in IIb, the word *after* produced a completely different error pattern. Both *after_2* and *after_3* produced errors significantly above chance showing that *before* had been overextended to cover *after* as well.

Further evidence that Stage IIb involved overextension of the meaning of *before* comes from the production task used in the same study. Children were asked either (a) 'When did [Event 1] happen?' or (b) 'When did [Event 2] happen?' For adults, appropriate answers would be 'Before [Event 2]' and 'After [Event 1]', respectively. Several of the children in the transitional answer stage used the word *before* quite appropriately in answer to *when-1* questions, but evinced a lot of hesitation and even used the word *before* when they tried to answer *when-2* questions. The transitional answer stage in the production task was highly correlated with Stage II of the comprehension task.

The interpretation of these data given in E. Clark (1971a) was that at this stage, the meaning of *before* was in fact extended to cover *after*. In other words, children interpreted *before* correctly, and treated *after* as if it meant the same thing as *before*. At Stage III, the two words have been correctly recognized as being opposite, rather than synonymous, in meaning.

The order of acquisition can be represented in terms of the semantic features added to the entries of temporal words, as follows: First of all, the child learns whether or not a word refers to time: + Time.[6] The first temporal words used spontaneously by the child have, in addition, the characteristic of referring to events that are cotemporaneous with the speech act or with the event being described, and can therefore be specified as + Time, + Simultaneous. Only after this stage does the child learn that there are words that refer to nonsimultaneous events, i.e., to events in sequence: These words can be described as − Simultaneous. However, when two or more events occur in sequence, the order (which came first?)

has to be specified. To begin with, — Simultaneous is always interpreted as + Prior. Thus the child at this stage will interpret *before* correctly, but if he has realized that *after* is also + Time and — Simultaneous, he will misinterpret it since — Simultaneous is further specified simply as + Prior. It is only later on that the feature — Prior is acquired (E. Clark, 1971a). The same sequence of acquisition for *before* and *after* (*avant que, après que*) was observed by Ferreiro (1971) in her research with French-speaking Swiss children.

The data on *before* and *after* look very similar to the *more-less* data and the *same-different* data reported in Donaldson and Wales (1970). This kind of overextension, then, appears to be a fairly widespread phenomenon in the acquisition of several different kinds of relational terms. What all these terms have in common is (a) they occur in pairs that are closely related in meaning, and (b) the term that is overextended always appears to be the unmarked member of the pair in the case of dimensional adjectives or else the one that is positive in some sense. Furthermore, (c) it is the meaning of the term that is overextended that is acquired first by the child.

Verbs and Complex Nouns

The third type of overextension that will be presented is also less noticeable than the first type, and is generally observed only in contexts similar to those discussed in connection with relational terms: where the child makes a mistake in carrying out instructions that use certain verbs, or else where he fails to give adequate definitions of certain complex relational nouns.

The data come mainly from two studies, the first, by C. Chomsky (1969), concerned with the acquisition of knowledge about the complements taken by certain verbs — this work has since been replicated by Kessel (1970); and the second, by Piaget (1928), concerned with the child's ability to give definitions of complex relational nouns. The children studied by C. Chomsky ranged in age from 5;0 to 10;0, while Piaget's subjects were between 5;0 and 12;0 years old. The children in these studies, then, are considerably older than those who used the first two types of overextension.

Ask and Tell. C. Chomsky (1969) studied children's comprehension of the English verbs *promise, ask* and *tell*, used with various complement structures. Misunderstandings among the younger children (who usually assigned the wrong NP as the subject of the complement verb) were attributed to a lack of syntactic knowledge on the children's part. However, in the present paper, an interpretation of the *ask* and *tell* data will be offered that takes a semantic point of view rather than a syntactic one (cf. also E. Clark, 1971b).

It was C. Chomsky's general finding that children under the age of 8;0 years consistently interpreted the verb *ask* as if it meant *tell*. For example, in response to an instruction like:

(a)   Tell X what to feed the doll.

the child will answer quite correctly with:

(a)   A banana.

However, when given instead the instruction:

(b)   Ask X what to feed the doll.

the child does *not* ask a question of the other child present, but instead simply *tells* him:

(b)   A banana.

A rather more extended dialogue from the many protocols that C. Chomsky quotes took the following form:

E:	Ask Linda what time it is.
BARBARA:	I don't know.
E:	Ask Linda her last name.
BARBARA:	La Croix.
E:	Ask Linda her teacher's name.
BARBARA:	Miss Turner.
E:	Now I want you to tell Linda some things. Tell Linda how many pencils there are.
BARBARA:	Three.
E:	And tell Linda what color this crayon is.
BARBARA:	Yellow.
E:	And ask Linda what's in this box.
BARBARA:	I don't know.
E:	Could you ask Linda? Maybe Linda knows.
BARBARA:	Do you, Linda?
LINDA:	No.

[From the protocol for Barbara, aged 5;3, Chomsky, 1969, p. 63f.]

C. Chomsky used several different forms of complement with both *ask* and *tell*. These are shown under the heading 'Sentence form' in Table 8.13, which summarizes the interpretations made of *ask* in the different constructions. The children fell into five different groups (Stages I-V) on the basis of their interpretations of *ask*. Their interpretations of all the instructions containing *tell* were always correct at all age-levels. Furthermore, the errors on *ask* (except for (3) in Stage IV) were all the result of interpreting *ask* as though it meant the same thing as *tell*. This can be seen very clearly in the protocol quoted above in which the 5-year-old persistently treated *ask* as *tell*, responding to all the experimenter's instructions accordingly.

Table 8.13: Ask and Tell[a]

	Interpretation Stage				
Sentence form	I	II	III	IV	V
(1) Ask x what time it is	tell	ask	ask	ask	ask
(2) Ask x his last name	tell	tell	ask	ask	ask
(3) Ask x what to feed the doll	tell	tell	tell	ask[b]	ask
(1') Tell x what time it is	tell	tell	tell	tell	tell
(2') Tell x your last name	tell	tell	tell	tell	tell
(3') Tell x what to feed the doll	tell	tell	tell	tell	tell

a   Based on C. Chomsky (1969)
b   *Ask* is interpreted as a question, but the wrong subject is assigned to the complement verb.
    What are *you* going to feed the doll?
instead of:
    What should *I* feed the doll?

If *tell* is interpreted in the imperative contexts given in Table 8.13 as meaning roughly something like 'I order you — you say to x — complement sentence', we can contrast it with the related analysis of *ask*: 'I order you — you say to x — you request x — x say to you — complement sentence'. This analysis contains the added information that this is a question that will need an answer, and not simply an assertion. From this rough performative analysis, it is clear that *ask* and *tell* overlap in meaning, but *ask* has some additional properties that are not found in *tell*. The meaning of *ask* involves learning the request feature and also the allocation of roles: The third person (*x*) and not the initial addressee is to supply the answer. One possible semantic interpretation of C. Chomsky's results, therefore, is that the meaning of *tell* is used for *ask* until the child learns the rest of the semantic information about the verb *ask* which will differentiate it in meaning from *tell*. This, then, is an instance of the synonymy form of overextension.

Brother and Sister. In *Judgment and Reasoning in the Child* (1928), Piaget describes a series of investigations that he undertook on the child's conceptions of various complex relational nouns like *brother* (or *sister*), *family, friend,* and *country.* His work on *brother* and *sister* has since been replicated with English-speaking children (Danziger, 1957; Elkind, 1962), and one of the replications found the same kind of results with three other kinship terms, viz., *daughter, uncle,* and *cousin.* The technique used in all these studies was to ask the children for definitions (e.g., 'What is a brother?'), and then to examine the difference between the definitions given at the various stages of conceptual development.

Piaget found that the definitions could be divided into three main classes: first, those that simply defined a brother as a boy (and a sister as a girl); at the second stage, the child would recognize that there had to be more than one child in the family, but he still did not realize that each sibling was a brother (or sister, according to sex) and would insist that only one of two siblings was a brother. At the third stage (rarely achieved before the age of 9;0), the child would recognize that terms like *brother* and *sister* are in fact reciprocal, so that if one has a brother, one is either a brother or a sister.

At the earliest stage, Piaget (1928) found that the words *brother* and *boy, sister* and *girl* are treated as synonyms:

(1)   Lo [aged 5;0)
      — What is a sister?
      — *A sister is a girl you know.*
      — Are all the girls you know sisters?
      — *Yes, and all the boys are brothers.*

(2)   Kan [aged 7;6)
      — What's a brother?
      — *It's a boy.*
      — Are all boys brothers?
      — *Yes.*

— Is your father a brother?
— *No, because he's a man.*

(3) Sob [aged 7;0]
— Is your father a brother?
— *Yes, when he was little.*
— Why was your father a brother?
— *Because he was a boy.* [pp. 104f]

From the examples (2) and (3), it can be seen that the first definitions of *brother* may exclude adults. Some of the children, though, simply defined *brother* on the basis of sex with no age constraints.

At the next stage, the children recognize that there have to be other children in the family;

(4) So [aged 8;0 — an only child, not sure if he himself is a brother]
— *A brother is when someone has a child, well the child who comes next is a brother.*

(5) Hal [aged 9;0]
— What's a brother?
— *When there's a boy and another boy, when there are two of them.*
— Has your father got a brother?
— *Yes.*
— Why?
— *Because he was born second.*
— Then what is a brother?
— *It is the second brother that comes.*
— Then the first one is not a brother?
— *Oh no, the second one that comes is called brother.* [p. 105]

Despite the recognition of the need for two children, the term *brother* is still restricted in that there is no reciprocal sense attached to it: It appears to apply only to the second child (or occasionally only to the first if the child being questioned had an older brother), not to both of them.

Finally, children realize that *brother*, besides involving sex and other siblings, defines a reciprocal relationship among siblings:

(6) Bern [aged 10;0]
— *A brother is a relation, one brother to another.* [p. 106]

At the first stage, then, *brother* and *boy* (like *ask* and *tell*) are treated as synonyms. The lexical entries for *brother* and *boy*, then, could both be represented as:

(7)
$$\begin{bmatrix} + \text{Male} \\ - \text{Adult} \end{bmatrix}$$

As the child gets older, he adds to the lexical entry more specific features which begin to differentiate the meaning of *brother* from that of *boy*. One of the first signs of this separation is the recognition that adults may also be brothers. The next feature of meaning that is added to *brother* can be characterized as *requires sibling*. In a feature notation, the entry for *brother* is now the following:

(8)
$$\begin{bmatrix} + \text{Male} \\ \pm \text{Adult} \\ + \text{Sibling} \end{bmatrix}$$

The word *brother* still does not, for the child, designate a reciprocal relationship. It is at this stage that he will claim that only one of two boys in a family is a brother, or only the smallest child is a brother, and so on. Then, at the last stage, the child adds to the meaning of the word *brother* the idea of reciprocity:

(9)
$$\begin{bmatrix} + \text{Male} \\ \pm \text{Adult} \\ + \text{Sibling} \\ + \text{Reciprocal} \end{bmatrix}$$

Piaget described this process as the development of the 'concept' of *brother*. I have argued, though, from a different point of view that it is the addition of the specific semantic features to the meaning of the word *brother* that eventually allows the child to differentiate between *boy* and *brother*.

Summary

In presenting the data from three different areas of research in language acquisition, I have shown that what the data have in common is that they are the result of some form of overextension, when overextension entails that the lexical entry for the meaning of a word in the child's vocabulary is incomplete. After the first stages of language acquisition, the overextensions that are made are fairly inconspicuous, and usually go by unnoticed.

The child's early referential overextensions show, first, that children use certain kinds of features criterially; second, these criterial features are derived from the child's percepts of objects and events; thirdly, the domain of the overextension of a word can be used to infer which features are being used. Last, the narrowing-down process toward the end of this period also provides some information about the features that the child is using by the constraints that are placed on the use of the new words that help break up a semantic domain. The more restricted use of new words suggests that the child has more detailed entries for these lexical items. As a result, more criteria have to be met before a word can be applied to an object or situation.

In the second kind of overextension discussed, the children were far more advanced linguistically. They no longer used noticeable overextensions, but where two words were very closely related, they confused their meanings. Of the relational terms that have been studied, the tendency was to use the meaning of the unmarked term (or where marking criteria did not apply, the term that was positive) to cover both words in the pair, e.g., *more-less, same-different, before-after*. The marked term, moreover, was wrongly interpreted, as if it meant the same thing as its unmarked counterpart. It was not until the children learned the more specific semantic feature(s) that closely related words became differentiated. Again, the children's errors (this time in interpretation rather than in spontaneous production of speech) are a good guide to which features they did know, and which they did not.

In the data from the pairs of dimensional terms, there was also evidence that the child knew that they were all related to each other as a set; the proof of this comes from his use of *big* and *small* as cover terms for unmarked and marked dimensional adjectives respectively. This usage also suggests that the meanings of the other adjectives had not yet been sufficiently fully specified for the child to differentiate in any detail between, for example, *big* and *tall*. The meaning of *big* is simply extended to cover the other terms because the child's lexical entries for them do not yet contain all the features needed to differentiate them from *big* (cf. further E. Clark, 1972).

The third kind of overextension described is somewhat similar to the second. The child is again in the position of having some incomplete lexical entries that lead him to treat some words synonymously (*tell-ask, boy-brother*) until he learns some of the other features that have to be added to the lexical entry for one of the words in order to differentiate their meanings. Again, the child's errors of interpretation or his inability to give adequate definitions allow one to infer what he does know about the meaning of a word and what remains for him to learn.

Sources of Semantic Features

In this section, I shall consider what we know about the kinds of semantic features that could be said to have been acquired and used by the child on the basis of the data presented. First, the features used in the early stages of semantic acquisition, as well as some used later, will be related to features in perceptual development. Then I shall touch on the part played later on by non-percept-based features, features that are derived from the social or cultural conventions of the group using a particular language.

Early Features – A Perceptual Basis?

One assumption of the present hypothesis is that the earliest semantic features probably belong to the universal set of semantic primitives. However, there is no way yet of knowing which features are primitive and which are not. Can the problem be approached from another direction? The primitives are assumed to be universal precisely because they derive from the human organism's interpretation of his perceptions and cognitions. Therefore, it is possible that the development of perception in infants might provide some clues about the kinds of features that might underlie early semantic features.

Since learning to attach meanings to words involves the interpretation and encoding of perceptual data, we might expect to find an analogous sequence of development in perception: the use of single criterial features followed later by the use of configurations of features. Gibson (1969) points out that the young infant at first singles out individual areas (single features) for attention when looking at objects: He focuses on high contrast edges, vertices, spots and moving parts. This initial attention to single features then develops into the use of what Gibson (1969) calls 'bundles of features': 'Distinctive features develop later out of these properties as contrasts are discovered . . . the specificity of discrimination is thereby increased. *Gestalten* or higher order structured units develop still later, as bundles of features are processed with greater simultaneity and relations between features are registered as units of structure [p. 345].'

In illustration of this progression within perceptual development, one can consider the infant's stages in coming to recognize human faces. At the earliest stage, one can elicit from the infant a smiling response to dots or lines; later he will require the dots to appear within some contour: Thus, eyes will have to appear within a given setting (the top half of the face). Soon after this, he begins to require there to be a mouth present, preferably in movement, and this has to be combined with eyes and facial contour. By the age of 5 months, the infant can distinguish between realistic heads and unrealistic ones. Gibson states further: 'Development seems to proceed from simple contours to differentiated features to structured relations or patterns to unique patterns of individual faces [p. 347].' This account of the development of perception going from attention to individual features to attention to configurations or structured relations between features is remarkably similar to what appears to go on in the use of early semantic features that are attached to a word. It is possible that the use of perceptual features that are then interpreted as the meaning of a word thus follow a developmental pattern for perception. To begin with, only single features are interpreted and put down as the meaning for a word, but later on, configurations of perceptual features are used as a structured whole to code (some of) the word's meaning.

In using perceptual information about objects, there also seem to be certain preferences among children: Some perceptual attributes are dominant. Ricciuti (1963), for example, found that contour dominated details of objects in a similarity judgment task. He asked children between the ages of 3;0 and 8;0 years to tell him which object was most similar to a standard where the set of objects offered to the child differed in contour (shape) or in detail (the squares and circles had ears or dots added to them). At all age-levels, the children most often chose the item that was similar in contour rather than in any detail. As second choices made clear, however, they did perceive the detail, but the contour was given priority in classifying objects as similar. This tendency to rely on contour or shape may account for shape being the most frequent basis for overextensions.

Since the different classes of overextensions are most easily classified on the basis of certain perceptual features (movement, shape, sound, size, taste, and texture), it should hardly be surprising that the use of perceptually derived features should display some of the characteristics found in the development of perception itself. While the studies reported in Gibson on the use of single (global) features prior to the use of bundles of features or combinations of features were of infants less than a year old, it is quite possible that this progression is recapitulated when the child has to begin interpreting his perceptual input in order to use it in attaching a meaning to a word. The child therefore begins by using a single general feature, such as shape or contour, and considers that to be the meaning of some term. As he becomes compelled to differentiate more meanings, he can no longer simply use a single perceptual feature: He must begin to use more than one and eventually will encode the information from a bundle or combination of features (whose relations to each other are structured) and use this in attaching meaning to lexical items.

In conclusion, the data on the child's first use of components of meaning in the referential uses of words suggest very strongly that the earliest semantic features could be derived directly from the interpreted bundles or combinations of perceptual features. Thus, the perceptual features themselves may well belong to the set of universal semantic primitives postulated by Bierwisch (1967, 1970a). While a great deal of research is obviously needed before we can make such claims conclusive, what data we have clearly point in that direction.

Features Used in Relational Terms I

The earliest semantic features used by the child appear to be derived mainly from the perceptual information that he has about his surroundings. While most of the instances reported in the literature (cf. Tables 8.1 to 8.6) involved the learning of words used to name things, I shall argue in this section that the meanings of relational terms may also be derived from their perceptual features. The child has to learn which properties of objects such terms describe, and what the conditions are for the use of particular relational words. In the case of the dimensional adjectives studied by Donaldson and Wales (1970), the conditions of use include, at the very least, learning which adjectives name the properties of objects and which name the relations between objects in space. The set of dimensional adjectives, in fact, belongs to a larger set of terms that is used to describe spatial relations in English. Learning the meanings of these terms involves learning which words talk about reference points, which about lines, and which about planes, i.e. one-, two-, and three-dimensional spaces, respectively; and furthermore which words deal with extent, with position, and with directionality. The child has also to make the further distinction between the properties of space and the intrinsic properties of objects used as reference points, e.g., the front and back of a tree (Fillmore, 1971) versus the front and back of a house (Leech, 1970; Teller, 1969).

Of the pairs of adjectives examined, *big-wee/small* has very few constraints on its application: it can be used in the description of any three-dimensional object. The pairs *tall-short* and *high-low* (extension and position), on the other hand, refer to one particular dimension (verticality). At the same time, one of the conditions for using these two adjective pairs is that the objects be three-dimensional. With the exception of *big-wee*, each pair of unmarked-marked terms applies to one specific dimension, e.g., *long-short, high-low*, etc. Measurement in the positive direction along the dimension is named by the unmarked term which also serves as the name of the dimension, e.g., *long-length, high-height*, etc. The marked terms, such as *short* or *low,* though, measure in a negative direction along the dimension. Each dimension is measured from a zero point (or primary reference point) so the positive direction goes away from the zero point.[7] In addition, each dimension may have several secondary reference points or standards against which an object is compared. The marked terms necessarily involve such a standard, and measure from this standard back to the zero point, in the negative direction along the dimension (for a more detailed discussion of these properties, cf. H. Clark, 1973).

In the acquisition of these terms, the data show that the pair *big-wee/small* is the best understood and the most used by children aged about 3½ years old. *Big-small* is the pair of terms that is the most general in meaning, referring simply to overall size, and it has the fewest conditions to fulfill for its use. It also appears to act as a cover term for the more specific pairs of dimensional adjectives that refer to particular dimensions.

Within the pairs of adjectives, there were decided asymmetries in their acquisition by children: The unmarked, positive terms such as *long* or *high* were understood better and used more than the corresponding marked, negative terms such as *short* or *low.* Is there any perceptual basis for these asymmetries (unmarked/positive adjectives versus marked/negative ones) found in the acquisition of dimensional adjectives? In fact, the structure of the human organism's perceptual apparatus does possess certain asymmetries in terms of the perceptual fields available. If the earth's surface is taken as a natural (horizontal) plane with gravity as a reference direction (vertical), then the human being standing upright has a symmetrical left-right field of vision (the body is symmetrical about its left-right axis), but has an asymmetrical front-back perceptual field: Those things in front are visible, those behind are not; and he also has an up-down asymmetry: Those things on or above the earth's surface are visible, but those below are (normally) out of sight. Thus, as H. Clark (1973) has argued, the asymmetries among the pairs of terms used to describe spatial relations in English appear to reflect the asymmetries present in the perceptual capacities of the human organism (cf. also Bierwisch, 1967; Teller, 1969), e.g., *up* is positive, *down* negative; *in front* is positive, *behind* negative, etc., where *positive* is roughly equivalent to 'within the field of vision' and *negative* to 'not within the field of vision'. However, what have been called negative terms here may simply involve reversal of direction, e.g., among dimensional adjectives such as *tall-short*, or among prepositional pairs such as *in-out* or *on-off*.

These asymmetries in the description of space apply also to the description of time in English where many temporal relations have a spatial model underlying them. This is the reason why *before* (parallel to *in front of*) may be called positive and *after* (parallel to *behind* or *in back of*) negative. Moreover, the same asymmetry, positive before negative, was found in the acquisition of the meanings of *before* and *after* as was found in the acquisition of dimensional adjective pairs in which the unmarked, positive members of the pairs were acquired before the marked, negative members.

One might argue, therefore, on the basis of the early data and of these data on relational terms that perceptual information is all that need be available in order for the child to be able to set up appropriate lexical entries for the vocabulary of his language. This view, though, would be an over-simplification for it ignores what have variously been called the functional, social, or cultural factors in the determination of word meanings. In addition to encoding perceived characteristics of an object, the meaning of the word used to name it may require some further specification of its function or culturally determined role. For example, on the basis of perceptual information, a child would see no reason to distinguish between a *chair* and a *throne*. The difference between them is simply a functional or cultural one within some societies that is defined by how the object is used in the social context, i.e., who sits there. This kind of culturally derived information will be called knowledge about roles. While the child begins by using perceptual information in attaching meanings to words, he eventually has to add to his perceptual information details about the roles that certain words name or assign to participants in particular contexts.

Features Used in Relational Terms II

For the data on certain verbs (C. Chomsky, 1969) and on some kinship terms (Piaget, 1928), both perceptually based information and information about roles have to be taken into account in studying the acquisition of their meanings by children. One of the things that the child has to learn about these more complex relational terms is which roles are implied and assigned by their use. As an example, let us take another verb that was studied by C. Chomsky (1969), the verb *promise*. At first, the child appears to treat *promise* as if it belongs to the class that includes *tell, say, assert, state*, etc., but in addition the word *promise* involves some notion of obligation.[8] In Chomsky's experiment, this knowledge alone would be enough to give the appearance of being able to define what a promise was, without actually knowing which roles it assigned; i.e., without yet understanding that the person who does the promising — whether in a first-person context (*I promise you that x*), or in a second- or third-person context — is always the one who is meant to carry out the promised action (E. Clark, 1971b). The roles assigned by *promise* are not understood correctly until about age 8;0 or 9;0. Learning what a verb like *promise* means necessitates learning which roles the verb assigns to the speaker and/or addressee, and which roles the speaker may expect to see carried out by a third person.

In the same way, the child has to learn which roles are assigned to the addressee by the verbs *ask* and *tell*. Within the imperative context of the experiments, the child (who was always the addressee) had to know whether he was to take the role of asserting something to a third person present in the room (*tell*), or whether he was to put a question to that third person (*ask*). These roles cannot be easily derived from the interpretation of the perceptual characteristics of the situation in which the child observes the use of such words. The child has to observe not only the contexts but further to infer from the consequences (reactions to the use of these words) exactly what kinds of roles exist and which roles are assigned to speaker and/or addressee by the use of a particular word. The exact interpretation of these roles is often dependent on the social structure and conventions of the speech community in which the child grows up.

The other data for which the acquisition of knowledge about roles is essential come from the work on the acquisition of the meanings of some kinship terms. Societies vary widely on the definitions given to different terms and on the number of terms used. The legal definitions depend in turn on the social organization, while biological factors are not always obvious and are not necessarily integrated into the social and legal systems. The child, therefore, has to learn many new social facts about the roles played by different people before he can find out what a particular kinship relation means. If we take the term studied in most detail by Piaget, we find that the child's first meaning for the word *brother* could very easily be said to be based on perceptually derived information, e.g., 'Brothers are boys', 'Brothers are little boys', and so on. However, the child also makes incorrect inferences from these facts, for example that the converse holds: 'All boys are brothers' or 'Only small boys are brothers'. At a later stage, the child adds further components to the meaning of the word, principally that there have to be at least two children in order for there to be a *brother* (although only one of them is a brother, even where the children are both male). This too, it can be claimed, is an observable fact from which the child could make appropriate inferences about the meaning of *brother*. About this time, some children begin to give social or functional definitions too: 'He's someone who lives with you'. Soon after this, the child learns that *brother* involves a reciprocal relationship. However, it is not clear whether he knows exactly what the role named *brother* consists of within the family structure, since he does not give adult definitions yet of the word *family* (Piaget, 1928). At this stage, his definitions are functional and perceptually derived: A *family* is 'people who live together in the same house.' The child has still to learn what all the different roles are, and how they are related to each other within the kinship system. Although Piaget's study was limited to the study of the terms *brother* and *sister*, with a little work on the definition of *family*, Danziger's (1957) study was somewhat more extensive. In his work also, the first meanings for kinship terms were those things that are perceptually derived (e.g., sex- and age-based characteristics), followed later by the addition of social or functional factors (living in the same house, eating together, etc.). Thus, acquiring the full (adult) meaning of the set of kinship terms within a language necessarily involves knowledge of the social structure as well as of the perceived attributes of the people who can appropriately be called *brother* or *sister*.

To summarize, the first semantic features used by the child appear to be based on his perceptions of the world. To this kind of semantic feature are later added those features of meaning that are contributed by social or functional factors within the cultural context. These social factors have been described in terms of the different roles that may be named or assigned to participants in some situation. While some roles are assigned on a temporary basis (e.g., by verbs like *promise* or *ask*), others are more permanent in character (e.g., *brother, father*).

The analysis of the kinds of meaning component or feature that knowledge of roles adds to the lexical entry for individual words has necessarily been less detailed than the discussion of semantic features derived from perceptual information. In mitigation, I can only report that very little is yet known about what I have called roles, either in terms of their semantic structure or in terms of the acquisition of knowledge about them by children learning their first language.

Conclusions

The present paper has attempted to characterize some of the knowledge that one has to have about a word in order to use it appropriately. In considering such knowledge from the developmental point of view, I have shown that one has to begin by finding out what it is that the child knows about the meaning of a word, and how this knowledge changes during the language acquisition process. The Semantic Feature Hypothesis assumed that the meanings of words are made up of features or components of meaning, and proposed that children learn word meanings gradually by adding more and more features to their lexical entries. This hypothesis was derived originally from a consideration of some of the diary data (E. Clark, 1971c). In the present paper, the general predictions made by this theory have been shown to be remarkably consistent with data from several different sources in the literature on children's language.

Nonetheless, the theory contains a number of lacunae that future work will have to fill. For example, there is no account of the internal structure (or lack of it) in the child's earliest lexical entries. Is the child's choice of the first semantic feature(s) attached to a word, over and above the perceptual basis, an arbitrary one or not? Another issue that has not been dealt with is the structuring or restructuring of the child's lexical entries as a result of language-particular constraints. For example, there are a number of selectional restrictions which in many languages are governed by the presence of features such as ± Animate or ± Human: At what point does the child pull these features out from among the other percept-based features and accord them special status? Furthermore, data on the internal organization of entries in the adult lexicon suggest that the features are arranged in much the same way for all speakers of a language (cf. the discussion of word-association data in H. Clark, 1970b): When does the child adopt this adult form of lexical organization? Yet another issue that will require further elucidation is the order of acquisition of semantic features. Where the entries appear to be hierarchically structured, children learn the most general features first and then the more specific ones (e.g., E. Clark, 1971a; Piaget, 1928). But what is the order of acquisition for those lexical entries that do not contain hierarchically related features?

These constitute only a few of the questions that remain to be answered within the framework of the present theory, and indeed within the framework of any developmental theory about the acquisition of semantic knowledge. Thus, although the data discussed in this paper do support the Semantic Feature Hypothesis, I want to point out that the hypothesis itself still needs further elaboration and testing.

In conclusion, I have tried to show that we cannot take for granted what children say. If we are to study language acquisition properly, then we cannot ignore semantics, for it is essential to know what the child means by what he says, and to know how he understands what he hears. One of the most basic steps the child has to take in acquiring his first language is to attach meaning to words, and therefore semantics is central to the study of language development. Furthermore, the acquisition of semantic knowledge needs to be better studied in relation to the development of the child's perceptual and cognitive abilities. Language, after all, is what provides the child with a means of encoding and communicating his percepts and thoughts about the world around him.

Notes

1.   This research was supported in part by NSF Grant GS-1880 to the Language Universals Project, Stanford University, and in part by NSF Grant GS-30040 to the author.

2.   I should like to thank H. Clark for drawing my attention to some of the data used to support the arguments in this paper, as well as for making comments on earlier versions of the manuscript.

3.   A number of studies in the literature have pointed out that proper names tend to be extremely stable even in the earliest stages of language acquisition. They are among the first words to have specific, identifiable referents and, according to several reports, are among the first words learned by the child (Perez, 1892, p. 299; Sully, 1896, p. 161). The stability of such words in the child's repertoire is further attested by Bloch (1921), Decroly (n.d.), Guillaume (1927b), and more recently by Leopold (1949a). Guillaume (1927b) makes the further claim that proper names are among the first words the child seems to segment out and recognize in the flow of adult conversations.

Both Bloch (1921) and Leopold (1949a), though, specifically exclude the terms *mama* and *papa* from the category of proper names since they exhibit none of the stable usage noted for proper names elsewhere in the child's early speech. In the earliest uses, *mama* (and often *papa* and *baba* too, cf. Jakobson, 1962) is simply a general expression of need based on hunger, discomfort or fright. This is reported, for instance, by Bloch (1921, p. 706), Grégoire (1937), Guillaume (1927b), Leopold (1949a), Lindner (1882), Moore (1896, p. 122), Nice (1925, p. 107), Preyer (1889), Scupin and Scupin (1907), and Smoczynski (1955). At the next stage, *papa* seems to become more specialized as the male parent, but *mama* continues to refer to needs in general. Leopold (1948) reports that shortly after this, his daughter used *papa* for all men for a period lasting about a month, and then narrowed the range of application to a single referent. The *mama-papa* forms and the confusions in their use are cited in most studies (cf. references above). *Mama* continues to be used for needs and for the provider of food (male or female) for some time (cf. Grégoire, 1937, pp. 86f.). On the other hand, a few reports claim proper name status for *mama* and *papa* also, e.g., Pavlovitch, 1920. In the few instances where a proper name is extended by the child, he appears to have assumed that the word was in fact a class name (Leopold, 1949a).

4.   This switching of features is reminiscent of Vygotsky's (1962) discussion of the phenomenon he called *chaining*, in which young children would move from the use of one attribute to another when asked to group different objects.

5.   In classifying the overextensions as examples of the use of certain classes of criterial features, I have emphasized the perceptual source of the phenomenon of overextension. This emphasis contrasts with the so-called functional viewpoint, first put forward by Dewey (1894), and more recently taken by by Lewis (1957), which posits that the extension of any term to an inappropriate referent occurs only because the child sees their potential equivalence of function. The sort of examples cited are the postulated extension of the word *ball* to the moon because the child knows that if the moon were within reach, it could be thrown like a ball! However,

the perceptually based explanation of such an extension is rather more satisfactory for the earliest stages since it has simply to assume that the child has the ability to use his eyes to match objects on the basis of something like shape; he does not have to know anything about the uses of objects in order to overextend items of vocabulary. The diary literature as a whole supports a perceptual basis rather than a functional one for such early overextensions.

6.   In an analysis that takes account of the close relation between spatial and temporal terms in English, the feature represented as + Time would probably be better characterized as + Location, − Place. The corresponding spatial terms would belong to the hierarchy dominated by + Location, + Place. The validity of this characterization is borne out by some of the responses to *when* questions given by children aged about 3;0 years. They treated *when* as if it meant *where*, i.e., as a question about + Location, + Place rather than as about + Location, − Place, given answers like 'just here' or 'here' (E. Clark, 1971a).

7.   The analysis and the terms 'primary and secondary reference points' are borrowed from H. Clark (1973).

8.   D.I. Slobin (personal communication) reports that a child of 4;6 years used *promise* in the following context: Early on in the day she had told her friend to come over to her house. Then later, when the friend did not come, she said: 'I promised that Amy would come over but she didn't.' This example (which is supported by others from the same source) clearly shows that knowledge of the role assigned by the word *promise* has not yet been acquired.

References

Ament, W. *Die Entwicklung von Sprechen und Denken beim Kinde.* Leipzig: Barth, 1899.

Anglin, J.M. *The growth of word meaning.* Cambridge, Massachusetts: MIT Press, 1970.

Bierwisch, M. Some semantic universals of German adjectivals. *Foundations of Language*, 1967, 3, 1-36.

Bierwisch, M. On certain problems of semantic representations. *Foundations of Language*, 1969, 5, 153-84.

Bierwisch, M. Semantics. In J. Lyons (ed.), *New horizons in linguistics.* Penguin Books, 1970a.

Bierwisch, M. On classifying semantic features. In M. Bierwisch & K.E. Heidolph (eds.), *Progress in linguistics.* The Hague: Mouton, 1970b.

Bloch, O. Les premiers stades du langage de l'enfant. *Journal de Psychologie*, 1921, 18, 693-712.

Bloom, L. One word at a time – the use of single-word utterances before syntax. The Hague: Mouton, in press.

Bowerman, M.F. Learning to talk: A cross-linguistic comparison of early syntactic development, with special reference to Finnish. Unpublished doctoral dissertation, Harvard University, 1970.

Bowerman, M. Structural relationships in children's utterances: syntactic or semantic? In T.E. Moore (ed.), *Cognitive development and the acquisition of language.* London: Academic Press, 1973, pp. 197-213.

Brown, R.W. How shall a thing be called? *Psychological Review*, 1958, 65, 14-21.

Brown, R. *A first language.* Cambridge, Massachusetts: Harvard University Press, in press.

Chamberlain, A.F. & Chamberlain, J.C. Studies of a child. *Pedagogical Seminary*, 1904, 11, 264-91.

Chomsky, C.S. *The acquisition of syntax in children from 5 to 10.* Cambridge, Massachusetts: MIT Press, 1969.

Clark, E.V. On the acquisition of the meaning of 'before' and 'after'. *Journal of Verbal Learning and Verbal Behavior*, 1971, 10, 266-75, (a).

Clark, E.V. Review of C.S. Chomsky: 'The acquisition of syntax in children from 5 to 10.' *Language*, 1971, 47, 742-9, (b).

Clark, E.V. Semantic development in language acquisition. Paper presented at the Third Child Language Research Forum, Stanford University, March, 1971, (c).

Clark, E.V. On the child's acquisition of antonyms in two semantic fields. *Journal of Verbal Learning and Verbal Behavior*, 1972, 11, 750-8.

Clark, H.H. The primitive nature of children's relational concepts. In J.R. Hayes (ed.), *Cognition and the development of language*. New York: Wiley, 1970, (a).

Clark, H.H. Word associations and linguistic theory. In J. Lyons (ed.), *New horizons in linguistics*. London: Penguin Books, 1970, (b).

Clark, H.H. Space, time, semantics and the child. In T.E. Moore (ed.), *Cognitive development and the acquisition of language*. London: Academic Press, 1973, pp. 27-63.

Danziger, K. The child's understanding of kinship terms: A study in the development of relational concepts. *Journal of Genetic Psychology*, 1957, 91, 213-32.

Decroly, O. *Epreuves de compréhension, d'imitation et d'expression*. (Revu et complété par J. Jadot-Decroly & J.-E Segers) Bruxelles: Collection Ivoire, Centre National d'Education, n.d.

Dewey, J. The psychology of infant language. *Psychological Review*, 1894, 1, 63-6.

Donaldson, M., & Balfour, G. Less is more: A study of language comprehension in children. *British Journal of Psychology*, 1968, 59, 461-72.

Donaldson, M., & Wales, R.J. On the acquisition of some relational terms. In J.R. Hayes (ed.), *Cognition and the development of language*. New York: Wiley, 1970.

Elkind, D. Children's conceptions of brother and sister: Piaget replication study V. *Journal of Genetic Psychology*, 1962, 100, 129-36.

Ferreiro, E. *Les relations temporelles dans le langage de l'enfant*. Geneva: Droz, 1971.

Fillmore, C.J. Toward a theory of deixis. Paper presented at the Pacific Conference on Contrastive Linguistics and Language Universals, University of Hawaii, January, 1971.

Gibson, E.J. *Principles of perceptual learning and development*. New York: Appleton, 1969.

Greenberg, J.H. *Language universals*. The Hague: Mouton, 1966.

Grégoire, A. *L'apprentissage du langage*. Two vols. Paris: Droz, 1937, 1949.

Guillaume, P. Les débuts de la phrase dans le langage de l'enfant. *Journal de Psychologie*, 1927, 24, 1-25.

Idelberger, H. Hauptoproblemen der kindlichen Sprachentwicklung. *Zeitschrift fur padagogische Psychologie*, 1903, 5, 241-97.

Imedadze, N.V. K psikhologicheskoy prirode rannego dvuyazychiya. *Voprosy Psikhologii*, 1960, 6, 60-8.

Jakobson, R. Why "mama" and "papa"? In *Roman Jakobson: Selected writings*. The Hague: Mouton, 1962.

Katz, J.J., & Fodor, J.A. The structure of a semantic theory. *Language*, 1963, 39, 170-211.

Kenyereš, E. Les premiers mots de l'enfant. *Archives de Psychologie*, 1926, 20, 191-218.

Kessel, F.S. The role of syntax in children's comprehension from ages six to twelve. *Society for Research in Child Development Monographs*, 1970, 35, (6).

Lakoff, G. Global rules. *Language*, 1970, 46, 627-39, (a).

Lakoff, G. Linguistics and natural logic. *Synthèse*, 1970, 22, 151-272, (b).

Lakoff, G. On generative semantics. In D.D. Steinberg & L.S. Jakobovits (eds.),

Semantics. London: Cambridge University Press, 1971.

Leech, G. *Towards a semantic description of English*. Bloomington, Indiana: Indiana University Press, 1970.

Leopold, W.F. *Speech development of a bilingual child: A linguist's record*. Vol. 1. Vocabulary growth in the first two years. Vol. 2. Sound learning in the first two years. Vol. 3. Grammar and general problems in the first two years. Vol. 4. Diary from age two. Evanston, Illinois: Northwestern University Press, 1939, 1947, 1949a, 1949b.

Leopold, W.F. Semantic learning in infant language. *Word*, 1948, 4, 173-80.

Lewis, M.M. *Infant speech*. London: Routledge & Kegan, 1951.

Lewis, M.M. *How children learn to speak*. London: Harrap, 1957.

Lindner, G. Beobachtungen und Bermerkungen uber die Entwicklung der Sprache des Kindes. *Kosmos*, 1882, 6, 321-42, 430-41.

Lyons, J. *Introduction to theoretical linguistics*. London: Cambridge University. Press, 1968.

Luria, A.R., & Yudovich, F.I. *Speech and the development of mental processes in the child*. New York: Humanities, 1959.

McCawley, J.D. The role of semantics in grammar. In E. Bach & R.T. Harms (eds.), *Universals in linguistic theory*. New York: Holt, 1968.

McNeill, D. *The acquisition of language*. New York: Harper, 1970.

Moore, K.C. The mental development of a child. *Psychological Review, Monograph Supplements*, 1896, 1 (3).

Nice, M.M. A child who would not speak. *Pedagogical Seminary*, 1925, 32, 105-42.

Ohman, S. Theories of the 'linguistic field'. *Word*, 1953, 9, 123-34.

Pavlovitch, M. *Le langage enfantin: Acquisition du serbe et du français par un enfant serbe*. Paris: Champion, 1920.

Perez, B. *Les trois prèmieres années de l'enfant*. Paris: Alcan, 1892.

Piaget, J. *Judgment and reasoning in the child*. London: Routledge & Kegan, 1928.

Postal, P.M. Review article: André Martinet, 'Elements of general linguistics'. *Foundations of Language*, 1966, 2, 151-86.

Postal, P.M. The surface verb 'remind'. *Linguistic Inquiry*, 1970, 1, 37-120.

Preyer, W. *The mind of the child*. New York: Appleton, 1889.

Rasmussen, V. *Et barns dagbog*. Kovenhavn: Gyldendal, 1922.

Ricciuti, H.N. Geometric form and detail as determinants of comparative similarity judgements in young children. In *A basic research program on reading*. Final Report, Co-operative Research Project N. 639, U.S. Office of Education, 1963, pp. 1-48.

Scupin, E., & Scupin, G. *Bubis erste Kindheit: Ein Tagebuch*. Leipzig: Grieben, 1907.

Shvachkin, N. Kh. 'Razvitye fouematicheskogo vospriyatiya rechi v rannem vozraste' (Development of phonemic speech perception in early childhood). *Izv. Akad. Pedog. Nauk RSFSR*, [1948] 13, 101-32. (English translation by Elena Derbach in C.A. Ferguson & D.I. Slobin, *Child language acquisition: Readings*. New York: Holt, in press.)

Sinclair-de Zwart, H. *Acquisition du langage et développement de la pensée, soussystèmes linguistiques et opérations concrètes*. Paris: Dunod, 1967.

Slobin, D.I. Universals of grammatical development in children. In G.B. Flores d'Arcais & W.J.M. Levelt (eds.), *Advances in psycholinguistics*. New York: American Elsevier, 1970, pp. 174-84.

Slobin, D. Suggested universals in the ontogenesis of grammar. Paper presented at the Conference on Developmental Psycholinguistics, Buffalo, August, 1971.

Smoczynski, P. Przyswajanie przez dziecko podstaw systemu jezykowego. *Soceitas Scientiarum Lodziensis*, 1955, Section 1, No. 19.

Sully, J. *Studies of childhood*. New York: Appleton, 1896.

Taine, H. Acquisition of language by children. *Mind*, 1877, 2, 252-9.

Tashiro, L. On the acquisition of some non-comparative terms. Senior Honors Thesis, Stanford University, 1971.

Teller, P. Some discussion and extension of Manfred Bierwisch's work on German adjectivals, *Foundations of Language*, 1965, 5, 185-217.

Vygotsky, L.S. *Thought and language*. Cambridge, Massachusetts: MIT Press, 1962.

Wales, R.J., & Campbell R. On the development of comparison and the comparison of development. In G.B. Flores d'Arcais & W.J.M. Levelt (eds.), *Advances in psycholinguistics*. Amsterdam: North-Holland, 1970.

9 THE DEVELOPMENT OF CONVERSATION BETWEEN MOTHERS AND BABIES

Catherine Snow

Source: Excerpt from Catherine Snow, 'The development of conversation between mothers and babies', *J. Child Lang.*, Vol. 4 (1977), pp. 1-22.

Abstract[1]

The speech of two mothers to their infants at several points between three and eighteen months of age was analysed. Simplicity of the speech, as measured by MLU, was about the same at all ages, and none of the other features of the mothers' speech style showed any abrupt change at the time the children started to talk. The changes that did occur started much earlier, at about seven months. These findings are incompatible with the explanation that mothers speak simply and redundantly in response to cues of attention and comprehension from the child listener.

Conversational Model

What, then, is the explanation for these adjustments in the mothers' speech? And what changes occur in the mother-infant interaction at 5-7 months which could explain the changes in mothers' speech style which take place then? Answering these questions requires looking more specifically at the functional aspects of the maternal utterances, and especially at the nature of the interaction the mothers were engaging in with their babies. I suggest that the interactions between these mothers and babies can best be described as conversational in nature, and that the changes in the maternal speech result from the development of the baby's ability to take her turns in the conversation. In order to support this contention, I will cite some examples of interactional sequences that occurred between Ann and her mother (similar sequences from the transcripts of Mary — the other child in the study — and her mother could also be quoted) and analyse them using the conversational model presented by Sacks, Schegloff & Jefferson (1974).

The hypothesis that the mothers were using a conversational model in interacting with their children rests on two crucial assumptions: that they were trying to communicate specific information to the babies, and that they were receiving (or trying to receive) specific information from them. The conversational mode differs from other communicational modes precisely in that it is RECIPROCAL — information is exchanged between

235

the partners in both directions. It is thus of special interest that the mothers would choose this reciprocal system for interacting with babies still so young that their ability to communicate was very limited. If the mothers' only purpose was to keep the babies quiet and contented or attentive by talking to them, then they could have chosen any of several other modes of interaction — telling stories, singing songs, reciting poems, talking nonsense, thinking aloud. In fact, the mothers made almost no use of a monologue mode; even when they did sing songs or recite nursery rhymes they did so as part of a game in which the baby also played a role, e.g., the Ride-a-cock-horse game described by Bruner (1975). Essentially, all of the mothers' speech was related in content to the baby or the baby's activities and direction of attention, and much of it was directed towards eliciting responses from the baby. It is for these reasons that it seems appropriate to describe the mothers as operating with the conversational mode in interacting with their babies.

Sacks *et al*. (1974) proposed a two-part system for the organization of turn-taking in conversation: a TURN-CONSTRUCTIONAL component, which produces the unit types which make up a speaker's turn; and a TURN-ALLOCATIONAL component, which operates through a set of rules to determine who will speak next. The turn-allocational component operates only at transition-relevant places, which are determined by the end of the unit-type selected by the current speaker. Unit-types may be words, phrases or clauses — they are, in fact, equivalent to the units traditionally called utterances. The end of an utterance is a transition-relevant place, i.e. a place where a new speaker may be selected or may select himself, or where the current speaker may continue with another unit-type. The most common technique for self-selection as the next speaker is by starting to talk first. The means by which the current speaker selects the next speaker include the 'adjacency-pairs', i.e. utterances which by their nature demand a reply from a specific person, such as a question addressed specifically, a compliment, an insult, or a greeting. The rules proposed by Sacks *et al*. are designed to account for turn-taking in multi-participant conversations. The mother-child interactions studied here were simpler, in that only two potential participants were present. They also differed in that, whereas getting one's turn is a major goal in adult conversations (Sacks *et al*. suggest that it is a motivation to go on listening carefully), getting the child to take her turn seemed to be the primary goal of the mothers studied. None the less, much of the mechanism suggested by Sacks *et al.*, especially the notion of speaker-selection by the use of adjacency-pairs, seems very useful in describing the mother-infant interactions discussed here and in accounting for many of the characteristics of the mothers' speech.

Three months

Before discussing the evidence supporting the conversational interpretation of mothers' speech to young babies, it is perhaps instructive to cite an example of a very typical exchange at 0;3:

(1)	Mother	Ann
		(smiles)
	Oh what a nice little smile!	
	Yes, isn't that nice?	
	There.	
	There's a nice little smile.	(burps)
	What a nice wind as well!	
	Yes, that's better, isn't it?	
	Yes.	
	Yes.	(vocalizes)
	Yes!	
	There's a nice noise.	

This sequence demonstrates several points. First of all, it gives an example of the short, simple baby-centred utterances typical of the mothers' speech at this time. Secondly, it includes three cases of specific maternal responses to infant behaviours. These are typical of many more instances; at 0;3, in fact, 100 per cent of both Ann's and Mary's burps, yawns, sneezes, coughs, coo-vocalizations, smiles and laughs were responded to by maternal vocalizations, suggesting that under conditions of reasonable proximity such responses were almost obligatory for these mothers. Thirdly, it exemplifies the nature of maternal responses to the class of infant behaviours in question: the behaviour is referred to specifically, either by naming, as above, or by using a relatively stereotyped content-related response, such as *That's better* or *Pardon you* to a burp, and *What's so funny?* or *Do you think that's nice?* to a smile. Such specific, content-related and predictable responses on the mothers' part have been taken as the criteria for referring to infant behaviours as unit-types within the Sacksian model, i.e. as the units which constitute a turn. Using this criterion of maternal responsiveness, it is possible to identify a fairly restricted class of infant behaviours which at 0;3 qualify as unit-types: smiles, laughs, burps, yawns, sneezes, coughs, coo-vocalizations, and looking attentively at something. These behaviours do not satisfy the normal adult criterion for a unit-type, that it be intentional and communicative.

However, they do all have in common that they are directly interpretable, i.e. that they can be responded to as if they were intended to communicate something specific. Infant behaviours which do not have this quality of signalling something unambiguous about the infant's state of mind, e.g. arm- or leg-waving, bouncing, head-movements, or crying, do not seem to function as infant unit-types in conversational interactions.

Responding, even responding consistently and reliably, to this class of infant unit-types does not provide the basis for very extensive turn-taking, partly because the babies did not emit such behaviours very often. The mothers devoted a much greater proportion of their utterances to trying to elicit specific responses, most often coos or smiles, from the babies. That these utterances had the very specific function for the mother of trying to elicit turns from the baby, thus justifying our referring to them as first-pair parts of adjacency pairs, is evidenced by the fact that the topic of the maternal utterances was shifted as soon as the elicitation was successful. Ann's mother at 0;3 devoted 124 consecutive utterances to the topic of burping, and shifted to the topic of what Ann was looking at as soon as Ann had indeed burped. The adjacency-pair nature of these turn sequences is, of course, apparent only to the mother. It is she who is imposing on the interaction the rules of conversation, of which her baby is still unaware (though it has been suggested that babies of this age are capable of elementary turn-taking; Bateson 1971, Jaffe, Stern & Perry 1973). The mothers' attempts to maintain a conversation despite the inadequacies of their conversational partners account for the most striking characteristics of the maternal speech style — its repetitiveness, the high frequency of questions (especially tag-questions and post-completers like *Hmm?*, which are described by Sacks *et al.* (1974) as devices for passing a turn on), and the frequency of sequences like (2) and (3), in which the mother takes both parts:

(2)   Mother
Oh you are a funny little one, aren't you, hmm?
Aren't you a funny little one?
Yes.

(3)   Mother
Where is it? (referring to the baby's wind)
Come on, come on, come on.
You haven't got any.
I don't believe you.

The mother here repaired the breakdown in the conversational exchange by filling in for the baby, taking the turn for her. A further conversation-repair device used by the mothers at 0;3 consisted of phrasing questions so that a minimal response on the baby's part could be treated as a reply. In (4) the mother shifted topics as if the baby had said she was finished, whereas all she had in fact done was refrain from crying when the bottle was removed.

(4)   Mother
   Are you finished?
   Yes? (removing bottle)
   Well, was that nice?

This sequence also exemplifies one of the most ubiquitous features of the mothers' speech at even the earliest age studied: the mothers constantly talked about the child's wishes, needs and intentions. A crying baby was always offered specific comforts, as if the mother's task was to find out something the baby already knew. Persistent crying was referred to as 'being stroppy', as if it reflected intentional naughtiness. The babies' behaviour was never described as random, and only rarely as a function of physiological variables. It was seen, just as adult behaviour is seen, as intended and intentional. This view of infant behaviour is of course prerequisite to the attempts to communicate with the baby, and to interpret the baby's behaviour as communicative, which have been described above. The presumption that any voluntary behaviour is produced intentionally is also common in interaction between adults. Austin (1962) gives the example of sequences (5a-d), in which the same event is described but with different levels of intention ascribed to the actor:

   (5a)   John pulled the trigger.
   (5b)   John shot at the donkey.
   (5c)   John hit the donkey.
   (5d)   John killed the donkey.

The tendency to report intentions and consequences instead of actual behaviour is thus not peculiar to mother-infant interaction; it is simply more striking there because non-voluntary behaviours such as burps are also interpreted as intentional and because the basis for assigning intention is so often unclear to the observer.

The mothers talked very little to the babies during bottle feeding while the bottle was in the mouth at 0;3 (see Table 9.1). Maternal utterances during the feeding sessions were restricted to the winding episodes, unless

Table 9.1: Amount of time spent and number of maternal utterances produced in the feeding and play portions of the sessions analysed

	Ann						Mary						
Age in weeks ...	12	29	49	79	87	13	22	29	38	44	52	75	81
Minutes of feeding	17.50	8.50	3.50	10.00	5.50	9.10	10.50	12.20	15.40	9.00	5.45	7.40	10.00
Minutes of play	3.45	13.00	16.20	10.00	14.10	12.20	10.30	9.10	5.40	12.30	15.45	12.20	10.00
Utterances, feeding	133	66	23	139	90	45	80	56	127	65	53	123	109
Utterances, play	100	150	231	130	280	157	149	112	69	148	235	276	198
Utterances, total	233	216	254	269	370	202	229	168	196	213	288	399	307

Table 9.2: Frequency of speaker-switching and mean length of maternal and child turns for Ann and Mary at 0;3, 0;7, 1;0 and 1;6

Age	0;3		0;7		1;0		1;6	
	Ann	Mary	Ann	Mary	Ann	Mary	Ann	Mary
Frequency of speaker-switching	18	24	56	30	70	72	222	226
Mean length of maternal turns in utterances	23.50	15.54	7.45	10.50	7.06	7.78	2.42	2.98
Mean length of child turns in unit-types	1.00	1.00	1.04	1.07	1.03	1.00	1.19	1.08

the baby did something special which elicited a response, such as ceasing to suck (eliciting *What's the matter?* or *Have you had enough?*) or staring at something in the room (eliciting *What are you looking at?* or *What can you see?*). The lack of maternal utterances during bottle feeding supports the contention that the mothers' speech was produced on the basis of a turn-taking model. The mothers' aim was to engage in adult-style conversation with true turns, and she therefore refrained from talking when the baby was prevented from answering. A similar pattern emerged during spoon feeding, when maternal utterances were produced between spoonfuls, not when the baby's mouth was full.

Interestingly, crying on the part of the baby did not seem to act as the first half of an adjacency-pair in the same way as burping, smiling, laughing, etc. The mothers did, of course, respond to crying, but they did not respond in specific and predictable ways, perhaps because crying gives too little information about what the appropriate response would be.

Seven months

The most striking change between 0;3 and 0;7 was that the babies were at 0;7 considerably more active partners. This is reflected in the figures given in Table 9.2, which show that the mean length of a maternal turn (i.e. the mean number of maternal unit-types which followed one another without intervention of a baby unit-type) declined drastically between 0;3 and 0;7, and that the frequency of speaker-switching increased concomitantly. The increased participation of the infant in the interaction occurred despite the facts that the baby's repertoire of unit-types had only expanded slightly, and that the mothers had become somewhat more demanding as to what kinds of vocalization they accepted as a unit-type.

At 0;7 the baby could initiate an adjacency-pair by smiling, laughing or burping, as at 0;3, and also by producing a kind of protest cry. This cry was observed when, for example, Ann's mother persisted in offering a spoonful of food which Ann had already refused, and when Ann's mother restrained her from moving out of camera range. It was more discrete than the crying at 0;3, and had much more the character of a signal which the mother had to respond to, e.g.

(6)	Mother	Ann
		(protest cry)
	Hey hey hey hey hey	(protest cry)
	Hey come on, lookit, look shh.	(looks at mother)
	There.	

The mother no longer responded to all child vocalizations, only to 'high-quality' vocalizations, i.e. a vocalic or consonantal babble. These high-quality babbles were quite frequent and did elicit sure responses, often in the form of imitations. Elaborated and lengthy babbling sequences were responded to with *What was that all about?* or *Oh, really?* Responses to the baby's babbles accounted for 7.2 per cent of Ann's and 4.4 per cent of Mary's mother's utterances at 0;7. The turn-taking character of babble-imitations is made especially clear in the transcript from Ann and her mother, because Ann's mother had introduced an imitation game, in which she set rules about the nature of the correct response. This is illustrated in (7):

(7) Mother	Ann
Ghhhhh ghhhhh ghhhhhh ghhhhhh	
Grrrrr grrrrr grrrrrr grrrrr	(protest cry)
Oh, you don't feel like it, do you?	aaaaa aaaaa aaaaa
No. I wasn't making that noise.	
I wasn't going aaaaa aaaaa.	aaaaa aaaaa
Yes, that's right.	

This imitation game was, in principle, symmetrical, with either partner privileged to imitate the other. In fact, as the quoted exchange indicates, Ann often failed to observe the rules, and her mother carried much of the structure of the game.

The babies had at 0;7 a somewhat larger repertoire of motor responses which could be recruited into the turn-sequences. Taking a bite of food was accepted by Ann's mother as a response to *Isn't it nice?*; looking about or reaching for an object as a response to *What's that?* or *Where's it gone?*; and looking at the mother as a response to the child's name. In example (8) Ann's mother refers to the object as *it* in her third utterance, as if Ann had named it, whereas all Ann had in fact done was to establish joint reference by looking at the object:

(8) Mother	Ann
Look, what's that?	
What's that?	(looks at object)
Well you thought it'd gone away, didn't you?	

Despite the fact that the children were more active in taking their turns at 0;7 than at 0;3, they still very often failed to do so. Occurrences of maternal questions without answers (9), and of such conversational repairs as mothers answering their own questions (10) and simplifying their own questions (11) were still frequent.

(9)   Mother   Ann
                                                (looks into corner of room)
   What can you see?
   What are you looking at?
   What are you looking at?
   What are you looking at, hmm?
   Hmmm?   haaa
   Haaa

(10)
   Mmmm, does that taste nice?
   I don't suppose it does, does it?
   Doesn't taste very nice.
   No, it doesn't

(11)
   Where's it gone?
   Where's it gone, little one?
   Where's it gone
   Hey?
   Where's it gone?
   's gone away, hasn't it?
   Hmm, has it gone away?   (looks at mother)
   Yes, it has.

Twelve months

The turn-taking activities at 1;0 did not differ greatly from those at 0;7, although in general the babies were both responding more reliably to maternal utterances and were initiating more adjacency-pairs with their own activities. The nature of the mothers' responses to the infant vocalizations had changed. Rather than simply producing imitations of the high-quality babbles, the mothers now sometimes expanded or explained the babble, implicitly accepting it as an attempt at a word:

(12)   Mother   Ann
                                                abaabaa
   Baba.
   Yes, that's you, what you are.

Hiding and finding objects had become a favourite game for Ann, one which ideally allows symmetrical turn-taking, but which was initiated only by the mother at this stage:

(13)   Mother   Ann
    (rattling container) What's in there?
    What's in there?   (drops object out)
    There it is.

(14)
    (dropping object into container) Inside.
    (looks into container) There it is.

The following sequence was initiated by Ann, but she failed to take her second turn, so her mother had to answer her own question:

(15)   Mother   Ann
                                        (straining to get out
                                        of her mother's arms)
    Oh. where do you want to go then?
    Hey!
    Where do you want to go?
    Where do you want to go?
    You want to go exploring.

Although the turn-taking activities did not change greatly in nature between 0;7 and 1;0, the number of and amount of time spent in shared activities increased steadily from 0;3 till 1;0. At 0;3 Ann and her mother had only two short periods of shared social activity – an episode of mutual looking, and the protoconversational sequence partially quoted above. By 1;0 they shared several different kinds of activities, some of which extended over several minutes, e.g. their imitation game, hiding and finding an object, retrieving an object from inaccessible places, and looking at Ann in a shiny surface.

Eighteen months

By the time she was 1;6, Ann was taking her turn quite often and most of her unit-types consisted of words. Her mother expected not only that she would take her turn, but that she would provide appropriate responses, e.g.

(16)   Mother   Ann
   Who's that?   Daddy.
   That's not daddy, that's Dougall.
   Say Dougall.

(17)   Hot.
   Hot, hot.   Tea.
   No, it's not tea, it's coffee.   Coffee.
   ? (incomprehensible utterance)   Coffee.
   You're not having coffee now, you're having dinner.

Such sequences of response, correction, and corrected response, which occurred for pronunciation corrections as well as content corrections, formed an important part of the turn-taking at 1;6.

Almost any clearly articulated word from Ann seemed to function as the initiator of an adjacency-pair at 1;6, and her mother would even interrupt an ongoing conversation with the observer in order to respond to them. Examples (18) and (19) show how Ann's words initiated new conversational topics:

(18)   Mother   Ann
                                                        (blowing noises)
   That's a bit rude.   Mouth.
   Mouth, that's right.   Face.
   Face, yes, mouth is in your face.
   What else have you got in your face?   Face. (closing eyes)
   You're making a face, aren't you?

(19)
   Don't know where it is. (talking about Ann's nose).   Titus Titus (the cat)
   Where, I can't see him.
   Oh, there he is.
   Oh yes, he's on the floor.
   Titus is . . .   Floor. (interrupting)
   Floor.   Floor.
   Yes, Titus is on the floor.

Even if the mother had nothing to say about the new topic, she never failed to respond by at least repeating the word. This insistence on politeness formulas and her consistency in responding to them provided another turn-taking situation, e.g.

(20)   Mother   Ann
(giving Ann a biscuit) What do you say?
What do you say?
No, you don't put it straight in your mouth.
What do you say?   Thank you.
There's a good girl.

and numerous cases of (21):

(21)   Mother   Ann
                                       Please.
Please what?

Ann's mother continued to use the question-reformulation technique to make it easier for Ann to take her turn:

(22)   Mother   Ann
What else have you got in your face?
Where's your nose?
Where's your nose?
Ann's nose?

(23)
Where's Titus?
He went out, didn't he?

However, despite the imperfect turn-taking, the interaction at 1;6 gave the strong impression of being a real conversation, both in terms of the frequency of speaker-switching and in terms of the apparent effectiveness of the communication. This impression was dependent on the mother's willingness to follow up on any conversational opening given by the child, and to fill in for the child whenever necessary. Ann still clearly violated some of the rules of turn-taking – for example, by interrupting a conversation going on between mother and observer, by introducing new topics before current topics were exhausted, and by failing to complete many adjacency-pairs introduced by the mother. The mother very effectively kept the conversation going, despite these inadequacies on the part of her conversational partner, by her constant willingness to cede a turn to the child, to accept any reasonable attempt at a word as a first pair part, to follow the child's shifts in conversational topic, to fill in for the child when she missed her turn, and to change the form of her own first pair parts until they did elicit a response.

Discussion

The hypothesis that mothers operate on the basis of a conversational model in interacting with their babies helps to explain some of the striking aspects of mother-infant interaction and some otherwise puzzling aspects of the mothers' speech register[†] as well. This hypothesis accounts for the fact that mothers talk to young babies at all, and explains why they talk to them most while in a face-to-face position or sharing activities, and least while feeding. Furthermore, it accounts for the very high frequency of questions in speech to babies: questions, especially tag-questions and other post-completers like *Hmm?*, are devices for passing the turn to the partner, which is precisely what the mothers are trying hardest to do. Another adjacency-pair used by mothers in much the same way is greetings; an analysis is currently under way of the situations in which mothers greet their infants, but preliminary observations confirm that mothers greet infants after only very short absences or separations, situations in which greeting an adult would be quite abnormal. Both questions and greetings enable the mother operating within the conversational mode to treat any response on the part of her child as a communicative response, because the mothers' conversational rules dictate that the unit-types which follow questions or greetings be responses. Very often, of course, the questions or greeting was not followed by any behaviour which could be interpreted as communicative, and then the mother was forced into conversational repair procedures such as repetition or taking the baby's turn.

The nature of adults' speech to 2-year-old children can also be better understood if it is recognized that such speech occurs within conversations and is largely directed towards keeping the conversation going (see Cherry 1976, Lieven 1975, Shugar 1975). For example, the mothers studied used turn-passing devices frequently, but never used turn-grabbing or turn-keeping devices (pre-starters such as *Well . . .* and *But . . .* and pause-fillers) which are quite frequent in adult-adult conversation. This fact may help to explain the absence of inappropriate pausing, segmentation ambiguities, and false starts in mothers' speech to 2-year-olds (Broen 1972). Mothers' desire to communicate reciprocally with their children, which underlies their use of the conversational mode, may well be a crucial factor in limiting the topics discussed and thus the semantic and syntactic complexity in mothers' speech. The question-reformulation sequences and similar sequences with imperatives may account for much of the utterance and constituent repetition in mothers' speech to 2-year-olds, as it does in mothers' speech to babies. Furthermore, recognition of the skill and

248   *The Development of Conversation*

insistence with which mothers introduce the conversational mode into their interactions with their children may help to explain how children acquire turn-taking skills, both in conversation and in other types of interaction, so early (Escalona 1973, Keenan 1974).

The way mothers talk to their babies is one reflection of their belief that the babies are capable of reciprocal communication. Their choice of the conversational mode not only reflects this belief, but also provides opportunities for reinforcing it by giving meaning within the rules of conversational turn-taking to the infant behaviours that occur. Another example of a similar process is provided by Newson & Pawlby (1974), who report that mothers who had been observed playing imitation games with their babies said that they did so because it gave them the feeling of being in contact with the babies. Maternal expectations about infants' abilities both arise from and are tested by the nature of the interaction mothers establish with their babies. An important question for future research is the extent to which the nature of the interaction established between mothers and infants in the first year of life contributes to the speed and the nature of later language acquisition.

Notes.

1.   The abstract summarises the early sections of the original article.

References

Austin, J.L. (1962). *How to do things with words.* Cambridge, Mass.: MIT.
Bateson, M.C. (1971). The epigenesis of conversational interactions. Paper presented to the Society for Research in Child Development, Minneapolis.
Broen, P. (1972). The verbal environment of the language-learning child. *ASHA Monogr.* 17.
Bruner, J. (1975). The ontogenesis of speech act. *J. Ch. Lang.* 2. 1-20.
Cherry, L. (1976). Interactive strategies in language development: a model of social cognition. Paper presented to the Conference on Language, Children, and Society, Columbus, Ohio.
Escalona, S. (1973). Basic modes of social interaction: their emergence and patterning during the first two years of life. *MPQ* 19. 205-32.
Jaffe, J., Sten, D. & Perry, J. (1973). 'Conversational' coupling of gaze behaviour in prelinguistic human development. *J. Psycholing. Res.* 2. 321-30.
Keenan, E. (1974). Conversational competence in children. *J. Ch. Lang.* x. 163-84.
Lieven, E. (1975). Conversations between mothers and young children: individual differences and their possible implication for the study of language learning. Paper presented to the Third International Symposium on First Language Acquisition, London.
Newson, J. & Pawlby, S. (1974). On imitation. Unpublished paper, University of Nottingham.

Sacks, H., Schegloff, E. & Jefferson, G. (1974). A simplest systematics for the organisation of turn-taking for conversation. *Lg* 50. 696-735.
Shugar, G.W. (1975). Text analysis as an approach to the study of early linguistic operations. Paper presented to the Third International Symposium on First Language Acquisition, London.

10 LEARNING AND USING THE AUXILIARY VERB IN ENGLISH

Gordon Wells

Source: specially written for this volume. Copyright © 1978 The Open University.

Auxiliary verbs serve many important functions in English: they are necessary for the syntactic realisation of questions and negative statements; they play a major part in the formulation of moral and hypothetical statements and they provide one of the chief means of expressing tentativeness and politeness. For this reason the presence or absence of these forms is one of the features that is most salient for those who have to make judgements about the maturity or immaturity of children's speech at the beginning of schooling. It is important to discover, therefore, at what age children typically develop control of these forms, and what factors affect their development and use.

There are two basic research strategies that can be used in seeking answers to questions about the sequential pattern of language development. The first involves eliciting specific types of linguistic behaviour under carefully controlled conditions, typically imitation or transformation of stimulus sequences, or some kind of response which demonstrates comprehension of particular forms or structures. Major's (1974) study of the modal auxiliaries in the language of children in kindergarten and grades 1, 2 and 3, adopted this research strategy. Its advantages are that it allows a particular aspect of language to be studied both systematically and economically, and typically a cross-sectional design is adopted in which developmental trends are inferred from differences between groups selected at different ages. There are, however, attendant disadvantages. The first is that the tasks are inevitably removed from the normal context of the child's spontaneous behaviour and, depending on the aspect of language to be investigated, more or less artificial in the demands that are made. The second disadvantage, which is related to the first, is that the children's performance on such tasks tells us little about their understanding or use of the forms or structures in spontaneous linguistic interaction, and even less about the environmental conditions that are related to their development and use. This research strategy is most effective, therefore, when previous observation has given rise to quite specific hypotheses which are best tested under controlled conditions.

The alternative strategy, and the one that has been most frequently

250

adopted, is to collect regular samples of spontaneously occurring speech and to extract from these the data that are relevant to the particular aspect of language to be investigated. The advantages of this strategy for the authenticity and contextual richness of the data obtained are obvious, but, once again, there are attendant disadvantages. Most serious is the lack of control that the researcher has over what is said: he is dependent on the chance occurrence of whatever contexts elicit the linguistic items in which he is interested. This means that large quantities of speech have to be collected and as wide a range of contexts sampled as possible. As a result this research strategy is extremely labour-intensive and in general it has been the practice to study many aspects of language development simultaneously, but with a very restricted number of children. A corollary of this is that authenticity and detail are bought at the price of limited generalisability of the findings of the research.

The study of the auxiliary verb system to be reported in this paper has been conducted by means of the second strategy, as part of a larger study of language development being carried out in the University of Bristol. Unlike most studies in this tradition, however, it involves a sample of 128 children selected to be representative of the pre-school population in terms of sex, class of family background and season of birth.[1] Ten recordings were made of each child at three-monthly intervals, each recording consisting of 24 ninety-second samples at intervals over one day between 9 a.m. and 6 p.m. During the whole of this time, the child wore a radio-microphone which allowed him to move freely around his home and the immediate vicinity. Neither the child nor his parents were aware when the samples were being recorded and no observer was present at any time during the day, contextual information being obtained in the evening by playing over the recording to the mother and asking her to recall, in as much detail as possible, the participants and activities relevant to each sample. The speech samples thus obtained were transcribed and checked and then analysed according to a comprehensive linguistic coding scheme (Wells, 1973).

The data for the present study consist of the speech samples obtained from all ten recordings of the 60 children in the younger age group who completed the study. Each child was recorded for the first time at the age of 15 months and the last recording was made at 45 months. A small number of children missed recordings as a result of sickness, but no child was included who missed more than one recording. The aim at each recording was to obtain about 100 utterances from the child as well as all utterances addressed to him. A small number of recordings, particularly those at the younger ages, fell well below this target in the case of some, less talkative, children. Many recordings on the other hand, contained far more than 100 utterances. The total corpus for the investigation consists of 89,599 child utterances and 60,592 utterances addressed to the children by adults.

Auxiliary Verb Forms and Meanings

In his description of the auxiliary verb, Palmer (1965) distinguishes two classes of auxiliaries: the primary auxiliaries *be, have* and *do*, and the secondary, or modal, auxiliaries *will, shall, can, may, must, ought, dare* and *need*. He also recognises a number of additional forms, quasi-auxiliaries, *be going to, had better, would rather, let's*, and forms such as *be able to, have to, have got to*, which behave very much like modal auxiliaries. Some of these forms, *dare, need, would rather* do not occur at all in the present child corpus and so have been omitted from the analysis; *let's* has been omitted on the grounds of its restricted use as a 'first person plural imperative' only. These exceptions apart, the forms to be investigated are those identified by Palmer, together with their 'past tense' forms, *would, should, could, might.*

In identifying the class of auxiliary verbs, Palmer makes use of four tests:

1.   Negation: Only auxiliary verbs have negative forms, e.g. *can't, won't* etc.

2.   Inversion: Auxiliary, but not full, verbs can be inverted with the subject in questions and in certain other sentence types, e.g. 'Hardly had he left, when . . .'

3.   Code: Palmer uses this term for the use of auxiliaries 'to avoid repetition' in elliptical responses, and with *so*, e.g. 'Are you coming?' – 'Yes I am'; 'Peter can swim and so can Henry.'

4.   Emphatic affirmation: Auxiliaries can occur as the stressed element in a sentence to give an emphatic affirmation in response to a doubtful statement or as the denial of a negative statement, e.g. 'I can jump across this stream'.

In sentences involving negation inversion, code or emphatic affirmation, *do* is the form that occurs if no other auxiliary is present.[2]

The fact that auxiliary verbs, and only auxiliary verbs, pass these tests is the justification for calling them a system, with respect to their syntactic functioning. The tests provide a set of generalisations about the way in which the members of the system function within the language as a whole. Another way of formulating these generalisations is as a set of rules, which applies to the auxiliary verbs as a class. In a Transformational Generative grammar these rules are of two kinds: a Phrase Structure rule, which introduces the class in the derivation of sentences: Aux⟶Tense (Modal) (hav-en) (be-ing); and a number of transformation rules, such as those for negation and inversion, which operate upon Phrase Markers containing an auxiliary introduced by the above rule or, in the absence of such an auxiliary, add the auxiliary form *do*.

Although not in one-to-one correspondence with the forms, the meanings associated with the auxiliary verbs can also be described as a system, or rather as a group of related systems. In the case of the primary auxiliaries we are concerned with two of the non-deictic temporal distinctions that are included under the general term Aspect (Lyons, 1977). Continuous Aspect (*be-ing*) has the meaning of 'in progress' or 'continuing', whilst Perfect Aspect (*hav-en*) has the meaning of 'having taken place at a previous time but having relevance for a later time'. Both Continuous and Perfect Aspect can be combined with either the past or the non-past tense. Continuous Aspect is also used with future orientation, typically about actions which the speaker intends to put into effect, e.g. 'I'm not playing any more'. Associated with Perfect Aspect because of its structural similarity, is the form *have got*: this is used idiomatically in British spoken English with the meaning of 'possession'.

With the modal auxiliaries we are concerned with various qualifications concerning the actuality of the event named by the full verb. A variety of approaches has been adopted in describing this group of meanings. The basic problem is to do justice to the different meanings associated with particular modal forms, whilst at the same time giving due recognition to what these meanings have in common. Palmer's (1965) analysis is the most helpful in this respect and the scheme to be proposed here is, in many ways, similar to his.

Modality can be conveniently thought of as a matrix, the cells of which are defined by the two dimensions of *Degrees* and *Types* of modality (Table 10.1). Four Degrees are proposed: *Possible, Predictable, Necessary* and *Actual*. The degree of Actual is typically unmarked — no modality is expressed. The place of this degree in the system becomes clear in a context where it is in contrast with one of the other degrees e.g. 'I think this scruffy mongrel *might* be yours' — 'It *is* mine'.

With the Types of Modality, the various relations between the modal verb and the subject of the sentence are contrasted. In the first two cases, the subject typically realises the semantic role of Agent with respect to the action. In the case of *Potential* the meaning of the modal concerns the agent's potentiality with respect to the action named by the full verb,

Table 10.1: Meanings Realised by Auxiliary Verbs

	INFERENCE	LIKELIHOOD	CONSTRAINT	POTENTIAL	PERFORMATIVE
POSSIBLE	TENTATIVE POSSIBLE might, could POSSIBLE may, can	TENTATIVE POSSIBLE might, could POSSIBLE may, can + CONTRAFACTUAL could, would	LACK OF CONSTRAINT: PERMITTED can, may CIRCUMSTANTIAL POSSIBILITY can, could	ABILITY can, be able to INTRINSIC POTENTIAL can, will	REQUEST/GRANT PERMISSION can, may could might REQUEST/OFFER ACTION can, may, could, will, shall would, would like
PREDICTABLE	PROBABLE will	PREDICT will, shall, be V+ing, be going to HABITUAL will, would		INTENTION/ VOLITION will, shall, be V+ing, be going to INSISTENCE will, would	COMMAND shall, will, can SUGGESTION REQUEST EVALUATE INTENTION shall, would like
NECESSARY	TENTATIVE CONCLUSIVE should, ought CONCLUSIVE must, have to, have got to		ADVISABLE had better OBLIGATION should, ought REQUIRED must, have got to, (will) have to + CONTRAFACTUAL should, ought		FORMULATION OF ADVISABILITY had better FORMULATION OF OBLIGATION should, ought FORMULATION OF REQUIREMENT must, have got to, have to, be to
NEUTRAL	CONDITIONAL could, would, should	CONTINUOUS/PERFECTIVE ASPECT be V+ing, have V+en	UNMODIFIED	POSSESSION have got	PASSIVE be V+en

typically his Ability or Intention to act. By contrast, in the case of *Constraint*, the modal focuses on the presence or absence of constraints on the agent's performance of the act. If the first two types of modality are agent-oriented, this is not the case with the next two types: in the *Likelihood* type the modal meanings are concerned with the probability of the event being actualised (or, in the case of logical discourse, of the proposition being true); whilst in the *Inference* type, the probability of an event which is not directly known is inferred with varying degrees of certainty from information which is directly available.

In contrast to the meanings covered by all these four types of modality, the *Performative* meanings of the modals are concerned with the acts that are performed in the uttering of the sentences containing them. The distinction is between what Halliday terms inter-personal and ideational meanings (Halliday, 1970). This is not to say that utterances containing modal auxiliaries with ideational meaning do not have an inter-personal function, for they certainly do, but rather that the function of such utterances is not essentially affected by the selection of the type of modal. With the Performative type, however, the selection of the modal defines the inter-personal roles that the speaker is assigning to the participants in the interaction: seeker and granter of permission, controller and controlled, etc. In each of these cases, the Performative use of the modal presupposes one of the ideational types of meanings: to seek or grant permission assumes the ability of the person being granted permission to carry out the action; to ask for an evaluation of an intention assumes the intention to act if the suggested act is approved, etc. Nevertheless, the meaning that is to the forefront in the Performative type of modality is the type of Inter-Personal action that is performed by the utterance of the sentence.

The distinction between these five types of modality can best be illustrated with respect to *can* and *may* which can occur in all five types:

Potential:	'I can write my own name now'
	'My new bike can go very fast'
Constraint:	'I can (may) play outside till tea-time'
	'There's nothing coming. We can cross now'
Likelihood:	'It may (could/might) rain. We'd better take our coats'
Inference:	(Doorbell rings) 'That may (could/might) be John. He said he'd call'
Performative:	'Can (may) I go out to play?
	'You can't have that.'

The types of modality can thus be thought of as providing answers to different types of question. For Potential and Constraint, the question is: 'Is it possible for X to . . .?'; for Likelihood and Inference, the question is: 'Is it possible that . . .?'; and for the Performative types of modality, the question is 'Does one of the discourse participants make it possible/ impossible for one of them to . . .?'

The modal matrix has fifteen possible cells, but two of these are not filled (Predictable:Constraint, and Necessary:Potential); a third cell, Necessary:Likelihood only occurs in logical discourse. The various modal verbs occur in more than one cell, but typically only within one degree. Aspectual and quasi-auxiliary forms are also to be found in certain cells of the matrix, thus demonstrating the close relationship between the various systems of meaning realised by auxiliary verbs.[3]

Finally, there are a number of other meanings in the total system. Firstly, the Contrafactual meanings realised by *could, would* and *should* in conjunction with *have*; secondly, the Conditional meanings of the same forms; thirdly, the use of the 'past tense' forms to achieve concord of tenses following a past tense form of a verb of 'saying', 'thinking' etc.; there is also *be* in the Passive construction, *be-en*. Finally there is the auxiliary *do,* which does not introduce any meaning of its own, but is merely an empty place-holder in the contexts of negation, inversion, code and emphatic affirmation.

Auxiliary Forms and Meanings in Child Speech

All child utterances from the longitudinal records of each child in the sample were examined, and a count made of the occurrence of each auxiliary form at each recording. The frequencies of each form, summed over all recordings and all children, are presented in Table 10.2 (column 1). Since not all forms were used by all children a calculation was made of the proportion of the sample having used each form at least once in an utterance judged not to be an immediate imitation of another's utterance by the time of the last recording at 42 months. This is expressed as a percentage in column 2. A third measure of acquisition is the age at which a particular form is first used. The criterion employed here was the age (in 3-month intervals) by which 50 per cent of the sample had used a particular form at least once. This is shown in column 3 for all forms that reached this criterion by the time of the last recording.

As will be seen, there is very considerable variation in the frequency of occurrence, the proportion of the sample having control by 42 months and the age at reaching criterion, for the various forms of auxiliary verb. Only two, *do* and *have-en* show mastery by 100 per cent of the sample, whilst the majority of the modal forms do not reach the criterion of

Table 10.2: Distribution of Auxiliary Forms

	Total Frequency	Proportion of Sample Using	Age in Months at Criterion
Do	1418	100	27
Have-en	1314	100	27
Can	1210	98	30
Be-ing	1149	97	30
Will	841	100	30
Be Going to	512	92	33
Have Got to	232	73	36
Shall	123	60	39
Could	66	50	42
Have to	55	42	
Must	52	45	
Might	32	32	
Should	26	25	
Would	25	22	
May	25	17	
Had Better	23	25	
Be + Passive	20	20	
Would like to	20	17	
Be Able to	3	5	
Ought	2	3	

mastery by more than 50 per cent of the children. The age at which the 50 per cent criterion reached is, therefore, only applicable to some of the auxiliary forms, and within these, the age at reaching criterion ranges from 27 months, in the case of *do* and *have-en*, to 42 months in the case of *could*. These data taken together, suggest a tentative order of acquisition such as the order in which the forms occur in Table 10.2.

For the investigation of auxiliary meanings each occurrence of an auxiliary verb was classified according to the meaning that it realised in the utterance in which it occurred. There was a small number of cases that were open to classification in more than one way, particularly involving the Likelihood and Constraint:Circumstantial meanings of *can*, and the Performative and Constraint meanings of *must* and other forms at this degree. In the case of *can*, this problem was resolved by combining these two categories of meaning under the general heading Possible and assigning

Table 10.3: Distribution of Auxiliary Meanings

	Total Frequency	Proportion of Sample Using	Age in Months at Criterion
Do — Support	1418	100	27
Contin. Aspect	930	97	30
Have Got	774	100	27
Can: Ability	638	98	30
Will: Intend	542	98	30
Perfect Aspect	540	98	30
Be Going to	512	92	33
Can: Perf. Permission	509	97	33
Contin. Intend	219	83	36
Will: Predict	212	82	36
Have Got to: Constraint	195	67	39
Shall: Performative	97	52	42
Will: Perf. Request	87	65	36
Have to: Constraint	53	42	
Have Got to: Perform.	37	35	
Can: Perf. Request	37	32	
Could: Constraint	33	33	
Might: Likelihood	32	32	
Can: Constraint	26	33	
Shall Intend	26	28	
Must: Constraint	23	25	
Must: Performative	22	18	
Should: Constraint	21	22	
Had Better: Constraint	20	22	
Be + Passive	20	20	
Would like to: Perf.	20	17	
May: Perf. Permission	19	15	
Could: Ability	15	20	
Could: Perf. Request	14	12	
Would: Conditional	13	17	
Must: Inference	7	10	
Would: Intend	7	7	
May: Likelihood	6	3	
Would: Perf. Request	5	2	
Could: Conditional	4	7	

Table 10.3 *(cont.)*

	Total Frequency	Proportion of Sample Using	Age in Months at Criterion
Be Able to: Constraint	3	5	
Had Better: Perform.	3	5	
Should: Performative	3	3	
Have to: Performative	2	3	
Ought: Constraint	2	3	
Should: Inference	2	2	

them to the Constraint type of modality. This seemed justified as the number of unambiguous cases of Likelihood *can* was extremely small. In the case of *must*, etc. the problem is more difficult. For an instance of one of these forms to be classified as Performative, it must occur in a declarative utterance in the present tense. The utterance must also be the realisation of an intention on the part of the speaker to get another person to act in a particular way by virtue of that person's understanding the utterance as a command, rather than as a statement about a constraint that he should be aware of. Clearly, the distinction is a fine one, and in a number of cases it is extremely difficult to decide whether the source of the requirement invoked by the child resides in his own authority as a participant, in causal relations in the environment, or in practical or moral obligations that are recognised by all participants in the activity. In practice, it is the context and the specific intonation of such utterances that are critical in arriving at a decision. Unless there was clear evidence that such utterances could be glossed as '. . . because I say so', (Performative), doubtful cases were assigned to the Constraint category.

The distribution of auxiliary verbs according to their meanings is presented in Table 10.3. As in Table 10.2, total frequencies are shown in column 1, proportion of the sample having used each meaning at least once by 42 months in column 2, and age at which 50 per cent of the sample had used each meaning (where relevant) in column 3.

As was to be expected, there are very substantial differences in frequency and extent of mastery of the different meanings. This is as true for different meanings associated with the same form as it is for meanings realised uniquely by particular forms. As with the auxiliary forms, the data suggest an order of acquisition corresponding to the order in which the meanings are presented in Table 10.3. However with both forms and meanings the strong association between frequency and extent of mastery may not be appropriately accounted for by treating it as a direct outcome of order of acquisition. This subject will be returned to below.

So far the data have been presented only for the sample as a whole. Considerable variation between individuals is to be expected, however, as in all other aspects of language development. In order to obtain some estimate of this, a criterion of individual mastery of auxiliary verb forms was chosen: age by which five different forms had been used. (The criterion of five forms was chosen after inspection of the data in Table 10.2, as this was the number of forms used by at least 95 per cent of the sample by 42 months). All but one child reached this criterion by the end of the study, and the mean age at which it was reached was 31.7 months (S.D.4.50, range 21-42+ months). Taking this age for each child as an index of rate of acquisition, tests were made for relationships between rate of acquisition and both sex and class of family background. In neither case was there a statistically significant relationship.

To estimate the extent of individual variation in the mastery of auxiliary meanings, a different criterion was selected: the range of meanings used by the age of 42 months. Once again, there was a considerable range: 4-30, with the mean number being 18.3 (S.D.4.90). A comparison between the sexes showed a trend for boys to have a greater range of meanings than girls, but this trend failed to reach significance ($X^2 = 5.25$, 3 d.f.). A positive relationship was found between range of auxiliary meanings and class of family background ($r = 0.361$, $p < 0.1$), but when correlations were calculated for the sexes separately, only that for the girls achieved significance ($r = 0.425$, $p < .05$).

The Significance of Frequency Data

Throughout the previous section, the results of the analyses carried out have been presented in a somewhat tentative manner, and no firm conclusions have been drawn from them, for, in order to take these results as conclusive evidence for or against a particular hypothesis, it would be necessary to have grounds for assuming that the sample of speech collected from each child on each occasion was fully representative of the child's behaviour at that time with respect to his acquisition of the linguistic system under investigation. There are essentially two questions to be resolved here: firstly, does the child display mastery of auxiliary verb forms or meanings that have not been picked up in the samples recorded? And secondly, is it possible that a child may master a particular form but not provide any evidence of such mastery until a considerably later date? This latter question raises in an acute form the competence-performance distinction. Chomsky (1964) criticised observational studies of language development on precisely such grounds: that they provide only indirect evidence about linguistic competence. Those who do not recognise the value of the competence-performance distinction, on the other hand, would argue that a child cannot be credited with having mastered a particular form or structure until he gives evidence of producing or responding to it appropriately. However, even if the child does use a particular form appropriately, it is still possible that the method of sampling may fail to pick up such occasions of use, thus leading to an underestimate of the child's ability.

The data in Tables 10.2 and 10.3 show a strong positive relationship between frequency of occurrence, proportion of the sample displaying mastery by 3½ years, and age by which 50 per cent of the sample are using a particular form or meaning. Two possible explanations suggest themselves for this relationship. Either the higher frequencies occur because the items in question are acquired earlier by a higher proportion of children — essentially an explanation in terms of order of acquisition; or the differential frequencies reflect the relative importance of the different aspects of children's experience that are made the subject of linguistic communication — with the implication that mere absence of a particular item does not permit an inference to be drawn about a child's ability to use it should the appropriate occasion arise.

Some progress towards deciding between these two explanations might be made by investigating the frequencies of the same forms in the speech of mature speakers in similar situations. Fortunately a corpus of adult speech of precisely this kind is to be found in the speech addressed to the children on the occasions on which the child recordings were made. This corpus of utterances was therefore analysed in the same way as the child corpus, and the frequency of, and the proportion of adults[4] using each form was calculated for all auxiliary forms. The results are compared with those from the children's corpus in Table 10.4.

There is clearly a broad similarity between the relative frequencies of the different auxiliary verb forms in the two corpora, in spite of the fact that the adults must be presumed to have mastered all the forms before the study began, whilst the children were developing mastery during the period covered by the investigation. This global difference in degree of mastery between the two groups is reflected in the fact that whereas 25.3 per cent of adult utterances contained an auxiliary verb, the proportion in the children's corpus was only 9.4 per cent overall. Nevertheless the distribution of the forms that occur in the two corpora is closely similar, yielding a correlation of r = 0.93. What is even more surprising is the

Table 10.4: Comparison of Children's and Adults' Distribution of Auxiliary Forms

	Total Child Frequency	Proportion of Child Using	Total Adult Frequency	Proportion of Adults Using
Do	1418	100	3374	100
Have-en	1314	100	2104	100
Can	1210	98	1201	100
Be-ing	1149	97	1997	100
Will	841	100	1869	100
Be Going to	512	92	881	98
Have Got to	232	73	383	98
Shall	123	60	302	92
Could	66	50	61	57
Have to	55	42	144	66
Must	52	45	174	87
Might	32	32	79	60
Should	26	25	82	55
Would	25	22	128	83
May	25	17	18	13
Had Better	23	25	124	75
Be + Passive	20	20	150	75
Would Like to	20	17	95	52
Be Able to	3	5	41	43
Ought	2	3	23	27

number of forms that are not recorded as being used at all by a sizeable proportion of the adult sample. Of course it cannot be inferred that these forms are never used by these adults in conversation with their children, only that they are used less than once in a typical sample of approximately 1,000 utterances.

It seems, therefore, that at least two factors account for the frequency distributions in the children's speech: order of acquisition and differential importance of the meanings realised by auxiliary verbs in the interactions that take place between children and their parents. For it is just those forms that figure most frequently in the adults' speech that are acquired first and used most frequently by the children.

Alternative Theories of Language Acquisition

The acquisition of so compact yet far-reaching a system as that of the auxiliary verb should provide an excellent opportunity to contrast a number of alternative theories of language acquisition. This final section will be concerned, therefore, with a re-examination of the data from this point of view.

Although now out of favour, a Behaviourist theory of the kind proposed by Skinner (1957) might seem to be the simplest way of accounting for the data obtained. In terms of this theory, the correlation between the distributional frequencies in the children's and adult's corpora could be explained by the effective shaping of the children's verbal behaviour by the adults around them. At a superficial level, this certainly seems to be the case. Interestingly, however, for those individual child-adult pairs that have already been examined, the correlations are of a much lower order ($r = 0.28$ to $r = 0.76$), which suggest that the children are not modelling their parents' behaviour in any simple way. Furthermore, as has been the case in most detailed studies of language development (e.g. Brown *et al.* 1969), there is little evidence for anything, on the part of the adults, that could be called reinforcing behaviour that is at all related to specific linguistic forms; nor is there evidence of imitation by the children of adult utterances containing the forms in question, if imitation is defined as repetition of whole or part of an adult utterance within a period of a few seconds following the adult utterance. The children are certainly learning to talk like the adults they hear, but a 'learning theory' account of language offers little in the way of explanation of the processes actually involved.

In the study of language acquisition, the strongest attack on the Behaviourist account has been made by those working within the framework of Transformational-Generative grammar (Chomsky, 1959; Bever *et al.* 1965). Arguing on the basis of the abstractness and complexity of the grammatical knowledge that every child acquires, they have rejected any account that is couched in terms of piecemeal learning of individual forms and sequences of forms, followed by some kind of generalisation and, instead, have proposed that the child be thought of as constructing his internal grammar through a process of applying his innate knowledge of linguistic universals to the speech data he hears, and hypothesising and testing rules of the kind that are to be found in a T-G grammar.

As we saw earlier, the grammatical functioning of the auxiliary verbs is governed by a set of rules, both Phrase Structure and Transformational, that are central to any version of T-G grammar. On the basis of this theory alone, therefore, one might hypothesise that, as a result of acquiring the base rule for the introduction of auxiliaries into the structure of sentences, a child would pass fairly rapidly from using no auxiliary verbs to using a wide selection of members of the class; one might also hypothesise that, although there would necessarily be an order in which particular auxiliaries would first appear in the speech of individual children, there would be no particular sequence in which they would emerge, when a large number of children were considered together. Both these hypotheses would be close to the position adopted by such writers as McNeill (1966) and Lenneberg (1967).

In order to test the first of these hypotheses, the criterion of five different auxiliary forms was taken as an indication that the child had a general rule governing the derivation of sentences containing an auxiliary verb and the interval of time over which this rule was established was calculated as the number of months from the first recorded use of any auxiliary verb (excluding *don't* as a negative imperative)[5] to the point at which the criterion was reached. The hypothesis to be tested was that this interval would not exceed three months (i.e. the interval between consecutive observations). In practice, the distribution was as follows:

	< 3 mths.	3 mths.	6 mths.	9 mths.	≥ 12 mths.
No. of children	4	21	19	13	3

from which it can be seen that the majority of children took more than three months to establish a rule for Aux governing at least five auxiliary verb forms.

The second hypothesis predicted that all auxiliary forms would be equally likely to be amongst the first to be acquired. The data in Table 10.2 showing the proportion of the sample using each form, and the age at which each reaches the criterion of 50 per cent mastery, can be used to test this hypothesis. From these data it is clear that, for the sample as a whole, all forms are not equally likely to be amongst the first to be used, and this remains true when the children are considered individually. At least four of the following forms — *do, have-en, be-ing, will, can, be going to* are amongst the first five to be used by every child, and these are precisely the forms that are used first by the sample as a whole.

However, before these findings are taken as evidence against the acquisition of general syntactic rules, further consideration must be given to the data from which they are derived. As has already been pointed out, spontaneous speech data do not permit non-occurrence of particular forms to be taken, at face value, as evidence for the inability of the children to produce these forms under all circumstances. It is possible therefore that the children do indeed acquire a general rule governing auxiliary verbs, together with one or more transformation rules associated with the sub-categories of Aux, and that these rules are called upon quite fully in comprehension, but to a much more limited extent in production. Unfortunately the present study does not allow this possibility to be investigated. Nevertheless, the fact that more than a third of the sample did reach the criterion within a three-month period suggests that, for these children at least, it is more appropriate to speak of the acquisition of a rule-governed system than of the piecemeal addition of unrelated forms. The early emergence of *do* gives further support to the 'syntactic rule' hypothesis, for, lacking semantic content, its acquisition can only be explained in terms of its syntactic functions.

On balance, therefore, the evidence does seem to be in favour of syntactic rule learning, but with the rule system being built up gradually over a period of several months. Then, as new forms are acquired, they are quickly used in the full range of syntactic structures governed by the rule system prevailing at the time.

A syntactic rule learning theory cannot, however, provide a complete explanation of the acquisition of the auxiliary verb system and in parti-cular it fails to account for the clear developmental sequence in which the auxiliary forms are acquired. Here, as in the acquisition of language in general, it seems somewhat surprising that acquisition of syntactic forms and structures should be considered to take place uninfluenced by the meanings that they serve to realise.[6] However, a number of studies sum-marised in Brown (1973), have shown that there is a very considerable degree of similarity in the semantic relations realised in early utterances in a wide variety of languages and, on this basis, Slobin (1973) argues that it is semantic knowledge, acquired initially independently of language, that forms the cognitive prerequisite for the acquisition of syntax. Cromer (1974) also in his review of the evidence in favour of the 'cognitive hypo-thesis', concludes that 'we are able to understand and productively to use particular linguistic structures only when our cognition abilities enable us to do so' (p. 246). He goes on to add, however, that the syntactic com-plexity of a structure must also be taken into account: even with the necessary cognitive ability to cope with the meaning of a particular struc-ture, the meaning/structure unit may still not be acquired if the structure itself is formally too complex.

To derive specific hypotheses from this theoretical approach with respect to the auxiliary verb system is not at all straightforward, for it requires the various form/meaning units (what have been described earlier as auxiliary verb meanings) to be placed in an order of cognitive complexity or difficulty. It is not at all clear, however, how some of these meanings, such as 'possibility', 'necessity', etc., can be recognised independently of their linguistic realisation, whilst the Performative meanings, as discussed earlier, introduce the domain of inter-personal as opposed to the ideational meaning, which is the type of meaning with which Slobin and Cromer were concerned. For these reasons, the hypotheses that follow are based on notional complexity, and must be treated as extremely tentative.

Taking the concrete-abstract distinction as a plausible dimension of cognitive difficulty, it might be hypothesised that the modal meanings, as a whole, will be more complex — and therefore acquired later — than the aspectual meanings, since the 'continuity' or 'presently-relevant-completed-ness' of an event is more directly observable than its 'probability'. On the same grounds, one might predict that *be going to*, with its 'predictable' meaning, will be more complex than either continuous or perfect aspect. Within the group of modal meanings as a whole, on the other hand, those within the Potential type of modality, because of their subject-as-agent orientation, might be predicted to be less complex than those within the Likelihood and Inference types; and within the degrees of modality, the meanings within the Possible degree to be less complex than those within Necessity, with those within the Predictable degree falling somewhere in between.

It will be recalled, however, that Cromer pointed out that cognitive-semantic ease or difficulty alone would not be sufficient to predict order of acquisition, as meanings of equivalent cognitive difficulty might be realised by forms or structures of unequal syntactic complexity. Within the class of auxiliaries, the only distinction of this sort that can be made is between the simple modal forms, *can, must*, etc. and the aspectual forms, *be going to, have got to* and *be able to. Do* presents special problems, however. Formally it is simple, but its absence of semantic meaning might suggest that it would be more difficult to acquire. The Passive, on the other hand, being semantically empty but formally complex, might be predicted to be one of the latest uses of the auxiliary to be acquired.

The data relevant to these hypotheses were presented in Table 10.3 above. From this table it can be seen that there is no evidence that modal meanings, as a class, are more complex than aspectual meanings: *can* in its Potential:Ability meaning and *will* in its Potential:Intention meanings are acquired simultaneously with, and occur as frequently as, aspectual meanings. It is possible, however, that the mastery of aspectual meanings is delayed by their greater formal complexity, and it is certainly the case that many children first realise these meanings in a reduced form, omitting the primary auxiliary component of the complete form. Whereas there are no simpler forms with the same meanings with which the aspectual verbs can be compared, in the case of *be going to* a partial comparison can be made with *will* in its Intention and Predict meanings. As can be seen, *will* (Intend) is acquired slightly earlier, and *will* (Predict) slightly later than *be going to*. Within the modal group, *have got to*, which is one of the more complex forms, precedes *must*, with which it is almost synonymous, whilst *be able to* appears considerably later than its near synonym *can* (Ability). Taking all these facts into account, there seems to be little reason for believing that the more complex forms, as such, present more difficulty in acquisition than the simpler modal forms.

As far as the two semantically empty forms are concerned, Passive behaves according to the prediction. Very few children appear to have acquired it, and for those who have, it comes relatively late. *Do*, on the other hand, is the first auxiliary form to be acquired, in spite of the fact that it has no meaning to assist in acquiring its syntactic function. This fact does not seem to accord easily with the general argument underlying the 'cognition hypothesis'.

In order to test the hypotheses related to the degrees and types of modality, the frequency of occurrence data are presented in Table 10.5 in the cells of the modal matrix described in the earlier part of the paper, with percentage of the sample achieving mastery being indicated in brackets.

Table 10.5: Distribution of Modals by Degree and Type of Modality

	Inference	Likelihood	Constraint	Potential	Performative	TOTAL
Possible	—	38 (33%)	62 (53%)	653 (98%)	399 (97%)	1352 (98%)
Predictable	—	212 (82%)		575 (98%)	189 (82%)	976 (100%)
Necessary	10 (12%)		313 (82%)		67 (55%)	390 (87%)
TOTAL	10 (12%)	250 (87%)	375 (87%)	1228 (100%)	855 (55%)	2718

As can be seen, the hypotheses about the order of acquisition of the degrees and types of modality are substantially supported by the data of both frequency and proportion of sample showing mastery by 3½ years. More children have acquired meanings in the degrees of Possible and Predictable than in the degree of Necessity; and Possible meanings occur with greater frequency than Predictable. With respect to types of modality, all children have Potential meanings, 87 per cent have Constraint meanings,

87 per cent Likelihood meanings, and only 12 per cent Inference meanings. Taken together with the frequency data for the different types, it appears therefore, that the general order of acquisition is: Potential, Constraint, Likelihood, Inference.

The Performative type of modality was omitted from the predictions based on the 'cognition hypothesis', on the grounds that that hypothesis is concerned with ideational rather than inter-personal meaning. However, since Performative modal meanings presuppose an additional ideational meaning, it might be expected that they would be a later acquisition than the corresponding non-performative meanings. And this does in fact seem to be the case. Although some children first use some forms with a Performative meaning, they usually have a parallel form for the equivalent non-Performative meaning, which first occurs before, or at the same time as, the Performative meaning, (e.g. *must* used Performatively whilst *have got to* is used for Constraint). In the case of 4 children only (7 per cent of the sample) is a Performative the first modal meaning to occur.

As with the syntactic rule theory, it is not possible from these results to arrive at an unequivocal conclusion with respect to the cognition hypothesis. In part this is due to the lack of independent data on the cognitive difficulty of the various meanings concerned and of the forms through which they are realised, and in part to the limitations of data based on samples of spontaneous speech. The data analysed do, however, offer some evidence for a sequential developmental pattern in the gradual mastery of the auxiliary verb system, a pattern which is related to the meanings rather than to the forms of the different auxiliary verbs. In very general terms, development can be represented as in Figure 10.1, with the key being a gradual broadening from an initial concern with the subject-as-agent in actual and potential events, through a less agent-oriented awareness of potential, and of constraint on potential in others, to a more

Figure 10.1: Development of Meanings Realised by the Auxiliary Verb System

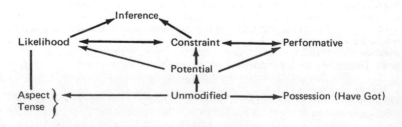

detached consideration of the likelihood of events and states of affairs, and finally to the use of existing knowledge to draw inferences about events not directly experienced.

From this investigation, therefore, it must be concluded that neither the 'syntactic rule' theory nor the 'cognition hypothesis' is fully compatible with the data, though both receive partial confirmation. Cutting across both these theoretical explanations of language development, and of the acquisition of the auxiliary verb system in particular, is the remarkably similar distribution of auxiliary forms and meanings in the corpora of both adults and children. This, taken together with the substantial proportion of auxiliary forms in the children's speech which realise what has been called a Performative meaning, suggests that an adequate theory of language acquisition must attend much more to the social functions that language performs from its very beginning in the life of the child, in negotiating the purposes and meanings that make up the intersubjective space that children and their parents inhabit (Wells, 1975; Halliday, 1976). One possible interpretation of the close matching of frequencies in the two corpora is that it is the result of interaction and progressive modification of the speech of both adults and children, each influencing and being influenced by changes in the other. Although there is already some evidence that such an interaction takes place in the case of accelerated language developers (Cross, 1977), such an explanation is still in need of further investigation for the population as a whole.

Notes

1.　Full details of the study are to be found in 'Journal of Child Language 1', 1: pp. 158-62 (1974). The research is supported by grant HR2024 from the Social Science Research Council.

2.　The verbs *be* and *have* can also function as full verbs. Even as full verbs, however, they still pass the above auxiliary verb tests, e.g. 'He isn't a policemen, is he?' 'I have a pet mouse and so has Jane'.

3.　In order to simplify the exposition, the complex pairing of positive and negative forms, e.g. *must* and *needn't* has been omitted. Perhaps significantly, there is no instance of *needn't* in the child corpus under investigation.

4.　The unit of analysis here was the individual child. Where several adults interacted with a particular child across the ten recordings, these adults were combined and their total contribution treated as a unitary input to that particular child. Thus n = 60 for both child and adult sample.

5.　The negative imperative *don't* was excluded as the first auxiliary as McNeill (1966) argues that if this is the only auxiliary form, it is probably no more than an alternative to the negative morpheme *no*, and not yet governed by transformation rules applying to Aux.

6.　Chomsky's (1965) position on this issue seems unequivocal. With reference to the importance of semantic reference, he writes 'it would not be at all surprising to find that normal language learning requires use of language in real-life situations in some way. But this, if true, would not be sufficient to show that information regarding situational context, plays any role in determining how language is acquired, once the [language acquisition] mechanism is put to work and the task of language learning is undertaken by the child'. (Chomsky, 1965, p. 33)

References

Bever, T.G., Fodor, J.A. & Weksel, W., 'On the acquisition of syntax: a critique of "contextual generalisation" '. *Psychological Review*, 72, 1965, pp. 467-82.

Brown, R., Cazden, C. & Bellugi, U., 'The child's grammar from I to III'. In J.P. Hill (ed.), *The Second Annual Minnesota Symposium on Child Psychology*, University of Minnesota Press, 1969, reprinted in Ferguson, C. and Slobin, D., *Studies in Child Language Development*, 1973.

Chomsky, N.A., review of Skinner's 'Verbal Behaviour', *Language*, 35, 1959, pp. 26-58.

Chomsky, N.A., discussion of Miller's and Ervin's paper, in U. Bellugi and R. Brown (eds.), *The Acquisition of Language*, Monogr. Soc. Res. Child Dev. 29, 1, pp. 35-42.

Chomsky, N.A., *Aspects of the Theory of Syntax*, MIT Press, 1965.

Cromer, R., 'The development of language and cognition: the cognition hypothesis', in B.M. Foss (ed.), *New Perspectives in Child Development*, Penguin Books, 1974.

Cross, T.G., 'Mothers' speech adjustments: the contribution of selected child listener variables', in C. Ferguson & C. Snow (eds.), *Talking to Children: Language Input and Acquisition*, Cambridge University Press, 1977.

Halliday, M.A.K., 'Language structure and language function', in J. Lyons (ed.), *New Horizons in Linguistics*, Penguin, 1970.

Halliday, M.A.K., 'Meaning and the construction of reality in early childhood', in H.L. Pick Jnr. & E. Saltzman (eds.), *Modes of Perceiving and Processing Information*, N.Y. Erlbaum Press, 1976.

Lenneberg, Erich H. (ed.), *Biological Foundations of Language*, Wiley, New York, 1967.

Lyons, J., *Semantics* Vol. 2, Cambridge University Press, 1977.

Major, D., *The Acquisition of Modal Auxiliaries in the Language of Children*, Janua Linguarum, Series Minor 195, Mouton, The Hague, 1974.

McNeill, D., 'Developmental psycholinguistics', in F. Smith & G.A. Miller (eds.), *The Genesis of Language*, MIT Press, 1966, pp. 15-84.

Palmer, F.R., *The English Verb*, Longmans, 1965.

Skinner, B.F., *Verbal Behaviour*, Appleton-Century-Crofts, 1957.

Slobin, D.I., 'Cognitive prerequisites for the development of grammar', in C.A. Ferguson & D.I. Slobin (eds.), *Studies in Child Language Development*, Holt Rinehart, 1973.

Wells, C.G., *Coding Manual for the Description of Child Speech*, University of Bristol School of Education, 1973 (rev. 1975).

Wells, C.G., *Interpersonal Communication and the Development of Language*, paper given to Third International Symposium on Child Language Development, London, September 1975.

SECTION TWO: LANGUAGE VARIATION

Introduction

The first four readings in this section can be interpreted in terms of the 'language-deficit/language-difference' debate.

The first two items can be considered as contributions to the language deficit thesis. So complicated is this particular issue that the authors themselves might well object to being labelled deficit theorists. Adlam and Bernstein are certainly *not* of the school which suggests that a normal child can be deficient in language in the sense that he is non-verbal. Both items are written in the Bernstein theory of codes tradition which suggests that one of the reasons for the relatively poor educational attainment of working-class children lies in the difference between the language of the child and the language of the school. The language of the child coming to school need not be deficient in any way for the experience he has known, but the school provides new experiences for which new language functions are necessary. It is in this sense that the first two readings can be placed in the deficit theory category.

As the title of the Diana Adlam extract suggests, the major concern of the first extract is with two very important ideas for language variation, *code* and *context*. Even more importantly, it is concerned with the *relationship* between these two ideas. Code, as presented in the Bernstein tradition, has often been misunderstood and misinterpreted, and Diana Adlam tries to clarify the issue by distinguishing *code* at the verbal planning level from *codings* at the language use level. She also distinguishes between *eliciting contexts* and *contexts of transmission*. She emphasises the importance of examining inter-relationships among these ideas, stressing the need to look at language across a range of contexts. As most recent work on Bernstein's theory of codes, this extract centres around the context-dependent/context-independent dimension. She sees the text, rather than the sentence, for instance, as the unit of analysis, and considers the influence of the method of collecting the data upon the results achieved.

The second article starts with a brief examination of the theoretical background of Bernstein's theory of codes, followed by a brief summary of previous work in the behavioural sciences which inspired it. Once again it is a question of 'relationship between', this time between speech forms and social relationships. Bernstein argues that speech both realises and controls social relationships. He sees social class as having a fundamental influence upon language performance as a major source of language variation. He points out, for instance, that socialisation guides a child towards either universalistic or particularistic meanings. There are close links with the previous reading, and the four contexts of socialisation, for example, which Bernstein regards of importance to the child's acquisition of language, are the same four contexts of transmission which Diana Adlam uses.

The third and fourth readings are language-difference ways of looking at language variation. They acknowledge social class and ethnic differences in language, but argue that these language variations are of equal value to the more standard language of white middle-class children. They emphasise the important effect of *context* on eliciting language, and are directly opposed to Bernstein's theory of codes.

Labov, for example, sets out to show that the language of black children can be equally as effective as that of middle-class white children. He tries to show that lower class language can be equally logical and handle abstract argument efficiently. In addition, he argues that not all middle-class language is as effective as it at first sounds. We are conditioned, he maintains, to accept middle-class speech as effective when it is often redundant and imprecise simply because we are used to the high status indicators it employs.

Central to the philosophy of the Cazden paper is the idea of 'situational relativity'. By this she means that variation in language is largely caused by differences in speech situation. Most of her article is concerned with citing and assessing the evidence for the influence of the speech situation on language use. Although she maintains that the 'different-language view' is inadequate in so far as it is oriented towards structure instead of patterns of use and relates language to characteristics of the child rather than to characteristics of the speech situation, this article is in the Labov rather than the Bernstein mould. She reinforces Hymes' plea (in the second paper in this volume) concerning the importance of communicative competence as opposed to linguistic competence.

The fifth article is broader in scope. The concern with social class and social background is still there, and it is fair to say that Wells comes down on the side of Labov rather than of Bernstein. Social background, however, is now considered along with other variables which are given prominence such as intelligence, sex and experience of linguistic interaction. Although social background is treated as just one of the areas in which research in language variation has been carried out, much of the Wells paper is an overview of this research. The opening sections, however, are an analysis of the theoretical and methodological considerations of such research which leads Wells to conclude that most research in this area is naïve.

11 CODE IN CONTEXT

Diana Adlam

Source: Diana Adlam *et al.*, *Code in Context* (Routledge and Kegan Paul, London 1977), pp. 1-37.

A paper which takes for its title the relationship between two concepts, both of which are currently more ambiguous than clear, is under some obligation to vindicate their use. We begin with an outline of two senses in which context may be considered.

Bernstein (1973) suggests that a child's orientation to language is first acquired in the family and is initially determined by the relationships existing therein. The communication patterns to which a child is exposed both reflect the social in the family and give a social basis to his construction of the world; and this in the sense that the child's orientation to language use will extend to his coding of objects as well as his experience of persons. Code is seen as a principle integrating semantic relevance with the form of its contextual realisation. Berstein has suggested four generalised socialising contexts which are critical in the socialisation of the child. These are the regulative, the instructional, the interpersonal and the imaginative contexts. Bernstein considers that communication elicited by these four familial contexts is governed by elaborated or restricted codes of varying strengths depending upon the extent to which familial communication to the child focuses upon relatively context-dependent or -independent meanings. He argues that different explorations of the grammar and lexes are related to such coding orientations. This first sense of context attempts to describe those on-going and constantly recurring situations in which code both regulates the form of the transmission and is itself transmitted to the child.

The term context is also used throughout this paper to describe those local situations in which speech is elicited or recorded from speakers. The eliciting context has received a great deal of attention in recent socio-linguistic work as investigators have become sensitised to the general problem of situational constraints on language use and have applied their ideas and findings to specifically educational contexts. Since Bernstein's concept of sociolinguistic code cannot be directly observed but must be inferred from speech in context, and since the concept of the child's coding orientation includes his own understanding or construction of this context then it follows, at least from the present theoretical perspective,

275

276 Code in Context

that neither code nor context can be fully apprehended without a consideration of the relations between them. A child's communicative competence is only made active in context and so cannot be understood without analysis of what is immediately critical for the form this activation takes. At the same time, the meaning of a context for a speaker and therefore his realisation of it is shaped by just this competence or code.

Having underlined the importance of the interaction, we must stress also that analytically the two are separable and that theoretically they are distinct. A child's coding orientation is not identical with his interpretation and realisation of contexts but may be defined independently as a general orientation to the selection and realisation of meaning on the part of an active speaker/hearer. Thus code is further proposed to have a number of non-linguistic implications. And contexts are not conceived as wholly phenomenal, since then we have a very shifting basis for comparison between groups of speakers and for anchoring descriptions of contextualised speech to a more sociological explanation of the ways in which different groups of speakers use language.

These two kinds of context, which we may call contexts of transmission and eliciting contexts, apparently operate at rather different levels of abstraction. Bernstein's four socialising contexts are closely related to the neo-Firthian[†] concept of generalised[†] language functions while it is clear that contexts of elicitation refer to specific situations or situation-types. The two are linked in the present framework by the hypothesis that the code acquired by the child through experience in the contexts of transmission will be realised in a predictable manner in any one context of elicitation. Where contexts of transmission are governed by different codes then children are expected to differ in their orientation to language use and these different coding orientations will be realised in the semantic and linguistic choices made by the child in a range of eliciting situations.

I Codes and Contexts of Transmission

In Bernstein's thesis class is seen as regulating the distribution of what counts as dominant or privileged meanings and the acceptable form of their realisation. According to this particular thesis class affects the form of transmission and the institutionalisation of elaborated codes in education as well as their distribution between families. Middle-class families are oriented to the meanings and communication patterns of the elaborated code because the class structure points such families towards a structure of social relationships which gives rise to an elaborated code. The structure of social relationships typical of many lower-working-class families gives rise to the semantic orientation and communication patterns of the restricted code again through the action of the wider class structure. Here, these more macro-elements of the thesis will concern us only indirectly. The theoretical consideration of most concern to us may be formulated as *the nature of the relationship between sociolinguistic codes and some specific sociolinguistic codings*. This question cannot, however, be divorced from the general framework, and more sociological aspects of the thesis will frequently be invoked. Bernstein has outlined the most relevant sociological concepts (Introduction to Adlam *et al.*, 1977), and a detailed account may be found in Cook-Gumperz (1973).

II Codes and Codings: the Theoretical Formulation

Bernstein defines code as a general orientation to the selection and organisation of meaning and to the form of its realisation in speech. Briefly, elaborated code users are orientated to more universalistic or context-independent[1] meanings which are explicitly realised in speech. Restricted code users are orientated towards more particularistic or context-dependent meanings which are implicitly realised in speech. Code, then, is seen as a tacit rule system† regulating the semantic and linguistic choices which a speaker makes in a wide range of situations. Code is not identical with these choices but is realised through them. This relationship of codes to actual speech is formulated as the relationship of codes to *context-specific codings* (or speech variants or texts) and is diagrammed in Figure 11.1.

In this first section we shall focus on how parental orientation to code will influence the density and nature of communication in the four generalised transmission contexts. It is of some importance to point out that the unit for analysis is the communicative structure of the family in which is embedded the specific communication of a parent or parents to children. However, parents talk to each other, and the form and content of their speech provides for the children a crucial structure of meanings.

Where the code is elaborated, the four contexts of transmission will be explored and realised in a way that differs systematically from their exploration and realisation through a restricted code. Inevitably the discussion will contain many concrete examples and the specific 'contexts of situation' shown in the diagram here refer to encounters between parent and child. In the next section when we come to consider the interview context the same diagram is relevant, but the contexts of situation under discussion are encounters between children and interviewers and the emphasis is more squarely on attributes of the interview situation. In both cases, however, the relationship of codes to context-specific codings is

Figure 11.1: The Relationship of Code to a Variety of Context-specific Codings

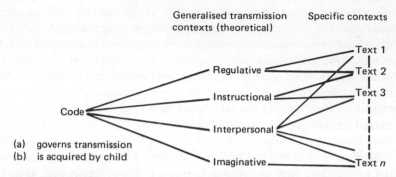

being explored.

It is suggested that in general elaborated codes are realised through elaborated codings, restricted codes give rise to restricted codings. Such a formulation raises the question of how the surface indices of restricted and elaborated codings are to be identified. What, in any one context, counts as restricted coding and what counts as elaborated coding? This question is fundamental and may be put more specifically.

1. The codes are defined in terms of quite high level concepts such as context-independence/context-dependence; explicit/implicit; universalistic/particularistic.

2. What we are faced with empirically is the talk of a child or parent or teacher in a concrete situation, about a specific topic and often with a well-defined aim.

The problem is how to relate the observable speech to the general concept of code. To say that elaborated coding will be relatively more context-independent than restricted coding does not tell us what are the actual lexical and grammatical indices of one or another variant in a given context. Methodologically the problem is 'solved' in the writing of a coding frame.[†]

The network type of coding frame developed by Bernstein and drawing on the work of linguist Michael Halliday starts with the more general theoretical distinctions and works through to specify the linguistic markers of these distinctions in the particular context under consideration. One facet of the theoretical problem can therefore be viewed as the nature of the activity involved in writing context-specific coding frames. By 'context-specific' here we mean that at the linguistic level the coding frame has very little generality beyond this one particular situation. Thus a second aspect of the problem consists in ensuring that varying examples of context-specific speech are coded at comparable levels. For instance, the markers of restricted coding in a control context may differ considerably from the markers of restricted coding in an instructional context (see below for an expansion of this point). In order to tie theory to data and to clarify the framework through which this is done, we must be able both to derive from theory the linguistic markers of restricted coding in the two contexts and to make sure that the two sets of markers are comparable one with the other. These twin aims are really two sides of the same coin. Only if the two sets of markers are realisations of the same more basic distinctions will the coding be comparable across contexts.

At first sight the above may appear obscure. This is partially because the discussion anticipates our presentation of some concrete illustrations of context-specific restricted and elaborated codings. It will be easier, once some such illustrations have been discussed, to examine the question of how the theoretical distinctions between the two codes may be realised and recognised in the distinctions made by speakers in their coding of contexts. It is important, however, that the theoretical problems are to the fore throughout the reading of the following examples and, at the risk of confusing the reader, some further points may be alluded to before the examples are given. All of these will be given fuller consideration presently.

Relating Varying Context-specific Codings

It was noted above that 'the markers of restricted coding in a control context may differ considerably from the markers of restricted coding in an instructional context'. In terms of Figure 11.1 the critical features of texts 1 through n may vary greatly while still being tied to the more general concept of code. Now in order to infer whether a child is primarily oriented to a restricted code or to an elaborated code it is clearly better to look at a range of his context-specific codings than to restrict the analysis to one single text. It will become evident that such an analysis is far from simple. It involves the correlating of what, at a surface level, are very different kinds of texts. The texts are of course related at a theoretical level because the same conceptual framework generated each individual coding frame. Keeping the different analyses comparable is a major methodological problem. Examining the consistency of speakers across contexts becomes a test of the thesis itself.

Context-specific Coding Considered as Text

We have said that a central problem in Bernstein's theory (or in 'operation-alising' this theory) is that of relating the more abstract or more socio-logical definitions of code to actual speech in context (codings). In the practical task of analysing such speech the converse problem presents itself. Having derived from theoretical distinctions the corresponding distinctions at the level of lexes and grammar there is a danger of concen-trating so exclusively on linguistic features that the object of concern (i.e. semantic orientation) is almost lost sight of completely. For example it may be decided that exophoric† pronouns are one index of restricted coding in a descriptive task while expanded nominal groups† are an index of elaborated coding in the same situation. The significant thing about a child's response then becomes whether his use of these categories is above or below average. Certainly this is important, but other features contribute to the nature of the text which he offers. Linguistic indices are more important in the pattern formed by them than in the use of any one individually. This notion of a text is crucial in sociolinguistic work and is discussed in detail on p. 290. For the moment let it be noted that from the perspective of the present paper it is a text rather than a phrase, clause or sentence that is taken as the unit of analysis in the investigation of speech. The notion of text is closer to concepts such as context-independent/dependent than are more purely linguistic measures and so provides a link between the two. The patterning of linguistic indices tells us the nature of the text that is offered.

Structured v. Naturalistic Data

Throughout, we will tend to take a particular situation (e.g. mother con-trolling her child, children explaining the rules of a game to an interviewer) and compare and contrast the texts offered by restricted and elaborated code users in this situation. Such an approach may obscure the basic fact that speakers (especially those with power, e.g. parents and teachers) *have a considerable degree of control over the contexts which they choose to code.* [2] Thus while we shall here illustrate how different speakers vary in their exploration and realisation of the same contexts it is also the case that the density of communication over the range of situation types encountered by members of a culture will vary according to code. Thus elaborated code transmitters may use language for the exploration and articulation of feelings and intent to a greater extent than do restricted code transmitters. The latter may centre more of their communications around control than is the case for elaborated code users. Both these examples may be derived from Bernstein's thesis and receive support from

Wootton's (1974) study of mother/child interaction. Although our discussion will inevitably centre on comparison and contrast in pre-given situations we shall, wherever possible, allude to corresponding theoretical predictions and empirical findings from less structured situations.

Code Realisation in the Four General Contexts of Transmission

In order to clarify the structure of relationships between codes and context-specific codings, Bernstein has delineated four critical socialising contexts. Further, this framework points to the theoretically most relevant siutations which the child encounters. It should be stressed that this notion of context does not correspond to the term as it is used in some current sociolinguistic work but is more akin to a generalised function of language as conceived by the neo-Firthian school of linguistics (see especially Halliday, 1973). Thus any one speech encounter might include two or more socialising contexts. Situations in which the child is being controlled would obviously be characterised as regulative contexts but might also be instructional and/or interpersonal. There is a fairly wide range of empirical speech events (at least in the life of the child) which may be characterised according to Bernstein's four contexts of transmission. Bernstein (1971, ch. 9) describes these contexts as follows:

1. The regulative context — these are authority relationships where the child is made aware of the rules of the moral order and their various backings.
2. The instructional context — where the child learns about the objective nature of objects and persons and acquires skills of various kinds.
3. The imaginative context (or innovating) — where the child is encouraged to experiment and re-create his world on his own terms and in his own way.
4. The interpersonal context — where the child is made aware of affective states — his own and others.

What, then, do the theoretical distinctions imply for specific interactions? Halliday (1973) discusses at some length the possible semantic options open to a mother in a situation where her child has returned home after playing in a forbidden place and with a 'trophy' of dubious origin and nature. How is the mother to convey her annoyance at the episode and prevent its recurrence? Halliday gives a whole series of options — she can tell him unequivocally that this is not allowed, she can point out that he has ruined his clothes, she can express disapproval of his playmates, she can threaten to tell his father, she can explain that the place is physically dangerous, etc., etc. The implication of Halliday's network of choices is that where communication is governed by a restricted code then the characteristic pattern of choices will differ from that where the communication is governed by an elaborated code. We must point out, however, that Halliday is here concerned with the construction of a network of choices within the regulative context. It is not possible to infer whether the speech variant is restricted or elaborated from the consideration of any *one* choice in the network. The following sets of statements would be drawn from different systems of the network describing choices in the regulative context. The first set would enter choices in the imperative system whereas the second set would enter choices in the appeal system. The latter makes available to the child information about the intentions and consequences of the child's acts as they relate to him (child-oriented appeals) or as they relate to the controller (parent-oriented appeals). (For a complete account of this system of classification see Cook-Gumperz, 1973.)

Don't do that again.

You'll get smacked.

I told you before about going there and if you do it again you'll lose a week's pocket money.

I'm going to tell your dad this time.

Just look at the state of your clothes, don't you think I've got enough to do without you adding to it?

You mustn't play on rubbish dumps — they're often full of broken glass and old tins and you might get cut.

The first set of statements conveys to the child information about explicit hierarchical relationships. He is given no basis for the ruling and so the verbal statement does not transcend the given context. The child can, of course, question 'Why can't I?', but the probability of 'Because I say so' as an answer is quite high.

The child confronted with statements of the second kind also learns that he is supposed to give up this particular play patch. But he learns something besides this. The meaning structure to which he is exposed goes beyond this single incident and he receives both an explicit basis for not repeating this action and an indication of other acts that might meet with nasty consequences — either for himself or for others. The meanings offered to this child transcend the given context while giving an explicit basis for the action within it. This is not to say that, faced with persistent disobedience, this mother might not eventually explode with 'Because I say so now be quiet', but the hypothesis is that the verbally explicit information is likely to be evoked, at least as a first strategy, in a wide range of regulative situations.

We would like to emphasise that abstracted, isolated statements such as those given above are in themselves no firm empirical basis for determining the underlying coding orientation. It is necessary to examine the total pattern of choices to make such an inference. This point will be expanded in our discussion of texts as a unit of analysis.

Consider now an instructional or explanatory context. There is considerable evidence that children differ in the sheer amount of adult instructional speech to which they are exposed outside school. Wootton (1974), in a naturalistic study of parent-child interaction in the home, found that pre-school working-class (WC) children spent much less time in verbal exchanges with their parents than did their middle-class (MC) contemporaries. Beyond this difference in amount of talk, WC mothers were less prepared than MC mothers to answer the children's requests for information or to offer such information spontaneously. Further, the utterances of the MC mother were apparently such as to encourage more 'advanced' questions – in content terms – from their children. A final, intriguing finding was that while WC mothers were often quite prepared to participate actively in their children's fantasy play, MC mothers frequently used such imaginings as an opportunity for the transmission of information. The WC mothers never did this.

Henderson (in Brandis and Henderson, 1970), using a much larger sample of questionnaire-based data, reports results congruent with Wootton's findings. WC mothers were consistently more likely than MC mothers to avoid their children's questions in a number of situations: fantasy questions, requests for information, questions about the meaning of words, etc.

Beyond the finding that MC mothers are more predisposed to make the instructional context a focal part of the child's verbally mediated socialisation, Bernstein suggests that the nature of the communication once such a context has been initiated will differ according to the dominant code. As with the control context it is expected that where the code is elaborated stress will be on the transmission of principles, and that instruction in context will include information relevant outside the particular situation. In such a context, verbal explicitness both realises the mother's intent and sensitises the child to the relevance of the principles that lie behind the immediate operation with which he is involved. Henderson's analysis (1970, *op. cit.*) of maternal communication styles provides considerable support for the notion that MC mothers are concerned to teach general rules whereas WC mothers tend to stress aspects of the particular situation. Henderson also gives evidence to suggest that the MC mothers couple this emphasis on general principles with considerable contextual specificity and that WC mothers tend to discriminate less between, for example, topics in terms of explanatory strategy.

Lineker's analysis (in Adlam *et al.*, 1977) of children's preferred means of explaining the rules of a game (hide-and-seek) provides interesting data as to how these social class differences in maternal orientation to explanation might be realised in the child's approach to such a context, as elicited in an experimental interview. Lineker finds that while MC children are strongly disposed to giving an overall review of the rules in terms of 'general' players and circumstances (e.g. 'someone's got to hide somewhere') many WC children move towards a description of a specific instance of the game in which they have themselves participated (e.g. 'little girl hides in the kitchen').

The interpersonal context enters quite explicitly into some of the control examples given above — as when the child's attention is drawn to the unhappiness which his behaviour has caused his mother. Bernstein and Henderson found that MC mothers relative to WC mothers judged that the transmission of interpersonal skills would be much more difficult without language than would the transmission of manual skills. Thus MC mothers emphasise the verbal exploration of affect and intent. Wootton, in the study referred to above, also found that MC mothers were far more likely to make explicit reference to feelings and personal states. In fact, Wootton (personal communication) found that WC *mothers* made less explicit reference to the interpersonal area than did MC *children* although in general adults make such references far more extensively than do children. These findings suggest that MC families place some emphasis on drawing the attention of their children to the affective states of others and on encouraging the children to be explicit about their individual meanings in this area. Detailed study of the interpersonal function of language has tended to focus on its role in regulative situations; in the present framework, on how control and interpersonal contexts relate together. An interesting aspect of Wootton's analysis was the finding that for all families, most references to intent were made outside control situations (although in both control and non-control situations the class differential was highly significant).

Both conceptually and empirically, the interpersonal and innovative contexts have been studied in less detail than have the regulative and instructional functions of language. This is especially true of the imaginative context, but even the current limited state of our knowledge would suggest that the most interesting sub-cultural differences in the exploration of this context occur in the extent to which it is made situation-specific for the child, and particularly in the way it is related to the other three language functions. Briefly, both Wootton's analysis and the SRU research suggest that there is far greater tension and interaction between the imaginative and instructional contexts for MC than for WC children. We have already mentioned that MC mothers are much more likely than WC mothers to use their children's fantasy play as an opportunity to transmit information. In the speech of the children also, WC children are much more likely than MC children to use narrative speech when asked explicitly for instruction or for description (which, it is suggested, involves a strong instructional element in the context of adult/child interaction). This is clearly shown in both Lineker's and Adlam's papers (in Adlam *et al., op. cit.*) and has been corroborated by others, including Lancia in Belgium. It has also been shown by Turner that in the interview context, MC children require very explicit requests before they will move into a hypothetical mode whereas WC children do this more freely. And Hasan (personal communication) finds that when asked to make up a bedtime story, MC children are more constrained and give more tightly and traditionally structured answers than do their WC peers. Taken together, this rather heterogeneous group of findings would suggest that MC children are learning to mark off contexts according to the social relationships and questions asked, whereas some WC children are in similar contexts predominantly oriented to narrative speech. While this may allow them sometimes to make more fluent and free use of the narrative mode, it also implies a different understanding of the parameters of speech contexts and a different classification and patterning of uses of language than that which is acquired by the MC child. It would appear that the tension that exists in MC transmission between report and innovation on the one hand, and instruction and investigation on the other, is a likely determining influence.

We have tried to show how different orientations to code will create different patterns of communication and control in the familial socialisation of the child. Where a restricted code governs transmission, the speech variants will tend towards restriction in all four socialising contexts. Similarly, where an elaborated code governs the transmission, the four general socialising contexts will tend to elicit elaborated variants or codings. This does not mean that where the code is restricted, there will never be any context-specific elaborated codings. Conversely, Bernstein has continually stressed that where the dominant code is elaborated, a whole range of situations will be more appropriately handled through restricted codings. This issue is fully considered below. Here it remains to discuss how the speech itself is to be described, and this can profitably be done in relation to child language. Two aspects of the problem will be singled out for analysis. First, the identification of the critical features of speech variants will be discussed. Since code is defined in terms of semantics, as a general orientation to meaning, then what is significant at the level of lexes and grammar may differ considerably from one situation to another. Second, we will consider the general problem of the appropriate unit of linguistic analysis for sociolinguistic work. It will be argued that any attempt to understand the relationship between social structure and language use should aim for a textual characterisation of speech; that detailed analysis of the mean frequency of certain lexical and grammatical items in the speech of any social group is not in itself an adequate characterisation of the nature of that speech from a social perspective. Both these discussions of course take up points initially raised in our consideration of the relationship between codes and codings at the beginning of this section.

III   Codes and Codings: the Description of Speech

The Critical Features of Speech Variants

The linguistic realisations of code have been described here in terms of an orientation to the *selection* and *realisation* of meaning on the part of speakers — to the creation of meaning and the form of its encoding in speech. But the two are not independent. In the examples drawn from the regulative and instructional contexts (pp. 282, 284) it was suggested that speakers could focus either on more local issues — particularistic meanings — or that they could focus on the principles behind the immediate event — universalistic meanings — as well. Thus in these two contexts children are being sensitised to different orders of meaning according to whether the dominant code is elaborated or restricted. Because they are more tied to the immediate situation, particularistic meanings have also been termed more context-dependent than the universalistic type, which are apparently more generally applicable and so more context-independent.

But this distinction of context-independence and context-dependence has also been used to describe the explicitness of the speech. Thus when the children were given Trotin[†] pictures to describe, there was variation in the extent to which they made their meanings explicit and specific. Some of the children gave speech that could be understood by listeners outside the immediate interaction, whereas others gave speech that was much more context-dependent in that the listener had need of the eliciting material in order fully to understand the child's utterance. The first of the following two statements is of this more context-dependent type, whereas the second is relatively less embedded in the eliciting situation:

he's doing that
the guard man's pushing a luggage cart

Now in practice, this distinction between the child's selection of meaning and his orientation to its realisation is quite blurred. If a child understands that he is to be verbally explicit in certain kinds of communication situations then this will affect what he talks about as well as how. Similarly, the choice of, say, an imperative control strategy itself constrains the form of the linguistic realisation. Beyond this, the form of an utterance can itself be of semantic significance, especially in the social meaning which it carries (see next section).

Figure 11.2: Linguistic Realisation of Code

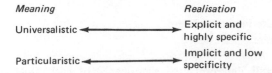

Meaning	Realisation
Universalistic ◄────────►	Explicit and highly specific
Particularistic ◄────────►	Implicit and low specificity

It is apparent that the semantic and lexical/grammatical aspects of language in use cannot be divorced. Semantic options will limit the range of possible formal choices, and formal options (influenced, for example, by the speaker/listener relationship) will affect meaning in a variety of ways. But it is the case that the relationship between universalistic meanings and explicit speech and between particularistic meanings and implicit speech is not of the order shown in Figure 11.2.

It is important to spell this out because the terms context-independent and context-dependent have been applied to both levels and it would be easy to infer that the relation between the levels was simple. But in Lineker's analysis (1977), many of the children who gave particularistic accounts of hide-and-seek used fairly explicit linguistic constructions. What, for example, is the difference in explicitness between the following?

someone's got to hide in a good place
little girl goes and hides in the cupboard

Conversely, the difference in meaning between the following cannot be described in terms of general/particular

he's doing that
the guard man's pushing a luggage cart

yet Adlam (Adlam *et al., op. cit.*) calls the first context-dependent, the second more context-independent.

However, if we consider the implicit variants of the two instructional examples, both transform into

she's got to hide there

In other words, making the realisation implicit, making an utterance implicit at the level of lexes and grammar, automatically renders the meaning more context-dependent. This would seem to imply that context-independent meaning must be realised explicitly. But the converse does not hold — context-dependent or particularistic meanings can be realised explicitly or implicitly; which is not to say that there is no important difference between

little girl goes and hides in the cupboard
she goes and hides there

The specific context will determine the significance of each facet of language for coding orientation.

Our model of the relationship between the semantic and lexico-grammatical levels then looks more like Figure 11.3.

The hypothesis that sociolinguistic code may be inferred from the nature of the speech variants[†] in the four socialising contexts (or, more precisely, specific situations relevant to these) demands that the level at which these variants are characterised is compatible between contexts. The terms context-independent and context-dependent are useful because whether the distinctive features of elaborated and restricted variants are expected largely at the level of meaning or largely at the level of realisation (e.g. Adlam, in Adlam *et al., op. cit.*), at the social level, the basis of the orientation remains the same. Both particularistic meanings and implicit speech are realisations of a social situation which, for the speaker, involves reduced distance between himself and other aspects of the setting. Both universalistic meanings and explicit speech are part of a speaker/setting relationship of increased distance; both the meaning and the form of its

Figure 11.3: The Relationship between the Semantic and Lexico-grammatical Levels of Speech

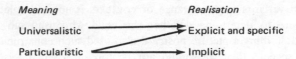

encoding in speech have less need of the eliciting context in order to be decoded by a listener. For this reason Bernstein can say that explicit speech is universalistic in nature in the sense that the meaning is more universally available, is available to more listeners. And implicit speech can be called particularistic in the sense that only particular others – those with whom the speaker has certain shared knowledge either in terms of their common history or in terms of the immediate context – can fully decode the message.

Because both the selection and realisation of meaning are of social origin, it is difficult to make the distinction at all. Indeed the grounds for so doing are more pragmatic than explanatory and our essential concern is to point to the different emphases or foci which investigation of child speech can adopt. Meaning reverberates on speech, syntactic and lexical choices can be viewed as more delicate semantic options, grammatical form is an index of semantic organisation. We tease out the levels in order to understand their interaction and to show that apparently disparate surface features of speech have a common social motivation and therefore may be equally relevant to social theory.

Having stressed the dialectical relationship between the social, semantic and grammatical aspects of speaking we can briefly take an analytic perspective and suggest that the three pairs of terms: universalistic/particularistic; implicit/explicit; context-independent/context-dependent, might be applied to the levels of, respectively, meaning, lexical/grammatical choice and text. This third level – that of text – includes the other two and, since it derives directly from the more general theory, is an important means of ensuring that the description of speech in one context is comparable with the description in another. The characterising of speech in context as an elaborated or a restricted variant will depend on the extent to which the speech shows a context-independent orientation to meaning and to its realisation. The context itself will determine what specific features of the utterance are to be the focus of attention. Thus the instructional task can focus on the child's overall approach to explanation; the control task can look at the child's tendency to use imperative as opposed to more informative and contingent strategies; the imaginative task is concerned both with linguistic cohesion and with questions of structure.

It should now be clear why Bernstein's concern with assessing the nature of the speech variants across a range of contexts is not a simple one. If the issue were to determine whether the child who used subordinate clauses in describing a picture postcard also used such constructions in his control speech, then we should not be too surprised if this were the case. However, it is not immediately apparent why children who opt for imperative control strategies should also explain hide-and-seek in terms of particular players and places. The 'consistency' predicted by Bernstein's framework refers to consistency in the contextual realisation of the child's general orientation to sociolinguistic code. To put it tritely, the linguistic realisation of code depends on context (as Bernstein has used it) as well as on code.

Our concern with arriving at a theoretically derived textual description of any one speech variant stems partly from just this surface discontinuity in the different contextual realisations of code. The notion that individual linguistic indices should be used only as a guide to the textual characteristics of speech will be considered in some detail. This is a basic tenet of the present perspective as well as having quite general relevance.

Textual Descriptions

Many studies to date have been concerned to demonstrate differences between sub-cultural groups in individual linguistic measures, e.g. number of pronouns or frequency of relative clauses. We are here arguing that such an approach gives inadequate information about the child's orientation to language use and that the appropriate unit of analysis for sociolinguistic research is a text. Clearly, word counts and the like will relate to a textual description of the speech. Indeed, such a description will usually be based on more detailed linguistic analyses. The point is that the significance of individual indices is given less by their incidence or frequency in the child's speech and more by how they pattern with other measures. Adlam in discussing the results of the analysis of descriptive speech (Adlam *et al.*, *op. cit.*) writes:

It may have been noted that in no case was a (linguistic) category used exclusively and extensively by one group of children — that, in fact, the differences observed were often superficially slight, representing variations in tendency, in orientation to one or another kind of speech. And this is what we would expect. The children are speaking the same language and they have all been given a standardised set of questions about a standardised task. *Nevertheless it is our conviction that quite small variations in the extent to which certain semantic and linguistic elements are employed, will combine and interact to give crucial differences in the overall patterning of the speech and that these will emerge quite clearly when we look at texts as a whole* (italics original).

Clearly it is of fundamental importance to explicate the linguistic indices which will differentiate texts in a theoretically relevant way. The problem is really one of losing the wood through an overriding concern with the taxonomic properties of trees and, to labour the metaphor, of then being unable to say very much about the conditions which generate different kinds of forest. In the above case, the theoretical dimension with which we were concerned was Bernstein's distinction between context-independent and context-dependent speech. These concepts refer to properties of texts but were operationalised through the identification of critical semantic and grammatical features. The problem of then using these quantitative measures as a basis for a more global description of each child's speech is not a simple one. Lineker's analysis (Adlam *et al., op. cit.*) is more satisfactory in this regard since her coding procedure made an initial distinction in terms of the child's overall approach to the task of instruction.

Staying for a moment with the descriptive task, in which children were asked about three detailed picture postcards depicting work by Trotin, we can make more concrete the distinction between textual and linguistic feature analyses. As stated above, the descriptive analysis was concerned with the explicitness and specificity of the child's speech, with the degree to which it could be understood independently of the eliciting context. Some children made their descriptions much more context-dependent than others. Context-dependent speech is characterised as relying on external situational features for its interpretation. Exophoric pronouns (e.g. he, she, this, that, *not* referring back to an item previously specified linguistically) have their referents in the context of situation and have therefore been explored as an index of context-dependence, especially in descriptive and narrative tasks (Hawkins, 1969; Hasan, 1968; Adlam in Adlam *et al., op cit.*). It has been shown that exophora differentiates texts intuitively and sub-cultural groups empirically in that working-class children in an interview context tend to make greater use of such pronouns and adverbs than do middle-class children. However, the incidence of exophorics does not in itself define a text as either context-independent or context-dependent. The way in which such constructions pattern with other linguistic features is the essential consideration.

Consider the following examples:

lady sitting there   man walking along
little girl's got a train   lady's going shopping   shops
trains   ladies   dogs   those men

This short excerpt contains one exophoric reference in 11 headworks, but it could not be characterised as showing a strong orientation to context-independent speech. A lack of exophoric reference means something quite different in the above text than it does in the following sample of speech:

people are at the station waiting for their train   maybe they're going on holiday   there's a house at the side with smoke coming out of the chimney   she's got a big suitcase to go in the train

Thus largely because of the second child's inclusion of certain indices such as highly specific reference to general statements, the two children differ considerably in the extent to which they have constructed context-independent texts. In terms of an analysis confined to the incidence of discrete linguistic categories, however, these children score similarly on a critical measure.

A further reason for making a text the linguistic unit of analysis is brought out very clearly when we examine the child's speech across contexts (Adlam and Turner in Adlam *et al., op. cit.*). For example, we may want to compare the child's orientation to descriptive speech with his speech in the control task. A preference for certain choices within the imperative form of control is suggested as one characteristic of trans-mission governed by a restricted code (Bernstein, 1971, ch. 9) but, follow-ing the argument applied to exophora in description, the child's preference for imperative strategies cannot be taken in isolation. For example, his tendency to explicate the reasons for the command is also of interest. It follows from this that attempts to investigate whether a child's coding orientation is consistent across contexts will gain a misleading picture if correlations are made, for example, between frequency of exophoric constructions and frequency of imperative forms. The appropriate analysis is one which compares the child's orientation to language use, in the two tasks. By aiming for a textual characterisation of speech we allow more meaningful comparisons of very different kinds of texts generated by very different sociolinguistic contexts.

The above discussion throws considerable doubt on the kind of single-phrase illustrations of restricted and elaborated code use sprinkled rather liberally throughout this paper. We can of course argue limitations of space but would be in fundamental agreement with such a criticism. It is at the level of complete interview transcripts (Adlam *et al., op. cit.*) that we seek to understand the child's use of language. Further, we are not only suggesting that the emphasis on individual structural aspects of speech is misplaced and that the textual patterning of such aspects is primary. The argument applies also to more semantically focused analyses as when the incidence of imperative control strategies was pointed out above to be only one index of restricted forms of control to be considered in the light of the child's tendency also to make more informative options. The categories used in the analysis of control, such as imperatives, reasoning and concessions, are primarily semantic rather than grammatical (given the fluidity of that distinction) but the necessity of centring on their overall patterning still holds.

In conclusion, it can be said that a central concern is to show how Bernstein's theory of restricted and elaborated codes can generate a useful description of socially based differences in how children use language in a variety of situations. And further, that such descriptions may be meaningfully compared across these situations. Adlam and Turner (Adlam *et al., op. cit.*) report a comparison of the orientation of 200 children to language use in control, descriptive and instructional contexts and find that the children do indeed show some consistency in whether their coding orientations are restricted or elaborated. Now these tasks (the control, descriptive and instructional) were constructed to correspond to Bernstein's initial socialising contexts as outlined above. It should be noted, however, that the collection of speech from the children was in a sense indirect. Their speech was not recorded in actual contexts of transmission, but in tasks expected to realise the coding orientation acquired in such contexts. And these tasks were presented in interview form. The question then arises whether or not the procedure of data collection exerted a critical influence on the data obtained. The answer to this is broadly that it did, but to understand the significance of the context of elicitation in Bernstein's theory we must discuss in more detail the social assumptions underlying the two codes. Such a discussion will profitably include extended reference to other sociolinguistic enquiries into the effect of context on language use.

IV   The Context of Situation

The notion of the context of situation is not new in linguistic writings, but having been obscured by the appearance of Chomskyan theory it

294	Code in Context

has only recently found a new stage in sociolinguistics. Firthian and neo-Firthian tradition in linguistics has always been concerned with linguistic function and with context, but we will here concentrate on how the notion of context has figured in recent sociolinguistic work, largely in America.

A wide range of empirical research now exists to show how aspects of the situation in which a speaker (or writer) finds himself will constrain what is said and how. Such work ranges from investigations of quite broad problems such as the appropriateness of evaluative statements in situations of varying formality through more linguistically oriented studies of the effects of topic, listener, locale, role relationships and function on a speaker's phonology, grammar, lexes and, amongst multilinguals and dialectals, variety. For example, Labov (1964) has shown that the presence of the post-vocalic /r/[†] in the speech of New Yorkers is a function both of the social status of the speaker and of the formality of the situation (casual speech through word lists). And it is well established that among bilinguals the code used will vary as a function of recipient, setting, topic etc. or some combination of these (Ervin-Tripp, 1964; Blom and Gumperz, 1972).

Just as context constrains what a speaker says and the form in which he clothes it, so a listener uses context in interpreting the meaning of what is said both directly and in the wider sense of using the speech as a clue to the social attributes or intentions of the speaker. Only references to the context of situation, for example, will decide whether a statement such as 'it's much too hot in here' is to be understood as simple description, a request to turn off the heating or open a window, or a reproach for wasting electricity, etc. If spoken by a guest who is not a close friend in the home of a middle-class English family, such a statement might also be considered inappropriate and its author abrupt or rude. Unless, of course, the speaker was a visitor from an exotic country, and the host 'enlightened' about cultural diversity, in which case the incident might be ignored. And so on. Gumperz and Hernandez-Chavez (1972) show how code-switching amongst bilinguals is used to signal changes in intimacy and distance during conversation. In their study, what seems at first sight to be random switching from Spanish to English is found to realise subtle variations in social meaning.

This is not the place to attempt an overview of the kind of research to which we alluded above. Rather it is important to see how the aims and findings of 'descriptive sociolinguistic' or ethnography-of-speaking[†] approaches to child language may be related to the present series of studies and their theoretical backing. The goal of much micro sociolinguistic work is a description of who says what in what form to whom, where, when and for which purpose. Such a formulation is most readily applicable in situations of multilingualism or dialect variation, since where this is absent or not the central concern it becomes extremely difficult to decide on what counts as variation in form (see, for example, Hasan [1973] on the distinctions code, register and dialect). It is more appropriate to rephrase the problem as it bears on the work of the SRU — where all the children are speaking the same language and dialect variation is not a primary focus of interest — as what constellation of contextual variables will evoke which *kinds of codings* in different groups of children. And this is not a trivial quibble over the formulation of the problem; it involves the basic distinction between code in Bernstein's sense and, for example, dialect or language variety, and also between the nature of the meanings carried by their use. Hasan (1973) makes this distinction between code and dialect as follows:

> Two outstanding differences between the two immediately draw attention to themselves: while the extra-linguistic factor(s) correlating with social dialect are incidental, those correlating with code are said to be causal; if the relationship between the two in the former case is simply that of co-occurrence, the relationship between the two in the case of code is that of logical dependence which presupposed co-occurrence. Secondly, while social dialect is defined by reference to its distinctive formal properties, the code is defined by reference to its semantic properties, thus involving consideration of the formal levels only indirectly. That is to say, it can be argued that the semantic properties of the codes can be predicted from the elements of the social structure which, in fact, give rise to them.

This distinction is, perhaps, best illustrated by considering situations where code use and dialect use overlap. In communities employing more than one language variety there is often concurrence between when a variety is used and what it is used for. Much of the research in this area has, in fact, demonstrated just this — that one variety is used in relaxed situations and that an alternative is used in and marks more formal contexts (Fishman, 1965; Blom and Gumperz, 1972). Whether a speaker uses a restricted or an elaborated code is also dependent on the social situation, on the role relationship between speaker and listener. Restricted coding realises relationships based on shared assumptions and shared meanings where explication in speech would be awkward and redundant; elaborate coding rests on different assumptions (e.g. takes less for granted in the speaker/listener relationship) and is used to explain, to instruct, to probe behind the apparent. However, because a dialect or language is the appropriate means of speech in informal situations and therefore is often used to realise a restricted code, this does not mean that such a variety *is* a restricted code. There is no fundamental reason why variety A, appropriate to informal contexts, could not be used to elaborate meanings of a universalistic kind and, conversely, why variety B, appropriate to formal contexts, could not embody the condensed implicit symbols of solidarity; which is not to say that such usage would come easily to speakers (see, for example, Ervin-Tripp's interview with Japanese women who, though fluent in English through intermarriage, had great difficulty in discussing matters of personal significance in the English tongue).

Coding orientation, then, follows logically from the nature of the eliciting context itself while dialect, although it can be used in very subtle ways to define and redefine contexts, is only incidentally related to them. We might say that while coding orientation *realises* the social context, dialect or variety is used to *mark* the social context.

This raises a whole number of issues, some of which we will explore in detail. First, the meanings carried and realised by code use are likely to be of a different nature to those carried and realised through dialect use. Second, the form of investigation appropriate to these two aspects of the relation between social structure and language is likely to be different. An ethnographic approach is almost dictated by what we have referred to as descriptive sociolinguistics, while it is unlikely to be very efficient in the adequate exploration of code. Third, the kinds of linguistic analysis needed and therefore the slant of the linguistic theory are likely to be different. In determining the dialect used by a speaker we look for a particular pattern of phonological, lexical and grammatical choices, and although the social context will be fundamental in determining which choices are made, the analysis of the speech can be carried out without reference to this context. We do not need information about locale, the topic of conversation or the person to whom it is directed to decide whether a person is using Welsh or English, although very detailed ethnographic data may be required in order to reveal the full range of meaning carried by that choice. An analysis of code use, however, is basically functional and therefore cannot be undertaken without reference to the eliciting context (see sections on 'Codes and Codings').

A fourth problem concerns the nature of context. Is it, in fact, a social or a social/psychological variable? And this raises also the question of the nature of social control. Is a child's linguistic performance subject to the kind of external control that acts upon cheekiness, sullenness and aggression, or does it point also to the social constraints on the realisation of mental structures, on the formation of consciousness?

Finally, we can look to how these two approaches to social aspects of language use might have some very definite convergences. The issue of the influence of such factors as topic or listener on whether a speaker uses Spanish or American English, Clydebank Glaswegian or BBC Standard is not identical to the problem of the influence of topic or listener on whether a speaker chooses to condense his verbally realised meanings or to articulate and elaborate their nature and origins. Nevertheless there are situational constraints on both these aspects of speech use, and the influences of context on coding orientation can be clarified considerably by the work which examines the more general issue of the social constraints on language use.

One implication of explicating the norms of appropriateness which obtain for a speaker or group of speakers across the spectrum of their uses of language is that we shall more adequately understand communicative interference. Not only will the realisation and interpretation of meaning within a community be made more comprehensible but situations where different patterns of rules for use of language lead to miscommunication will also become clearer.

Studies of the use of terms of address provide neat examples of this kind of confusion (Brown and Gilman, 1960; Kantorovich, 1966; Ervin-Tripp, 1964). As long as we share a system of rules with those around us, it is easy to manipulate terms of address to imply deference or show solidarity, but where a newcomer to a group has a different system of sociolinguistic rules, misinterpretation is likely to result. For example, if the speaker but not the listener has a system in which familiarity, not merely solidarity, is required for use of a first name, he will use 'Mr Smith' instead of 'John' and be regarded as aloof by his listener. Again, he will feel first-name usage by the other in the dyad to be intrusive.

Such situations of mis-match are particularly important in education. Children whose speech patterns are not that of the school may find that they are not understood in the classroom, that the full meaning of their speech fails to reach the teacher and that their responses to her are somehow not appropriate. And as Hymes (1972) has pointed out, 'If one rejects a child's speech, one probably communicates rejection of the child'.

The plight of children whose natural language or dialect is punished or forbidden in the school has been documented by a number of writers and it has also been shown, most clearly by Labov, that even where a child's communicative skills are not actively prohibited, the context of the classroom may be one in which he finds it impossible or irrelevant to make any use of these at all. Hence arose the myth of the non-verbal child. Polgar (1960) describes how Eskimo children interpreted the normal loudness of voice and directness of their American teacher as anger and how she, in turn, took their respectful, fearful silence to be a sign of sullenness and unwillingness to learn.

Again, however, 'interference' can exist at the level of dialect and at the level of code and in both cases there may be variation in its recognition as well as its implications. Differences in orientation to meaning, however, are likely to be more difficult both to recognise and to manage. Interference at the level of code may often assume a more subtle and perhaps more insidious form than that which leads a teacher to try to change a child's accent or grammar. Bernstein (1975) has suggested that in the open classrooms of British primary schools many working-class children understand differently from middle-class children what is required of them and what they must achieve. A number of ways in which what he refers to as the 'invisible pedagogy' may be selectively visible can be suggested. There may, for example, be different tacit understandings as to what counts as a question — from child or adult — and what counts as an acceptable answer — again from child or adult. The question form in the setting of the classroom may provoke, from the child whose socialisation is geared to the modes of instruction which the school prefers, a very different selection and organisation of meanings and speech from that evoked in the child to whom the open classroom appears to have less to do with instruction and more to do with play. In this case the question form might be said to mark the setting as one in which elaborated coding is appropriate.

The understanding that many of the factors which influence a child's language in the classroom are social before they are linguistic, has brought a new set of questions to bear on the problem of the educational testing situation and the relative failure of many WC children on standard attainment measures. Allied to this is the place of the experimental setting in educational research and its limitations in telling us anything at all about any child, but especially about the child who finds such a context culturally confusing or alien. Specifically it must be asked whether the experimental interview is a suitable medium for the investigation of child language.

Labov, for example, has demonstrated how the formality of the interview setting can intimidate a lower-working-class black child to the point where he says practically nothing. By manipulating physical (sitting on the floor eating crisps), psychological (having present the speaker's best friend) and social (reducing the height and therefore status difference between interviewer and interviewee) aspects of the interaction, such a non-verbal child could be transformed into an enthusiastic and fluent speaker. Less dramatically, Heider, Cazden and Brown (1968) showed how social-class differences in the extent to which meanings were made explicit could be made to disappear by giving WC children twice as many probes as MC children. Cazden (1971) gives a useful summary of how children's speech varies as aspects of the eliciting context — topic, task, listener, instructions — are changed.

We can examine some implications of this work in the light of our concern with the effects of context on a child's coding orientation, bearing in mind that the studies cited above have been interested in various kinds of speech use and noting that conclusions drawn from one perspective — e.g. the effect of the situation on the realisation of grammatical competence — have often been applied, and sometimes inappropriately, to the whole question of language use.

It has, for example, been suggested that the kind of research reported by Labov and others implies that every effort should be made to overcome the effects of context, otherwise we shall never get at what the child really knows. This view would appear either to emphasise grammatical rather than communicative competence or else to confuse the two, but its origins are not hard to trace. The importance of demonstrating linguistic competence in Black children springs firstly from a concern to correct the picture of the verbally destitute child painted by deficit theory; and secondly, from a more academic interest in explicating the relationship, in terms of transformational grammar, between standard English and Black vernacular. In pursuing the second aim and demonstrating that Black children have as complex a grammatical competence as any child, Labov has succeeded also in achieving the first. But as Hymes (1972) points out, the demonstration of grammatical competence does not sign the death warrant of the notion of linguistic disadvantage.

Certainly it is scientifically absurd to describe children as coming to school 'linguistically deprived' so far as the presence of regular grammar and the capacity for creative use of language in social life are concerned.

But there is the rub. Children may indeed be linguistically deprived if the language of their natural competence is not that of the school; if the contexts that elicit or permit use of that competence are absent in the school; if the purposes to which they put language and the ways in which they do so, are absent or prohibited in the school.

What much of the research directed at the deficit hypothesis shows is, in fact, that 'the contexts that elicit or permit use of that (Black children's) competence are absent in the school' and the importance of these findings cannot be sufficiently stressed. However, we are still a long way from understanding *how* speakers use a particular dialect or language in different contexts. To show that when ghetto children speak freed of the social constraints of the schoolroom or interview their speech is fluent and dense, and that an underlying logic informs what they say, is to illustrate the completeness of their grammatical competence and to tell us something about which contexts will evoke full use of this competence and which contexts will suppress it almost completely. But an analysis of this kind cannot tell us very much about how the child uses that competence as a coding device. The purposes to which he puts language in different contexts and the extent to which his coding orientation clashes or fits with the orientation expected in the classroom are problems raised only obliquely.

We have said that the selection and realisation of meanings governed by code has its basis in the ongoing social relationship. It is thus apparent that the contexts used to elicit speech that will reflect differences in the code used (either by the same speaker across situations or between speakers in objectively similar situations) must be amenable to differences in coding. We can expand this notion.

A restricted code realises social relationships which are predicated on shared knowledge, where the meanings are implicitly realised and communicated because their verbal explication would be redundant, inappropriate and tedious. Such are the situations which obtain between friends in relaxed atmospheres although to be sure some topics may make the assumption of shared knowledge less certain and their introduction may change the context to one which demands more elaborated coding. In general, however, an encounter between people whose social histories have much in common in a setting which has had many counterparts in the course of their shared histories, and where the content of the talk is neither new nor especially problematic, is a paradigmatic setting for the use of restricted coding.

Now if all speakers will be strongly oriented to restricted coding in this kind of situation, what is the nature of contexts realised through elaborated coding — how are we to characterise such contexts and what are the implications of this for research? Elaborated coding realises contexts where the role relationship that obtains between speaker and listener is such that meanings, principles and processes must be made explicit, where reference to a 'common grid' is either difficult or to be suspended (e.g. as when children learn that although a relevant adult knows very well the answer to the question he has just asked, still the child must answer as if the information was novel). It therefore follows that in order to investigate the presence and extent of orientation to an elaborated code, speech should be elicited in situations which will activate such an orientation. The relationship between speaker and listener, which may be partly given by aspects of the physical situation, is critical if the child who is oriented to elaborated code use in appropriate situations is to understand this situation as appropriate. It is further clear that since sociolinguistic code use *is* the social realised in the linguistic, it is on the social context as the child constructs it that we must focus. Situations to which some children respond with elaborated code use are understood differently *at the social level* by these children than by children who realise the same objective context through restricted codings.

It can now be seen that the kinds of situation used by Labov in order to elicit 'natural' speech from Black children are much more likely to be realised through restricted codings than through elaborated codings. Since the speech was analysed grammatically rather than functionally, it is impossible to test this hypothesis without access to the data — it would be a valuable undertaking. Interesting, however, is the finding in the studies reported here that those children who interpreted the interview context as one in which the relationships between speaker and listener and between speaker and topic were ones of reduced distance and who we, therefore, infer were oriented to a restricted code in this context, were frequently the children who gave the longest and most fluent texts. Often it was the most explicit children or those offering context-independent responses who spoke least. This suggests that their understanding of the context as one in which very little could be taken for granted in the speaker/hearer relationship included a concern with 'accuracy'. The analogy with aspects of the classroom needs no emphasising and it is reasonable to assume that the nature of the speech elicited by an interviewer will shed some light on the way children talk to teachers. Bernstein highlights the role of the interview as follows.

The setting, tasks, social relationships and meanings are independent of the child's normal settings, tasks, relationships and meanings. In this sense, the experimental setting is a *context-independent* setting for the child. Now some children in this setting produce speech or responses which differ markedly from the speech or meanings of other children. Why do the children differ in their interpretation of the context? It certainly has nothing to do with the children's tacit understanding of grammar, and little to do with differences in the children's vocabulary. I suggest that what we are witnessing are differences in the *ground*† *rules* the children are using to generate their meanings and so their speech. One group of children are applying rules for the creation of context-independent speech whereas another group of children are doing this to a lesser extent.

And Adlam (in Adlam *et al., op. cit.*) adds:

In terms of the given context, there is nothing inefficient about context-dependent speech or relatively implicit meaning. Again, it is not to be supposed that children whose tacit understanding leads to the production of a restricted variant in the interview situation are incapable of any degree of elaboration. But the assumption is that such children would require very explicit instructions in order to produce an elaborated variant under these conditions. What is important is that different groups of children spontaneously and consistently offer different orders of meaning and different linguistic realisations, and that these differences are indicative of different orientations to the setting as a whole.

The child's orientation to meaning — his relationship to listener and to task — is constrained in this as in any other situation but it is in just such formally framed interactions that we expect differences in the nature of his socialisation to be made manifest in his speech.

The interview is an eliciting context which might be expected to realise differences in the nature of the transmission contexts which the child has experienced. Those children for whom communication in the home is regulated by an elaborated code will tend towards elaborated coding in such a context; those children for whom cultural transmission is governed by a restricted code will tend towards restricted coding in the same situation. And this is because the children differently construct the context itself.

This formulation, in the light of much of the work in the general sociolinguistic field, leads to two kinds of question. The first may be put quite bluntly. It says 'What if you are wrong?' This issue includes the possibility that, in fact, the empirical research has not measured differences in the child's general orientation to meaning but only (although it is quite a big 'only') differences in willingness to make particular linguistic choices in this one context. It is conceivable, in other words, that those children who made restricted codings in the interview context would without difficulty switch to elaborated code use in another situation. This is the problem posed by Labov and others, and although we have argued above that such studies have demonstrated the effect of context on use of grammatical knowledge rather than on coding orientation, the issue remains that contextual constraints on coding orientation may not be completely confined to the kinds of 'perceived role relationships' which we have discussed. If the children were intimidated by the situation then they would say very little and be disinclined to use language for purposes of exploration and explicitness – their 'restricted codings' would be a mark of anxiety or rejection rather than a realisation of shared assumptions and reduced personal distance. Empirically, this appears quite unlikely. In the research of the SRU it is the middle-class more often than the working-class children who show the greatest constraint. The most 'verbal' (in terms of quantity and rapidity of speech) children are almost without exception working-class and, interestingly, it is often just these children who are most readily characterised as giving restricted variants. While it is clearly the case that the verbal reticence of the children in Labov's research was due to their anxiety in or disdain for the interview context, this does not appear to have been a factor in the British work. To say that children are using language in an implicit, context-dependent way is not to say that they are not using language at all. On the other hand, if the context is such that the child will not make use of this natural language then clearly nothing at all can be said about his orientation to its use as a coding device. Quite simply, we have to try to understand the different levels at which the context of situation can influence language use and then to try to understand which of these is critical in any one empirical situation.

Before leaving this question additional empirical evidence may be mentioned (see Adlam and Turner in Adlam *et al., op. cit.,* for extended discussion) which argues against the suggestion that social class differences in coding orientation are a function of the interview situation pure and simple. The consistency of responses across tasks – where consistency is measured in terms of orientation to meaning and speech use and only indirectly concerns grammatical and lexical features – and the tendency for a child's speech to correlate with his mother's attitude to language use both suggest that the concept of a general coding propensity is necessary for an adequate understanding of the social aspects of language in use.

The second range of issues highlighted by our concern with situational constraints on coding orientation in fact follows from the above discussion and centres on how we are to delineate and characterise the specific features of the context which are important for the elicitation of elaborated coding. Bernstein has said that what is critical is the child's perception of his own social role – not only vis-à-vis his listener but also vis-à-vis the topic in itself and as it is to be communicated to his listener. Presumably, however, this understanding of the social relationship is itself influenced by features such as setting, the form and content of discourse, etc. We have emphasised that the child's speech in context cannot be understood without reference to the child's social history as evinced in his orientation to code. Neither can it be understood without reference to the eliciting context, and it is possible that there exist some very specific features of situations which mark them, for some children, as situations in which the role relationship is one of distance and the appropriate coding is elaborated. But clearly such features could only be so interpreted by a child who had experience of and could handle the necessary role. Other children would understand them differently. We are thinking here of highly specific features – perhaps single phrases like 'Tell me about . . .'

Perhaps the primary value of the focus on social relationships is to stress that it is the context as constructed by the child that is important. Paradoxically, this argues for collecting speech in quite standardised situations, for only then can we argue that systematic variation in speech is a reflection of different interpretations of and orientation to meaning in the same situation. It also suggests that we look at the same child's speech over a range of situations in order to see what for him are the critical differentiating features. The SRU has made a start in this direction and the intention is to make a more comprehensive exploration over the next three years.

In summary, an elaborated coding orientation is identified with a general propensity to take on a social role of distance – at the intra-personal as well as the interpersonal level. In one sense, it is just because he has this context-independent orientation that the individual is led to interpret a wide range of contexts as situations where things must be objectified and made explicit. Context-independent meanings and speech are the realisation of a social perception rooted in the individual's history and beyond. Context-dependent meanings and implicit speech are the realisation of a different order of social relationships, also rooted in the individual's history. At the same time, there will be certain age-, sex- or class-specific contextual features which will intensify or mark the appropriateness of one or other of these orientations once established. Such features may be said to act upon code use in a similar way to that in which they act upon other aspects of language use, but it should be stressed that they do so by underlining what is relevant in the social relationship. And it is the linguistic realisation of the role relation that is seen as necessary for coding orientation but not for other sociolinguistic dimensions. Bernstein's basic proposition is that the typical form and therefore interpretation of the social will differ quite consistently between sub-cultural groups, and that this is reflected in the selection of relevant meanings and the form of their realisation in a wide and significant range of situations.

V Code in Context

Two related forms of contextual constraint on language use have been explored in the discussion so far. Clearly these constraints are not peculiar to Bernstein's theoretical framework but their influence on speech is given a specific, and we believe useful, focus when seen in terms of subcultural differences in the structure of transmission. First, it was suggested that within a transmission system whatever the dominant code, the content and purpose of any one interaction will exert a fundamental influence on the discourse. The features of language which command attention will vary according to which socialising context or language function is to hand. Beyond this, whether the dominant code is restricted or elaborated will affect both the semantic areas which are given emphasis within each context, and the extent to which each of the four socialising contexts is initiated and explored by the mother with her child. It is further suggested that such variation in contents and contexts will influence the form of the communication.

If the first kind of contextual influence on speech may be broadly identified with 'function' or 'topic', the second discussion considered aspects of the context of situation, taking the speaker/listener relationship as fundamental. It was seen that the nature of this relationship exerts a strong influence on many aspects of language use, including the degree to which meanings are made explicit and specific in speech. Further it was suggested that since the code governing transmission in the home is rooted in the social structure which includes the material basis of the family, the child's acquisition of sociolinguistic competence must include acquisition of knowledge about social roles and relationships. Thus his interpretation of what is appropriate in the context of any one interaction will depend, at least initially, on his experience of social relationships in the family. A specific hypothesis is that the child's tendency to assume that language must carry the burden of communication between himself and another is significantly determined by the forms of communication which mediate socialisation.

Transmission, Acquisition and Realisation

As a theory of cultural transmission Bernstein's framework addresses itself to three broad issues. First, what are the principles regulating the transmission of cultural meanings; what is made relevant for the child and how is it made relevant? Second, how is the nature and process of acquisition to be described; what does the child learn at the tacit as well as the overt level? And finally, how is this acquisition realised in specific contexts; how can such contextually specific realisations be understood so that our conception of the acquisition matrix becomes clearer?

Such questions obviously have relevance beyond their application to linguistic and communicative skills, which might be considered as one very critical facet of acquisition. But at every level we assume that much of what the child learns he learns in a tacit way, and that even in an explicitly instructional situation the child learns much more than the adults intended teaching. Specific ways of speaking, individual practical tasks, particular means of solving problems – such skills are not learned discretely, in isolation, but are also the basis on which the child builds a set of rules that orient him to selected aspects of new situations and thereby relate different experiences in a coherent way. Constrained by the transmission system, his actions are nevertheless born of his own construction of the reality which that system makes available to him.

There is thus a tension set up between principles of transmission and the process of acquisition. The socialiser has certain notions about what the child should learn and also how best to teach him. These generate specific practices to which the child is exposed but which cannot be divorced from the ideas which lie behind them nor from the tacit cultural knowledge which will affect both the conscious ideology and the actual teaching practices.

The child towards whom this transmission is directed will learn something of its specific contents but will infer also a way of organising and acting upon experience that accords not only with the explicit and tacit cultural knowledge of the socialiser but also with the prevailing stock of rules and strategies he has himself built up. There may be a considerable gap between what is transmitted and what is acquired. A great deal of what is taught may be transformed, ignored or simply not seen. A great deal is certainly acquired that is never intentionally transmitted. Occasions on which there is direct match between the adult's conscious transmission and what is learned by the child are surely rare. The distinction between transmission and acquisition is of crucial importance. Nevertheless, it is a distinction that it is dangerous to overplay. The way in which transmission constrains acquisition is our central concern. To frame the basic question in this way is not to see the child as passive nor to imply that the main function of socialisation is to limit, inhibit and conventionalise.

Only by recognising and understanding the nature and modality of control is it feasible to raise questions about the possibilities available and the potential for exploration open to an active child in a social world.

The present model sees transmission agencies as concerned, both explicitly and at a covert level, to make aspects of the environment selectively relevant for the socialised such that he comes to attend to some features more readily than others; such that he has certain expectations about what may or may not occur; such that he has a tacit understanding of what is an appropriate response from him. The process may be thought of as analogous to or an extension of the process of perception. What is perceived, its spatial and temporal relations to other perceptions, what appears ambiguous as well as modes of resolving that ambiguity — all are shaped by the structure of transmission. And similarly with the cultural transmission of ways of thinking, acting and believing as well as the contexts and contents typically articulated thereby. On the basis of such selectively focused experiences, the child acquires an understanding which enables him to make sense of new situations and act within them accordingly. Clearly this has implications for what happens when a child of one culture meets situations controlled by the principles and members of another.

There are perhaps two complementary methods of trying to understand the social basis of the acquisition matrix and its nature. First, we may attempt to uncover what lies behind transmission and regulates its form. What are the principles governing activity and speech, social relationships and material setting in the child's interaction with the cultural world? Such an approach centres on what is made relevant for the child and how it is made relevant. Second, it is possible to consider the problem of what is acquired by looking more directly at the child; at the situationally specific realisations of the acquisition matrix. We would expect on the basis of the above argument that, for example, his speech and his activities will be consistent across situations in accordance with the ground rules he has acquired. The problem then becomes one of the basis and various manifestations of that consistency. In particular, a social perspective is interested to show how a variety of situationally specific behaviour can be seen as realisations of an acquisition matrix that is rooted in the social context of transmission.

Notes

1.   In an important sense there are no context-independent meanings.

Meanings arise in contexts and are constrained by them. Formal education can be considered as an agency which regulates the selection, form and focusing of meanings, practices, social relationships and contexts which give access to elaborated codes. Thus context-independent meanings are always regulated by the recontextualising procedures of education.

2.   This is oversimplication. The material and economic structure will constrain quite strongly the contexts that, for example, a mother or teacher may explore with a child. A small room with six boisterous children severely limits the time which a mother may devote to anything other than control. The focus on instruction, 'play and learn' and discovery characteristic of the middle classes demands the provision of books and special toys, plenty of space and an adult with time to guide and to answer questions.

References

Adlam, D.S. *et al*. (1977) *Code in Context*, Routledge & Kegan Paul, London.

Adlam, D.S. (1977), 'The descriptive context', in D.S. Adlam *et al*., *Code in Context*, Routledge & Kegan Paul, London.

Adlam, D.S. and Turner, G. (1977), 'Code in context', in D.S. Adlam *et al*., *Code in Context*, Routledge & Kegan Paul, London.

Bernstein, B. (1971), *Class, Codes and Control*: Vol. 1. *Theoretical Studies Towards a Sociology of Language*, Routledge & Kegan Paul, London.

Bernstein, B. (1973), 'A brief account of the theory of codes', Appendix I in *Social Relationships and Language: Some Aspects of the Work of Basil Bernstein*, The Open University, E 262, Block 3.

Bernstein, B. (1975), *Class, Codes and Control*: Vol. 3. *Towards a Theory of Educational Transmission*, Routledge & Kegan Paul, London.

Blom, J.P. and Gumperz, J. (1972), 'Some social determinants of verbal behaviour', in J.J. Gumperz and D. Hymes (eds.), *Directions in Sociolinguistics*, Holt, Rinehart & Winston, New York.

Brandis, W. and Henderson, D. (1970), *Social Class, Language and Communication*, Routledge & Kegan Paul, London.

Brown, R. and Gilman, A. (1960), 'The pronouns of power and solidarity', in T. Sebeok (ed.), *Style and Language*, MIT Press, Cambridge, Mass.

Cazden, C. (1971), 'The situation: a neglected source of social class difference in language use', in J.B. Pride and J. Holmes (eds.), *Sociolinguistics*, Penguin, Harmondsworth.

Cook-Gumperz, J. (1973), *Social Control and Socialization*, Routledge & Kegan Paul, London.

Ervin-Tripp, S. (1964), 'An analysis of the interaction of language, topic and listener', *American Anthropologist*, 66, no. 6, part 2, 86-102.

Fishman, J.A. (1965), 'Who speaks what language to whom and when?'. *Linguistique*, no. 2, 67-88.

Gumperz, J. and Hernandez-Chavez, E. (1972), 'Bilingualism, bidialectalism, and classroom interaction', in C. Cazden, P. John and D. Hymes (eds.), *Functions of Language in the Classroom*, Teachers College Press, New York.

Halliday, M.A.K. (1973), *Explorations in the Functions of Language*, Edward Arnold, London.

Halliday, M.A.K. and Hasan, R. (1976), *Cohesion in English*, Longmans, London.

Hasan, R. (1968), *Grammatical Cohesion in Spoken and Written English*, Part 1, Nuffield Programme in Linguistics and English Teaching, Paper no. 7, Longmans, London.

Hasan, R. (1973), 'Code, register and social dialect', in B. Bernstein, *Class, Codes and*

Control, vol. 2.
Hawkins, P.R. (1969), 'Social class, the nominal group and reference', in B. Bernstein (1973).
Heider, E.R., Cazden, C. and Brown, R. (1968), *Social Class Differences in the Effectiveness and Style of Children's Coding Ability*, Project Literacy Reports, no. 9, Cornell University Press, Ithaca, N.Y.
Hymes, D. (1972), Introduction to C. Cazden, P. John and D. Hymes (eds.), *Functions of Language in the Classroom*, Teachers College Press, New York.
Kantorovich, I. (1966), *Ty and Vy: A Writer's Notes*, quoted by S. Ervin-Tripp, 'Sociolinguistics', in J. Fishman (ed.), *Advances in the Sociology of Language*, vol. 1, Mouton, The Hague.
Labov, W. (1964), 'Phonological correlates of social stratification', *American Anthropologist*, 66, no. 2, 164-76.
Lineker, L. (1977), 'The instructional context', in D.S. Adlam *et al.*, *Code in Context*, Routledge & Kegan Paul, London.
Polgar, S. (1960), Quoted by Hymes, D. (1971), 'Competence and performance in linguistic theory', in R. Huxley and E. Ingram (eds.), *Language Acquisition: Models and Methods*, Academic Press, New York.
Wootton, A.J. (1974), 'Talk in the homes of young children', *Sociology*, 8, 278-95.

SOCIAL CLASS, LANGUAGE AND SOCIALIZATION

Basil Bernstein

Source: Basil Bernstein, *Class, Codes and Control*, Vol. 1 (Routledge & Kegan Paul, London 1974), 2nd edition, pp. 170-89.

Introduction

It may be helpful to make explicit the theoretical origins of the thesis I have been developing over the past decade. Although, initially, the thesis appeared to be concerned with the problem of educability, this problem was embedded in and was stimulated by the wider question of the relationships between symbolic orders and social structure. The basic theoretical question, which dictated the approach to the initially narrow but important empirical problem, was concerned with the fundamental structure and changes in the structure of cultural transmission. Indeed, any detailed examination of what superficially may seem to be a string of somewhat repetitive papers, I think would show three things.

(1)   The gradual emergence of the dominance of the major theoretical problem from the local, empirical problem of the social antecedents of the educability of different groups of children.

(2)   Attempts to develop both the generality of the thesis and to develop increasing specificity at the contextual level.

(3)   Entailed in (2) were attempts to clarify both the logical and empirical status of the basic organizing concept, code. Unfortunately, until recently these attempts were more readily seen in the *planning* and *analysis* of the empirical research than available as formal statements.

Looking back, however, I think I would have created less misunderstanding if I had written about socio-linguistic codes rather than linguistic codes. Through using only the latter concept it gave the impression that I was reifying syntax and at the cost of semantics; or worse, suggesting that there was a one-to-one relation between meanings and a given syntax. Also, by defining the codes in a context free fashion, I robbed myself of properly understanding, at a theoretical level, their significance. *I should point out that nearly all the empirical planning was directed to trying to find out the code realizations in different contexts.*

The concept of socio-linguistic code points to the social structuring of meanings *and* to their diverse but *related* contextual linguistic realizations. A careful reading of the papers always shows the emphasis given to the form of the social relationship, that is to the structuring of relevant meanings. Indeed, role is defined as a complex coding activity controlling the creation and organization of specific meanings and the conditions for their transmission and reception. The general socio-linguistic thesis attempts to explore how symbolic systems are both realizations and regulators of the structure of social relationships. The particular symbolic system is that of speech *not* language.

It is pertinent, at this point, to make explicit earlier work in the social sciences which formed the implicit starting point of the thesis. It will then be seen, I hope, that the thesis is an integration of different streams of thought. The major starting points are Durkheim and Marx, and a small number of other thinkers have been drawn into the basic matrix. I shall very briefly, and so selectively, outline this matrix and some of the problems to which it gave rise.

Durkheim's work is a truly magnificent insight into the relationships between symbolic orders, social relationships and the structuring of experience. In a sense, if Marx turned Hegel on his head, then Durkheim attempted to turn Kant on his head. For in *Primitive Classification* and in *The Elementary Forms of the Religious Life*, Durkheim attempted to derive the basic categories of thought from the structuring of the social relation. It is beside the point as to his success. He raised the whole question of the relation between the classifications and frames of the symbolic order *and* the structuring of experience. In his study of different forms of social integration he pointed to the implicit, condensed, symbolic structure of mechanical solidarity and the more explicit and differentiated and symbolic structures of organic solidarity. Cassirer, the early cultural anthropologists, and, in particular, Sapir (I was not aware of Von Humboldt until much later), sensitized me to the cultural properties of speech. Whorf, particularly where he refers to the fashions of speaking, frames of consistency, alerted me to the selective effect of the culture (acting through its patterning of social relationships) upon the *patterning* of grammar *together* with the pattern's semantic and thus cognitive significance. Whorf more than anyone, I think, opened up, at least for me, the question of the deep structure of linguistically regulated communication.

In all the above work I found two difficulties. If we grant the fundamental linkage of symbolic systems, social structure and the shaping of experience it is still unclear *how* such shaping takes place. The *processes* underlying the social structuring of experience are not explicit. The second difficulty is in dealing with the question of change of symbolic systems. Mead is of central importance in the solution of the first difficulty, the HOW. Mead outlined in general terms the relationships between role, reflexiveness and speech and in so doing provided the basis of the solution to the HOW. It is still the case that the Meadian solution does not allow us to deal with the problem of change. For the concept, which enables role to be related to a higher order concept, 'the generalized other',† is, itself, not subject to systematic enquiry. Even if 'the generalized other' is placed within a Durkheimian framework, we are still left with the problem of change. Indeed, in Mead change is introduced only at the cost of the re-emergence of a traditional Western dichotomy in the concepts of the 'I' and the 'me'. The 'I' is both the indeterminate response to the 'me' and yet, at the same time, shapes it. The Meadian 'I' points to the voluntarism in the affairs of men, to the fundamental creativity of man, made possible by speech; a little before Chomsky.

Thus Meadian thought helps to solve the puzzle of the HOW but it does not help with the question of change in the structuring of experience; although both Mead implicitly and Durkheim explicitly pointed to the conditions which bring about pathological structuring of experience.

One major theory of the development of and change in symbolic structures is, of course, that of Marx. Although Marx is less concerned with the internal structure and the process of transmission of symbolic systems, he does give us a key to their institutionalization and change. The key is given in terms of the social significance of society's productive system and the power relationships to which the productive system gives rise. Further, access to, control over, orientation of and *change* in critical symbolic systems, according to the theory, is governed by power relationships as these are embodied in the class structure. It is not only capital, in the strict economic sense, which is subject to appropriation, manipulation and exploitation, but also *cultural* capital in the form of the symbolic systems through which man can extend and change the boundaries of his experience.

I am not putting forward a matrix of thought necessary for the study of the basic structure and change in the structure of cultural transmission, *only* the specific matrix which underlies my own approach. Essentially and briefly I have used Durkheim and Marx at the macro-level and Mead at the micro-level to realize a socio-linguistic thesis which could meet with a range of work in anthropology, linguistics, sociology and psychology.

I want first of all to make clear what I am not concerned with. Chomsky, in *Aspects of the Theory of Syntax*, neatly severs the study of the rule system of language from the study of the social rules which determine their contextual use. He does this by making a distinction between competence and performance. Competence refers to the child's tacit understanding of the rule system, performance relates to the essentially social use to which the rule system is put. Competence refers to man abstracted from contextual constraints. Performance refers to man in the grip of the contextual constraints which determine his speech acts. Competence has its source in the very biology of man. There is no difference between men in terms of their access to the linguistic rule system. Here Chomsky like many other linguists before him, announces the communality of man; all men have equal access to the creative act which is language. On the other hand, performance is under the control of the social – performances are culturally specific acts, they refer to the choices which are made in specific speech encounters. Thus, according to Hymes, Chomsky indicates the tragedy of man, the potentiality of competence and the degeneration of performance.

Clearly, much is to be gained in rigour and explanatory power through the severing of the relationship between the formal properties of the grammar and the meanings which are realized in its use. But if we are to study speech, *la parole*, we are inevitably involved in a study of a rather different rule system; we are involved in a study of rules, formal and informal, which regulate the options we take up in various contexts in which we find ourselves. This second rule system is the cultural system. This raises immediately the question of the relationship between the linguistic rule system and the cultural system. Clearly, specific linguistic rule systems are part of the cultural system, but it has been argued that the linguistic rule system in various ways shapes the cultural system. This very briefly is the view of those who hold a narrow form of the linguistic relativity[†] hypothesis. I do not intend to get involved in that particular quagmire. Instead, I shall take the view that the code which the linguist invents to explain the formal properties of the grammar is capable of generating any number of speech codes, and there is no reason for believing that any one language code is better than another in this respect. On this argument, language is a set of rules to which all speech codes must comply, but which speech codes are realized is a function of the culture acting through social relationships in specific contexts. Different speech forms or codes symbolize the form of the social relationship, regulate the nature of the speech encounters, and create for the speakers different orders of relevance and relation. The experience of the speakers is then transformed by what is made significant or relevant by the speech form. This is a sociological argument because the speech form is taken as a consequence of the form of the social relation or, put more generally, is a quality of a social structure. Let me qualify this immediately. Because the speech form is initially a function of a given social arrangement, it does not mean that the speech form does not in turn modify or even change that social structure which initially evolved the speech form. This formulation, indeed, invites the question: Under what conditions does a given speech form free itself sufficiently from its embodiment in the social structure so that the system of meanings it realizes points to alternative realities, alternative arrangements in the affairs of men? Here we become concerned immediately with the antecedents and consequences of the boundary maintaining principles of a culture or sub-culture. I am here suggesting a relationship between forms of boundary maintenance at the cultural level and forms of speech.

I am required to consider the relationship between language and socialization. It should be clear from these opening remarks that I am not concerned with language, but with speech, and concerned more specifically with the contextual constraints upon speech. Now what about socialization? I shall take the term to refer to the process whereby a child acquires a specific cultural identity, *and* to his responses to such an identity. Socialization refers to the process whereby the biological is transformed into a specific cultural being. It follows from this that the process of socialization is a complex process of control, whereby a particular moral, cognitive and affective awareness is evoked in the child and given a specific form and content. Socialization sensitizes the child to the various orderings of society as these are made substantive in the various roles he is expected to play. In a sense, then, socialization is a process for making people safe. The process acts selectively on the possibilities of man by creating through time a sense of the inevitability of a given social arrangement, and through limiting the areas of permitted change. The basic agencies of socialization in contemporary societies are the family, the peer group, school and work. It is through these agencies, and in particular through their relationship to each other, that the various orderings of society are made manifest.

Now it is quite clear that given this view of socialization it is necessary to limit the discussion. I shall limit our discussion to socialization within the family, but it should be obvious that the focusing and filtering of the child's experience within the family in a large measure is a microcosm of the macroscopic orderings of society. Our question now becomes: What are the sociological factors which affect linguistic performances within the family critical to the process of socialization?

Without a shadow of doubt the most formative influence upon the procedures of socialization, from a sociological viewpoint, is social class.

The class structure influences work and educational roles and brings families into a special relationship with each other and deeply penetrates the structure of life experiences within the family. The class system has deeply marked the distribution of knowledge within society. It has given differential access to the sense that the world is permeable. It has sealed off communities from each other and has ranked these communities on a scale of invidious worth. We have three components, knowledge, possibility and invidious insulation. It would be a little naïve to believe that differences in knowledge, differences in the sense of the possible, combined with invidious insulation, rooted in differential *material* well-being, would not affect the forms of control and innovation in the socializing procedures of different social classes. I shall go on to argue that the deep structure of communication itself is affected, but not in any final or irrevocable way.

As an approach to my argument, let me glance at the social distribution of knowledge. We can see that the class system has affected the distribution of knowledge. Historically, and now, only a tiny percentage of the population has been socialized into knowledge at the level of the meta-languages† of control and innovation, whereas the mass of the population has been socialized into knowledge at the level of context-tied operations.

A tiny percentage of the population has been given access to the principles of intellectual change, whereas the rest have been denied such access. This suggests that we might be able to distinguish between two orders of meaning. One we could call universalistic, the other particularistic. Universalistic meanings are those in which principles and operations are made linguistically explicit, whereas particularistic orders of meaning are meanings in which principles and operation are relatively linguistically implicit. If orders of meaning are universalistic, then the meanings are less tied to a given context. The meta-languages of public forms of thought as these apply to objects and persons realize meanings of a universalistic type. Where meanings have this characteristic then individuals have access to the grounds of their experience and can change the grounds. Where orders of meaning are particularistic, where principles are linguistically implicit, then such meanings are less context independent and *more* context bound, that is, tied to a local relationship and to a local social structure. Where the meaning system is particularistic, much of the meaning is embedded in the context and may be restricted to those who share a similar contextual history. Where meanings are universalistic, they are in principle available to all because the principles and operations have been made explicit, and so public.

I shall argue that forms of socialization orient the child towards speech codes which control access to relatively context-tied or relatively context-independent meanings. Thus I shall argue that elaborated codes orient their users towards universalistic meanings, whereas restricted codes orient, sensitize, their users to particularistic meanings: that the linguistic realization of the two orders are different, and so are the social relationships which realize them. Elaborated codes are less tied to a given or local structure and thus contain the potentiality of change in principles. In the case of elaborated codes the speech may be freed from its evoking social structure and it can take on an autonomy. A university is a place organized around talk. Restricted codes are more tied to a local social structure and have a reduced potential for change in principles. Where codes are elaborated, the socialized has more access to the grounds of his own socialization, and so can enter into a reflexive† relationship to the social order he has taken over. Where codes are restricted, the socialized has less access to the grounds of his socialization, and thus reflexiveness may be limited in range. *One of the effects of the class system is to limit access to elaborated codes.*

I shall go on to suggest that restricted codes have their basis in condensed† symbols, whereas elaborated codes have their basis in articulated symbols; that restricted codes draw upon metaphor, whereas elaborated codes draw upon rationality; that these codes constrain the contextual use of language in critical socializing contexts and in this way regulate the orders of relevance and relation which the socialized takes over. From this point of view, change in habitual speech codes involves changes in the means by which object and person relationships are realized.

I want first to start with the notions of elaborated and restricted speech variants. A variant can be considered as the contextual constraints upon grammatical-lexical choices.

Sapir, Malinowski, Firth, Vygotsky and Luria have all pointed out from different points of view that the closer the identifications of speakers the greater the range of shared interests, the more probable that the speech will take a specific form. The range of syntactic alternatives is likely to be reduced and the lexis to be drawn from a narrow range. Thus, the form of these social relations is acting selectively on the meanings to be verbally realized. In these relationships the intent of the other person can be taken for granted as the speech is played out against a back-drop of common assumptions, common history, common interests. As a result, there is less need to raise meanings to the level of explicitness or elaboration. There is a reduced need to make explicit through syntactic choices the logical structure of the communication. Further, if the speaker wishes to individualize his communication, he is likely to do this by varying the expressive associates of the speech. Under these conditions, the speech is likely to have a strong metaphoric element. In these situations the speaker may be more concerned with how something is said, when it is said; silence takes on a variety of meanings. Often in these encounters the speech cannot be read by those who do not share the history of the relationships. Thus the form of the social relationship acts selectively in the meanings to be verbalized, which in turn affect the syntactic and lexical choices. The unspoken assumptions underlying the relationship are not available to those who are outside the relationship. For these are limited, and restricted to the speakers. The symbolic form of the communication is condensed, yet the specific cultural history of the relationship is alive in its form. We can say that the roles of the speakers are communalized roles. Thus, we can make a relationship between restricted social relationships based upon communalized roles and the verbal realization of their meaning. In the language of the earlier part of this paper, restricted social relationships based upon communalized roles evoke particularistic, that is, context-tied, meanings, realized through a restricted speech variant.

Imagine a husband and wife have just come out of the cinema, and are talking about the film: 'What do you think?' 'It had a lot to say' 'Yes, I thought so too — let's go to the Millers, there may be something going there'. They arrive at the Millers, who ask about the film. An hour is spent in the complex, moral, political, aesthetic subtleties of the film and its place in the contemporary scene. Here we have an elaborated variant; the meanings now have to be made public to others who have not seen the film. The speech shows careful editing, at both the grammatical and lexical levels. It is no longer context-tied. The meanings are explicit, elaborated and individualized. Whilst expressive channels are clearly relevant, the burden of meaning inheres predominantly in the verbal channel. The experience of the listeners cannot be taken for granted. Thus each member of the group is on his own as he offers his interpretation. Elaborated variants of this kind involve the speakers in particular role relationships, and *if you cannot manage the role, you can't produce the appropriate speech*. For as the speaker proceeds to individualize his meanings, he is differentiated from others like a figure from its ground.

The roles receive less support from each other. There is a measure of isolation. *Difference* lies at the basis of the social relationship, and is made verbally active, whereas in the other context it is *consensus*. The insides of the speaker have become psychologically active through the verbal aspect of the communication. Various defensive strategies may be used to decrease potential vulnerability of self and to increase the vulnerability of others. The verbal aspect of the communication becomes a vehicle for the transmission of individuated symbols. The 'I' stands over the 'we'. Meanings which are discrete to the speaker must be offered so that they are intelligible to the listener. Communalized roles have given way to individualized roles, condensed symbols to articulated symbols. Elaborated speech variants of this type realize universalistic meanings in the sense that they are less context-tied. Thus individualized roles are realized through elaborated speech variants which involve complex editing at the grammatical and lexical levels and which point to universalistic meanings.

Let me give another example. Consider the two following stories which Peter Hawkins, Assistant Research Officer in the Sociological Research Unit, University of London Institute of Education, constructed as a result of his analysis of the speech of middle-class and working-class five-year-old children. The children were given a series of four pictures which told a story and they were invited to tell the story. The first picture showed some boys playing football; in the second the ball goes through the window of a house; the third shows a woman looking out of the window and a man making an ominous gesture, and in the fourth the children are moving away.

Here are the two stories:

(1)   Three boys are playing football and one boy kicks the ball and it goes through the window the ball breaks the window and the boys are looking at it and a man comes out and shouts at them because they've broken the window so they run away and then that lady looks out of her window and she tells the boys off.

(2)   They're playing football and he kicks it and it goes through there it breaks the window and they're looking at it and he comes out and shouts at them because they've broken it so they run away and then she looks out and she tells them off.

With the first story the reader does not have to have the four pictures which were used as the basis for the story, whereas in the case of the second story the reader would require the initial pictures in order to make sense of the story. The first story is free of the context which generated it, whereas the second story is much more closely tied to its context. As a result the meanings of the second story are implicit, whereas the meanings of the first story are explicit. It is not that the working-class children do not have in their passive vocabulary the vocabulary used by the middle-class children. Nor is it the case that the children differ in their tacit understanding of the linguistic rule system. Rather, what we have here are differences in the use of language arising out of a specific context. One child makes explicit the meanings which he is realizing through language for the person he is telling the story to, whereas the second child does not to the same extent. The first child takes very little for granted, whereas the second child takes a great deal for granted. Thus for the first child the task was seen as a context in which his meanings were required to be made explicit, whereas the task for the second child was not seen as a task which required such explication of meaning. It would not be difficult to imagine a context where the first child would produce speech rather like the second. What we are dealing with here are differences between the children in the way they realize in language-use apparently the same context. We could say that the speech of the first child generated universalistic meanings in the sense that the meanings are freed from the context and so understandable by all, whereas the speech of the second child generated particularistic meanings, in the sense that the meanings are closely tied to the context and would be fully understood by others only if they had access to the context which originally generated the speech.

It is again important to stress that the second child has access to a more differentiated noun phrase, but there is a restriction on its *use*. Geoffrey Turner, Linguist in the Sociological Research Unit, shows that working-class, five-year-old children in the same contexts examined by Hawkins, use fewer linguistic expressions of uncertainty when compared with the middle-class children. This does not mean that working-class children do *not* have access to such expressions, but that the eliciting speech context did not provoke them. Telling a story from pictures, talking about scenes on cards, *formally framed* contexts, do not encourage working-class children to consider the possibilities of alternate meanings and so there is a reduction in the linguistic expressions of uncertainty. Again, working-class children have access to a wide range of syntactic choices which involve the use of logical operators,† 'because', 'but', 'either', 'or', 'only'. The constraints exist on the conditions for their *use*. Formally framed contexts used for eliciting context-independent universalistic meanings may evoke in the working-class child, relative to the middle-class child, restricted speech variants, because the working-class child has difficulty in managing the role relationships which such contexts require. This problem is further complicated when such contexts carry meanings very much removed from the child's cultural experience. In the same way we can show that there are constraints upon the middle-class child's use of language. Turner found that when middle-class children were asked to role-play in the picture story series, a higher percentage of these children, when compared with working-class children, initially refused. When the middle-class children were asked 'What is the man saying?' or linguistically equivalent questions, a relatively higher percentage said 'I don't know'. When this question was followed by the hypothetical question 'What do you think the man might be saying?' they offered their interpretations. The working-class children role-played without difficulty. It seems then that middle-class children at five need to have a very precise instruction to *hypothesize in that particular* context. This may be because they are more concerned here with getting their answers right or correct. When the children were invited to tell a story about some doll-like figures (a little boy, a little girl, a sailor and a dog) the working-class children's stories were freer, longer and more imaginative than the stories of the middle-class children. The latter children's stories were tighter, constrained within a strong narrative frame. It was as if these children were dominated by what they took to be the *form* of a narrative and the context was secondary. This is an example of the concern of the middle-class child with the structure of the contextual frame. It may be worthwhile to amplify this further. A number of studies have shown that when working-class black children are asked to associate to a series of words, their responses show considerable diversity, both from the meaning and form-class of the stimulus word. Our analysis suggests this may be because the children for the following reasons are less constrained. The form-class of the stimulus word may have reduced associative significance and this would less constrain the selection of potential words *or* phrases. With such a weakening of the grammatical frame there is a greater range of alternatives as possible candidates for selection. Further, the closely controlled, middle-class, linguistic socialization of the young child may point the child towards both the grammatical significance of the stimulus word and towards a tight logical ordering of semantic space. Middle-class children may well have access to deep interpretative rules which regulate their linguistic responses in certain formalized contexts. The consequences may limit their imagination through the tightness of the frame which these interpretative rules create. It may even be that with *five*-year-old children, the middle-class child will innovate *more* with the arrangements of objects (i.e. bricks) than in his linguistic usage. His linguistic usage is under close supervision by adults. He has more *autonomy* in his play.

To return to our previous discussion, we can say, briefly, that as we move from communalized to individualized roles, so speech takes on an increasingly reflexive function. The unique selves of others become palpable through speech and enter into our own self; the grounds of our experience are made verbally explicit; the security of the condensed symbol is gone. It has been replaced by rationality. There is a change in the basis of our vulnerability.

So far, then, I have discussed certain types of speech variants and the role relationships which occasion them. I am now going to raise the generality of the discussion and focus upon the title of the paper. The socialization of the young in the family proceeds within a critical set of interrelated contexts. Analytically, we may distinguish four contexts.

(1)　The regulative context — these are authority relationships where the child is made aware of the rules of the moral order and their various backings.
(2)　The instructional context, where the child learns about the objective nature of objects and persons, and acquires skills of various kinds.
(3)　The imaginative or innovating contexts, where the child is encouraged to experiment and re-create his world on his own terms, and in his own way.
(4)　The interpersonal context, where the child is made aware of affective states — his own, and others.

I am suggesting that the critical orderings of a culture or sub-culture are made substantive — are made palpable — through the forms of its linguistic realizations of these four contexts — initially in the family and kin.

Now if the linguistic realization of these four contexts involves the predominant use of restricted speech variants, I shall postulate that the deep structure of the communication is a restricted code having its basis in communalized roles, realizing context-dependent meanings, i.e. particularistic meaning orders. Clearly the specific grammatical and lexical choices will vary from one to another.

If the linguistic realization of these four contexts involves the predominant usage of elaborated speech variants, I shall postulate that the deep structure of the communication is an elaborated code having its basis in individualized roles realizing context-independent universalistic meanings.

In order to prevent misunderstanding an expansion of the text is here necessary. It is likely that where the code is restricted, the speech in the regulative context may well be limited to command and simple rule-announcing statements. The latter statements are not context-dependent in the sense previously given, for they announce general rules. We need to supplement the context-independent (universalistic) and context-dependent (particularistic) criteria with criteria which refer to the extent to which the speech in the regulative context varies in terms of its *contextual specificity*. If the speech is context-specific then the socializer cuts his meanings to the *specific* attributes/intentions of the socialized, the specific characteristics of the problem, the specific requirements of the context. Thus the general rule may be transmitted with degrees of *contextual specificity*. When this occurs the rule is individualized (fitted to the local circumstances) in the process of its transmission. Thus with code elaboration we should expect:

(1)   Some developed grounds for the rule
(2)   Some qualification of it in the light of the particular issue
(3)   Considerable *specificity* in terms of the socialized, the context and the issue

This does *not* mean that there would be an *absence* of command statements. It is also likely that with code elaboration the socialized would be *given* opportunities (role options) to question.

Bernstein and Cook (1965) and Cook (1971) have developed a semantic coding grid which sets out with considerable delicacy a general category system which has been applied to a limited regulative context. G. Turner, linguist to the Sociological Research Unit, is attempting a linguistic realization of the same grid.

Figure 12.1: Realization of the Regulative Context

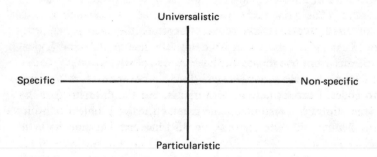

We can express the two sets of criteria diagrammatically. A limited application is given by Henderson (1970).

It may be necessary to utilize the two sets of criteria for *all* four socializing contexts.

If we look at the linguistic realization of the regulative context in greater detail we may be able to clear up another source of possible misunderstanding. In this context it is very likely that syntactic markers of the logical distribution of meaning will be extensively used.

'If you do that, then . . .'
'Either you . . . or . . .'
'You can do that, but if . . .'
'You do that and you'll pay for it.'

Thus it is very likely that all young children may well in the *regulative* context have access to a range of syntactic markers which express the logical/hypothetical, irrespective of code restriction or elaboration. However, where the code is restricted it is expected that there will be reduced specificity in the sense outlined earlier. Further, the speech in the control situation is likely to be well organized in the sense that the sentences come as wholes. The child responds to the total *frame*. However, I would suggest that the informal *instructional* contexts within the family may well be limited in range and frequency. Thus the child, of course, would have access to, and so have *available*, the hypotheticals, conditionals, disjunctives etc., but these might be rarely used in *instructional* contexts. In the same way, as we have suggested earlier, all children have access to linguistic expressions of uncertainty but they may differ in the context in which they receive and realize such expressions.

I must emphasize that because the code is restricted it does not mean that speakers at no time will not use elaborated speech variants; only that the use of such variants will be infrequent in the socialization of the child in his family.

Now, all children have acccess to restricted codes and their various systems of condensed meaning, because the roles the code presupposes are universal. But there may well be selective access to elaborated codes because there is selective access to the role system which evokes its use. Society is likely to evaluate differently the experiences realized through these two codes. I cannot here go into details, but the different focusing of experience through a restricted code creates a major problem of educability only where the school produces discontinuity between its symbolic orders and those of the child. Our schools are not made for these children; why should the children respond? To ask the child to switch to an elaborated code which presupposes different role relationships and systems of meaning without a sensitive understanding of the required contexts may create for the child a bewildering and potentially damaging experience.

So far, then, I have sketched out a relationship between speech codes and socialization through the organization of roles through which the culture is made psychologically active in persons. I have indicated that access to the roles and thus to the codes is broadly related to social class.

However, it is clearly the case that social class groups today are by no means homogeneous groups. Further, the division between elaborated and restricted codes is too simple. Finally, I have not indicated in any detail how these codes are evoked by families, and how the family types may shape their focus.

What I shall do now is to introduce a distinction between family types and their communication structures. These family types can be found empirically within each social class, although any one type may be rather more modal at any given historical period.

I shall distinguish between families according to the strength of their boundary maintaining procedures. Let me first give some idea of what I mean by boundary maintaining procedures. I shall first look at boundary maintenance as it is revealed in the symbolic ordering of space. Consider the lavatory. In one house, the room is pristine, bare and sharp, containing only the necessities for which the room is dedicated. In another there is a picture on the wall, in the third there are books, in the fourth all surfaces are covered with curious postcards. We have a continuum from a room celebrating the purity of categories to one celebrating the mixture of categories, from strong to weak boundary maintenance. Consider the kitchen. In one kitchen, shoes may not be placed on the table, nor the child's chamber pot — all objects and utensils have an assigned place. In another kitchen the boundaries separating the different classes of objects are weak. The symbolic ordering of space can give us indications of the relative strength of boundary maintaining procedures. Let us now look at the relationship between family members. Where boundary procedures are strong, the differentiation of members and the authority structure is based upon clear-cut, unambiguous definitions of the status of the member of the family. The boundaries between the statuses are strong and the social identities of the members very much a function of their age, sex and age-relation status. As a short-hand, we can characterize the family as *positional*.

On the other hand, where boundary procedures are weak or flexible, the differentiation between members and the authority relationships are less on the basis of position, because here the status boundaries are blurred. Where boundary procedures are weak, the differentiation between members is based more upon *differences between persons*. In such families the relationships become more egocentric and the unique attributes of family members are made more and more substantive in the communication structure. We will call these *person-centred* families. Such families do not reduce but increase the substantive expression of ambiguity and ambivalence. In person-centred families, the role system would be continuously evoking, accommodating and assimilating the different interests and attributes of its members. In such families, unlike positional families, the members would be making their roles rather than stepping into them. In a person-centred family, the child's developing self is differentiated by continuous adjustment to the verbally realized and elaborated intentions, qualifications and motives of others. The boundary between self and other is blurred. In positional families, the child takes over and responds to the formal pattern of obligation and privilege. It should be possible to see, without going into details, that the communication structures within these two types of family are somewhat differently focused. We might then expect that the reflexiveness induced by positional families is sensitized to the general attributes of persons, whereas the reflexiveness produced by person-centred families is more sensitive towards the particular aspects of persons. Think of the difference between Dartington Hall or Gordonstoun public schools in England, or the difference between West Point and a progressive school in the USA. Thus, in person-centred families, the insides of the members are made public through the communication structure, and thus more of the person has been invaded and subject to control. Speech in such families is a major medium of control. In positional familes, of course, speech is relevant but it symbolizes the boundaries given by the formal structure of the relationships. So far as the child is concerned, in positional families he attains a strong sense of social identity at the cost of autonomy; in person-centred families, the child attains a strong sense of autonomy but his social identity may be weak. Such ambiguity in the sense of identity, the lack of boundary, may move such children towards a radically closed value system.

If we now place these family types in the framework of the previous discussion, we can see that although the code may be elaborated, it may be differently focused according to the family type. Thus, we can have an elaborate code focusing upon persons or an elaborated code in a positional family may focus more upon objects. We can expect the same with a restricted code. Normally, with code restriction we should expect a positional family; however, if it showed signs of being person-centred, then we might expect the children to be in a situation of potential code switch.

Where the code is elaborated, and focused by a person-centred family, then these children may well develop acute identity problems concerned with authenticity, with limiting responsibility — they may come to see language as phony, a system of counterfeit masking the absence of belief. They may move towards the restricted codes of the various peer group subcultures, or seek the condensed symbols of affective experience, or both.

One of the difficulties of this approach is to avoid implicit value judgments about the relative worth of speech systems and the cultures which they symbolize. Let it be said immediately that a restricted code gives access to a vast potential of meanings, of delicacy, subtlety and diversity of cultural forms, to a unique aesthetic the basis of which in condensed symbols may influence the form of the imagining. Yet, in complex industrialized societies its differently-focused experience may be disvalued and humiliated within schools, or seen, at best, to be irrelevant to the educational endeavour. For the schools are predicated upon elaborated code and its system of social relationships. Although an elaborated code does not entail any specific value system, the value system of the middle class penetrates the texture of the very learning context itself.

Elaborated codes give access to alternative realities, yet they carry the potential of alienation, of feeling from thought, of self from other, of private belief *from role obligation.*

Finally I should like to consider briefly the sources of change of linguistic codes. The first major source of change I suggest is to be located in the division of labour. As the division of labour changes from simple to complex, then this changes the social and knowledge characteristics of occupational roles. In this process there is an extension of access, through education, to elaborated codes, but access is controlled by the class system. The focusing of the codes I have suggested is brought about by the boundary maintaining procedures within the family. However, we can generalize and say that the focusing of the codes is related to the boundary maintaining procedures as these affect the major socializing agencies — family, age group, education and work. We need, therefore, to consider together with the question of the degree of type of complexity of the division of labour, the value orientations of society which, it is hypothesized, affect the boundary maintaining procedures. It is the case that we can have societies with a similar complexity in their division of labour but which differ in their boundary maintaining procedures.

I suggest then that it is important to make a distinction between societies in terms of their boundary maintaining procedures if we are to deal with this question of the focusing of codes. One possible way of examining the relative strength of boundary maintenance is to consider the strength of the *constraints* upon the choice of values which legitimize authority/power relationships. Thus in societies where there is weak constraint upon such legitimizing values, that is, where there is a variety of formally permitted legitimizing values, we might expect a marked shift towards person type control; whereas in societies with strong constraints upon legitimizing values, where there is a severe *restriction* upon the

choice, we might expect a marked shift towards positional control.
I shall illustrate these relationships with reference to the family:

Figure 12.2: Sources of Change of Linguistic Codes

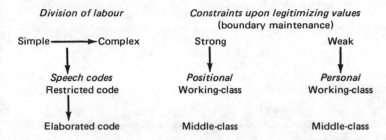

Thus the division of labour influences the availability of elaborated codes; the class system affects their distribution; the focusing of codes can be related to the boundary maintaining procedures, i.e. the value system. I must point out that this is only a coarse interpretative framework.

Conclusion

I have tried to show how the class system acts upon the deep structure of communication in the process of socialization. I refined the crudity of this analysis by showing how speech codes may be differently focused through family types. Finally, it is conceivable that there are general aspects of the analysis which might provide a starting point for the consideration of symbolic orders other than languages. I must point out that there is more to socialization than the forms of its linguistic realization.

References

Bernstein, B. (1970), 'Education cannot compensate for society', *New Society* No. 387, February.
Bernstein, B. (1962), 'Family role systems, socialisation and communication', manuscript, Sociological Research Unit, University of London Institute of Education; also in 'A socio-linguistic approach to socialisation', *Directions in Sociolinguistics*, Gumperz, J.J. and Hymes, D. (eds.), New York: Holt, Rinehart & Winston.
Bernstein, B. and Cook, J. (1965), 'Coding grid for maternal control', available from Department of Sociology, University of London Institute of Education.
Bernstein, B. and Henderson, D. (1969), 'Social class differences in the relevance of language to socialisation', *Sociology* 3, No. 1.
Bright, N. (ed.) (1966), *Sociolinguistics*, Mouton Press.

Carroll, J.B. (ed.) (1956), *Language, Thought and Reality: selected writings of Benjamin Lee Whorf*, New York: Wiley.

Cazden, C.B. (1969), 'Sub-cultural differences in child language: an interdisciplinary review', *Merrill-Palmer Quarterly* 12.

Chomsky, N. (1965), *Aspects of Linguistic Theory*, Cambridge M.I.T.

Cook, J. (1971), 'An enquiry into patterns of communication and control between mothers and their children in different social classes', Ph.D. Thesis, University of London.

Coulthard, M. (1969), 'A discussion of restricted and elaborated codes', *Educ. Rev.* 22, No. 1.

Douglas, M. (1970), *Natural Symbols*, Barrie & Rockliff, The Cresset Press.

Fishman, J.A. (1960), 'A systematization of the Whorfian hypothesis', *Behavioral Science* 5.

Gumperz, J.J. and Hymes, D. (eds.) (1971) *Directions in Sociolinguistics*, New York: Holt, Rinehart & Winston. (In press.)

Halliday, M.A.K. (1969), 'Relevant models of language', *Educ. Rev.* 22, No. 1.

Hawkins, P.R. (1969), 'Social class, the nominal group and reference', *Language and Speech* 12, No. 2.

Henderson, D. (1970),,'Contextual specificity, discretion and cognitive socialisation: with special reference to language', *Sociology* 4, No. 3.

Hoijer, H. (ed.) (1954), 'Language in Culture', *American Anthropological Association Memoir* No. 79; also published by Univ. of Chicago Press.

Hymes, D. (1966), 'On communicative competence', Research Planning Conference on Language Development among Disadvantaged Children, Ferkauf Graduate School, Yeshiva University.

Hymes, D. (1967), 'Models of the interaction of language and social setting', *Journal of Social Issues* 23.

Labov, W. (1965), 'Stages in the acquisition of standard English', in Shuy, W. (ed.), *Social Dialects and Language Learning*, Champaign, Illinois: National Council of Teachers of English.

Labov, W. (1966), 'The social stratification of English in New York City', Washington D.C. Centre for Applied Linguistics.

Mandelbaum, D. (ed.) (1949), *Selected Writings of Edward Sapir*, Univ. of California Press.

Parsons, T. and Shils, E.A. (eds.) (1962), *Toward a General Theory of Action*, Harper Torchbooks (Chapter 1, especially).

Schatzman, L. and Strauss, A.L. (1955), 'Social class and modes of communication', *Am. J. Soc.* 60.

Turner, G. and Pickvance, R.E. (1971), 'Social class differences in the expression of uncertainty in five-year-old children', *Language and Speech* (in press).

Williams, F. and Naremore, R.C. (1969), 'On the functional analysis of social class differences in modes of speech', *Speech Monographs* 36, No. 2.

13 THE LOGIC OF NONSTANDARD ENGLISH

William Labov

Source, as printed: *Language in Education*, prepared by the Language and Learning Course Team (Routledge & Kegan Paul, London 1972), pp. 198-211.

In the past decade, a great deal of federally sponsored research has been devoted to the educational problems of children in ghetto schools. In order to account for the poor performance of children in these schools, educational psychologists have attempted to discover what kind of disadvantage or defect they are suffering from. The viewpoint which has been widely accepted, and used as the basis for large-scale intervention programs, is that the children show a cultural deficit as a result of an impoverished environment in their early years. Considerable attention has been given to language. In this area, the deficit theory appears as the concept of 'verbal deprivation': Negro children from the ghetto area receive little verbal stimulation, are said to hear very little well-formed language, and as a result are impoverished in their means of verbal expression: they cannot speak complete sentences, do not know the names of common objects, cannot form concepts or convey logical thoughts.

Unfortunately, these notions are based upon the work of educational psychologists who know very little about language and even less about Negro children. The concept of verbal deprivation has no basis in social reality: in fact, Negro children in the urban ghettos receive a great deal of verbal stimulation, hear more well-formed sentences than middle-class children, and participate fully in a highly verbal culture; they have the same basic vocabulary, possess the same capacity for conceptual learning, and use the same logic as anyone else who learns to speak and understand English.

The notion of 'verbal deprivation' is a part of the modern mythology of educational psychology, typical of the unfounded notions which tend to expand rapidly in our educational system. In past decades linguists have been as guilty as others in promoting such intellectual fashions at the expense of both teachers and children. But the myth of verbal deprivation is particularly dangerous, because it diverts attention from real defects of our educational system to imaginary defects of the child; and as we shall see, it leads its sponsors inevitably to the hypothesis of the genetic inferiority of Negro children which it was originally designed to avoid.

329

The most useful service which linguists can perform today is to clear away the illusion of 'verbal deprivation' and provide a more adequate notion of the relations between standard and non-standard dialects. In the writings of many prominent educational psychologists, we find a very poor understanding of the nature of language. Children are treated as if they have no language of their own in the pre-school programs put forward by Bereiter and Engelmann (1966). The linguistic behavior of ghetto children in test situations is the principal evidence for their genetic inferiority in the view of Arthur Jensen (1969). In this paper, I will examine critically both of these approaches to the language and intelligence of the populations labelled 'verbally' and 'culturally deprived'.[1] I will attempt to explain how the myth of verbal deprivation has arisen, bringing to bear the methodological findings of sociolinguistic work, and some substantive facts about language which are known to all linguists. I will be particularly concerned with the relation between concept formation on the one hand, and dialect differences on the other, since it is in this area that the most dangerous misunderstandings are to be found.

Verbality

The general setting in which the deficit theory has arisen consists of a number of facts which are known to all of us: that Negro children in the central urban ghettos do badly on all school subjects, including arithmetic and reading. In reading, they average more than two years behind the national norm.[2] Furthermore, this lag is cumulative, so that they do worse comparatively in the fifth grade than in the first grade. Reports in the literature show that this bad performance is correlated most closely with socio-economic status. Segregated ethnic groups, however, seem to do worse than others: in particular, Indians, Mexican-Americans and Negro children. Our own work in New York City confirms the fact that most Negro children read very poorly; however, our studies in the speech community show that the situation is even worse than has been reported. If one separates the isolated and peripheral individuals from the members of the central peer groups, the peer group members show even worse reading records, and to all intents and purposes are not learning to read at all during the time they spend in school (Labov and Robins, 1969).

In speaking of children in the urban ghetto areas, the term 'lower-class' is frequently used as opposed to 'middle-class'. In the several sociolinguistic studies we have carried out, and in many parallel studies, it is useful to distinguish a 'lower-class' group from 'working-class'. Lower-class families are typically female-based or 'matri-focal', with no father present to provide steady economic support, whereas for the working-class there is typically an intact nuclear family with the father holding a semi-skilled or unskilled job. The educational problems of ghetto areas run across this important class distinction; there is no evidence, for example, that the father's presence or absence is closely correlated with educational achievement.[3] The peer groups we have studied in South Central Harlem, representing the basic vernacular culture, include members from both family types. The attack against 'cultural deprivation' in the ghetto is overtly directed at family structures typical of lower-class families, but the educational failure we have been discussing is characteristic of both working-class and lower-class children.

In the balance of this paper, I will therefore refer to children from urban ghetto areas, rather than 'lower-class' children: the population we are concerned with are those who participate fully in the vernacular culture of the street and who have been alienated from the school system.[4] We are obviously dealing with the effects of the caste system of American society — essentially a 'color marking' system. Everyone recognizes this. The question is, by what mechanism does the color bar prevent children from learning to read? One answer is the notion of 'cultural deprivation' put forward by Martin Deutsch and others: the Negro children are said to lack the favorable factors in their home environment which enable middle-class children to do well in school. (Deutsch *et al.*, 1967; Deutsch, Katz and Jensen, 1968). These factors involve the development of various cognitive skills through verbal interaction with adults, including the ability to reason abstractly, speak fluently, and focus upon long-range goals. In their publications, these psychologists also recognize broader social factors.[5] However, the deficit theory does not focus upon the interaction of the Negro child with white society so much as on his failure to interact with his mother at home. In the literature we find very little direct observation of verbal interaction in the Negro home; most typically, the investigators ask the child if he has dinner with his parents, and if he engages in dinner-table conversation with them. He is also asked whether his family takes him on trips to museums and other cultural activities. This slender thread of evidence is used to explain and interpret the large body of tests carried out in the laboratory and in the school.

The most extreme view which proceeds from this orientation — and one that is now being widely accepted — is that lower-class Negro children have no language at all. The notion is first drawn from Basil Bernstein's writing that 'much of lower-class language consists of a kind of incidental "emotional" accompaniment to action here and now' (Jensen, 1968, p. 118). Bernstein's views are filtered through a strong bias against all forms of working-class behavior, so that middle-class language is seen as superior in every respect — as 'more abstract, and necessarily somewhat more flexible, detailed and subtle'. One can proceed through a range of such views until one comes to the practical program of Carl Bereiter, Siegfried Engelmann and their associates (Bereiter *et al.*, 1966; Bereiter and Engelmann, 1966). Bereiter's program for an academically oriented pre-school is based upon their premise that Negro children must have a language with which they can learn, and their empirical finding that these children come to school without such a language. In his work with four-year-old Negro children from Urbana, Bereiter reports that their communication was by gestures, 'single words', and 'a series of badly-connected words or phrases', such as *They mine* and *Me got juice*. He reports that Negro children could not ask questions, that 'without exaggerating . . . these four-year-olds could make no statements of any kind'. Furthermore, when these children were asked 'Where is the book?', they did not know enough to look at the table where the book was lying in order to answer. Thus Bereiter concludes that the children's speech forms are nothing more than a series of emotional cries, and he decides to treat them 'as if the children had no language at all'. He identifies their speech with his inter-pretation of Bernstein's restricted code: 'the language of culturally deprived children . . . is not merely an underdeveloped version of standard English, but is a basically non-logical mode of expressive behavior' (Bereiter *et al.*, 1966, p. 113). The basic program of his pre-school is to teach them a new language devised by Engelmann, which consists of a limited series of questions and answers such as *Where is the squirrel? The squirrel is in the tree*. The children will not be punished if they use their vernacular speech on the playground, but they will not be allowed to use it in the schoolroom. If they should answer the question *Where is the squirrel?* with the illogical vernacular form *In the tree* they will be repre-hended by various means and made to say, *The squirrel is in the tree*.

Linguists and psycholinguists who have worked with Negro children are apt to dismiss this view of their language as utter nonsense. Yet there is no reason to reject Bereiter's observations as spurious: they were certainly not made up: on the contrary, they give us a very clear view of the behavior of student and teacher which can be duplicated in any class-room. In our own work outside of the adult-dominated environments of school and home,[6] we do not observe Negro children behaving like this, but on many occasions we have been asked to help analyze the results of research into verbal deprivation in such test situations.

Here, for example, is a complete interview with a Negro boy, one of hundreds carried out in a New York City school. The boy enters a room where there is a large, friendly white interviewer, who puts on the table in front of him a block or a fire engine, and says 'Tell me everything you can about this'. (The interviewer's further remarks are in parentheses.)

[12 seconds of silence]
(What would you say it looks like?)
   [8 seconds of silence]
A space ship.
(Hmmmm.)
   [13 seconds of silence]
Like a je-et.
   [12 seconds of silence]
Like a plane.
   [20 seconds of silence]
(What color is it?)
Orange. [2 seconds] An' whi-ite. [2 seconds] An' green.
   [6 seconds of silence]
(An' what could you use it for?)
   [8 seconds of silence]
A je-et.
   [6 seconds of silence]
(If you had two of them, what would you do with them?)
   [6 seconds of silence]
Give one to somebody.
(Hmmmm. Who do you think would like to have it?)
   [10 seconds of silence]
Cla-rence.
(Mm. Where do you think we could get another one of these?)
At the store.
(Oh ka-ay!)

We have here the same kind of defensive, monosyllabic behaviour which is reported in Bereiter's work. What is the situation that produces it? The child is in an asymmetrical situation where anything he says can literally be held against him. He has learned a number of devices to *avoid* saying anything in this situation, and he works very hard to achieve this end. One may observe the intonation patterns which Negro children often use when they are asked a question to which the answer is obvious. The answer may be read as 'Will this satisfy you?'

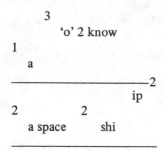

If one takes this interview as a measure of the verbal capacity of the child, it must be as his capacity to defend himself in a hostile and threatening situation. But unfortunately, thousands of such interviews are used as evidence of the child's total verbal capacity, or more simply his 'verbality'; it is argued that this lack of verbality *explains* his poor performance in school. Operation Headstart and other intervention programs have largely been based upon the 'deficit theory' — the notions that such interviews give us a measure of the child's verbal capacity and that the verbal stimulation which he has been missing can be supplied in a pre-schoool environment.

The verbal behavior which is shown by the child in the test situation quoted above is not the result of the ineptness of the interviewer. It is rather the result of regular sociolinguistic factors operating upon adult and child in this asymmetrical situation. In our work in urban ghetto areas, we have often encountered such behavior. Ordinarily we worked with boys 10-17 years old; and whenever we extended our approach downward to 8- or 9-year olds, we began to see the need for different techniques to explore the verbal capacity of the child. At one point we began a series of interviews with younger brothers of the 'Thunderbirds' in 1390 5th Avenue. Clarence Robins returned after an interview with 8-year-old Leon L., who showed the following minimal response to topics which arouse intense interest in other interviews with older boys.

CR: What if you saw somebody kickin' somebody else on the ground, or was using a stick, what would you do if you saw that?
Leon: Mmmm.
CR: If it was supposed to be a fair fight —
Leon: I don't know.
CR: You don't know? Would you do anything . . . huh? I can't hear you.
Leon: No.
CR: Did you ever see somebody got beat up real bad?
Leon: . . . Nope ? ? ?

CR: Well — uh — did you ever get into a fight with a guy?
Leon: Nope.
CR: That was bigger than you?
Leon: Nope.
CR: You never been in a fight?
Leon: Nope.
CR: Nobody ever pick on you?
Leon: Nope.
CR: Nobody ever hit you?
Leon: Nope.
CR: How come?
Leon: Ah 'on' know.
CR: Didn't you ever hit somebody?
Leon: Nope.
CR: [incredulous] You never hit nobody?
Leon: Mhm.
CR: Aww, ba-a-a-be, you ain't gonna tell me that.

It may be that Leon is here defending himself against accusations of wrong-doing, since Clarence knows that Leon has been in fights, that he has been taking pencils away from little boys, etc. But if we turn to a more neutral subject, we find the same pattern:

CR: You watch — you like to watch television? . . . Hey, Leon . . . you
   like to watch television? [Leon nods] What's your favorite program?
Leon: Uhhmmmm . . . I look at cartoons.
CR: Well, what's your favorite one? What's your favorite program?
Leon: Superman . . .
CR: Yeah? Did you see Superman — ah — yesterday, or day before yester-
   day: when's the last time you saw Superman?
Leon: Sa-aturday . . .
CR: You rem — you saw it Saturday? What was the story all about? You
   remember the story?
Leon: M-m.
CR: You don't remember the story of what — that you saw of Superman?
Leon: Nope.
CR: You don't remember what happened, huh?
Leon: Hm-m.
CR: I see — ah — what other stories do you like to watch on T.V.?
Leon: Mmmm ? ? ? . . . umm . . . [glottalization]
CR: Hmm? [4 seconds]

Leon: Hh?
CR: What's th' other stories that you like to watch?
Leon: ^{2}Mi-ighty^2 Mouse^2 ...
CR: And what else?
Leon: Ummmm ... ahm ...

This nonverbal behavior occurs in a relatively *favorable* context for adult-child interaction; since the adult is a Negro man raised in Harlem, who knows this particular neighborhood and these boys very well. He is a skilled interviewer who has obtained a very high level of verbal response with techniques developed for a different age level, and he has an extraordinary advantage over most teache:s or experimenters in these respects. But even his skills and personality are ineffective in breaking down the social constraints that prevail here.

When we reviewed the record of this interview with Leon, we decided to use it as a test of our own knowledge of the sociolinguistic factors which control speech. We made the following changes in the social situation: in the next interview with Leon, Clarence

1 brought along a supply of potato chips, changing the 'interview' into something more in the nature of a party;
2 brought along Leon's best friend, 8-year-old Gregory;
3 reduced the height imbalance (when Clarence got down on the floor of Leon's room, he dropped from 6ft 2in. to 3ft 6in.);
4 introduced taboo words and taboo topics, and proved to Leon's surprise that one can say anything into our microphone without any fear of retaliation.

The result of these changes is a striking difference in the volume and style of speech.

CR: Is there anybody who says *your momma drink pee?*
{ Leon: [rapidly and breathlessly] Yee-ah!
{ Greg: Yup!
Leon: And your father eat doo-doo† for breakfas'!
CR: Ohhh!! [laughs]
Leon: And they say *your father — your father eat doo-doo for dinner*!
Greg: When they sound† on me, I say *CBM*.†
CR: What that mean?
{ Leon: Congo-booger-snatch! [laughs]
{ Greg: Congo-booger-snatcher! [laughs]

Greg: And sometimes I'll curse with *BB*.
CR: What that?
Greg: Black boy! [Leon – crunching on potato chips] Oh that's a *MBB*.
CR: MBB. What's that?
Greg: 'Merican Black Boy!
CR: Ohh . . .
Greg: Anyway, 'Mericans is same like white people, right?
Leon: And they talk about Allah.
CR: Oh yeah?
Greg: Yeah.
CR: What they say about Allah?
Leon: Allah – Allah is God.
Greg: Allah –
CR: And what else?
Leon: I don' know the res'.
Greg: Allah i – Allah is God, Allah is the only God, Allah –
Leon: Allah is the *son* of God.
Greg: But can he make magic?
Leon: Nope.
Greg: I know who can make magic.
CR: Who can?
Leon: The God, the *real* one.
CR: Who can make magic?
Greg: The son of po' – [CR: Hm?] I'm sayin' the po'k chop God! He only
    a po'k chop God![7] [Leon chuckles]

The 'nonverbal' Leon is now competing actively for the floor; Gregory and
Leon talk to each other as much as they do to the interviewer.

    One can make a more direct comparison of the two interviews by
examining the section on fighting. Leon persists in denying that he fights,
but he can no longer use monosyllabic answers, and Gregory cuts through
his facade in a way that Clarence Robins alone was unable to do.

CR: Now, you said you had this fight, but I wanted you to tell me about
    the fight that you had.
Leon: I ain't had no fight.
{ Greg: Yes, you did!   He said Barry.
{ CR: You said you had one! you had a fight with Butchie.
{ Greg: An he say Garland . . . an' Michael.
{ CR: an' Barry . . .

{ Leon: I di'n'; you said that, Gregory!
{ Greg: You did.
{ Leon: You know you said that!
{ Greg: You said Garland, remember that?
{ Greg: You said Garland!   Yes you did!
{ CR: You said Garland, that's right.
Greg: He said Mich — an' I say Michael.
{ CR: Did you have a fight with Garland?
{ Leon: Uh-uh.
CR: You had one, and he beat you up, too!
Greg: Yes he did!
Leon: No, I di — I never had a fight with Butch! . . .

The same pattern can be seen on other local topics, where the interviewer brings neighborhood gossip to bear on Leon and Gregory acts as a witness.

CR: . . . Hey Gregory! heard that around here . . . and I'm 'on' tell you who said it, too . . .
Leon: Who?
{ CR: about you . . .
{ Leon: Who?
{ Greg: I'd say it!
CR: They said that — they say that the only person you play with is David Gilbert.
{ Leon: Yee-ah! yee-ah! yee-ah! . . .
{ Greg: That's who you play with!
{ Leon: I 'on' play with him no more!
{ Greg: Yes you do!
Leon: I 'on' play with him no more!
Greg: But remember, about me and Robbie?
Leon: So that's not —
Greg: and you went to Petey and Gilbert's house, 'member? *Ah haaah*!!
Leon: So that's — so — but I would — I had came back out, an' I ain't go to his house no more . . .

The observer must now draw a very different conclusion about the verbal capacity of Leon. The monosyllabic speaker who had nothing to say about anything and cannot remember what he did yesterday has disappeared. Instead, we have two boys who have so much to say they keep interrupting each other, who seem to have no difficulty in using the English language to express themselves. And we in turn obtain the volume of speech and the rich array of grammatical devices which we need for analyzing the structure of nonstandard Negro English (NNE): negative concord (*I 'on' play with him no more*), the pluperfect (*had came back out*), negative perfect (*I ain't had*), the negative preterite (*I ain't go*), and so on.

One can now transfer this demonstration of the sociolinguistic control of speech to other test situations — including IQ and reading tests in school. It should be immediately apparent that none of the standard tests will come anywhere near measuring Leon's verbal capacity. On these tests he will show up as very much the monosyllabic, inept, ignorant, bumbling child of our first interview. The teacher has far less ability than Clarence Robins to elicit speech from this child; Clarence knows the community, the things that Leon has been doing, and the things that Leon would like to talk about. But the power relationships in a one-to-one confrontation between adult and child are too asymmetrical. This does not mean that some Negro children will not talk a great deal when alone with an adult, or that an adult cannot get close to any child. It means that the social situation is the most powerful determinant of verbal behavior and that an adult must enter into the right social relation with a child if he wants to find out what a child can do: this is just what many teachers cannot do.

The view of the Negro speech community which we obtain from our work in the ghetto areas is precisely the opposite from that reported by Deutsch, Engelmann and Bereiter. We see a child bathed in verbal stimulation from morning to night. We see many speech events which depend upon the competitive exhibition of verbal skills: sounding, singing, toasts, rifting,† louding† — a whole range of activities in which the individual gains status through his use of language.[8] We see the younger child trying to acquire these skills from older children — hanging around on the outskirts of the older peer groups, and imitating this behavior to the best of his ability. We see no connection between verbal skill at the speech events characteristic of the street culture and success in the schoolroom.

Verbosity

There are undoubtedly many verbal skills which children from ghetto areas must learn in order to do well in the school situation, and some of these are indeed characteristic of middle-class verbal behavior. Precision in spelling, practice in handling abstract symbols, the ability to state explicitly the meaning of words, and a richer knowledge of the Latinate vocabulary, may all be useful acquisitions. But is it true that *all* of the middle-class verbal habits are functional and desirable in the school situation? Before we impose middle-class verbal style upon children from other cultural groups, we should find out how much of this is useful for the main work of analyzing and generalizing, and how much is merely stylistic — or even dysfunctional. In high school and college middle-class children spontaneously complicate their syntax to the point that instructors despair of getting them to make their language simpler and clearer. In every learned journal one can find examples of jargon and empty elaboration — and complaints about it. Is the 'elaborated code' of Bernstein really so 'flexible, detailed and subtle' as some psychologists believe (Jensen, 1968, p. 119)? Isn't it also turgid, redundant, and empty? Is it not simply an elaborated *style*, rather than a superior code or system?[9]

Our work in the speech community makes it painfully obvious that in many ways working-class speakers are more effective narrators, reasoners and debators than many middle-class speakers who temporize, qualify, and lose their argument in a mass of irrelevant detail. Many academic writers try to rid themselves of that part of middle-class style that is empty pretension, and keep that part that is needed for precision. But the average middle-class speaker that we encounter makes no such effort; he is enmeshed in verbiage, the victim of sociolinguistic factors beyond his control.

I will not attempt to support this argument here with systematic quantitative evidence, although it is possible to develop measures which show how far middle-class speakers can wander from the point. I would like to contrast two speakers dealing with roughly the same topic — matters of belief. The first is Larry H., a 15-year-old core member of the Jets, being interviewed by John Lewis. Larry is one of the loudest and roughest members of the Jets, one who gives the least recognition to the conventional rules of politeness.[10] For most readers of this paper, first contact with Larry would produce some fairly negative reactions on both sides: it is probable that you would not *like* him any more than his teachers do. Larry causes trouble in and out of school; he was put back from the eleventh grade to the ninth, and has been threatened with further action by the school authorities.

JL: What happens to you after you die? Do you know?
Larry: Yeah, I know.
JL: What?
Larry: After they put you in the ground, your body turns into — ah — bones, an' shit.
JL: What happens to your spirit?
Larry: Your spirit — soon as you die, your spirit leaves you.
JL: And where does the spirit go?
Larry: Well, it all depends . . .

JL: On what?

Larry: You know, like some people say if you're good an' shit, your spirit goin' t' heaven . . . 'n if you bad, your spirit goin' to hell. Well, bullshit! Your spirit goin' to hell anyway, good or bad.

JL: Why?

Larry: Why? I'll tell you why. 'Cause you see, doesn' nobody really know that it's a God, y'know, 'cause I mean I have seen black gods, pink gods, white gods, all color gods, and don't nobody know it's really a God. An' when they be sayin' if you good, you goin' t' heaven, tha's bullshit, 'cause you ain't goin' to no heaven, 'cause it ain't no heaven for you to go to.

Larry is a paradigmatic speaker of nonstandard Negro English (NNE) as opposed to standard English (SE). His grammar shows a high concentration of such characteristic NNE forms as negative inversion (*don't nobody know* . . .), negative concord (*you ain't goin' to no heaven* . . .), invariant *be* (*when they be sayin'* . . .), dummy *it* for SE *there* (*it ain't no heaven* . . .), optional copula deletion (*if you're good* . . . *if you bad* . . .), and full forms of auxiliaries (*I have seen* . . .). The only SE influence in this passage is the one case of *doesn't* instead of the invariant *don't* of NNE. Larry also provides a paradigmatic example of the rhetorical style of NNE: he can sum up a complex argument in a few words, and the full force of his opinions comes through without qualification or reservation. He is eminently quotable, and his interviews give us many concise statements of the NNE point of view. One can almost say that Larry *speaks* the NNE culture (see Labov, Cohen, Robins and Lewis, 1968, vol. 2, pp. 38, 71-3, 291-2).

It is the logical form of this passage which is of particular interest here. Larry presents a complex set of interdependent propositions which can be explicated by setting out the SE equivalents in linear order. The basic argument is to deny the twin propositions

(A) If you are good.   (B) then your spirit will go to heaven.
(−A) If you are bad.   (C) then your spirit will go to hell.

Larry denies (B), and asserts that *if* (A) *or* (−A), *then* (C). His argument may be outlined as follows:

(1)   Everyone has a different idea of what God is like.
(2)   Therefore nobody really knows that God exists.
(3)   If there is a heaven, it was made by God.

(4)   If God doesn't exist, he couldn't have made heaven.
(5)   Therefore heaven does not exist.
(6)   You can't go somewhere that doesn't exist.
(−B)   Therefore you can't go to heaven.
(C)   Therefore you are going to hell.

The argument is presented in the order: (C), because (2) because (1), therefore (2), therefore (−B) because (5) and (6). Part of the argument is implicit: the connection (2) therefore (−B) leaves unstated the connecting links (3) and (4), and in this interval Larry strengthens the propositions from the form (2) *Nobody knows if there is* . . . to (5) *There is no* . . . Otherwise, the case is presented explicitly as well as economically. The complex argument is summed up in Larry's last sentence, which shows formally the dependence of (−B) on (5) and (6):

An' when they be sayin' if you good, you goin' t' heaven,
[*The proposition, if* A, *then* B]
Tha's bullshit,
[*is absurd*]
'cause you ain't goin' to no heaven
[*because* −B]
'cause it ain't no heaven for you to go to.
[*because* (5) *and* (6)] .

This hypothetical argument is not carried on at a high level of seriousness. It is a game played with ideas as counters, in which opponents use a wide variety of verbal devices to win. There is no personal commitment to any of these propositions, and no reluctance to strengthen one's argument by bending the rules of logic as in the (2-5) sequence. But if the opponent invokes the rule of logic, they hold. In John Lewis' interviews, he often makes this move, and the force of his argument is always acknowledged and countered within the rules of logic. In this case, he pointed out the fallacy that the argument (2-3-4-5-6) leads to (−C) as well as (−B), so it can be used to support Larry's assertion (C):

JL: Well, if there's no heaven, how could there be a hell?
Larry: I mean — ye — eah. Well, let me tell you, it ain't no hell, 'cause this
    is hell right here, y'know!
JL: This is hell?
Larry: Yeah, this is hell right here!

Larry's answer is quick, ingenious and decisive. The application of the (3-4-5) argument to hell is denied, since hell is here, and therefore conclusion (C) stands. These are not ready-made or preconceived opinions, but new propositions devised to win the logical argument in the game being played. The reader will note the speed and precision of Larry's mental operations. He does not wander, or insert meaningless verbiage. The only repetition is (2), placed before and after (1) in his original statement. It is often said that the nonstandard vernacular is not suited for dealing with abstract or hypothetical questions, but in fact speakers from the NNE community take great delight in exercising their wit and logic on the most improbable and problematical matters. Despite the fact that Larry H. does not believe in God, and has just denied all knowledge of him, John Lewis advances the following hypothetical question:

JL: . . . But, just say that there is a God, what color is he? White or black?
Larry: Well, if it is a God . . . I wouldn' know what color, I couldn' say, — couldn' nobody say what color he is or really *would* be.
JL: But now, jus' suppose there was a God —
Larry: Unless'n they say . . .
JL: No, I was jus' sayin' jus' suppose there is a God, would he be white or black?
Larry: . . . He'd be white, man.
JL: Why?
Larry: Why? I'll tell you why. 'Cause the average whitey out here got everything, you dig? And the nigger ain't got shit, y'know? Y'understan'? So — um — for — in order for *that* to happen, you know it ain't no black God that's doin' that bullshit.

No one can hear Larry's answer to this question without being convinced that they are in the presence of a skilled speaker with great 'verbal presence of mind', who can use the English language expertly for many purposes. Larry's answer to John Lewis is again a complex argument. The formulation is not SE, but it is clear and effective even for those not familiar with the vernacular. The nearest SE equivalent might be: 'So you know that God isn't black, because if he was, he wouldn't have arranged things like that.'

The reader will have noted that this analysis is being carried out in standard English, and the inevitable challenge is: why not write in NNE, then, or in your own nonstandard dialect? The fundamental reason is, of course, one of firmly fixed social conventions. All communities agree that SE is the 'proper' medium for formal writing and public communication.

Furthermore, it seems likely that SE has an advantage over NNE in explicit analysis of surface forms, which is what we are doing here. We will return to this opposition between explicitness and logical statement in the section on grammaticality. First, however, it will be helpful to examine SE in its primary natural setting as the medium for informal spoken communication of middle-class speakers.

Let us now turn to the second speaker, an upper-middle-class, college educated Negro man being interviewed by Clarence Robins in our survey of adults in Central Harlem.

CR: Do you know of anything that someone can do, to have someone who has passed on visit him in a dream?

Charles M: Well, I even heard my parents say that there is such a thing as something in dreams some things like that, and sometimes dreams do come true. I have personally never had a dream come true. I've never dreamt that somebody was dying and they actually died, (Mhm) or that I was going to have ten dollars the next day and somehow I got ten dollars in my pocket. (Mhm). I don't particularly beieve in that, I don't think it's true. I do feel, though, that there is such a thing as – ah – witchcraft. I do feel that in certain cultures there is such a thing as witchcraft, or some sort of *science* of witchcraft; I don't think that it's just a matter of believing hard enough that there is such a thing as witchcraft. I do believe that there is such a thing that a person can put himself in a state of *mind* (Mhm), or that – er – something could be given them to intoxicate them in a certain – to a certain frame of mind – that – that could actually be considered witchcraft.

Charles M. is obviously a 'good speaker' who strikes the listener as well-educated, intelligent and sincere. He is a likeable and attractive person – the kind of person that middle-class listeners rate very high on a scale of 'job suitability' and equally high as a potential friend.[11] His language is more moderate and tempered than Larry's; he makes every effort to qualify his opinions, and seems anxious to avoid any misstatements or over-statements. From these qualities emerges the primary characteristic of this passage – its *verbosity*. Words multiply, some modifying and qualifying, others repeating or padding the main argument. The first half of this extract is a response to the initial question on dreams, basically:

1 Some people say that dreams sometimes come true.
2 I have never had a dream come true.
3 Therefore I don't believe (1).

Some characteristic filler phrases appear here: *such a thing as, some things like that, particularly*. Two examples of dreams given after (2) are after-thoughts that might have been given after (1). Proposition (3) is stated twice for no obvious reason. Nevertheless, this much of Charles M's response is well-directed to the point of the question. He then volunteers a statement of his beliefs about witchcraft which shows the difficulty of middle-class speakers who (a) want to express a belief in something but (b) want to show themselves as judicious, rational and free from superstitions. The basic proposition can be stated simply in five words:

But I believe in witchcraft.

However, the idea is enlarged to exactly 100 words, and it is difficult to see what else is being said. In the following quotations, padding which can be removed without change in meaning is shown in brackets.

1 'I [do] feel, though, that there is [such a thing as] witchcraft.' *Feel* seems to be a euphemism for 'believe'.

2 '[I do feel that] in certain cultures [there is such a thing as witch-craft].' This repetition seems designed only to introduce the word *culture*, which lets us know that the speaker knows about anthropology. Does *certain cultures* mean 'not in ours' or 'not in all'?

3 '[or some sort of *science* of witchcraft.]' This addition seems to have no clear meaning at all. What is a 'science' of witchcraft as opposed to just plain witchcraft?[12] The main function is to introduce the word 'science', though it seems to have no connection to what follows.

4 'I don't think that it's just [a matter of] believing hard enough that [there is such a thing as] witchcraft.' The speaker argues that witchcraft is not merely a belief; there is more to it.

5 'I [do] believe that [there is such a thing that] a person can put himself in a state of *mind* . . . that [could actually be considered] witch-craft.' Is witchcraft as a state of mind different from the state of belief denied in (4)?

6 'or that something could be given them to intoxicate them [to a certain frame of mind] . . .' The third learned word, *intoxicate*, is introduced by this addition. The vacuity of this passage becomes more evident if we remove repetitions, fashionable words and stylistic decorations:

But I believe in witchcraft.
I don't think witchcraft is just a belief.
A person can put himself or be put in a state of mind that is witchcraft.

Without the extra verbiage and the OK words like *science, culture* and *intoxicate*, Charles M. appears as something less than a first-rate thinker. The initial impression of him as a good speaker is simply our long-conditioned reaction to middle-class verbosity: we know that people who use these stylistic devices are educated people, and we are inclined to credit them with saying something intelligent. Our reactions are accurate in one sense: Charles M. is more educated than Larry. But is he more rational, more logical, or more intelligent? Is he any better at thinking out a problem to its solution? Does he deal more easily with abstractions? There is no reason to think so. Charles M. succeeds in letting us know that he is educated, but in the end we do not know what he is trying to say, and neither does he.

In the previous section I have attempted to explain the origin of the myth that lower-class Negro children are nonverbal. The examples just given may help to account for the corresponding myth that middle-class language is in itself better suited for dealing with abstract, logically complex and hypothetical questions. These examples are intended to have a certain negative force. They are not controlled experiments: on the contrary, this and the preceding section are designed to convince the reader that the controlled experiments that have been offered in evidence are misleading. The only thing that is 'controlled' is the superficial form of the stimulus: all children are asked 'What do you think of capital punishment?' or 'Tell me everything you can about this.' But the speaker's interpretation of these requests, and the action he believes is appropriate in response is completely uncontrolled. One can view these test stimuli as requests for information, commands for action, as threats of punishment, or as meaningless sequences of words. They are probably intended as something altogether different; as requests for display;[13] but in any case the experimenter is normally unaware of the problem of interpretation. The methods of educational psychologists like Deutsch, Jensen and Bereiter follow the pattern designed for animal experiments where motivation is controlled by such simple methods as withholding food until a certain weight reduction is reached. With human subjects, it is absurd to believe that an identical 'stimulus' is obtained by asking everyone the 'same question'. Since the crucial intervening variables of interpretation and motivation are uncontrolled, most of the literature on verbal deprivation tells us nothing about the capacities of children. They are only the trappings of science: an approach which substitutes the formal procedures of the scientific method for the activity itself. With our present limited grasp of these problems, the best we can do to understand the verbal capacities of children is to study them within the cultural context in which they were developed.

It is not only the NNE vernacular which should be studied in this way, but also the language of middle-class children. The explicitness and precision which we hope to gain from copying middle-class forms are often the product of the test situation, and limited to it. For example, it was stated in the first part of this paper that working-class children hear more well-formed sentences than middle-class children. This statement may seem extraordinary in the light of the current belief of many linguists that most people do not speak in well-formed sentences, and that their actual speech production or 'performance' is ungrammatical.[14] But those who have worked with any body of natural speech know that this is not the case. Our own studies of the 'Grammaticality of Every-day Speech' show that the great majority of utterances in all contexts are complete sentences, and most of the rest can be reduced to grammatical form by a small set of 'editing rules'.[15] The proportions of grammatical sentences vary with class backgrounds and styles. The highest percentage of well-formed sentences are found in casual speech, and working-class speakers use more well-formed sentences than middle-class speakers. The widespread myth that most speech is ungrammatical is no doubt based upon tapes made at learned conferences, where we obtain the maximum number of irreducibly ungrammatical sequences.

It is true that technical and scientific books are written in a style which is markedly 'middle-class'. But unfortunately, we often fail to achieve the explicitness and precision which we look for in such writing; and the speech of many middle-class people departs maximally from this target. All too often, 'standard English' is represented by a style that is simultaneously overparticular and vague. The accumulating flow of words buries rather than strikes the target. It is this verbosity which is most easily taught and most easily learned, so that words take the place of thought, and nothing can be found behind them.

When Bernstein described his 'elaborated code' in general terms, it emerges as a subtle and sophisticated mode of planning utterances, achieving structural variety, taking the other person's knowledge into account, and so on. But when it comes to describing the actual difference between middle-class and working-class speakers, we are presented with a proliferation of 'I think', of the passive, of modals and auxiliaries, of the first person pronoun, of uncommon words; these are the bench marks of hemming and hawing, backing and filling, that are used by Charles M., devices which often obscure whatever positive contribution education can make to our use of language. When we have discovered how much middle-class style is a matter of fashion and how much actually helps us express our ideas clearly, we will have done ourselves a great service; we will then be in a position to say what standard grammatical rules must be taught to nonstandard speakers in the early grades.

Grammaticality

Let us now examine Bereiter's own data on the verbal behavior of the children he dealt with. The expressions *They mine* and *Me got juice* are cited as examples of a language which lacks the means for expressing logical relations – in this case characterized as 'a series of badly connected words'. (Bereiter, 1966, pp. 113 ff.) In the case of *They mine*, it is apparent that Bereiter confuses the notions of logic and explicitness. We know that there are many languages of the world which do not have a present copula, and which conjoin subject and predicate complement without a verb. Russian, Hungarian and Arabic may be foreign; but they are not by that same token illogical. In the case of nonstandard Negro English we are not dealing with even this superficial grammatical difference, but rather with a low-level rule which carries contraction one step farther to delete single consonants representing the verbs *is*, *have*, or *will* (Labov, Cohen, Robins and Lewis, 1968, sect. 3.4). We have yet to find any children who do not sometimes use the full forms of *is* and *will*, even though they may frequently delete it. Our recent studies with Negro children four to seven years old indicate that they use the full form of the copula *is* more often than pre-adolescents 10 to 12 years old, or the adolescents 14 to 17 years old.[16]

Furthermore, the deletion of the *is* or *are* in nonstandard Negro English is not the result of erratic or illogical behavior: it follows the same regular rules as standard English contraction. Wherever standard English can contract, Negro children use either the contracted form or (more commonly) the deleted zero form. Thus *They mine* corresponds to standard *They're mine*, not to the full form *They are mine*. On the other hand, no such deletion is possible in positions where standard English cannot contract: just as one cannot say *That's what they're* in standard English, *That's what they* is equally impossible in the vernacular we are considering. The internal constraints upon both of these rules show that we are dealing with a phonological process like contraction, sensitive to such phonetic conditions as whether or not the next word begins with a vowel or a consonant. The appropriate use of the deletion rule, like the contraction rule, requires a deep and intimate knowledge of English grammar and phonology. Such knowledge is not available for conscious inspection by native speakers: the rules we have recently worked out for standard contraction (Labov, Cohen, Robins and Lewis, 1968, sect. 3.4) have never appeared in any grammar, and are certainly not a part of the conscious knowledge of any standard English speakers. Nevertheless, the adult or child who uses these rules must have formed at some level of psychological organization clear concepts of 'tense marker', 'verb phrase', 'rule ordering', 'sentence embedding', 'pronoun', and many other grammatical categories which are essential parts of any logical system.

Bereiter's reaction to the sentence *Me got juice* is even more puzzling. If Bereiter believes that *Me got juice* is not a logical expression, it can only be that he interprets the use of the objective pronoun *me* as representing a difference in logical relationship to the verb: that the child is in fact saying that *the juice got him* rather than *he got the juice*! If on the other hand the child means 'I got juice', then this sentence form shows only that he has not learned the formal rules for the use of the subject form *I* and oblique form *me*. We have in fact encountered many children who do not have these formal rules in order at the ages of four, five, six or even eight.[17] It is extremely difficult to construct a minimal pair to show that the difference between *he* and *him*, or *she* and *her*, carries cognitive meaning. In almost every case, it is the context which tells us who is the agent and who is acted upon. We must then ask: what differences in cognitive, structural orientation are signalled by the fact that the child has not learned this formal rule? In the tests carried out by Jane Torrey it is evident that the children concerned do understand the difference in meaning between *she* and *her* when another person uses the forms; all that remains is that the children themselves do not use the two forms. Our knowledge of the cognitive correlates of grammatical differences is certainly in its infancy; for this is one of very many questions which we simply cannot answer. At the moment we do not know how to construct any kind of experiment which would lead to an answer; we do not even know what type of cognitive correlate we would be looking for.

Bereiter shows even more profound ignorance of the rules of discourse and of syntax when he rejects *In the tree* as an illogical, or badly-formed answer to *Where is the squirrel?* Such elliptical answers are of course used by everyone; they show the appropriate deletion of subject and main verb, leaving the locative which is questioned by *wh* + *there*. The reply *In the tree* demonstrates that the listener has been attentive to and apprehended the syntax of the speaker.[18] Whatever formal structure we wish to write for expressions such as *Yes* or *Home* or *In the tree*, it is obvious that they cannot be interpreted without knowing the structure of the question which preceded them, and that they presuppose an understanding of the syntax of the question. Thus if you ask me 'Where is the squirrel?' it is necessary for me to understand the process of *wh*-attachment, *wh*-attraction to the front of the sentence, and flip-flop of auxiliary and subject to produce this sentence from an underlying form which would otherwise have produced *The squirrel is there.* If the child had answered *The tree*, or *Squirrel the tree*, or *The in tree*, we would then assume that he did not understand the syntax of the full form, *The squirrel is in the tree.* Given the data that Bereiter presents, we cannot conclude that the child has no grammar, but only that the investigator does not understand the rules of grammar. It does not necessarily do any harm to use the full form *The squirrel is in the tree*, if one wants to make fully explicit the rules of grammar which the child has internalized. Much of logical analysis consists of making explicit just that kind of internalized rule. But it is hard to believe that any good can come from a program which begins with so many misconceptions about the input data. Bereiter and Engelmann believe that in teaching the child to say *The squirrel is in the tree* or *This is a box* and *This is not a box* they are teaching him an entirely new language, whereas in fact they are only teaching him to produce slightly different forms of the language he already has.

What's Wrong with Being Wrong?

If there is a failure of logic involved here, it is surely in the approach of the verbal deprivation theorists, rather than in the mental abilities of the children concerned. We can isolate six distinct steps in the reasoning which has led to programs such as those of Deutsch, Bereiter and Engelmann:

1. The lower-class child's verbal response to a formal and threatening situation is used to demonstrate his lack of verbal capacity, or verbal deficit.

2. This verbal deficit is declared to be a major cause of the lower-class child's poor performance in school.

3. Since middle-class children do better in school, middle-class speech habits are seen to be necessary for learning.

4. Class and ethnic differences in grammatical form are equated with differences in the capacity for logical analysis.

5. Teaching the child to mimic certain formal speech patterns used by middle-class teachers is seen as teaching him to think logically.

6. Children who learn these formal speech patterns are then said to be thinking logically and it is predicted that they will do much better in reading and arithmetic in the years to follow.

In the previous sections of this paper, I have tried to show that these propositions are wrong, concentrating on (1), (4), and (5). Proposition (3) is the primary logical fallacy which illicitly identifies a form of speech as the *cause* of middle-class achievement in school. Proposition (6) is the one which is most easily shown to be wrong in fact, as we will note below.

However, it is not to naive to ask, 'What is wrong with being wrong?' There is no competing educational theory which is being dismantled by this program; and there does not seem to be any great harm in having children repeat *This is not a box* for twenty minutes a day. We have already conceded that NNE children need help in analysing language into its surface components, and in being more explicit. But there are serious and damaging consequences of the verbal deprivation theory which may be considered under two headings: (1) the theoretical bias, and (2) the consequences of failure.

(1) It is widely recognized that the teacher's attitude towards the child is an important factor in his success or failure. The work of Rosenthal on 'self-fulfilling prophecies' shows that the progress of children in the early grades can be dramatically affected by a single random labelling of certain children as 'intellectual bloomers' (Rosenthal and Jacobson, 1968). When the everyday language of Negro children is stigmatized as 'not a language at all' and 'not possessing the means for logical thought', the effect of such a labelling is repeated many times during each day of the school year. Every time that a child uses a form of NNE without the copula or with negative concord, he will be labelling himself for the teacher's benefit as 'illogical', as a 'nonceptual thinker'. Bereiter and Engelmann, Deutsch and Jensen are giving teachers a ready-made, theoretical basis for the prejudice they already feel against the lower-class Negro child and his language. When they hear him say *I don't want none* or *They mine*, they will be hearing through the bias provided by the verbal deprivation theory: not an English dialect different from theirs, but the primitive mentality of the savage mind.

But what if the teacher succeeds in training the child to use the new language consistently? The verbal deprivation theory holds that this will lead to a whole chain of success in school, and that the child will be drawn away from the vernacular culture into the middle-class world. Undoubtedly this will happen with a few isolated individuals, just as it happens in every school system today, for a few children. But we are concerned not with the few but the many, and for the majority of Negro children the distance between them and the school is bound to widen under this approach.

Proponents of the deficit theory have a strange view of social organization outside of the classroom: they see the attraction of the peer group as a 'substitute' for success and gratification normally provided by the school. For example, Whiteman and Deutsch introduce their account of the deprivation hypothesis with an eye-witness account of a child who accidentally dropped his school notebook into a puddle of water and walked away without picking it up.

> A policeman who had been standing nearby walked over to the puddle and stared at the notebook with some degree of disbelief (Whiteman and Deutsch, 1968, pp. 86-7).

The child's alienation from school is explained as the result of his coming to school without the 'verbal, conceptual, attentional and learning skills requisite to school success'. The authors see the child as 'suffering from feelings of inferiority because he is failing; . . . he withdraws or becomes hostile, finding gratification elsewhere, such as in his peer group.'

To view the peer group as a mere substitute for school shows an extraordinary lack of knowledge of adolescent culture. In our studies in South Central Harlem we have seen the reverse situation: the children who are rejected by the peer group are quite likely to succeed in school. In middle-class suburban areas, many children do fail in school because of their personal deficiencies; in ghetto areas, it is the healthy, vigorous popular child with normal intelligence who cannot read and fails all along the line. It is not necessary to document here the influence of the peer group upon the behavior of youth in our society; but we may note that somewhere between the time that children first learn to talk and puberty, their language is restructured to fit the rules used by their peer group. From a linguistic viewpoint, the peer group is certainly a more powerful influence than the family (Gans, 1962). Less directly, the pressures of peer group activity are also felt within the school. Many children, particularly those who are not doing well in school, show a sudden sharp down turn in the fourth and fifth grades, and children in the ghetto schools are no exception. It is at the same age, at nine or ten years old, that the influence of the vernacular peer group becomes predominant.[19] Instead of dealing with isolated individuals, the school is then dealing with children who are integrated into groups of their own, with rewards and value systems which oppose those of the school. Those who know the sociolinguistic situation cannot doubt that reaction against the Bereiter-Engelmann approach in later years will be even more violent on the part of the students involved, and that the rejection of the school system will be even more categorical.

The essential fallacy of the verbal deprivation theory lies in tracing the educational failure of the child to his personal deficiencies. At present, these deficiencies are said to be caused by his home environment. It is traditional to explain a child's failure in school by his inadequacy; but when failure reaches such massive proportions, it seems to us necessary to look at the social and cultural obstacles to learning, and the inability of the school to adjust to the social situation. Operation Headstart is designed to repair the child, rather than the school; to the extent that it is based upon this inverted logic, it is bound to fail.

(2)   The second area in which the verbal deprivation theory is doing serious harm to our educational system is in the consequences of this failure, and the reaction to it. If Operation Headstart fails, the interpretations which we receive will be from the same educational psychologists who designed this program. The fault will be found not in the data, the theory, nor in the methods used, but rather in the children who have failed to respond to the opportunities offered to them. When Negro children fail to show the significant advance which the deprivation theory predicts, it will be further proof of the profound gulf which separates their mental processes from those of civilized, middle-class mankind.

A sense of the 'failure' of Operation Headstart is already in the air. Some prominent figures in the program are reacting to this situation by saying that intervention did not take place early enough. Bettye M. Caldwell notes that:

. . . the research literature of the last decade dealing with social-class differences has made abundantly clear that all parents are not qualified to provide even the basic essentials of physical and psychological care to their children (Caldwell, 1967, p. 16).

The deficit theory now begins to focus on the 'long-standing patterns of parental deficit' which fill the literature. 'There is, perhaps unfortunately,' writes Caldwell, 'no literacy test for motherhood.' Failing such eugenic measures, she has proposed 'educationally oriented day care for culturally deprived children between six months and three years of age'. The children are returned home each evening to 'maintain primary emotional relationships with their own families', but during the day they are removed to 'hopefully prevent the deceleration in rate of development which seems to occur in many deprived children around the age of two to three years' (Caldwell, 1967, p. 17).

There are others who feel that even the best of the intervention programs, such as those of Bereiter and Engelmann, will not help the Negro child no matter when they are applied – that we are faced once again with the 'inevitable hypothesis' of the genetic inferiority of the Negro people. Many readers of this paper are undoubtedly familiar with the paper of Arthur Jensen in the *Harvard Educational Review* (1969) which received early and widespread publicity. Jensen begins with the following quotation from the United States Commission on Civil Rights as evidence of the failure of compensatory education.

The fact remains, however, that none of the programs appear to have raised significantly the achievement of participating pupils, as a group, within the period evaluated by the Commission (p. 138).

Jensen believes that the verbal deprivation theorists with whom he had been associated — Deutsch, Whiteman, Katz, Bereiter — have been given every opportunity to prove their case — and have failed. This opinion is part of the argument which leads him to the overall conclusion that 'the preponderance of the evidence is . . . less consistent with a strictly environmental hypothesis than with the genetic hypothesis'; that racism, or the belief in the genetic inferiority of Negroes, is a correct view in the light of the present evidence.

Jensen argues that the middle-class white population is differentiated from the working-class white and Negro population in the ability for 'cognitive or conceptual learning', which Jensen calls Level II intelligence as against mere 'associative learning' or Level I intelligence:

certain neural structures must also be available for Level II abilities to develop, and these are conceived of as being different from the neural structures underlying Level I. The genetic factors involved in each of these types of ability are presumed to have become differentially distributed in the population as a function of social class, since Level II has been most important for scholastic performance under the traditional methods of instruction.

Thus Jensen found that one group of middle-class children were helped by their concept-forming ability to recall twenty familiar objects that could be classified into four categories: animals, furniture, clothing, or foods. Lower-class Negro children did just as well as middle-class children with a miscellaneous set, but showed no improvement with objects that could be so categorized.

The research of the educational psychologists cited here is presented in formal and objective style, and is widely received as impartial scientific evidence. Jensen's paper has already been reported by Joseph Alsop and William F. Buckley Jr. as 'massive, apparently authoritative . . .' (*NY Post* 3/20/69). It is not my intention to examine these materials in detail; but it is important to realize that we are dealing with special pleading by those who have a strong personal commitment. Jensen is concerned with class differences in cognitive style and verbal learning. His earlier papers incorporated the cultural deprivation theory which he now rejects as a basic explanation.[20] He classifies the Negro children who fail in school as 'slow-learners' and 'mentally-retarded', and urged that we find out how much their retardation is due to environmental factors and how much is due to 'more basic biological factors' (Jensen 1968, p. 167). His conviction that the problem must be located in the child leads him to accept and reprint some truly extraordinary data. To support the genetic hypothesis he cites the following table of Heber for the racial distribution of mental retardation.

Table 13.1: Estimated Prevalence of Children with IQs below 75

SES	White	Negro
1	0.5	3.1
2	0.8	14.5
3	2.1	22.8
4	3.1	37.8
5	7.8	42.9

This report, that almost half of lower-class Negro children are mentally retarded, could be accepted only by someone who has no knowledge of the children or the community. If he had wished to, Jensen could easily have checked this against the records of any school in any urban ghetto area. Taking IQ tests at their face value, there is no correspondence between these figures and the communities we know. For example, among 75 boys we worked with in Central Harlem who would fall into Heber's SES 4 or 5, there were only three with IQs below 75: one spoke very little English, one could barely see, and the third was emotionally disturbed. When the second was retested, he scored 91, and the third retested at 87.[21] There are of course hundreds of realistic reports available to Jensen: he simply selected one which would strengthen his case for the genetic inferiority of Negro children, and deliberately deleted the information that this was a study of an area selected in advance because of its high incidence of mental retardation.[22]

The frequent use of tables and statistics by educational psychologists serves to give outside readers the impression that this field is a science, and that the opinions of the authors should be given the same attention and respect that we give to the conclusions of physicists or chemists. But careful examination of the input data will often show that there is no direct relationship between the conclusions and the evidence (in Jensen's case, between IQ tests in a specially selected district of Milwaukee and intelligence of lower-class Negro children). Furthermore, the operations performed upon the data frequently carry us very far from the common-sense experience which is our only safeguard against conclusions heavily weighted by the author's theory. As another example, we may take some of the evidence presented by Whiteman and Deutsch for the cultural deprivation hypothesis. The core of Martin Deutsch's environmental explanation of low school performance is the Deprivation Index − a numerical scale based on six dichotomized variables. One variable is 'The educational aspirational level of the parent for the child'. Most people would agree that a parent who did not care if a child finished high school would be a disadvantageous factor in the child's educational career. In dichotomizing this variable Deutsch was faced with the fact that the educational aspiration of Negro parents is in fact very high − higher than for the white population, as he shows in other papers.[23] In order to fit this data into the Deprivation Index, he therefore set the cutting point for the deprived group as 'college or less'. (Whiteman and Deutsch, 1968, p. 100.) Thus if a Negro child's father says that he wants his son to go all the way through college, the child will fall into the 'deprived' class on this variable. In order to receive the two points given to the 'less deprived' on the index, it would be necessary for the child's parent to insist on graduate school or medical school! This decision is never discussed by the authors: it simply stands as a *fait accompli* in the tables. Readers of this literature who are not committed to one point of view would be wise to look as carefully as possible at the original data which lie behind each statement, and check the conclusions against their own knowledge of the people and community being described.

No one can doubt that the inadequacy of Operation Headstart and of the verbal deprivation hypothesis has now become a crucial issue in our society.[24] The controversy which is beginning over Jensen's article will undoubtedly take as given that programs such as Bereiter and Engelmann's have tested and measured the verbal capacity of the ghetto child. The cultural sociolinguistic obstacles to this intervention program are not considered; and the argument proceeds upon the data provided by the large, friendly interviewers that we have seen at work in the extracts given above.

That educational psychology should be strongly influenced by a theory so false to the facts of language is unfortunate; but that children should be the victims of this ignorance is intolerable. It may seem that the fallacies of the verbal deprivation theory are so obvious that they are hardly worth exposing; I have tried to show that it is an important job for us to undertake. If linguists can contribute some of their available knowledge and energy towards this end, we will have done a great deal to justify the support that society has given to basic research in our field.

Notes

1.   I am indebted to Rosalind Weiner of the Early Childhood Education group of Operation Headstart in New York City, and to Joan Baratz, of the Educational Development Corp., Washington DC, for pointing out to me the scope and seriousness of the educational issues involved here, and the ways in which the cultural deprivation theory has affected federal intervention programs in recent years.

2.   A report of average reading comprehension scores in New York City was published in the *New York Times* on 3 December 1968. The schools attended by most of the peer group members we have studied showed the following scores:

School	Grade	Reading score	National norm
JHS 13	7	5.6	7.7
	9	7.6	9.7
JHS 120	7	5.6	7.7
	9	7.0	9.7
IS 88	6	5.3	6.7
	8	7.2	8.7

The average is then more than two full years behind grade in the ninth grade.

3.   There are a number of studies reported recently which show no relation between school achievement and presence of a father in the nuclear family. Preliminary findings to this effect are cited from a study by Bernard Mackler of CUE in Thos. S. Langer and Stanley T. Michaels, *Life Stress and Mental Health* (New York: Free Press), Chapter 8. Jensen (1969) cites James Coleman's study *Equality of educational opportunity*, p. 506, and others to illustrate the same point.

4.   The concept of 'nonstandard Negro English', and the vernacular culture in which it is embedded, is presented in detail in Labov, Cohen, Robins and Lewis (1968), sections 1, 2, 3 and 4.1 See Volume 2, section 4.3, for the linguistic traits which distinguish speakers who participate fully in the NNE culture from marginal and isolated individuals.

5.   For example, in Deutsch, Katz and Jensen (1968) there is a section on 'Social and Psychological Perspectives' which includes a chapter by Proshansky and Newton on 'The Nature and Meaning of Negro Self-Identity' and one by Rosenthal and Jacobson on 'Self-Fulfilling Prophecies in the Classroom'.

6.   The research cited here was carried out in South Central Harlem and other ghetto areas in 1965-1968 to describe structural and functional differences between nonstandard Negro English and standard English of the classroom. It was supported by the Office of Education as Co-operative Research Projects 3091 and 3288. Detailed reports are given in Labov, Cohen and Robins (1965), Labov (1967) and Labov, Cohen, Robins and Lewis (1968).

7.   The reference to the *pork chop God* condenses several concepts of black nationalism current in the Harlem community. A *pork chop* is a Negro who has not lost the traditional subservient ideology of the South, who has no knowledge of himself in Muslim terms, and the *pork chop God* would be the traditional God of Southern Baptists. He and his followers may be pork chops, but he still holds the power in Leon and Gregory's world.

8.   For detailed accounts of these speech events, see Labov, Cohen, Robins and Lewis (1968, section 4.2).

9.   The term *code* is central in Bernstein's description of the differences between working-class and middle-class styles of speech. The restrictions and elaborations of speech observed are labelled as 'codes' to indicate the principles governing selection from the range of possible English sentences. No rules or detailed description of the operation of such codes are provided as yet, so that this central concept remains to be specified.

10.   A direct view of Larry's verbal style in a hostile encounter is given in Labov, Cohen, Robins and Lewis (1968), Vol. 2, pp. 39-43. Gray's Oral Reading Test was being given to a group of Jets on the steps of a brown-stone house in Harlem, and the landlord tried unsuccessfully to make the Jets move. Larry's verbal style in this encounter matches the reports he gives of himself in a number of narratives cited in section 4.8.

11.   See Labov, Cohen, Robins and Lewis (1968), section 4.6, for a description of subjective reaction tests which utilize these evaluative dimensions.

12.   Several middle-class readers of this passage have suggested that *science* here refers to some form of control as opposed to belief; the 'science of witchcraft' would then be a kind of engineering of mental states; other interpretations can of course be provided. The fact remains that no such subtleties of interpretation are needed to understand Larry's remarks.

13.   The concept of a 'request for verbal display' is here drawn from Alan Blum's treatment of the therapeutic interview in The Sociology of Mental Illness, mimeographed (to appear in *For Thomas Szaz*).

14.   In a number of presentations, Chomsky has asserted that the great majority of the sentences which a child hears are ungrammatical ('95 per cent'). In Chomsky (1965, p. 58), this notion is presented as one of the arguments in his general statement of the 'nativist' position; 'A consideration of the character of the grammar that is acquired, *the degenerate quality and narrowly limited extent of the available data* (my emphasis) the striking uniformity of the resulting grammars, and their independence of intelligence, motivation, and emotional state, over wide ranges of variation, leave little hope that much of the structure of the language can be learned . . .'

15.   The editing rules are presented in Labov (1966).

16.   From work on the grammars and comprehension of Negro children four to eight years old being carried out by Professor Jane Torrey of Connecticut College in extension of the research cited above in Labov, Cohen, Robins and Lewis (1968).

17.   From the research of Jane Torrey cited in footnote 16.

18.   The attention to the speaker's syntax required of the listener is analyzed in detail by Harvey Sacks in his unpublished 1968 lectures.

19.   For the relationship between age and membership in peer groups, see Wilmott (1966).

20.   In Deutsch, Katz and Jensen (1968), Jensen expounds the verbal deprivation theory in considerable detail. For example: 'During this "labelling" period . . . some very important social-class differences may exert their effects on verbal learning. Lower-class parents engage in relatively little of this naming or "labelling" play with their children . . . That words are discrete labels for things seems to be better known by the middle-class child entering first grade than by the lower-class child. Much of this knowledge is gained in the parent-child interaction, as when the parent looks at a picture book with the child . . .' (p. 119).

21.   Heber's studies of 88 Negro mothers in Milwaukee are cited frequently throughout Jensen (1969). The estimates in this table are not given in relation to a particular Milwaukee sample, but for the general population. Heber's study was specifically designed to cover an area of Milwaukee which was known to contain a large concentration of retarded children, Negro and white, and he has stated that his findings were 'grossly misinterpreted' by Jensen (*Milwaukee Sentinel*, 11 June 1969).

22.   The IQ scores given here are from group rather than individual tests and must therefore not be weighted heavily: the scores are from the Pintner-Cunningham test, usually given in the first grade in New York City schools in the 1950s.

23.   Table 15.1 in Deutsch *et al.* (1967, p. 312, section C), shows that some degree of college training was desired by 96, 97 and 100 per cent of Negro parents in Class levels I, II and III respectively. The corresponding figures for whites were 79, 95 and 97 per cent. In an earlier version of this paper, this discussion could be interpreted as implying that Whiteman and Deutsch had used data in the same way as Jensen to rate the Negro group as low as possible. As they point out (personal communication), the inclusion of this item in the Deprivation Index had the opposite effect, and it could easily have been omitted if that had been their intention. They also argue that they had sound statistical grounds for dichotomizing as they did. The criticism which I intended to make is that there is something drastically wrong with operations which produce definitions of deprivation such as the one cited here. It should of course be noted that Whiteman and Deutsch have strongly opposed Jensen's genetic hypothesis and vigorously criticized his logic and data.

24.   The negative report of the Westinghouse Learning Corporation and Ohio University on Operation Headstart was published in the *New York Times* (on 13 April 1969). This evidence for the failure of the program was widely publicized and it seems likely that the report's discouraging conclusions 'will be used by conservative Congressmen as a weapon against any kind of expenditure for disadvantaged' children, especially Negroes. The two hypotheses mentioned to account for this failure is that the impact of Headstart is lost through poor teaching later on, and more recently, that poor children have been so badly damaged in infancy by their lower-class environment that Headstart cannot make much difference. The third 'inevitable' hypothesis of Jensen is not reported here.

References

Bereiter, C. *et al.* (1966). An academically oriented pre-school for culturally deprived children, in F.M. Hechinger, (ed.), *Pre-School Education Today*. Doubleday, 105-37.

Bereiter, C. and Engelmann, S. (1966). *Teaching Disadvantaged Children in the Pre-School*. Prentice-Hall.

Caldwell, B.M. (1967). What is the optional learning environment for the young child? *Amer. J. Orthopsychiatry*, vol. 37, no. 1, 8-21.

Chomsky, N. (1965). *Aspects of the Theory of Syntax*. MIT Press.

Deutsch, M. *et al.* (1967). *The Disadvantaged Child*. Basic Books.

Deutsch, M., Katz, I., and Jensen, A.R. (eds.) (1968). *Social Class, Race and Psychological Development*. Holt.

Gans, H. (1962). The peer group society, in *The Urban Villagers*, Free Press.

Jensen, A. (1968). Social class and verbal learning, in Deutsch, Katz and Jensen, *Social Class, Race and Psychological Development*. Holt.

Jensen, A. (1969). How much can we boost IQ and scholastic achievement? *Harvard Educational Review*, 39, 1.

Labov, W. (1966). On the grammaticality of everyday speech. Paper given at the annual meeting of the Linguistic Society of America, New York City, December.

Labov, W. (1967). Some sources of reading problems for Negro speakers of nonstandard English, in A. Frazier, (ed.), *New Directions in Elementary English*. National Council of Teachers of English, 140-67. Reprinted in Joan C. Baratz and R.W. Shuy, (eds.) *Teaching Black Children to Read*. Washington DC, Center for Applied Linguistics, 29-67.

Labov, W., Cohen, P. and Robins, C. (1965). *A Preliminary Study of the Structure of English Used by Negro and Puerto Rican Speakers in New York City*. Final Report, Co-operative Research Project no. 3091. Office of Education, Washington DC.

Labov, W., Cohen, P., Robins, C. and Lewis, J. (1968). *A Study of the Non-Standard English of Negro and Puerto Rican Speakers in New York City*. Final Report, Co-operative Research Project no. 3288, Office of Education, Washington, DC, vols. 1 and 2.

Labov, W., and Robins, C. (1969). A note on the relation of reading failure to peer-group status in urban ghettos, *The Teachers' College Record*, vol. 70, 5.

Rosenthal, R., and Jacobson, L. (1968). Self-fulfilling prophecies in the classroom: teachers' expectations as unintended determinants of pupils' intellectual competence, in Deutsch, Katz and Jensen, *Social Class, Race and Psychological Development*. Holt.

Whiteman, M., and Deutsch, M. (1968). Social disadvantage as related to intellective and language development, in Deutsch, Katz and Jensen, *Social Class, Race and Psychological Development*. Holt.

Willmott, P. (1966). *Adolescent Boys of East London*. Routledge & Kegan Paul.

14 THE NEGLECTED SITUATION IN CHILD LANGUAGE RESEARCH AND EDUCATION[1]

Courtney Cazden

Source: Frederick Williams (ed.), *Language and Poverty* (Markham Publishing Company, Chicago 1970), pp. 81-101.

Some Current Inadequacies

Study of the acquisition of language has been based on the assumption that what had to be described and explained was the acquisition of a repertoire of responses (in the terminology of behaviorism) or the acquisition of a finite set of rules for constructing utterances (in the terminology of developmental psycholinguistics). On this assumption, the school language problems of lower-class children can have two explanations: either they have acquired less language than middle-class children, or they have acquired a different language. The less-language explanation has been given various names — *cultural deprivation, deficit hypothesis, vacuum ideology* — all with the same connotation of a nonverbal child somehow emptier of language than his more-socially-fortunate age-mates. The different-language explanation is forcefully argued by William Stewart and Joan Baratz.[2] It states that all children acquire language but that many children — especially lower-class black children — acquire a dialect of English so different in structural (grammatical) features that communication in school, both oral and written, is seriously impaired by that fact alone.

For different reasons neither of these explanations is adequate. Consider first the less-language explanation. There is growing evidence that if we are referring to what is called grammatical competence (the child's implicit knowledge of language structure), social-class differences are simply not great enough to explain the language problems which teachers report from the classroom. Four pieces of evidence can be offered.

First, LaCivita, Kean, and Yamamoto (1966) report a study in which lower-middle- and upper-class elementary-school children from three schools in Youngstown, Ohio, were asked to give the meaning of nonsense words in sentences such as the following:

'Ungubily the mittler *gimmled*.' (grammatical signal -*ed* only cue)
'A twener *baikels* meedily.' (grammatical signal plus position cue)

They hypothesized that lower-class children would have less understanding of grammatical structure and thus be less able to give a word that was the same part of speech as the underlined nonsense word (in the above instances, a verb). This hypothesis was not confirmed. Older children were better than younger children, and position cues aided comprehension, but the lower-class children were at no disadvantage.

Second, Shriner and Miner (1968) tested the ability of middle-class and lower-class white four-year-old children to generalize noun and verb endings (plural, possessive, and tense) to nonsense syllables, and found no difference between the two groups.

Third, Slobin (1968, p. 13) reports beginning returns from a cross-cultural study of the acquisition of language in Mexico, India, Samoa, Kenya, and the Negro ghetto in Oakland, California:

> Though we have not yet analyzed the language development of the children studied in these diverse groups, it is the impression of the field workers that they all appear to acquire language at a normal rate and are clearly not 'linguistically deprived'. This is certainly true of the Oakland children whom we have begun to study in some detail.

Finally, when measures of mean length of utterance (in morphemes, see Slobin 1967) as found in a study (Cazden 1965) of Negro children in a Boston day-care center are compared with the same measure as reported in studies of generally middle-class white children (Brown, Cazden, and Bellugi 1969; Bloom in press), the results indicate that the lower-class Negro children seem to be undergoing grammatical development at a similar rate. Although this comparison certainly may not apply to all lower-class children, it does raise questions about prior comparisons where such children were thought to have less language due to depressed test scores, but where their capabilities in spontaneous speech went unexamined. The speech of Gerald, one of the Negro children, is particularly interesting. At thirty three months, his average length of utterance is longer than that of any of the other Negro or white children. Following are the nine longest in his first two hundred utterances (unpublished speech samples from Cazden 1965):

> 'I'm looking for a cup.'
> 'I waiting for a other cup.'
> 'You put it up on there like dis.'
> 'Look at what I made with this one.'
> 'Den gon' put dis one back in here cause it fell out.'
> 'I'm gonna knock dese things in.'

'Soon I get finish I gon' do dat way.'
'Can I take if off and put it on?'

Whatever Gerald's communication problems in any particular situation — and I will suggest later that a problem could arise — they are not caused by deficiencies in his grammatical competence.

Turn now to the different-language explanation. It is clearly true, but still inadequate. Dialects do differ in structural features, and these must be taken into account in planning curriculum materials and instructional techniques. Due largely to the work of Labov, *et al.* (1968, vol. 1; see also the preceding paper in this volume), we are now getting the kind of analyses of at least one dialect, which he calls nonstandard Negro English, that will make such planning possible.

Both the less-language and different-language views of child language are inadequate on two counts. First, they speak only of patterns of structural forms and ignore patterns of use in actual speech events. Second, they speak as if the child learns only one way to speak, which is reflected in the same fashion and to the same extent at all times. On both theoretical and practical grounds, we can no longer accept such limitations.

The Importance of the Social Context of Speech

When Kagan (1967) issues a call for 'relativism' in psychology, Psathas (1968, p. 136) answered:

> When Kagan uses the term 'relativistic', he says that it 'refers to a definition in which context and state of the individual are part of the defining statement'. The 'neglected situation' as Goffman (1964) has called it and the state of the individual, particularly his internal symbol manipulating state, need to be considered. They would involve Kagan in sociology and anthropology much more than he recognizes. The 'context' that he refers to is one that has *socially* defined stimulus value. The social definitions for a situation are pregiven, i.e., exist before the psychologist or experimenter enters on the scene. He must, therefore, understand what these are and how they are perceived by the subject before he can claim to understand why the subject behaves the way he does. The 'state of the individual' includes not only his biological and physiological state but his interpretive structuring of the world as he experiences it, based on his previous socialization experiences as a member of the culture.

Applied to language this means that we have to describe more than the child's grammatical competence; we have to describe what Hymes (in press) calls communicative competence – how the child perceives and categorizes the social situations of his world and differentiates his ways of speaking accordingly.

The important point here is not a contrast between competence or knowledge on the one hand, and performance or behavior on the other hand, though many people including the author (Cazden 1967) have formulated the question in this way. A child's manifest verbal behavior, or performance, has both grammatical and pragmatic aspects; such behavior is a reflection of implicit knowledge (or competence) both of a grammar and of its use.

> The acquisition of competency for use, indeed, can be stated in the same terms as acquisition of competence for grammar. Within the developmental matrix in which knowledge of the sentences of a language is acquired, children also acquire knowledge of a set of ways in which sentences are used. From a finite experience of speech acts and their interdependence with socio-cultural features they develop a general theory of the speaking appropriate in their community, which they employ, like other forms of tacit cultural knowledge (competence) in conducting and interpreting social life. (Hymes in press)

We are a long way from understanding the range of communicative competences that different children have or how they develop. In fact, research on this enlarged question about the child's acquisition of language has only begun, as in the cross-cultural study mentioned earlier (Slobin 1967). Eventually, through such research, we will achieve a valid picture of social-class and ethnic differences in child language.

Practically, perhaps the best focus for attention is with the effect of the speech situation, since that is what we as educators, or social planners in some other sense, can change. At any one moment, a child decides to speak or be silent, to adopt communicative intent A or communicative intent B, to express idea x or idea Y, in form 1 or form 2. The options the child selects will be a function of characteristics of the speech situation as he perceives it on the basis of his past experience.[3] We observe that a particular child in a particular situation either makes or fails to make a particular utterance. Traditionally, we have related that utterance only to some characteristics of the child, such as his social-class background, while ignoring characteristics of the situation which are at least equally influential. At a time when much attention is focused on how different children – for example, from middle- or lower-class groups – respond to a single

Table 14.1: Studies of the Effects of Situation on Child Language

Characteristic of Language	Characteristics of the Situation				
	Topic	Task	Listener(s)	Interaction	Mixed
Fluency/ Spontaneity	Strandberg (1969) Strandberg and Griffith (1968) Williams and Naremore (1969a) Berlyne and Frommer (1966)	Heider, Cazden, and Brown (1968) Brent and Katz (1967)	Labov, et al., (1968, vol. 2)		Cowe (1967) Cazden (1965) Kagan (1969) Jensen (1969) Labov, et al., (1968 vol. 2) Pasamanick and Knobloch (1955) Resnick, Weld, and Lally (1969)
Length/ Complexity	Strandberg and Griffith (1968) Cowan et al., (1967) Moffett (1968) Williams and Naremore (1969a, b) Labov, et al., (1968, vol. 2)	Brent and Katz (1967) Cazden (1967) Lawton (1968) Robinson (1965) Williams and Naremore (1969a, b)	Cazden (1967) Smith (1935)	Plumer (1969)	Cowe (1967)
Content or Style		Labov, et al., (1968, vol. 2) Lawton (1968)			
Approximation to Standard English		Labov, et al., (1968, vol. 1)			

situation — in an experiment or in school — it should be useful to focus attention on how the same children respond differentially in different speech situations. As Robinson (1968) points out, the tendency in child-language research has been to ignore situational (contextual) variables or to combine speech data from several contexts. Instead, he (p. 6), suggests 'it may be wiser methodologically to accumulate the [social-class] differences within contexts and to see what higher-order generalizations can be made about them'.

Although the research which we will report is all about monolingual children, the notions of a diversified speech repertoire† and situational relativity apply even more obviously to bilinguals.[4]

Situation Variables

The research literature on child language includes some descriptions of how language usage varies with characteristics of speech situation. Although not all of these studies deal with lower-class children, all do provide evidence of the situational relativity of children's speech, and each gives some idea of the variables which must be considered. These variables and the published studies in which they are reported are summarized in Table 14.1. The columns in the table represent a very gross categorization of situational differences (or the independent variables in the research): topic, task, listener(s), interaction, and situations with mixed characteristics. Rows represent more easily definable characteristics of language (the dependent variables): fluency and/or spontaneity; length and/or complexity; characteristics of speech content such as abstractness; and degree of approximation to standard English. Unless otherwise specified, all differences reported are differences in the way the same child or group of children speak in different situations; occasionally, differences between similar groups of children are reported. All but three (Moffat 1968; Robinson 1965, and my unpublished observations) deal with oral language.

Topic

Four studies used different kinds of pictures. Strandberg (1969) found that four- and five-year-old children, above average in intelligence (with different children in each stimulus group), talked more about either a toy or a twenty-second silent film of that toy than they did about a still-color photograph of it. There was no difference, however, in either average length or complexity of the responses. Strandberg and Griffith (1968) gave four- and five-year-old children in a university laboratory school cameras loaded with color film. Later, they elicited conversations about the (remarkably successful) pictures the children took. The children talked more spontaneously (i.e., required fewer adult probes) and talked in longer and more complex utterances about the pictures they took at home of personally significant objects (e.g., a favorite climbing tree or a closeup of Mother's mouth) than they did about pictures taken under adult direction during the period of orientation to the camera. Since the pictures taken at home were also frequently of only one object, the authors conclude that the difference lies in the degree of personal involvement. Although topic is confounded with order in this study (since all the children told stories about the preselected objects first), it seems unlikely that this accounts for all the difference. Following are examples of one five-year-old's stories, first about an assigned picture and then about one of his choice:

> That's a horse. You can ride it. I don't know any more about it. It's brown, black and red. I don't know my story about the horse.

> There's a picture of my tree that I climb in. There's — there's where it grows at and there's where I climb up — and sit up there — down there and that's where I look out at. First I get on this one and then I get on that other one. And then I put my foot under that big branch that are strong. And then I pull my face up and then I get ahold of a branch up at that place — and then I look around. (Strandberg and Griffith, personal communication 1969)

Cowan, *et al.* (1967) presented elementary school children of mixed socioeconomic status with ten colored pictures from magazine covers. The effect of the particular picture on the mean length of response was strong across all age, sex, socioeconomic class, and experimenter conditions. One picture of a group standing around a new car elicited significantly shorter responses; one picture of a birthday party elicited significantly longer responses, while the other eight pictures were undifferentiated between the two extremes. Although the researchers cannot specify the source of the stimulus effect, they conclude that 'the implicit assumption that magnitude of mean length of response is a property of the subject independent of his setting should be permanently discarded' (Cowan, *et al.* 1967, p. 202).

Finally, Berlyne and Frommer (1966) studied the properties of different pictures and stories in eliciting one particular form of speech: questions. They presented children from kindergarten and grades three, five, and six at a university laboratory school with stories, pictures, and stories accompanied by pictures, and then invited the children to ask questions about them. Novel, surprising, and incongruous items elicited more questions, and the provision of answers (an interaction characteristic) had little effect.

Two studies compare narratives about television programs with other topics. Williams and Naremore (1969a, b; see also, Williams in press) analyzed forty interviews with Negro and white fifth- and six-graders selected from the extremes of the socioeconomic distribution of children in the Detroit Dialect Study (Shuy, *et al.* 1967). All informants had responded to three topics: games ('What kinds of games do you play around here?'); TV ('What are your favorite TV programs?'); and aspirations ('What do you want to be when you finish school?'). Social-class differences were found in the proportion of utterances which went beyond a simple yes-no answer or naming, on a ranking of the degree of connectedness of the utterances in a response, and on verbal indices of specific grammatical features. For the most part, however, the social-class differences were found when children were talking on the television topic.

> Although it is at best a subjective interpretation, the concentration of status differences in three of the clause indices on the TV topic seems to be a reflection of the tendency of the H.S. [high-status] children to engage in story telling or narrative while the L.S. [low-status] children tended to itemize instances of what they had seen or preferred . . . The language used by the child in an interview is as much a reflection of his engagement within the constraints of a communication situation as it is a reflection of his linguistic capabilities. (Williams and Naremore 1969b, p. 791.)

Labov has collected narratives of television programs and personal experience from preadolescent boys attending vacation day camps in Central Harlem. Following are two such narratives, by two different eleven-year-old boys, the first about 'The Man From Uncle' and the second about a personal fight (Labov, *et al.* 1968, vol. 2, pp. 298-9).

(First Boy)
a. This kid — Napoleon got shot
b. and he had to go on a mission.
c. And so this kid, he went with Solo.
d. So they went
e. And this guy — they went through this window.
f. and they caught him.
g. And then he beat up them other people.

h. And they went
i. and then he said that this old lady was his mother
j. and then he — and at the end he say that he was the guy's friend.

(Second Boy)
a. When I was in fourth grade — no it was in third grade —
b. This boy he stole my glove.
c. He took my glove
d. and said that his father found it downtown on the ground. (And you fight him?)
e. I told him that it was impossible for him to find downtown 'cause all those people were walking by and just his father was the only one that found it?
f. So he got all (mad).
g. So then I fought him.
h. I knocked him all out in the street.
i. So he say he give.
j. and I kept on hitting him.
k. Then he started crying.
l. and ran home to his father
m. And the father told him
o. that he didn't find no glove.

Labov, *et al.* (1968, vol. 2, p. 297) summarize that the main difference between the two sets of narratives is the absence of evaluation in the TV narratives: '. . . the means used by the narrator to indicate the point of the narrative, its *raison d'etre*, why it was told, and what the narrator is getting at'. Absence of evaluation in accounts of vicarious experience reduces structural complexity. Although the construction of the narrative clause in English is a relatively simple construction, explanations (one of the devices for evaluation) may be exceedingly complex. Note, as an example, utterance *e* in the second boy's narrative. It does not seem farfetched to suggest a common element in the findings of Strandberg and Griffith (1968), and Labov, *et al.* (1968): the greater the degree of affect or personal involvement in the topic of conversation, the greater the likelihood of structural complexity.

Two final examples of the effect of topic on linguistic structure deal with written language. First, Moffet's observations on a science lesson (1968, p. 180):

While watching some third-graders write down their observations of candle flames − deliberately this time, not merely in note form − I noticed that sentences beginning with if- and when-clauses were appearing frequently on their papers. Since such a construction is not common in third-grade writing, I became curious and then realized that these introductory subordinate clauses resulted directly from the children's *manipulation of what they were observing*. Thus: 'If I place a glass over the candle, the flame goes out.' And: 'When you throw alum on the candle, the flame turns blue.' Here we have a fine example of a physical operation being reflected in a cognitive operation and hence in a linguistic structure . . . The cognitive task entailed in the candle tests created a need for subordinate clauses, because the pupils were not asked merely to describe a static object but to describe changes in the object brought about by changing conditions (*if* and *when*).

Second are the author's observations of the written compositions by five-year-old children in two English Infant Schools in neighborhoods similarly mixed in socioeconomic status. In the first school, all the children were given their first writing books (blank, unlined pages for pictures and related stories), asked to draw a picture and then dictate a story for the teacher to write. All the resulting stories were simple sentences, and all but one was of the form 'This is a _____' The exception was the sentence 'This boy is dead'. In the second school, children were using experimental beginning-reading materials developed by Mackay and Thompson (1968). Each child had a word folder with a preselected store of basic words plus some blanks for his personal collection. He also had a stand on which words from the folder could be set up as a text. These children composed sentences very different from those in the first school and (more importantly) very different from each other, for example, the following:

'My Mum takes me to school.'
'Is my sister at school and is my baby at home?'
'My cousin is skinny.'
'I like Sian she gave me one of David's doggies.'
'On Tuesday the movie camera man is coming.'
'I ask Helen to come to my birthday.'

Whereas the presence of the pictures somehow constrained the first group of children to the simplest and most routine labels, absence of a picture seemed to free the second group of children to work with far more of their linguistic knowledge.

Task

In some studies, differences are found which seem to relate more to what the child is asked to do with the topic than to the topic itself. For instance, Brent and Katz (1967) asked white Head Start children to tell stories about pictures from the WISC (Wechsler Intelligence Scale for Children) picture-arrangement task, then removed the pictures and asked the children to tell the stories again. They found that the stories told without the pictures were superior. The children produced longer stories without prompting, and ideas were related more logically and explicitly. Brent and Katz (1967, pp. 4-5) suggest that:

> . . . the actual presence of the pictures, which constitute a *spatially distributed* series of *perceptually discrete* events, may in fact, interfere with our younger subjects' ability to form a *temporally distributed* and *logically continuous* story — a task which required a conceptual and linguistic 'bridging-the-gap' between discrete frames.

Since the order of story telling is confounded with the picture presence/absence, we cannot tell whether telling the story first with a picture present contributes to the more successful (and second) attempt when the picture is removed.

Lawton (1968), in a study of British boys aged twelve to fifteen years, tried to elicit both descriptive and more abstract speech by the instructions: 'Describe your school and then answer: What do you think is the real purpose of education?' All the boys used more subordinate clauses and complex constructions on the abstraction task than on the description task.

Four studies report differences which result from different degrees of structure or constraint in the directions. With the same boys, Lawton (1968) also conducted a discussion of capital punishment, replicating an earlier study of Bernstein (1962). He also gave them assignments to write on four topics such as 'My life in ten years time'. In the more open, unstructured discussions, middle-class boys used more abstract arguments and hypothetical examples, while the working-class boys used more concrete examples and cliches or anecdotes. But in the abstract sections of the interviews, social-class differences were much smaller.

> The inference I would draw is that in an 'open' situation the working-class boys tend to move towards concrete, narrative/descriptive language, but in a 'structured' situation where they have little or no choice about making an abstract response, they will respond to the demand

made upon them. They may have found the task extremely difficult, but it was not impossible for them. (Lawton, 1968, p. 138)

Comparable results were obtained by Williams and Naremore (1969a) and Heider, *et al.* (1968). One way in which Williams and Naremore (see the earlier description of the study) scored interviews on games, aspirations, and TV was by type of questions asked by the interviewer and the corresponding type of child response.

Probe Constraints:

Simple: Do you play baseball?
Naming: What television programs do you watch?
Elaboration: How do you play kick-the-can?

Response Style:

Simple: Yeah.
Naming: Baseball
Qualified naming: I usually watch the Avengers and lots of cartoons.
Elaboration: Last night the Penguin had Batman trapped on top of this tower . . .

Results show that following the first two probes, 'the lower-status children had more of a tendency to supply the minimally acceptable response, whereas their higher-status counterparts had a greater tendency to elaborate their remarks' (Williams and Naremore 1969a, p. 86). The researchers' general interpretation held that:

The mark of a lower status child was that he had some tendency to provide the type of response which would minimally fulfill the field worker's probe, [but] not go on to assume a more active role in the speech situation, including elaboration of more of his own experience. (Williams and Naremore 1969a, pp. 87-8)

The above differences, however, were not as evident when the field workers imposed a definite constraint for elaboration in their probes.

Heider, *et al.* (1968) report an experiment in which lower- and middle-class white ten-year-old boys were asked to describe a picture of one animal out of a large array. Criterial or essential attributes were the name of the animal, its number of spots, whether it was standing or lying down, and the position of its head. The frequencies of criterial attributes named by the children were almost identical for the two groups. However, there was a significant social-class difference in the number of requests the listener had to make for more information before the picture was adequately specified — nearly twice as many requests to the lower-class children as to the middle-class children. The lower-class children's performance was far superior to what it would have been if the amount of probing or feedback had been standardized for the two groups as it often is both in experiments and in classrooms.

Robinson (1965), another British researcher, gave two letter-writing assignments to middle-class and working-class twelve- and thirteen-year-old boys and girls in a comprehensive school. One assignment, to tell a good friend news of the past fortnight, presumably elicited informal language (or restricted code) from all subjects. The other assignment, advising a Governor of the school how some money he had donated might be spent, presumably elicited formal language (or elaborated code) from anyone who could use it. Contrary to expectations, there were no significant differences between the middle-class and working-class formal letters, and differences only in lexical diversity (number of different nouns, adjectives, and so on) between the informal letters where the topic was less constrained.

While the results of Lawton (1968), Williams and Naremore (1969a), Heider, *et al.* (1968), and Robinson (1965) suggest that working-class children display greater abstraction, elaboration, or informational analysis when it is demanded in a situation highly structured by an adult interviewer, one can find exceptions to the possible generalization suggested here. For example, in an earlier report (Cazden 1967), a lower-class Negro child of first-grade age provided the longest utterances (in morpheme count) in informal speech tasks, as against a middle-class white child who gave longest responses on highly structured tasks. Although this earlier study was only a pilot venture, it did reveal the strong potential interaction between children's backgrounds and the characteristics of speech situations. Presumably, there are more such interactions to be discovered if we knew where and how to look for them.

We can also differentiate speech situations on an informal-formal continuum from the least self-conscious and most excited speech in peer-group situations, to accounts of fights provided in interviews, to more usual interview materials, to reading sentences aloud, to reading lists of unconnected words (Labov, *et al.* 1968, vol. 1). As a speaker moves with increasing formality from the least self-conscious, excited speech to pronunciations of individual words, he tends to become more standard in his English usage.

Listener(s)

One important characteristic of the listener is age in relation to the speaker. In an early study, Smith (1935) found that children eighteen to seventy months old spoke longer sentences at home with adults than at play with other children. Presumably, this was because at home the children gave fewer answers to questions and fewer imperatives, and had greater opportunity for more connected discourse with less active play and less frequent interruptions. In the study cited above (Cazden 1967), it was found that both children spoke their shortest sentences, on the average, in two experimental situations with their peers — playing an arithmetic game, and in a telephone conversation.

In some recent unpublished research, two students at Harvard[5] found that children themselves modify their speech as they talk to different persons. One three-year-old spoke her longest utterances to her mother, her shortest utterances to her eighteen-month-old sister, while her speech to herself was between these in length. Three girls of nine, eleven, and thirteen years modified the complexity of their speech to younger boys (roughly eighteen and thirty months) more according to their perception of the child's language ability than strictly according to his age. But younger listeners are not the only ones to inhibit speech complexity in a child. Labov, *et al.* (1968 vol. 2, p. 117) reports the following utterance from a boy who is typically very fast and fluent in speech, but in the presence of older (sixteen-year-old) gang members, appears at a loss for words: 'He gon' getchyou with 'is li's . . . he got li-' he got leg like di-like . . .'

Interaction

Here we have only one report from a pilot study and one hypothesis now being tested. Oliver Cooperman, a Harvard medical student working at the University of London on the effects of various conditions of residential care on preschool-age children, conducted a pilot study of various aspects of children's conversations. He found conversation more likely to occur and to include a greater number of exchanges with an adult when it was initiated by the child rather than by the adult, and adult commands to initiate action (to 'do X') more frequently provoked verbal reply than commands to desist (to 'stop doing X').

Plumer (1969) is currently conducting research on dialogue strategies within twelve families with children seven or eight years old — six with sons with high verbal ability (as measured on standardized tests) and six with sons with average verbal ability. Recording equipment is given to each family, and dialogue is recorded from a wireless microphone worn by the child under study. Each family records a total of seven hours during one week, including twenty-minute sessions at breakfast, supper, and bedtime. One measure used will be the length of a dialogue (the number of verbal exchanges between the initiation and termination of a topic) and one analysis will be the relation of length of dialogue to complexity of the child's utterances.

A major assumption underlying this study is that the longer the dialogue the more likely the child is to hear and use a wide range of the resources and strategies of his language. The ability to elaborate and qualify − or to follow elaboration and qualification − is most likely to be learned in an extended dialogue after an initial exchange has set up the need for clarification and elaboration. (Plumer 1969, pp. 7-8)

If either Cooperman's or Plumer's observation and expectations are borne out in further research, they would have important implications for planning classrooms for maximally productive conversation. For instance, initiation of conversation probably takes place more often in a classroom where children carry major responsibility for planning their activities. But this may only be productive for language usage if personal involvement, and thereby conversation on a topic, is sustained over some period of time.

Mixed Aspects of Situations

Two kinds of situations seem to contain a mixture of relevant aspects: various activities in any classroom and in testing situations themselves. Cowe (1967) has recorded the conversations of kindergarten children in nine activities. In both amount and maturity of speech, housekeeping play and group discussion held the greatest potential for language usage, while play with blocks, dance, and woodworking held least. She suggests that factors influencing speech are adult participation, something concrete to talk about, physical arrangements, and noise. I have made similar observations when selecting play materials for a tutorial language program (Cazden 1965).

Testing situations contain the effects of interpersonal formality and power relationship mixed with the cognitive demands of particular tasks. Pasamanick and Knobloch (1955) and Resnick, Weld, and Lally (1969) report evidence that the verbal expressiveness of working-class Negro two-year-olds is artificially depressed in testing situations. Even Jensen (1969 p. 100), arguing that social-class differences in intelligence are largely inherited, reports from his own clinical experience that he regularly raised IQ scores on the Stanford-Binet (largely a test of verbal performance) eight to ten points by having children from an impoverished background come in for two, three, or four play sessions in his office so that the child could get acquainted and feel more at ease. And Kagan (1969, p. 276), in answer to Jensen, reports the experience of Francis Palmer in New York City:

> Dr. Palmer administered mental tests to middle and lower class black children from Harlem. However, each examiner was instructed not to begin any testing with any child until she felt that the child was completely relaxed, and understood what was required of him. Many children had five, six, and even seven hours of rapport sessions with the examiner before any questions were administered. Few psychological studies have ever devoted this much care to establishing rapport with the child. Dr. Palmer found few significant differences in mental ability between the lower and middle class populations. This is one of the first times such a finding has been reported and it seems due, in part, to the great care taken to insure that the child comprehended the nature of the test questions and felt at ease with the examiner.[6]

Labov, and his colleagues (*et al.* 1968, vol. 2, pp. 340-1) provide a dramatic example. Attacking the conditions under which much of the data on verbal deprivation is collected, he quotes an entire interview with a preadolescent boy in a New York City school, and contrasts it with his own methods and findings.

The child is alone in a school room with the investigator, a young, friendly white man, who is instructed to place a toy on the table and say 'Tell me everything you can about this'. The interviewer's remarks are in parentheses.

> (Tell me everything you can about *this*) (*Plunk*).
> [12 seconds of silence]
> (What would you say it looks like?)
> [8 seconds of silence]
> A space ship.
> (Hmmmm)
> [13 seconds of silence]
> Like a je-et.
> [12 seconds of silence]
> Like a plane.
> [20 seconds of silence]
> (What color is it?)

Orange (2 seconds) An' whi-ite. (2 seconds). An' green.
    [6 seconds of silence]
An' what could you use it for?
    [8 seconds of silence]
A je-et.
    [6 seconds of silence]
(If you had two of them, what would you do with them?)
    [6 seconds of silence]
Give one to somebody.
(Hmmm. Who do you think would like to have it?)
    [10 seconds of silence]
Cla-rence.
(Mm. Where do you think we could get another one of these?)
At the store.
(Oh ka-ay!)

The social situation which produces such defensive behavior is that of an adult asking a lone child questions to which he obviously knows the answers, where anything the child says may well be held against him. It is, in fact, a paradigm of the school situation which prevails as reading is being taught (but not learned).

We can obtain such results in our own research, and have done so in our work with younger brothers of the Thunderbirds in 1390 Fifth Avenue. But when we change the social situation by altering the height and power relations, introducing a close friend of the subject, and talking about things we know he is interested in, we obtain a level of excited and rapid speech.

New Goals in Oral Language Education

Even if we had the kind of understanding of communicative competence among diverse groups of children which Hymes (in press) calls for, we would still be far from a theory of oral language education. That theory requires, in addition, decisions about which goals are important, what communicative competence we seek. Sociolinguistic interference from contrasting communicative demands both in and outside school is almost certainly more important than grammatical interference (Hymes in press; Labov, *et al.* 1968, vol 2). To reduce this interference, we have to know what communicative capabilities the child brings and what we want him to be able to do.

Discussions of the goals of education, like analyses of child language, too often focus on language form when they should be concerned with language use. In arguing against oral language programs for teaching standard English to speakers of a nonstandard dialect, Kochman (1969, p. 2) says:

> My first quarrel with such a program is that it does not develop the ability of a person to use language, which I would further define as performance capability in a variety of social contexts on a variety of subject matter . . . Underlying this approach seems to be a misapplication of Basil Bernstein's terms which falsely equate *restrictive code* and *elaborated code* with, respectively, nonstandard dialect and standard dialect. It ought to be noted, as Bernstein uses the term, code is not to be equated with *langue*, but *parole*, not with *competence* but *performance*. What is restrictive or elaborated is not in fact the code as sociolinguists use the term, but the message.[7]

To reject attempts to teach a single, socially prestigious language form is not to reject all attempts at change. Cultural differences in language use can be interpreted as deficiencies when children confront the demands of particular communicative situations.

> Cultural relativism, inferred from an enormous variety of existing cultures, remains a prerequisite of objective analysis . . . But the moral corollary of cultural relativism — moral relativism — has been quietly discarded, except as a form of intellectual indulgence among those who claim the privilege of non-involvement. (Wolf 1964, pp. 21-2)

Educators certainly cannot claim any privilege of noninvolvement, and they must decide what goals they seek. Taking as his goal the education of a person who knows enough not to remain a victim, Olson (1967, p. 13) says,

> A teacher must possess extraordinary knowledge and humanity if he is to distinguish what the school demands of children simply to symbolize its capacity for authority over them, from what it legitimately 'demands' or 'woos out of them' to equip them for a niche in a technological society.

Pieces of an answer can be suggested. On the basis of his experience as a teacher in a village school for Kwakiutl Indian children on Vancouver Island, Wolcott (1969) suggests teaching specific skills rather than trying to make over the child into one's own image. Marion Blank (1970, pp. 62-80) argues for education in the use of language for abstract thinking. Kochman (personal communication 1969) recommends opportunity for the use of language in 'low-context' situations where speaker and listener do not share a common referent and where a greater burden of communication falls on words alone, a skill that thirty-three-month-old Gerald needs help in acquiring.[8] Cazden and John (1969) argue for coordinate education for cultural pluralism, in which patterns of language form and use (and beliefs and values as well) in the child's home community are maintained and valued alongside the introduction of forms of behavior required in a technological society.

In the end, the goals of education are in large part matters of value, and decisions about them must be shared by educators and spokesmen for the child and his community. Such decisions, combined with knowledge of communicative competence and how it develops, will enable us to design more productive situations for oral language education in school.

Notes

1.   With thanks to Goffman (1964) for both title and ideas.
2.   Their positions can be seen in Stewart (1970, pp. 359-79) and Baratz (1970, pp. 11-24). See also Stewart and Wilson (1969).
3.   See Herman (1961) for an analysis of the three-fold influences on language choice of bilingual speakers: personal needs, the immediate situation, and the background situation.
4.   See Macnamara (1967) for papers on bilingualism, including one by Hymes on 'Models of the Interaction of Language and Social Setting'.
5.   M.J. Yurchak and E. Bernat.
6.   See also Severson and Guest (1970, pp. 309-34).
7.   The distinction between *langue* and *parole* is meant to contrast between our description of the system of a language and the performance of that language in actual speech.
8.   See also Erickson (1969).

References

Baratz, J.C. Teaching reading in an urban negro school system. In F. Williams, ed., *Language and Poverty*. Chicago: Markham Publishing Company, 1970.

Berlyne, D.E., and Frommer, F.D. Some determinants of the incidence and content of children's questions. *Child Development* 1966, 37: 177-89.

Bernstein, B. Social class, linguistic codes and grammatical elements. *Language and Speech* 1962, 5: 221-40.

Blank, M. Some philosophical influences underlying preschool intervention for disadvantaged children. In F. Williams, ed., *Language and Poverty*. Chicago: Markham Publishing Company, 1970.

Bloom, L.M. *Language Development: Form and Function in Emerging Grammars*. Cambridge, Mass.: M.I.T. Press, in press.

Brent, S.B., and Katz. E.W. A study of language deviations and cognitive processes. Progress Report No. 3, Office of Economic Opportunity Job Corps contract 1209, Wayne State University, 1967.

Brown, R., Cazden, C.B., and Bellugi, U. The child's grammar from I to III. In J.P. Hill, ed., *1967 Minnesota Symposium on Child Psychology*. Minneapolis: University of Minnesota Press, 1969.

Cazden, C.B. Environmental assistance to the child's acquisition of grammar. Doctoral dissertation, Harvard University, 1965.

———. On individual differences in language competence and performance. *J. Special Education* 1967, 1: 135-50.

Cazden, C.B., and John, V.P. Learning in American Indian children. In S. Ohannessian, ed., *Styles of Learning Among American Indians: An Outline for Research*. Washington, D.C.: Center for Applied Linguistics, 1969.

Cowan, P.A., Weber, J., Hoddinott, B.A., and Klein, J. Mean length of spoken response as a function of stimulus, experimenter, and subject. *Child Development*. 1967, 38: 191-203.

Cowe, E.G. A study of kindergarten activities for language development. Doctoral dissertation, Columbia University, 1967.

Erickson, F.D. 'F'get you Honky': A new look at Black dialect and the schools. *Elementary English* 1969, 46: 495-99.

Goffman, E. The neglected situation. In J.J. Gumperz and D. Hymes, eds., *The Ethnography of Communication, American Anthropologist* 1964, 66: No. 6, Part 2, 133-6.

Heider, E.R., Cazden, C.B., and Brown, R. Social class differences in the effectiveness and style of children's coding ability. Project Literacy Reports, No. 9, pp. 1-10. Ithaca, N.Y.: Cornell Uninversity, 1968.

Herman, S.R. Explorations in the social psychology of language choice. *Human Relations* 1961, 14: 149-64.

Hymes, D. On communicative competence. In R. Huxley and E. Ingram, eds., *The Mechanisms of Language Development*. London: CIBA Foundation, in press.

Jensen, A.R. How much can we boost IQ and scholastic achievement? *Harvard Educational Review* 1969, 39: 1-123.

Kagan, J. On the need for relativism. *American Psychologist* 1967, 22: 131-42.

———. Inadequate evidence and illogical conclusions. *Harvard Educational Review* 1969, 39: 274-77.

Kochman, T. Social factors in the consideration of teaching standard English. Paper read at convention of Teachers of English to Speakers of Other Languages (TESOL). March 1969, Chicago.

Labov, W., Cohen, P., Robins, C., and Lewis, J. A study of non-standard English of Negro and Puerto Rican speakers in New York City. Final report, U.S. Office of Education Cooperative Research Project No. 3288, Vols. 1, 2. Mimeographed. Columbia University 1968.

LaCivita, A.F., Kean, J.M., and Yamamoto, K. Socioeconomic status of children and acquisition of grammar. *J. Educational Research* 1966, 60: 71-4.

Lawton, D. *Social Class, Language and Education*. New York: Schocken, 1968.

Macnamara, J., ed. Problems of bilingualism. *J. Social Issues* 1967, 23: No. 2.

Mackay, D., and Thompson, B. The initial teaching of reading and writing: some notes toward a theory of literacy. Programme in Linguistics and English Teaching, Paper No. 3. London: University College and Longmans Green, 1968.

Moffett, J. *Teaching the Universe of Discourse*. Boston: Houghton Mifflin, 1968.

Olson, P.A. Introduction. The craft of teaching and the school of teachers. Report of the first national conference, U.S. Office of Education Tri-University Project in Elementary Education, September 1967, Denver.

Pasamanick, B. and Knobloch, H. Early language behavior in Negro children and the testing of intelligence. *J. Abnormal and Social Psychology* 1955, 50: 401-2.

Plumer, D. Parent-child verbal interaction: a naturalistic study of dialogue strategies. Interim report, Harvard Graduate School of Education, 1969.

Psathas, G. Comment, *American Psychologist* 1968, 23: 135-7.

Resnick, M.B., Weld, G.L., and Lally, J.R. Verbalizations of environmentally deprived two-year-olds as a function of the presence of a tester in a standardized test situation. Paper presented at the meeting of the American Educational Research Association, February 1969, Los Angeles.

Robinson, W.P. The elaborated code in working-class language. *Language and Speech* 1965, 8: 243-52.

————. Restricted codes in sociolinguistics and the sociology of education. Paper presented at Ninth International Seminar, University College, December 1968, Dar es Salaam, Tanzania.

Severson, R.A., and Guest, K.E. Toward the standardized assessment of the language of disadvantaged children. In F. Williams, ed., *Language and Poverty*. Chicago: Markham Publishing Company, 1970.

Shriner, T.H., and Miner, L. Morphological structures in the language of disadvantaged and advantaged children. *J. Speech and Hearing Research* 1968, 11: 605-10.

Shuy, R.W., Wolfram, W.A., and Riley, W.K. Linguistic correlates of social stratification in Detroit speech. U.S. Office of Education Cooperative Research Project No. 6-1347, 1967.

Slobin, D.I., ed. A field manual for cross-cultural study of the acquisition of communicative competence (second draft). Berkeley, California: University of California, 1967.

Slobin, D.I. Questions of language development in cross-cultural perspective. Paper prepared for symposium on Language Learning in Cross-Cultural Perspective at Michigan State University, September 1968.

Smith, M.E. A study of some factors influencing the development of the sentence in preschool children. *J. Genetic Psychology* 1935, 46: 182-212.

Stewart, W.A. Toward a history of American negro dialect. In F. Williams, ed., *Language and Poverty*. Chicago: Markham Publishing Company, 1970.

Stewart, W.A., and Wilson, J.M.P. Anthology on educational problems of the disadvantaged. *Florida Foreign Language Reporter* 1969, 7: No. 1.

Strandberg, T.E. An evaluation of three stimulus media for evoking verbalizations from preschool children. Master's thesis, Eastern Illinois University, 1969.

Strandberg, T.E., and Griffith, J. A study of the effects of training in visual literacy on verbal language behavior. Unpublished paper. Eastern Illinois University, 1968.

Williams, F. Social class differences in how children talk about television: some observations and speculations. *J. Broadcasting*, in press.

Williams, F., and Naremore, R.C. On the functional analysis of social class differences in modes of speech. *Speech Monographs* 1969, 36: 77-102. (a)

————. Social class differences in children's syntactic performance: a quantitative analysis of field study data. *J. Speech and Hearing Research* 1969, 12: 777-93. (b)

Wolcott, H.F. The teacher as an enemy. Unpublished paper. University of Oregon, 1969.

Wolf, E.R. *Anthropology*. Englewood Cliffs, N.J.: Prentice-Hall, 1964.

15 VARIATION IN CHILD LANGUAGE

Gordon Wells

Source: P. Fletcher and M. Garman (eds.), *Studies in Language Acquisition* (Cambridge University Press, forthcoming)

In spite of the confident assertions about, for example, sex and class differences in language development, to be found in overviews of the subject, most of the work on variation has been extremely naïve — mainly because researchers have only just begun to understand the theoretical and methodological problems that have to be resolved before any worthwhile results can be obtained. As a result, I shall devote the first sections of this paper to a consideration of these problems, before going on to discuss the main areas in which research on variation has been carried out. Inevitably, no more than an overview can be presented here, but, where appropriate, references will be given to books and articles in which the topics are more fully discussed.

1. Types of Variation

Let us imagine that we pick a group of children and attempt to describe them — their personalities, the sort of homes they come from, their favourite activities, whom they spend their time with, and so on. We shall quickly find that they are all different — different, probably, with respect to each of the headings that we consider, and certainly different in the combined profiles that we might attempt to construct. Let us now imagine that we also record one, or a number of, samples of speech from each of these children in the course of their everyday activities, and without anyone being aware that we are making the recordings. When we come to describe these speech samples, we shall even more quickly realise that each one is different, and that a large part of this difference is directly related to the differences that we have already observed in the activities, preferences, etc. of the children, and in the situations in which the speech samples were recorded.

The researcher into child language is thus on the horns of a dilemma: either to reduce the problem to manageable proportions by strictly limiting the number of variables that are taken into account, or to attempt to take account of as many as possible, at the risk of being overwhelmed by the complexity of the task. The dilemma of course arises from the fact that, in order to take the first course, the researcher needs information about the full range of sources of variation, in order to control those that he does not wish to investigate; but this is only possible if the full range of variation has already been investigated and a theory developed, which provides a basis for the principled control of unwanted variation.

In practice, most researchers have attended to only one or two sources of variation, usually those that are most amenable to description, making the simplifying assumption that the remaining variation is arbitrary or coincidental. Such a strategy has had the effect of leaving completely unexplored such pervasive parameters as the situation in which speech occurs (Cazden, 1970), and of reducing to polarised dichotomies such parameters as social background (e.g. Bernstein, 1971), which are, in reality, made up of a cluster of interacting parameters, each varying continuously over the total population. As a result, there is as yet no over-all theory of variation, merely a number of relatively unrelated findings that still await integration. Given this situation, it may be helpful to start by making a number of broad distinctions between different types of variation, and by considering the ways in which they may be related.

Firstly, there is the child's actual language behaviour. Of course this is not a unitary phenomenon, and there are many aspects of language behaviour which display variation. On the whole, physical properties of speech − pace, volume, pitch, etc. − are not usually treated as significant, but almost all the linguistic dimensions are potential topics for investigation. The problem is in knowing how to quantify the dimensions to be investigated. The most frequently used general measure is Mean Length of Utterance (MLU), originally measured in words, but in more recent studies in morphemes, following Roger Brown's procedures (Brown *et al.* 1969; Slobin, 1967). The validity of this measure has been the subject of a considerable amount of critical discussion,[1] but because of its global nature and the ease with which it can be calculated, it probably remains the most satisfactory, although crude, general indicator of stage of development, at least in the first few years (Brown, 1973: pp. 53-4). Other measures that have been used include vocabulary size (Nelson, 1973); vocabulary comprehension (Huttenlocher, 1973; Brimer and Dunn, 1963); sentence comprehension (Reynell, 1969; Lee, 1969) and a variety of measures based on samples of spontaneous speech, including syntactic complexity (Menyuk, 1969), semantic modification, semantic range and pragmatic range (Wells, in press). A further possibility involves the construction of a profile from several of these measures, but this raises difficult problems of quantifying what are essentially qualitative differences.

Variation on these linguistic measures is of little interest in itself, however; what is of interest is the co-variation between linguistic behaviour and other child attributes with respect to which variation is found in the population. Since language changes and develops over time, age is obviously the first such attribute to consider. A typical strategy here is to assume the existence, over the population as a whole, of a linear correlation between age and linguistic development, and to examine *rate* of development (defined as score at a given age on one of the measures discussed above) in relation to other non-linguistic attributes. A second strategy is to look at changes in linguistic behaviour over time in particular individuals in an attempt to identify *styles* of development (Nelson, 1973; Ramer, 1976), which are then related to other child attributes.

It is possible to divide the other attributes that have been the subject of investigation into four main groups, as shown in Figure 15.1. Only one group is, strictly speaking, concerned with attributes of the children

Figure 15.1: Types of Variation

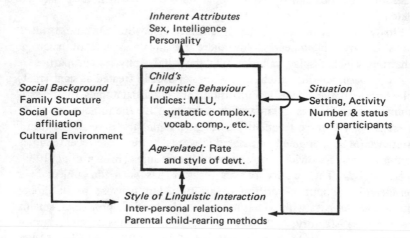

themselves, those that might be called *inherent* attributes: sex, intelligence, personality, etc. The remaining three cover different aspects of the children's environment: long-term characteristics of children's *social background*; factors in the social and physical *situation* in which the children's linguistic behaviour occurs; and the style of *linguistic interaction* which provides the context for their acquisition and use of language.

Clearly such a classification is no more than a matter of convenience for purposes of exposition. Variation in children's linguistic behaviour or in rate or style of development is not caused uniquely by any one of these groups of attributes, but is the outcome of an interaction between all of them, as the diagram attempts to indicate. Variation is also reciprocal: for example, as will be discussed in a later section, the style of interaction that the child experiences depends on his own inherent attributes and on attributes of his own language behaviour, as well as on the characteristics of those with whom he interacts and the situations in which these interactions occur. At least this degree of complexity must be attributed to the patterns of co-variation that characterise children's linguistic development, and this should be borne in mind in interpreting the research findings that are already available.

2. Methodological Problems of Data Collection and Analysis

The systematic study of linguistic variation is a comparatively recent development, and has so far been largely restricted to investigation of the linguistic correlates of social differentiation in the population of mature speakers of varieties of American English (e.g. Labov, 1972; 1977). Although his work is not of direct relevance to the subject of variation in early child language, there are many important lessons to be learned from the methodology that he has developed, and in particular from his discussion of the problems that have to be faced in any text-based study of language. Three of these will be briefly considered.

2.1 Obtaining Reliable Data

Labov refers to this problem as the 'Observer Paradox', as in the absence of an observer it is difficult to obtain interpretable data, but the very presence of an observer may so alter the situation that the speech that is observed lacks the qualities of spontaneity and naturalness which are essential for the investigation. Child language researchers, rightly convinced of the need for the richest possible contextual information to assist in the interpretation of the children's utterances, have usually convinced themselves that the effect of their presence is minimal; but we should remain sceptical. I have suggested elsewhere (Wells, 1977a) on the basis of our own recorded data, that the frequency of 'expansions' for example, may owe a great deal to the presence of an adult who is relatively unfamiliar with the child, for whose benefit the mother, quite unconsciously, expands or interprets all the child's utterances that may be difficult for the visitor to understand. There are probably other systematic changes in parents', if not in children's, behaviour when an observer is present. What is incontrovertible, I believe, is that the presence of an observer, however well known to the family, will have effects on the speech that occurs, and that these effects will differ according to the type of home, thus introducing a form of interference which makes it difficult to study the linguistic interaction between the child and other members of the family, the interaction which provides the most important context for the child's linguistic development.

A second problem associated with reliability concerns the child's physical and emotional state when the speech sample is obtained. Even when there is no bias introduced by an observer, it is important to ensure that the data are not distorted by the child being ill or upset or in any way not 'on form'. Whilst it is probably not possible to measure this in any very precise way, the mother will usually be able to say whether or not her child is behaving as usual.

The same problems arise, but in an even stronger form, when the data for study are obtained in experimental or test-like situations. Labov (1970) has vividly described the way in which many children respond to the questioning of unknown adult research workers by a stubborn refusal to utter anything more than monosyllables, and Rose and Blank (1974) have shown how children may be led to produce apparently illogical or inappropriate responses as a result of their misperception of the artificial testing context in which the questions or instructions are presented. The problem is that the language behaviour that is called for in such test or experimental situations is likely to be artificially divorced from a meaningful context in the child's experience, and thus the behaviour that occurs does not provide reliable evidence for the question under investigation, namely, his ability to use language to communicate with the familiar members of his home environment.

2.2   Obtaining Representative Data

As well as being reliable, the data for analysis should also be representative. This issue needs to be considered on two distinct levels. Firstly there is the need to sample from the child population in such a way that variation within that population is adequately represented. Where there are *a priori* theoretical grounds for distinguishing particular sub-groups, this is relatively straightforward; but in the absence of theoretically motivated distinctions, it is necessary to draw a sample of randomly selected individuals which is large enough for significant groupings within the population to be empirically determined from a *post hoc* analysis of the data. Although this issue is well understood in the field of experimental psychology, it has frequently been ignored in child language research, presumably because of the dominating interest in the universal characteristics of language development.

On a second level, there is a need to sample from the population of situations in which speech occurs. Since what people say is usually relevant to the communication situation as they perceive it, we can expect the characteristics of a speech sample to be influenced by the nature of the situation in which it is recorded. This may be most apparent with respect to the lexical selections that are made, but it will also be true of functional categories, and to a certain extent of syntactic structures also. For example, requests for permission are more probable in the presence of an adult than amongst children, and clauses linked by causal conjunction more probable when playing with construction toys, for example, than when playing a rough-and-tumble game.

Except perhaps in laboratory-like conditions, however, it is difficult to control the kaleidoscopic shifting from one context to another that makes up a typical child's day; and even if it were possible, we do not yet know enough about the significant parameters of situations to sample from them in such a way as to maximise the chances of obtaining a speech sample that represents a child's range of control over all aspects of language. Some long-term social and situational sources of variation which have linguistic repercussions are quite outside the control of the researcher. For example, in a study of the emergence of early semantic relations within the sentence, I found that the expression of possession was likely to emerge earlier in children with older siblings (Wells, 1974). Of course it is possible to control this particular source of variation by studying only first-born children (although this would make the study unrepresentative in other important ways), but the example is indicative of the enormous range of differences in the patterns of organisation of family life which subtly influence the range of experiences, and through them the specific structures, meanings and functions of language, which provide the context for the child's acquisition of language as a means of communication and reflection.

2.3 The Quantification of Linguistic Data

Even when the researcher has satisfactorily resolved the problems of obtaining reliable and representative data, he is still faced with the problem of quantifying them in some appropriate way. In his introduction to his study of the copula in Black English vernacular, Labov writes:

> The study of variation is necessarily quantitative, and quantitative analysis necessarily involves counting. At first glance, counting would seem to be a simple operation, but even the simplest type of counting raises a number of subtle and difficult problems. The final decision

as to what to count is actually the solution to the problem in hand; this decision is approached only through a long series of exploratory maneuvers (Labov, 1977: p. 82).

It is just such a series of exploratory manoeuvres that are necessary when analysing children's speech. Firstly, there are problems in the allocation of tokens[†] to types.[†] For example, in the relatively unstructured speech of an 18-month-old, is the *'s* in *What's that?* to be counted as a token of the contracted copula, or is it to be treated as an inseparable part of an un-analysed question-asking utterance type? If it is recognised as a copula, is the contracted copula to be treated as a separate type from the uncon-tracted copula, as in *What is that?*, or are instances of contracted and uncontracted equally token of the same type – the copula? Similarly, with somewhat older children, it has been observed that relative clauses occur almost excusively in relation to verb complements (Limber, 1973). Is it necessary, therefore, to set up more than one relative clause type, one for verb complements, another for subject relative clauses, and so on; or should it be argued that there is only one type, with the imbalance in position of occurrence being attributed to pragmatic factors, such as the tendency for the subject of a sentence to express 'given' information, with a consequent lack of necessity for it to be fully specified linguisti-cally?

Having resolved such problems, a decision still has to be made as to whether it is the occurrence of types that will be treated as significant or whether some frequency of tokens will be treated as the measure of control. When a particular element is well established, it may well be that it is variation in frequency that is of interest, but where the focus is on the point at which a particular element is acquired, one single token of the type may have to be taken as the appropriate evidence, because a criterion set in terms of a greater token frequency would seriously underestimate the number of children having control of the type in question. In the case of certain types, such as the morphemes studied by Brown (1973), for example, the frequency of obligatory linguistic contexts may be high enough to set a criterion such as 90 per cent presence, below which the child is judged not yet to have attained mastery. But for other elements, the frequency in the language as a whole may be so low that the prob-ability of actually observing them in a speech sample of a particular size may be too small for presence or absence to be reliably informative. For example, in a sample of approximately 18,000 utterances that we have obtained from 60 children, each recorded 3 times between 36 and 42 months, 12 children used a passive verb a total of 19 times, no child producing more than 3 tokens, and several children producing 1 token on the first occasion but none on the two subsequent occasions. Here, there is no obligatory context in which to look for proportional occurrence, and given so low an absolute frequency there can be no certainty that children who are not observed to use a passive do in fact lack control of this type. A possible solution here is to use cumulative frequency over a number of observations.

2.4 Problems of Size

As will be apparent by now, the biggest problem facing research on child language that tries to take systematic account of even one or two of the multiple sources of variation, whilst at the same time obtaining data amenable to detailed linguistic analysis, is the sheer size of the sample required. Early research, such as the normative studies reviewed by McCarthy (1954) and the later study by Templin (1957), was based on a substantial number of children (480 in Templin's case), but the corpora obtained were neither reliable nor representative as samples of naturalistic speech,[2] and the linguistic analysis was extremely crude. More recent research, in the tradition inaugurated by Brown *et al.* (1969), and Miller and Ervin (1964) has succeeded in obtaining corpora of data large enough to allow a detailed linguistic analysis, but at the price of restricting the number of children to a handful and by ignoring most of the social and situational causes of variation.

The Bristol study, with a sample of 128 children, representative of the urban child population in terms of sex, month of birth and class of family background, and with recordings made of each child once every three months at frequent intervals over a normal day at home without an observer present, has attempted to overcome the problems of reliability and representativeness, but the quantity of child speech obtained at each recording (120 utterances on average) and the intervals between recordings still pose problems for certain types of quantitative analysis, as suggested above.[3]

Thus, if it is an essential prerequisite of work on variation in child language that the data for study should be obtained in such a way that they meet the criteria that have just been discussed, it must be concluded that there is as yet little or no research in this field that will support any confident generalisation. Yet the nature and extent of this variation is a subject of considerable importance, not only because an understanding of it is needed as a basis for sampling decisions, whatever the focus of the research, but also because of the educational significance that has been attributed to certain aspects of linguistic variation, although in the absence of adequate empirical evidence. Because of the limitations of all the studies to be referred to with respect to at least one of the issues discussed above, none of the findings can be taken as conclusive, though many of them are suggestive of fruitful hypotheses for further evaluation. In the remainder of this paper I shall consider these findings under the major headings distinguished in Section 1.

3.   Inherent Attributes

3.1   Sex

References to the superiority of girls with respect to almost all aspects of language development abound in the literature, although it is extremely rare to find such extreme differences as those reported by Ramer (1976), in whose sample all the girls but none of the boys were characterised by a style of acquisition associated with rapid development. Reviewing the literature in 1954, McCarthy wrote:

> The vast accumulation of evidence in the same direction from a variety of investigators working in different parts of the country (USA) employing different analyses and linguistic indices, certainly is convincing proof that a real sex difference in language development exists in favor of girls . . . (McCarthy, 1954: p. 580).

However only a few years later, Templin, summarising her own findings, had this to say:

> When the performance of boys and girls is compared over the entire age range, girls tend to receive higher scores more frequently than the boys, but the differences are not consistent and are only infrequently statistically significant,

and she goes on to suggest that:

> It may be that the differences which have appeared in the literature have been overemphasised in the past. It may also be that over the years differences in language ability of the two sexes have actually become less pronounced in keeping with the shift towards a single standard in child care and training in the last few decades (Templin, 1957: pp. 145-7).

A similar conclusion is reached in a more recent review by Cherry (1975),

Variation in Child Language 391

and our own research strongly supports the view that what differences there are between the sexes are in rate rather than style of acquisition, but they are rarely significant.

However it is the last sentence of the quotation from Templin that is most interesting, for it heralds a new trend in studies of sex differences, towards an investigation of the differential treatment of the two sexes as an explanation of what had previously been taken to be a genetic superiority. Under this hypothesis, the relatively greater loquacity and fluency of girls (Smith & Connolly, 1972) would be attributed to differential expectations of, and communication with, the two sexes by their parents. There is some evidence for this in the responses in our maternal interview when the children were aged 3½ years.

In this context another finding from the Bristol research is of particular interest. Using the corpus of speech collected at 3¼ years, sequences of conversation were distinguished according to whether they were initiated by the child or by another person. All sequences were also categorised according to the context in which they occurred and the dominant purpose of the conversation. 70 per cent of all sequences whose initiator could be determined were initiated by the child, and for these sequences there were only small and mainly insignificant differences between boys and girls with respect to context or purpose. In the remaining 30 per cent of sequences, the vast majority of which were initiated by the mother (and a few cases by the father), there were highly significant differences in the contexts in which adults chose to initiate conversations with boys and girls (Table 15.1). The most striking contrasts are in the contexts of play with adult participation, helping and non-play activities.

Table 15.1: Proportions of Conversations Initiated by Adults with Boys and Girls in Different Contexts

	Boys	Girls
Toileting, Dressing & Meals	14.4	12.1
Playing Alone	8.1	3.4
Play with other child	2.7	2.6
Helping & Non-play Act	28.8	56.8
Play with Adult	18.1	5.2
Talking & Reading	22.5	19.0
Watching TV	5.4	0.9
Total	100%	100%

$x^2 = 25.037$ p $<$ .001

Adults initiate a far greater proportion of sequences with boys in contexts of play (a ratio of 3.5:1); in contrast, over half the sequences with girls were in helping and non-play contexts (a ratio of 2:1 compared with the boys). This suggests that adults emphasise more 'useful' and domestic activities in their interaction with girls, whilst the emphasis with boys is towards a more free-ranging, exploratory manipulation of the physical environment. It is perhaps surprising that no clear differentiation is apparent at this age in the children's own speech as a result of the sex-role stereotyping behaviour of the adults; certainly it becomes apparent at school age (Adlam, 1977) but this may be as much the result of sex differentiation in peer-group activities amongst school-children as a result of the speech addressed to them by adults. This is a subject that we intend to pursue in the subsequent phases of the study.

3.2   Intelligence and Personality

If sex differences turn out to owe as much to environmental factors as to biological differences, the same is probably even more true of the relationships between intelligence and personality on the one hand, and language on the other. Interpretation of the undoubted correlations between intelligence and linguistic development reviewed by McCarthy (1954) is made more difficult by the fact that most tests of intelligence, even those purporting to test non-verbal intelligence, require certain minimal skills in communication, usually through language, for their administration, if only so that the subject can be made aware that a response is required and that it should take a particular form. Furthermore, neither intelligence nor language is a unitary phenomenon and developments in the two domains interpenetrate each other in an interactive way which suggests that any effort to establish a global, unidirectional, causal relationship, in whichever direction, is almost certainly misguided. It seems much more plausible, instead, to hypothesise a continuum of causality extending in both directions, on which observed correlations between particular tests and linguistic sub-skills might be located. The relationship between size of vocabulary and a test of intelligence such as the English Picture Vocabulary Test (Brimer and Dunn, 1963), which depends on the comprehension of pictured objects and events, for example, would probably fall at the language → measured intelligence end, whilst the relationship between the ability to recognise spatial or temporal sequences or configurations, as measured by Raven's Progressive Matrices, and rate of acquisition of the hierarchical structure of syntax, particularly subordination and embedding, would probably fall towards the intelligence → language end.

Mention has already been made of the variation among children in their experience of test-like situations and the effect that this can have on test performance. Attention has recently also been focused on the problems of cultural bias in tests of intelligence and in many of the instruments that have been used to assess linguistic skills and maturity (Labov, 1970). It is clear, therefore, that the co-variation between intelligence and language must also be firmly related to environmental variation, and particularly to social and cultural differences in the valuation that is put upon different types of intellectual and linguistic performance.

Finally in this section, brief mention should be made of the variation associated with what I called earlier personality. Here again the relationship is difficult to untangle, since communication style is one of the bases on which judgements of personality are made (Argyle & Kendon, 1967; Crystal, 1975). To the extent also that personality is learned through interaction with the social environment, the directionality of causation is likely to be complex. In practice, this aspect of variation has so far received little attention at any level, although some of the work in literary stylistics bears on this issue. In the field of child language, Nelson's (1973) investigation of the effect of interaction strategies takes account of certain variables in both mother and child that could be included under the heading of personality, and finds that degree of match or mismatch between mother and child on these variables is 'most potent in accounting for the child's progress during the second year' (p. 113). It seems likely that the differences between the active outgoing child and the placid retiring child will influence many aspects of the linguistic interactions that they experience, and that this in turn may have an effect on both rate and style of language learning, just as it has already been shown to affect some aspects of social learning.

4. Social Background

This is probably the most controversial of all the dimensions of variation in child language and more has certainly been written on this subject and its supposed implications for educability than on all the other dimensions of variation added together. For this reason, only selected aspects will be considered here; for a comprehensive and critical review of the literature, the reader is referred to two recent books: Dittmar (1976) and Edwards (1976a).

Since the formal organisation of language and the meanings and purposes it serves to communicate are learned chiefly through social interaction, it seems self-evident that in so far as this varies from one social group to another there will be variation in child language which can be related to group membership. And on this point there is very little disagreement. Where the disagreement is to be found is on: 1) the nature and size of the variation; 2) the parameters that should be used to distinguish significant social groupings; 3) the mechanisms responsible for the relationship between social group membership and linguistic variation.

The greater part of the debate has taken socio-economic status, or social-class, as the point of departure (they are usually treated as if they were equivalent), thus pre-empting a serious consideration of possible alternative parameters. Research findings were initially presented in terms of rate of development, with children from lower SES groups showing a developmental lag, frequently at a statistically significant level (McCarthy 1954; Templin, 1957). An evaluative element was soon added, and the developmental lag became a linguistic deficit (Deutsch, 1967; Loban, 1963), then, under the influence of Bernstein's formulation of the class:code relationship, a difference in style of acquisition was introduced, the middle class being said to develop an exploratory and explicit use of language in contrast to the expressive and implicit use of the lower class. (Bernstein, 1960, 1965; Bereiter and Engelmann, 1966).

At about this point, in reaction to the extreme 'deficit' claims, two new strands entered the debate. On the one hand Labov used evidence from his studies of non-standard English to point out that many of the characteristics of lower-class speech that were being treated as indices of deficit, were in fact systematic differences of dialect. In a now famous polemical article (Labov, 1970), he dismissed the supposed superiority of middle-class speech and argued strongly that, although working-class Negro children differed in the form of English that they spoke and in the value that they placed upon particular uses of language, they were just as linguistically proficient as the middle-class white children who had been taken as the point of comparison.

On the other hand, and at about the same time, Bernstein reformulated his theory in terms which made it clear that the codes regulated habitual 'performance' and were not to be taken as a description of underlying 'competence', or if so, only of 'communicative competence' (Bernstein, 1971: p. 146). However, this reformulation is less radical than might appear, for restriction to a restricted code is still seen as the probable cause of cognitive deficit:

> for this code orients its speakers to a less complex conceptual hierarchy and so to a lower order of causality. . . Thus the relative backwardness of many working-class children who live in areas of high population density or in rural areas may well be a culturally induced backwardness

transmitted by the linguistic process. Such children's low performance on verbal IQ tests, their difficulty with 'abstract' concepts, their failures within the language area, their general inability to profit from the school, all may result from the limitations of a restricted code (Bernstein, 1971: p. 151).

It is true that the distinction between speech variant and code, and the introduction of the notion of critical socialising contexts, gave greater precision to the theory, but the results of the empirical studies carried out by his research team continued to be presented in terms of the relative inferiority of working-class children's speech: shorter utterances, less syntactic complexity, greater use of pronouns than of nouns and particular reliance on exophoric reference — all realisations of the restricted code user's orientation to particularistic, context-dependent meanings.

These two new developments have been seen by many to be in direct opposition to each other. But this is not the case. Labov's argument, that non-standard dialects are as adequate for the development of logical thought as any other dialect of English, is surely correct. Bernstein's thesis, however, is not concerned with differences between dialects, but with underlying code orientations to different orders of meaning, particularistic and universalistic, in whatever dialect, standard or non-standard. In principle, therefore, it is perfectly possible for there to be standard dialect speakers, whose speech is regulated by a restricted code, and speakers of non-standard dialects, whose speech is regulated by an elaborated code. The main reasons for the assumed incompatibility of the two arguments are firstly, the fact that the majority of the non-standard dialect speakers considered by Labov are working-class, and secondly, that Bernstein has persistently argued that the restricted and elaborated codes have social origins in orientation to the means of production: the restricted code both springs from, and transmits, the social structure experienced by the working class. The working class are, almost by definition, restricted code speakers.

If we now recapitulate the various arguments that have been developed, there appear to be two main hypotheses concerning the relationship between social class and language development:

a) that lower class children are relatively retarded in acquiring control of the dialect of their community
b) that lower-class children are more likely to use restricted speech variants and to have restricted code orientation towards context-dependent, particularistic meanings.

The evidence for and against both hypotheses is, as might be expected, difficult to disentangle. In the case of the first, dialect differences have certainly clouded the issue, for in some of the earlier studies, which claimed to find substantial class differences, non-standard departures from Standard English were treated as evidence of a developmental lag in acquiring the standard form. The conditions under which the speech samples were collected may also have affected children from different social classes differentially, as Labov (1972) argues. In a number of studies, also, the samples have been drawn from the population in such a way as to maximise the chances of finding the expected class differences.

In the Bristol project we have tried to guard against all these forms of bias: by stratifying an original random sample to give equal representation to four divisions on a continuum of social class; by sampling from a wide range of the naturally occurring contexts in which speech occurs in the children's daily lives, with no researcher present during the recording; and by treating local dialect forms, where they occur, in the same way as the equivalent standard forms. The results of the analyses carried out so far do not lend strong support to the hypothesis of a developmental lag.

No significant class differences have been found with respect to the amount of speech produced in the time-based samples, in the contexts in which child-speech occurs, or in the range of pragmatic functions realised. It seems, therefore, that in very general terms, language plays the same sort of role for children of all social classes. Only one clear test of the hypothesis has been carried out so far with respect to rate of acquisition of syntax: age at reaching the criterion for control of the auxiliary verb system. On this there was no significant difference in rate, neither was there any class difference in style. However there was a significant correlation between class of family background and number of different auxiliary verbs, both forms ($r = .331$, $p < .01$) and meanings ($r = .363$, p. $< .01$) that had been used by the age of 3½ years. (Wells, in preparation).

With respect to MLU, the results are equally indeterminate: at some ages, and with respect to some measures of MLU only, there are significant correlations between class and MLU. But even when statistically significant, such correlations are only of the order of $r = .3$, showing that class alone accounts for only a minor part of the variance in MLU. The one index on which there is a clear-cut relationship with class is score on the test of oral comprehension, ($r = .589$, p. $< .001$).

However, before accepting these latter results as supporting evidence for the hypothesis, it is necessary to distinguish carefully between what children can do and what they actually do. With the comprehension test results there is at least a possibility that the scores of some of the lower-class children were depressed by the test situation itself rather than by lack of linguistic ability, in spite of attempts to put them at their ease. Unfortunately, no independent measure exists of differential ability to cope with test situations, so we have not been able to isolate the two sources of variation. As far as MLU is concerned, there are two important qualifications to be made to the results as they stand. Firstly, although it is possible to treat different dialect forms as equivalent when considering the acquisition of grammatical rules, it is less easy to make adjustments for the same forms when measuring utterance length. Some of the class difference in MLU is therefore probably caused by certain features of the local dialect, which is most marked in the speech of some of the lower-class children. In this dialect a number of grammatical morphemes are frequently omitted, such as -*s* on third person singular non-past verbs, *be* and *have* in affirmative, declarative sentences containing *be going to, have got, have got to,* and perfective aspect. On the other hand the same dialect adds *to* in certain locative constructions, such as *Where's he to?* On balance, however, the tendency is towards deletion of elements; but in the absence of the necessary variation studies of this dialect, of the kind pioneered by Labov, it is not possible to estimate what allowance should be made when calculating MLU for such speakers.

Secondly, measures of MLU are derived from spontaneous behaviour and so are an index of what the speaker chooses to do rather than of what he can do. Beyond a certain level of development, a speaker selects the forms through which he realises his meaning intention according to what he considers appropriate in the context. If lower-class children more frequently select grammatically less explicit forms in a variety of contexts, this will certainly depress their MLU; but this should not be taken as an indication of less mature language development, unless there is also evidence that they *cannot* use the same range of grammatical options in contexts in which they judge them to be appropriate. In so far as this question has been properly investigated, the evidence does not support the hypothesis that lower-class children show a general developmental delay in grammatical development, although there is considerable evidence that they do not habitually exploit their grammatical resources to as full an extent as their middle-class peers (Edwards, 1976a).

On the second hypothesis, the evidence is less conclusive. Much of the relevant research has been carried out by Bernstein and his colleagues, and although many of their results lend support to the hypothesis of a relationship between class and code, the contexts from which the speech data were obtained were both non-spontaneous and highly specific, so it is difficult to assess how far the results were distorted by the differential responses of the two groups to the task-situations and by their differential perception of the task-demands, as Adlam (1977) admits in her discussion of these investigations. Hawkins' (1969) study of the different uses of the nominal group in telling a story from pictures is a good example of the problem. The restricted code stories that were typical of the working-class group, with their high proportion of exophoric reference, could be taken as entirely appropriate in the situation, since child and researcher were both able to see the pictures. Furthermore, the relationship between the hypothesised underlying code, with its somewhat speculative cognitive implications, and the speech variants actually observed in specific situational contexts has continued to elude really satisfactory articulation. Although the speech of working-class children frequently is less syntactically complex, and lexically less specific than that of middle-class children, in the contexts chosen for examination, the fact that, under what they consider to be appropriate circumstances, working-class children can be explicit, producing utterances of appropriate grammatical complexity and lexical specificity to achieve their communication goals (Edwards, 1976b; Francis, 1974) makes it inappropriate to continue to characterise the differences in terms of a binary distinction of their class or code, and must cast doubt on the usefulness of the construct 'code' itself. Or, if the concept is to be retained, we should allow for a plurality of codes, in the same way as we do with registers. Certainly, much greater attention must be paid to aspects of context than has typically been the case in such studies (but cf. Adlam (1977) for an attempt to relate code and context).

It is in relation to education that the putative relationship between class and restriction in the uses of language has assumed the greatest importance, for large-scale policy decisions (e.g. Plowden, 1967; Halsey, 1972) have been based on evidence such as that produced by Bernstein's Sociological Research Unit, and by similar research in the United States (e.g. Hess & Shipman, 1965; 1968; Deutsch, 1967). In her research in this tradition into class differences in the use of language Tough (1977) even labels her two contrasted groups of 3-year-olds in terms of predicted educational 'advantage' and 'disadvantage', although the chief criterion for selection was parental status: professional as opposed to unskilled or semi-skilled occupation. In this research it is not code as such which is the focus of investigation, but the relative frequency with which children from the two groups make use of different functions of language. The major functions distinguished are self-maintaining,[†] directive,[†] interpretative[†] and projective,[†] with distinctions of uses within these categories being arranged in a notional order of complexity. Comparing samples of speech recorded in a play situation, Tough found marked differences between the two groups, to the point that only one child in the disadvantaged group 'had scores on some measures that were better than the scores of one or two children in the advantaged group' (1977: p. 85). Although the meaning of 'better' is not defined, these results lead her to conclude that 'these children, coming from differing home environments, had established different priorities for expressing meaning, and different orientations towards the use of language' (p. 87).

Once again, however, these conclusions were reached on the basis of data that failed to meet the criteria discussed in the opening section of this paper. The speech samples were obtained from only one situation, with the observer present and taking notes, and the frequency data were not submitted to statistical analysis. In an attempt to carry out a partial replication of Tough's research, I carried out a similar analysis of samples of spontaneous speech at home for a sub-sample of the Bristol children, who were drawn from the full spectrum of family background (Wells, 1977b). After applying statistical tests to both sets of data, I found that the Bristol sample showed a much less clear-cut picture. In the first place, the frequency of uses considered to be most complex by Tough was so low for the samples as a whole that no statistical significance could be attached to differences between groups. And in the second place, although there were still some significant differences between classes with respect to the more frequently occurring categories, there were few of the linear trends indicative of simple correlation, and some of those that did occur were in the opposite direction from that predicted by Tough. As with the first hypothesis, therefore, the evidence is conflicting and certainly does not allow firm conclusions to be drawn on the relationship between class and language use.

Nevertheless one point of very general significance does emerge from the comparison of these two studies and that is the distorting effect that is produced when social variation is reduced to an opposition between two monolithic classes, and claims made that ignore the very large degree of variation that certainly exists within these classes. There is a persistent tendency to reduce variation to dichotomy and nowhere is this tendency more prevalent than in discussion of class and code differences.

Class, or occupational status, which is the index most frequently used to identify it, is not the only form of social variation, however, nor even a very informative one in trying to account for variation of rate or style of language acquisition. At best it is correlated with a variety of other characteristics of children's homes — income, type of neighbourhood, size and composition of family, level of parents' education, and parental attitudes to society in general – any one of which is likely to have more influence on the child's learning environment than class-membership as defined by the Registrar-General's I-V scale.

Although class, defined chiefly in occupational terms, is central to Bernstein's exposition of primary socialisation, it does not seem to me to be a necessary component of a theory which seeks to explain the role of language in the social transmission of knowledge and values. If class membership were treated as just one among a number of group affiliations, which would include membership of groups organised around religion, sports, politics, etc., all of which influence a family's values and orientations to other members of the family and to larger groupings within society, then Bernstein would surely be right in arguing that these values and orientations are largely embodied and transmitted through interpersonal communication, and that their realisation in particular, contextualised, conversations constitutes the means whereby the child learns both his language and the social structure of reality that both includes and is expressed by language.

5.   Experience of Linguistic Interaction

Given this emphasis on the social context of language acquisition, it is natural that attention should have come to focus more and more on characteristics of caretakers' conversation with their children. The qualitative modifications of mothers' speech to young children are now well documented (Ferguson and Snow, 1977) and have been discussed by Catherine Snow (in press). She documents the almost universal tendency of caretakers to reduce the length and complexity of their utterances to young children and the various strategies they use to induct children into the conversational strategies of turn-taking and joint topic construction, which are also discussed by John Dore, in his paper on conversation (in press). Naturally, most of this research has been searching for the universal characteristics of the linguistic input to the child. Here, however, I shall examine the evidence for variation in input.

5.1   *Conversational Experience*

The conversations in which a child participates simultaneously provide a model of the language to be acquired and an opportunity for him to try out his existing language system in a context where shared experience makes it possible for his partner to provide feedback that should be optional for further acquisition. Variation in conversational experience might be expected, therefore, to show a very strong relationship with variation in development. Unfortunately, to date, although there is evidence of both types of variation, there has been little study of their inter-relationship.

Amount of conversational experience varies quite widely as a result of differences in domestic arrangements and in individual differences in loquacity. Although there were no class differences in amount of speech in the Bristol sample, there were considerable differences between individuals, the most talkative child producing 3½ times as many utterances as the least talkative, whilst the difference between amount of speech addressed to the children was in the ratio of 15:1. However sheer quantity was not related to level of development. In the earlier pilot study (Wells, 1975), a qualitative distinction was made between three groups of contexts in which conversation occurred: *mothering* (which included such contexts as bathing, dressing, feeding and cuddling), *independent* (all contexts where the child was alone, with other children only, or receiving no more than sporadic and divided attention from an adult) and *joint enterprise* (contexts of shared activity, such as doing the housework together, play with adult participation, looking at books together or just talking). Comparing the proportion that occurred in each of the three groups of contexts, a significant relationship was found between rate of development at 2½ years and proportion of speech addressed to the child in contexts of joint enterprise. It also happened that, of the 8 children compared, the four faster developers were all first-born children, and it was suggested that it was the greater opportunity that the mothers of these children had to engage in talk in the context of shared activities, compared with the mothers of the children with one or more siblings, that accounted in large part for the first-born children's more rapid development. This finding still has to be confirmed with respect to the larger sample, but in analyses to date, effect of birth order alone has not been found to relate to variation in rate of acquisition.

The systematic modification of caretaker speech to young children has already been mentioned. The extent of this modification has been investigated in a number of experimental studies, and has been found to vary with the age of the child: caretaker speech increasing in MLU, grammatical complexity, proportion of disfluency and vocabulary type-token ratio with increasing age of the child (Snow, 1972; Brown, 1973; Fraser and Roberts, 1975). Fraser and Roberts (1973) also found similar trends in analyses of naturalistic speech data from the Bristol project. Whether or not variation in the extent of such modification for children at a given age or stage of development affects rate or style of development is a topic that still has to be investigated, although Cross's (1977) study of mothers' speech to accelerated language developers suggests that the effect of such modifications will be greatest when they are finely tailored to the child's linguistic level and the maturity of his communication strategies.

Cross makes the important point that effective communication is inter-active, and that, in the case of these accelerated children, the mothers' communication strategies were in part determined by those of the child. Nelson (1973) also stresses the importance of matching between the strategies of caretaker and child at different stages of development. Taking the three dichotomous variables, *match/mismatch* between the child's cognitive structure and the semantic structure of the adult lexicon, selection by the child of a *referential/expressive* hypothesis concerning the central functioning of language, and *acceptance/rejection* as the mother's dominant feedback to the child's utterances, she identified eight inter-action patterns and examined the relationship between these and rate of vocabulary acquisition. 'Match-Referential-Acceptance' was found to be most strongly associated with rapid acquisition and, as might be expected, 'Mismatch-Expressive-Rejection' with slowest acquisition. Of the three variables, cognitive-linguistic match or mismatch appeared to be most powerful in accounting for progress during the second year, but the parental feedback variable was considered to have the greatest long-term effects. It seems, therefore, that the child's initial strategies may be important in getting him off to a good start, but that in the longer term it is the quality of caretaker feedback in interaction with the child that contributes more to rate of development.

The characteristics of caretaker feedback was one of the topics investi-gated by Brown and his colleagues in their study of Adam, Eve and Sarah (Brown *et al.*, 1969). In one of their investigations they examined the effect of what they called 'training variables',[†] and found no conclusive evidence for a relation between linguistic development and either frequency with which particular constructions were modelled in parental speech or with parental approval or disapproval of the syntactic form of children's utterances. Parents, it seems, are more concerned with the truth-value than the syntactic well-formedness of their children's speech — which they conclude 'renders mildly paradoxical the fact that the usual product of such a training schedule is an adult whose speech is highly grammatical but not notably truthful' (Brown *et al.*, 1969: p. 330). In their earlier work (Brown & Bellugi, 1964), they had been struck by the frequency with which parents expanded their children's grammatically incomplete utterances, and the effect of a systematic regime of expansions was investigated by Cazden (1965) in a controlled comparison with a regime of language modelling through semantically appropriate responses. Two groups of negro children, aged 28-38 months, received one or other treatment for 40 minutes each day for 3 months, whilst a third, control, group received no specific treatment. Contrary to expectation, the expansion treatment was not found to aid in the acquisition of grammar, whilst those children who had received the modelling treatment made greater progress. A re-examination of the spontaneous data from the Harvard children confirmed these results. Reviewing all these studies in the conclusion to 'A First Language', Brown wrote:

> In sum, then, we do not presently have evidence that there are selection pressures of any kind operating on children to impel them to bring their speech into line with adult models. It is, however, entirely possible that such pressures do operate in situations unlike the situations we have sampled, for instance away from home or with strangers. It is also possible that one should look more closely at the small number of child utterances which turn up in most samples where the adult just does not seem able to make out what the child means. Perhaps these are the leading edge where the pressures operate (Brown, 1973: p. 412).

If parental feedback to the grammatical form of children's utterances does not seem to be the explanation of variation in rate of development, what else might be? Perhaps the answer lies in the direction indicated by the relatively greater success of the modelling condition in Cazden's experiment. One of the explanations suggested to account for that result was that 'richness of verbal stimulation might be more important than the grammatical contingency of the adult response' (Brown *et al.*, 1969: p. 324). This is surely the case, but might not an even more important quality of parental speech be its relevance to the meaning-intention of the child, and the extent to which conversation is jointly constructed by parent and child together? This seems to be implied by the findings of Cross and Nelson referred to above, and perhaps also in the quotation from Brown. Our own longitudinal records provide ample evidence of variation of this kind and in a comparison of typical speech samples from two girls, from otherwise similar backgrounds, I have shown how the reciprocal negotiation of meaning which characterises the conversational experience of one, but not the other, of these children also provides an opportunity for extending control over the formal features of language (Wells, 1976).

We have not as yet been able to test this hypothesis with respect to our whole sample, but Evans (1977) has made some progress in this direction by investigating, for 20 of the children, the effect on a number of indices of linguistic development at the beginning of schooling of the level of communicative relevance in mothers' responses to children's utterances at earlier stages of development. Using the recordings made at 3¼ and 3½ years, she classified and scored each maternal response to a child utterance in child-initiated sequences according to the following scale: *Inappropriate*: 0; *Procedural* (check/expansion, correction, request for repetition or clarification, etc.): 1; *Plateau* (confirmation, yes/no response, command, evaluation, etc.): 2; *Developing*: Instruction/suggestion: 2; Yes/No Question: 3; Statement/Explanation: 4; Content Question: 5. Two over-all scores were calculated for each mother: the mean level of response and a 'richness of interaction' score (mean response X mean number of exchanges per sequence), and these were correlated with MLU, syntactic complexity and oral comprehension (EPVT) at age 4 years 9 months, and with reading attainment at ages 6 and 7 years. With the exception of MLU, all correlations were positive and significant, thus lending support to the hypothesis that the quality of response that a mother gives to a child's speech in the early years has a significant influence on his subsequent linguistic development.

However, before we conclude that experience of this kind is crucial for satisfactory development, we should pause to consider whether such emphasis on the mother does not reflect a cultural bias resulting from the predominance of studies carried out in Western societies. Blount (1977) points out that older children are the primary socialisers of younger children in non-Western societies, and even in Western societies there is considerable variation in the age at which children are allowed to roam outside the home in peer-groups, and the amount of time that they spend in such activities. From this it would appear that conversation with an *adult* caretaker is not essential for the acquisition of language, although it may still be the case that some systematic modification of the input to young children such as has been found in parental speech is essential, but that it is a characteristic of caretaker speech, whatever the age or status of the caretaker. However, in those societies where parental caretaking is the norm, the evidence does seem to suggest that differences between children in the quality of their conversational experience are related to their rate of language development. It seems likely that the same will be true for differences between children in the uses to which they habitually put their linguistic resources, but this has not yet been investigated in any detail.

6.   Conclusion

In this paper, I have reviewed most of the sources of variation in child language that have been investigated in any detail, and, as I suggested at the beginning, the results are somewhat inconclusive. There is a wide range of variation in rate of development and probably also in habitual use of linguistic resources, once a certain stage of development has been reached. The evidence for different styles of development is more equivocal, but here too there is evidence of variation in fine points of detail; whether or not there are clearly differentiated styles or merely an indefinitely large number of interactions between relatively independent dimensions, still remains to be investigated on a large enough scale to permit conclusions to be reached. Evidence concerning relationships between rate and style of language development and non-linguistic variables is also inconclusive. The co-variation of language ability and measured intelligence is quite strong, but because of their interdependence it is difficult to arrive at any conclusion about the direction of causality. Brown (1973) is prepared to predict that 'rate of development will prove to be dependent on what the intelligence testers call g or general intelligence' because he thinks that 'a reasonable conceptual definition of comparative intelligence is the rate at which individuals build general rule systems or theories comprehending sets of data to which they are exposed' (pp. 408-9), but he is also aware of the difficulty of constructing valid independent measures of intelligence for children below school age.

Variation with sex and social background was at one time taken for granted and, in the case of social class differences, inflated to almost ludicrous proportions. However, more recent studies, which have taken account of contextual factors and distinguished between 'competence' and 'performance' in the Chomskyan sense, have thrown considerable doubt on the existence of substantial differences between the sexes or between different social classes in rate of development, whilst leaving more open the question of differences in habitual behaviour. Adlam (1977) and Turner (in press), both members of the Bernstein group, have developed very subtle techniques for studying the variation that is attributable to context, as perceived by different social classes; but although they have found systematic differences, the small number of contexts investigated, taken in conjunction with findings of other studies which show no systematic class differences, must leave the existence of the hypothesised restricted-elaborated code dichotomy very much unproven.

The main conclusion that can be drawn from such an overview, and one that is supported by the analyses carried out on the Bristol data, is that there is a central core of English that all children are acquiring in the same order, with the only important type of variation being that of rate of acquisition. This also seems to be true for children learning other languages. However, from an early age there develops a variation in the range of options within each child's linguistic repertoire from which selection is habitually made and in the relative frequency with which specific options are selected. This variation has not yet been shown conclusively to be attributable, to any significant extent, to any of the gross demographic variables, but is the outcome of the pattern of habitual events that is treated as socially salient by caretakers, and made the subject of conversation in the daily lives of particular families. Variation in the richness and explicitness of children's conversational experience has been found to be related to both rate of development and habitual language use, but development seems to follow the normal course, although at a slower rate, even in the absence of rich conversational experience, except in the most extreme cases.

I started this paper on a methodological note, and it is on this note that I wish to conclude. Much of the evidence that has been reviewed in the preceding pages has had to be qualified because of methodological weaknesses in the investigations through which it was obtained. There is thus clearly a need for further research, on all the topics considered, that attempts more satisfactorily to meet the criteria of reliability of sampling, representativeness of contexts and amenability to appropriate statistical analysis. Whilst detailed studies of small groups of children are invaluable for the generation of hypotheses, these can only be satisfactorily tested on relatively large and representative samples. The difficulties involved in carrying out such studies are substantial, but without them we shall remain at the level of little more than unsupported conjectures.

In most of the studies considered, the strategy of investigation has been to start with single or interrelated parameters of non-linguistic variation and to use these in an attempt to explain the variation in different aspects of language development. But, as we have seen, the explanatory power of this approach has not been very great. An alternative strategy which has, so far, only been attempted in a small number of studies (e.g. Cross (1977), Nelson (1973)) is to start by grouping the children according to attributes of their linguistic development and to work outwards, through variation in their conversational experience, to the attributes of the families associated with different styles of caretaker-child interaction. My hunch is that the results of such an approach will be less easy to describe, in terms of broad demographic groupings, but of significantly greater value to those who wish to use the outcome of research on variation in child language to apply scarce educational resources where they can be of greatest value.

Notes

1.   Crystal *et al*. (1976) contains a summary of these criticisms and Brown (1973) and Wells (1976b) offer a qualified defence.
2.   Templin's method of obtaining her speech data, which she claims was as nearly as possible a replication of that used by McCarthy, is described as follows: 'Children were taken into a room with an adult examiner and, after rapport was established, fifty remarks of the child, usually consecutive, were taken down' (1957: p. 15). It is worth remembering, also, that 'taken down' means taken down in writing on the spot.
3.   For a fuller account of this study, cf. *Journal of Child Language*, 1, 1: pp. 158-62, 1974.

References

Adlam, D.S. 1977. *Code in Context*. Routledge & Kegan Paul.
Argyle, M. & Kendon, A. 1967. The experimental analysis of social performance. In *Advances in Experimental Social Psychology*, ed. L. Berkowitz, pp. 55-98. Academic Press.
Bereiter, C. *et al*. 1966. An academically orientated preschool for culturally deprived children. In *Pre-School Education Today,* ed. F.M. Hectinger, Garden City, N.Y. Doubleday.
Bernstein, B. 1960. Language and social class, *British Journal of Sociology* 11: pp. 261-76.
Bernstein, B. 1965. A sociolinguistic approach to social learning. In *Penguin Survey of the Social Sciences*, ed. J. Gould. Penguin.
Bernstein, B. 1971. *Class, Codes and Control*. Vol. I. Routledge & Kegan Paul.
Blount, B.G. 1977. Ethnography and caretaker-child interaction. In *Talking to Children: Language Input and Acquisition*, ed. C. Ferguson & C. Snow, pp. 297-308, Cambridge University Press.
Brimer, M.A. & Dunn, L. 1963. *English Picture Vocabulary Test*. N.F.E.R.
Brown, R. & Bellugi, U. 1964. Three processes in the child's acquisition of syntax, *Harvard Educational Review* 34: pp. 133-51.
Brown, R., Cazden, C. & Bellugi-Klima, U. 1969. The child's grammar from I to III. In *Studies in Child Language Development*, ed. C. Ferguson & D. Slobin, pp. 295-333. Holt, Rinehart & Winston.
Cazden, C. 1965. *Environmental Assistance to the Child's Acquisition of Grammar*. Unpublished Ph.D. Thesis, Harvard University.
Cazden, C. 1970. The neglected situation in child language research and education, *Journal of Social Issues*, 25: pp. 35-60.
Cherry, L. 1975. Teacher-child verbal interaction: an approach to the study of sex differences. In *Language and Sex: Difference and Dominance*, eds. B. Thorne & N. Henley, Rowley Mass: Newbury House.
Cross, T.G. 1977. Mother's speech adjustments: the contribution of selected child listener variables. In *Talking to Children: Language Input and Acquisition,* eds. C. Ferguson & C. Snow, pp. 151-88. Cambridge University Press.
Crystal, D. 1975. *The English Tone of Voice*. Arnold.
Deutsch, M; (ed.) 1967. *The Disadvantaged Child*. Basic Books.
Dittmar, N. 1976. *Sociolinguistics*. Arnold.
Dore, J. (in press). Conversation and pre-school language development. In *Studies in Language Acquisition*, ed. P. Fletcher and M. Garman, Cambridge University Press, Cambridge.
Edwards, A.D. 1976a. *Language in Culture and Class*. Heinemann.

Edwards, A.D. 1976b. Speech codes and speech variants: social class and task differences in children's speech, *Journal of Child Language*, 3, 2: pp. 247-66.

Evans, J. 1977. *The Significance of Adult Feedback on Child Language Development*. Unpublished M.Ed. Dissertation, University of Bristol School of Education.

Ferguson, C.A. & Snow, C.E. 1977. (eds.) *Talking to Children: Language Input and Acquisition*, Cambridge University Press.

Francis, H. 1974. Social class, reference and context, *Language and Speech*, 17: pp. 193-8.

Fraser, C. & Roberts, N. 1973. *How Adults Talk to Children*, Final Report to the Nuffield Foundation.

Fraser, C. & Roberts, N. 1975. Mothers' speech to children of four different ages, *Journal of Psycholinguistic Research*, 4, 1: pp. 9-16.

Halsey, A.H. 1972. *Educational Priority Vol. I*. HMSO.

Hawkins, P.R. 1969. Social class, the nominal group and reference. *Language and Speech*, 12: pp. 125-35.

Hess, R. & Shipman, V. 1965. Early experience and the socialisation of cognitive modes in children. *Child Development*, 36: pp. 869-86.

Hess, R. & Shipman, V. 1968. Maternal influences upon early learning. In *Early Education*, ed. R. Hess & R. Beer, Aldine.

Huttenlocher, J. 1973. The origins of language comprehension. In *Theories in Cognitive Psychology*, ed. R.L. Solso, Lawrence Erlbaum.

Labov, W. 1970. The Logic of Non-Standard English. In *Language and Poverty*, ed. F. Williams. Chicago: Markham Publishing Co.

Labov, W. 1972. *Sociolinguistic Patterns*. Univ. Pennsylvannia Press.

Labov, W. 1977. *Language in the Inner City*. Oxford: B. Blackwell. Originally published by Univ. Pennsylvania Press, 1972.

Lee, L. 1969. *The Northwestern Syntax Screening Test*. Evanston, Illinois: Northwestern University.

Limber, J. 1973. The genesis of complex sentences. In *Cognitive Development and the Acquisition of Language*, ed. T.E. Moore, pp. 169-86. Academic Press.

Loban, W. 1963. *The Language of Elementary School Children*. U.S. National Council Teacher. English. Report No. 1.

McCarthy, D. 1954. Language Development in Children. In *Manual of Child Psychology*, ed. L. Carmichael, pp. 492-630. New York, Wiley.

Menyuk, P. 1969. *Sentences Children Use*. M.I.T. Press.

Miller, W.R. & Ervin, S.M. 1964. The development of grammar in child language. In the Acquisition of Language, eds. U. Bellugi & R. Brown, *Monograph of the Society for Research in Child Development*, 29 (1): pp. 9-35.

Nelson, K. 1973. Structure and strategy in learning to talk, *Monographs of the Society for Research in Child Development*, 38, pp. 1-2, serial no. 149.

Plowden, Lady. 1967. *Children and their Primary Schools*. HMSO.

Ramer, A.L.H. 1976. Syntactic styles in emerging language, *Journal of Child Language*. 3, 1: pp. 49-62.

Reynell, J. 1969. *The Reynell Developmental Language Scales*. NFER.

Rose, S.A. & Blank, M. 1974. The potency of context in children's cognition: an illustration through conservation, *Child Development*, 45: pp. 499-502.

Slobin, D.I. (ed.) 1967. *A Field-Manual for Cross-Cultural Study of the Acquisition of Communicative Competence*. University of California, Berkeley.

Smith, P. & Connolly, K. 1972. Patterns of play and social interaction in pre-school children. In *Ethological Studies of Child Behaviour*, ed. N.B. Jones, Cambridge University Press.

Snow, C.E. 1972. Mother's speech to children learning language, *Child Development*, 43: pp. 549-65.

Snow, C.E. (in press). Conversations with children. In *Studies in Language*

Acquisition, ed. P. Fletcher and M. Garman, Cambridge University Press, Cambridge.

Templin, M.C. 1957. *Certain Language Skills in Children*. Minn: University of Minnesota.

Tough, J. 1977. *The Development of Meaning*, Unwin Education Books.

Turner, G. (in press) *The Regulative Context: a Sociolinguistic Enquiry*. Routledge & Kegan Paul.

Wells, C.G. 1974. Learning to code experience though language, *Journal of Child Language*, 1, 2: pp. 243-69.

Wells, C.G. 1975. The contexts of children's early language experience, *Educational Review*, 27, 2: pp. 114-25.

Wells, C.G. 1976. Describing children's language development. In *Collecting, Using and Reporting Talk for Educational Research*, ed. C. Adelman (in press).

Wells, C.G. 1977a. A naturalistic approach to the study of language development. *Research Intelligence*, 3, 1: pp. 34-5.

Wells, C.G. 1977b. Language use and educational success: an empirical response to Joan Tough's The Development of Meaning (1977), *Research in Education* (in press).

Wells, C.G. (in press). What makes for successful language development. In *Advances in the Psychology of Language*, ed. R. Campbell & P. Smith. Plenum Publishing Co.

Wells, C.G. (in preparation). *The Acquisition and Use of the Auxiliary Verb in English by Children and their Parents.*

Acculturation. The influence and effect upon a society of exposure to another culture; the assimilation of part or whole of an alien culture. See *creolization.*

Achromatic. Without constant and/or measurable pitch.

Action. In *case grammar*, that part of a sentence traditionally identified as The Verb Phrase, which involves a change of state, e.g. 'John *kicked* the ball'; 'His hands *got* dirty.' See *Agent.*

Agent. The animate perceived instigator of the action identified by the verb. See *case-grammar*, action, object.

Auditory processing mechanisms. Strategies by which the brain analyses strings of sounds into meaningful words, phrases and sentences.

Base structure. The structure at which meaning is represented in a sentence. See *Transformational-generative grammar*, *case grammar* and the diagram on p. 109.

Behaviourist. A psychological theory which views learning as the forming of chains of small units of behaviour, linked by general principles of association. Links are formed by the habitual association of events in space and time, and strengthened or weakened by rewards and punishments. See *empiricist-associationist.*

Benefactor. In *case grammar*, the animate being who benefits from whatever is communicated, e.g. 'This present is *for Grandma*'.

Bound. Those units which do not have independent forms as words, but always occur in combination forms, such as the plural in English, which can occur on the endings 'book*s*', 'coach*es*', or involve a change in word form such as 'children', 'mice', etc.

Case-grammatical. Referring to a theory introduced by Charles Fillmore, which sees *deep structure* as representing sentences as a verb and one or

410

more noun-phrases, each associated with the verb in a particular case-relationship, such as agentive, instrumental, locative, etc. See *Agent, action, object.*

Centre-embedded. See *embedded.*

Chronological age. Actual physical age, often used to form a comparison between measures of intellectual development, physical development, and the expected norms for that age.

Citation style. The form words take when read in a list, rather than as combined in a sentence.

Code repertoire. Members of a society have access to different varieties and forms of language, these different forms being considered more or less appropriate for different purposes. The range of varieties found within a community is its code repertoire.

Coding frame. The description of those linguistic features which characterise the operation of a code in a given context.

Collective monologues. A type of 'dialogue' where children take turns talking but without any apparent intention that others should hear and respond. Anyone will serve as an audience.

Componential analysis. An approach which views all units as consisting of smaller simultaneously occurring units, so that every element is composed of a 'bundle' of features.

Concrete operations. Operational thinking which focuses on concrete things and events in the world. See *operational thinking.*

Conservation. In a classical conservation experiment, performed by Piaget, if young children are presented with two equal rows of pellets

A   .   .   .   .   .
B   .   .   .   .   .

they can judge them as equal. If the experimenter then rearranges the pellets to

A . . . . .
B . . . . .

children will select row A as having more pellets. What children lack is the realisation that quantity is invariant, even though the shape or appearance can vary. The concept that quantity can be conserved is not attained till the age of 6 or 7. See *decentration, reversibility, identity.*

Count noun. Nouns in English belong to three main classes: (1) Proper; (2) Mass (distinguished by their non-occurrence with 'a' and 'plurals', e.g. butter, sand, cement, etc.); (3) Count (distinguished by occurring with singular and plural forms, countable, e.g. ball, knife, coat, etc.).

Cycling rules. These rules assign stress to elements in sentences by operating on successively more major constituents to give firstly stresses within words, then stresses on elements of phrases, and finally stresses to elements of sentences as each cycle is repeated.

Creolization. When two different languages and cultures are in contact, a pidgin form sharing features of both languages may arise. Creolization is the process by which a pidgin becomes the native language of subsequent generations.

Decentration. The young child can attend to only one dimension at a time. When decentration is accomplished the child can attend to two dimensions simultaneously and recognise that change in one dimension is compensated for by a reverse change in the other dimension. See *conservation, reversibility, identity.*

Declarative. Sentences with a particular syntactic form, in English usually with the subject preceding the verb, contrasting with interrogative and imperative sentence types.

Deep. The level at which meaning is represented in the underlying structure of language. A universal deep structure would represent meaning as arising from the same elements in all languages. See *transformational-generative grammar, case grammar, surface structure.*

Deixis. The use of spatial, temporal and interpersonal features of linguistic and non-linguistic context to provide joint reference.

Deletion. A transformation which removes part of the structure of a string. It is always recoverable from context and surface form. e.g. I told John *to come* (It's John who is to come).

Directive. Language whose function is primarily concerned with organising the child's own activity and that of others.

Do-Do. Excrement or shit.

Empiricist-associationist. A psychological theory which assumes that humans learn language through general learning principles which are the same in many species. Learning is accomplished through the formation of chains of association. See *behaviourist.*

Encoding. The process in psychological terms, by which one type of representation is changed into another, as in the encoding of thought as language; the encoding of words as sound strings, etc.

Ethnography of speaking. An approach to linguistic analysis which treats the subject as a member of an 'alien culture' which can be studied in the manner of anthropological research, using field- and discovery-research techniques.

Exophoric pronouns. Pronouns which refer to entities outside the actual discourse. That is, the references are not explicit in the preceding or following text, e.g., upon being shown a picture of a boy playing football, the child says '*He's* kicking the ball' rather than, 'there is a boy in the street. *He's* kicking the ball.'

Expanded nominal groups. A minimal nominal group may be just a pronoun or an article and noun, c.g. 'He,' 'the boy'. An expanded group has additional, optional modification or qualification, e.g. 'The *red-haired* boy' 'The boy *in the yellow shirt.*'

Free recall. A standard psychological experiment where subjects are presented with items to remember and are later asked to repeat as many as they can with no cues given by the experimenter.

Generalised language functions. One aspect of a language-in-context analysis, which classifies utterances in terms of 'what they do' rather than in terms of their internal structure. Examples of functions would be 'controlling, informational, explanational,' etc.

Ground rules. The internalised principles used by speakers to formulate thought and language; the underlying cognitive and interactional systems.

Head. The centre of a construction, often the noun in a phrase, e.g. '*Yesterday*, the Post Office *Engineer* brought the new *telephone* for the *kitchen.*'

Holophrases. Early child utterances which consist of one word only, e.g. 'Mummy', 'There', 'Up'.

Homogeneous speech community. An idealised community where there is no variation in linguistic forms or styles, no slangs, jargons, etc., which are not common to every speaker.

Hypothetico-deductive. A theory which operates with abstract models rather than trying to develop analyses from observed data.

Identity. The recognition of the constancy of an object despite changes in its position and shape. See *decentration, conservation, reversibility.*

Illocutionary. The meaningfulness of an utterance, in the sense of its having reference.

Inference rules. A set of operating principles or procedures for discovering a grammar.

Internalised speech. The process of thinking in word meanings.

Interpretative. Language whose function is primarily concerned with logical reasoning and predicting and anticipating possibilities, alternatives and solutions.

Linguistic relativity hypothesis. The belief that the language of a society determines the way in which members of the society perceive the world: the belief that language determines cognition.

Location. In *case grammar*, the case which identifies the location or spatial orientation of the state or *action* identified by the verb. See *Agent, location.*

Locutionary. The meaningfulness of an act, in the sense of it being a command, request, question, statement, promise, etc.; the speaker's communicative intention.

Logical operators. A class of items which serve to link two or more items in a formally logical relationship, such as causality, inference, disjunction, etc.

Louding. See *sound.*

Mental grammar. The means of representing language within the human mind. Linguistic models attempt to recapture the features exhibited by speakers' knowledge and use of language but it is not known if language is handled in the same manner by the brain.

Mentalistic. Concerned with discovering a mental reality underlying actual behaviour.

Meta-language. The superordinate language which permits conceptualisation of concepts, e.g. the language one uses to talk about power or general economic issues.

Minimum units of content. In Hjelmslev's linguistics theory semantics is viewed as inseparable from the real world of experience which is called 'content'. The pattern of meanings within content is hierarchical, each 'content form' being subdivisible until the smallest or minimal units of content are reached.

Modulation. Items which provide variation around dimensions of core meanings, such as options for tense (past-present), number (singular-plural) etc.

Morphs. The minimal units in a language which carry meaning. They may either be free, i.e. words, which can occur on their own, or *bound.*

Multiple-branching. A construction with no internal structure, e.g. 'tall, young, handsome, intelligent man'. In terms of *tree-structure*, the adjectives in the first example are branches arising from the same node on the tree.

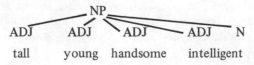

Neo-Firthian. An approach illustrated by the work of Halliday (see *system-structure*) which treats language as consisting of a number of linguistic levels, all of which contribute simultaneously to a description of an utterance's meaning.

Nesting. A construction where a phrase falls totally within another, e.g. 'I rang *the man who wrote the book* up.'

Object. Things affected by the action or state of the verb. See *case grammatical, action, Agent*.

Operational thinking. Thinking which is controlled by an abstract cognitive system which underlies all cognitions and perceptions. See *sensori-motor*.

Orectic intentions. Intentions by the child to obtain what he desires.

Over-extensions. The incorrect analysis by a learner of a language of the structure of words and combinations of words as revealed in generalisations from particular forms.

Perceptual device. A processing strategy of the brain (i.e. a psycholinguistic factor) which relies on the saliency of features of the speech signal.

Performative. A feature of the structure of the mind which accounts for why data is perceived in certain ways.

Pharyngeal fricative. A sound resembling a continuous 'H'.

Phonologically marked. Forms which are identifiable by the contrast in their pronunciation in one context with that in another. For instance, to pronounce 'Paris' as 'Paree' in an English conversation would be to use a marked form.

Possession. In *case grammar*, the case of the animate being who has control and rights over whatever is communicated by the rest of the sentence. Possession is closely linked semantically with *location*.

Post-vocalic /r/. The 'r' which occurs after vowels at the end of words, e.g. car, steer, lover, etc. Its absence in Southern English speech is prestigious (viz. West Country accents) while its absence in New York speech indicates low status.

Pragmatics. The study of the use of language in context. Pragmatics studies how situation, speaker role, topic, listener role and other variables effect the use of language.

Production span capacities. Limits on the length and complexity of utterances which can be produced. This lengthens with age as a child's language develops.

Production task. A standard psychological task where the subject is shown an array or picture and asked to describe it in his own words.

Progressive aspect. Characterising 'on-goingness' in time. Marked in English by various forms using -ing, e.g. 'I *was walking* the dog when I met him.'

Projective. Language whose function is primarily concerned with projecting into the experiences, feelings and reactions of others.

Recursion. Some of the rules which produce sentences are capable of being used more than once in developing a particular sentence, e.g. there is no limit in principle to the number of adjectives which can occur between the article and the noun: 'The big, bright, bouncy, yellow . . . etc. ball.'

Reflexive. Open to introspection and self-awareness of society and one's role in it.

Relational terms. Words which operate on a single dimension, such as 'short', 'medium', 'long' on the dimension of length, or 'before', 'at the same time', 'after' on a dimension of time.

Reversibility. The recognition that something can change in shape or arrangement and then change back to the original: events in the environment can be physically or mentally undone.

Rewriting rule. A transformational rule which, in a given context, changes a form. The statement is usually expressed as A → Z/X-Y (A becomes Z when it occurs between Z and Y).

Rifting. See *sound.*

Saccades. Sudden jumps in eye fixation occurring in rhythmic sequences.

Second formant transition. Formants refer to the resonant frequencies in the acoustic components of the speech signal, determined by the configurations of the organs of articulation during vowel production. Several formants characterise each vowel; contrasts between consonants are often perceived in part from differences in the transitions from the consonant to the vowel rather than in a contrast in the acoustic signal when the two consonants are compared.

Self-embedding. A construction where a phrase is *nested* in another and both are of the same type, e.g. 'The man *whom the boy whom the students recognised pointed out* is a friend of mine, where both are relative clauses.

Self-maintaining. Language whose function is primarily concerned with maintaining the rights and property of the self.

Semantic field. The range of entities over which the conceptual meaning of a word operates. In a language like Russian for example, where there is one word for greenish blue and another word for purplish blue, but no word for both, the semantic field of each of these words is narrower than the semantic field of the English word 'blue'.

Semantic markers. The hierarchical set of features which serves to identify the unique meaning of a word, e.g.

> 'bachelor'   male
>   adult
>   human
>   unmarried

Semiotic. A term referring to any of a number of systems of communication, of which language is only one. Another important semiotic system is kinesic: gestures and facial expressions.

Sensori-Motor schemas. The means by which an infant gradually disengages himself from the rest of the world by developing the ability to distinguish himself from other things, and objects from one another. The motor patterns the child develops to interact with the world provide the beginning of symbolisation.

Sentence frame completion task. A standard psychological experiment where subjects are given a sentence with a word missing and are asked to fill in the gap; e.g. He sat down on the ———— .

Separable verb prefixes. A number of prefixes which can occur either as independent forms or as part of verbs, e.g. to *up*date, bring *up* to date.

Set theory. Theory which organises elements as members of sets sharing common features. An item may simultaneously belong to a number of sets.

Sound, rift, loud. Verbal games, found in black inner city communities in the USA, involving the exchange of ritualised insults, rhyming insults, etc.

Stage 1. Roger Brown has classified child language development in terms of 5 stages, based on the MLU (mean length of utterance) of a child's speech:

Stage 1	1.1 – 2.0
Stage 2	2.0 – 2.5
Stage 3	2.5 – 3.0
Stage 4	3.0 – 3.5
Stage 5	3.5 – 4.0

Stratificational. A model developed by Sydney Lamb, which views language as a series of hierarchical sub systems relating sound to meaning. Each subsystem has its own structural organisation; one subsystem operates at each structural layer or 'stratum'.

Structural index. This contains the features, both contextual and inherent, which determine whether a transformation should be applied.

Structured recall. A standard psychological experiment where subjects are presented with items to remember and are later asked to repeat as many as they can. Their task is aided by being provided with reference categories to help storage and retrieval.

Surface. The level at which elements are represented as speech. In *transformational-generative* grammar, transformations modify *deep structure* into surface structure. Understanding of sentences requires recovery of deep structure from surface structure.

System-structure. A model developed by Michael Halliday, which views language as a series of system networks, each network representing the choices associated with a given type of constituent (e.g. clause system network, noun-phrase system network, etc.).

Tagmemic. A model of language developed by Kenneth Pike, which provides a simultaneous description about an item's function in a larger structure and about the class to which it belongs that could also fulfil that function. Information is provided in terms of matrices — a network of intersecting dimensions in which significant points are plotted.

'The generalised other'. An imagined construct the individual makes when he can conceive of other people's reacting to him in ways sufficiently similar for him to think of them as a single person.

Tokens. An instance of any item in a classification system. See *type.*

Transformational-generative grammar. A theory, first introduced by Noam Chomsky, which represents language in terms of rules which produce deep and surface structures. The rules which manipulate elements of *tree structures* are called transformational rules.

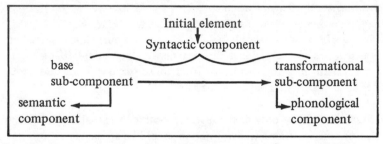

See also *deep structures, surface structures* and diagram on p. 109.

Trager-Smith-Joos. A model which separates levels of linguistic analysis such as phonetics, phonology, morphology and syntax, and treats each level independently of any other. All analyses must begin at the lowest, phonetic, level, and proceed upwards towards syntax.

Tree-structure. A model used in *transformational-generative grammar* which shows the constituent parts and subparts of each element of a sentence as branches on a tree.

Trotin cards. A set of Belgian paintings which show very detailed views of such events as weddings, street scenes, etc. There is a great deal of material which the subject can describe if he chooses.

Types. The classification assigned to a particular occurrence of an item. In the utterance 'the man bit the dog', there are two *tokens* of 'the' classified as one *type* of article. In 'the man in the yellow shirt bit a dog', there are two tokens of 'the' and one of 'a', classified as belonging to two types of article.

Velar stop. A sound made when stopping the airflow by raising the back of the tongue to the rear of the palate, resembling a 'k' or 'g'.

INDEX

acoustic cues 22-4, 25, 26
Anglin, J.M. 189-91, 197-8
aphasia and language 113
authority relationships 281-3, 323, 326-7
auxiliary verbs 250-69; acquisition of 263-9; and cognition hypothesis of language acquisition 265-6, 268-9; and recognition of language *v.* production 260-1; and sentence structure 158-63; and syntax acquisition 263-5; definition of 252-3; meaning of 253-6, 265-6; modal auxiliaries 252, 253-6, 266-8; primary auxiliaries 252, 253; use by children *v.* use by adults 261-2; use of auxiliary forms by children 256-7, 260, 264; use of auxiliary meanings by children 257-60, 266-8

babbling 18-20, 242
Bar-Adon, A. 172
Bates, E. *et al.* 66
behaviourism 104-5, 263
Bellugi, U. 121, 122
Benveniste, F. 83-4
Bereiter, C. 332, 333, 348, 349-50
Bernstein, B. 73,275-7, 278-9, 280, 281, 283, 284, 285-6, 289, 290, 293, 298, 301-2, 304, 305-6, 310-27, 331-2, 347, 394-5, 397,400
Bierwisch, M. 191-2
bilingualism *see* multilingualism
black children and language: and defensive strategies 333-6; and descriptive tasks 332-3; and educational achievement 330-1, 334, 351-3; and genetic inferiority theory 353-6; and interviews 298-300, 332-9, 340-3; and linguistic competence 299-300, 331-2, 333-4, 336, 337, 338-9, 341, 342, 343, 362-3; and logic 341-3; and Non-standard Negro English (NNE) 340-3; and peer groups 351-2; and teachers' attitudes 351; and verbal deprivation theory 329, 331, 350-4, 356-7
Bloom, L. 96, 112-13

Bloomfield, L. 40-1
Brown, R. 103-4, 118-19, 167-84, 403

Caldwell, B.M. 353
Cazden, C.B. 41, 50, 299, 361-79
Chao, Y.R. 172
Chase, S. 103
Chomsky, N. 36, 38, 38-40, 47-8, 50, 53-4, 63-4, 70, 95, 104, 106, 110, 120, 131, 132, 149, 215-18, 261, 263, 312-13
code, sociolinguistic 275-307; and coding 277; and grammar 313; and multingualism 294, 295-6; and situational context 275-7, 281-5, 286-9, 291-2, 293-305, 321-2; and social interaction 294, 296-300, 311, 313-14; and socialisation 305-7, 315; and socio-economic background 276-7, 283-5, 291, 298-300, 303, 316, 327, 339-40, 394-5, 398; and variation in language 286-8; coding grid for 278-9, 322; definition of 277; implicit *v.* explicit 286-9, 291-2, 301-2, 303, 304, 318-19; restricted *v.* elaborated 278-9, 282-3, 285-6, 293, 300-4, 316, 317, 323, 325-6, 340, 394-5
cognition hypothesis of language acquisition 102-26; and aphasia 113; and auxiliary verbs 265-6, 268-9; and concepts 103-4, 119-20, 125-6; and decentering 116-17; and grammar acquisition 118-19, 121-4; and 'productive span capacity' 112-13; and 'reversibility' 115-16; and sensorimotor development 114-15; and short-term memory 111-12; descriptive diagram of 108-10; historical background of 102-8; *see also* next entry
cognitive development and language 131-47; and grammar acquisition 134-5; and linguistic universals 152-5; and syntax acquisition 137-47; and vocabulary acquisition 145; *see also* previous entry
communicative intention *see* intention,